My dear cat Coro is the same age as *D.Gray*. Coro was born and abandoned in front of a station in Nishi Tokyo about the time the series began. A kind soul took him in and he ended up a member of my family.

—Katsura Hoshino

Shiga Prefecture native Katsura Hoshino's hit manga series *D.Gray-man* has been serialized in *Weekly Shonen Jump* since 2004. Katsura's debut manga, "Continue," appeared for the first time in *Weekly Shonen Jump* in 2003.

Katsura adores cats.

D.GRAY-MAN

VOL. 22
SHONEN JUMP ADVANCED
Manga Edition

STORY AND ART BY
KATSURA HOSHINO

English Adaptation/Lance Caselman
Translation/John Werry
Touch-up Art & Lettering/HudsonYards
Design/Matt Hinrichs
Editor/Gary Leach

D.GRAY-MAN © 2004 by Katsura Hoshino. All rights reserved.
First published in Japan in 2004 by SHUEISHA Inc., Tokyo. English translation rights arranged by
SHUEISHA Inc.

The rights of the author(s) of the work(s) in this publication to be so identified have been asserted
in accordance with the Copyright, Designs and Patents Act 1988. A CIP catalogue record for this
book is available from the British Library.

Printed in the U.S.A.

Published by VIZ Media, LLC
P.O. Box 77010
San Francisco, CA 94107

10 9 8 7 6 5 4 3 2 1
First printing, July 2012

www.viz.com

www.shonenjump.com

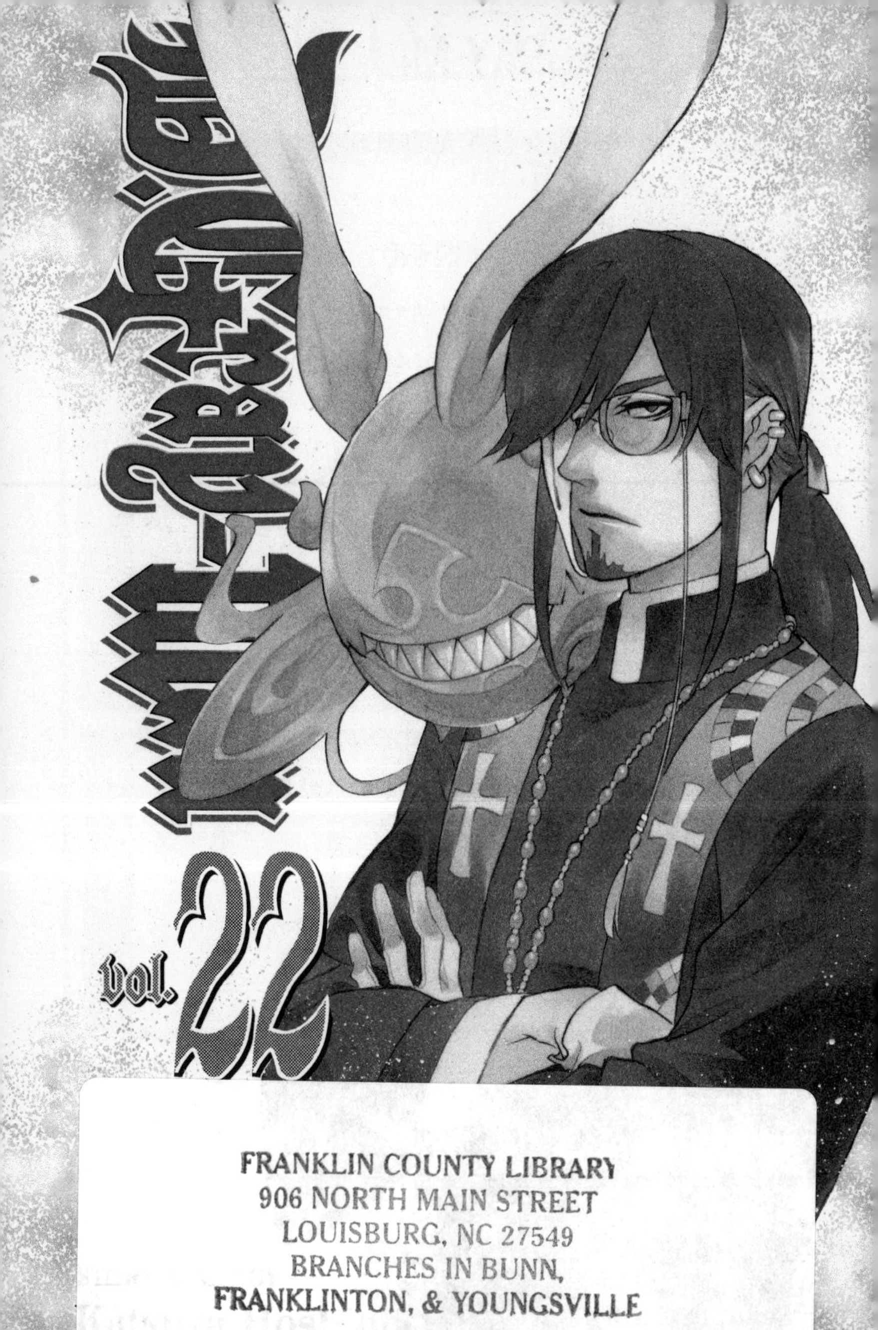
D.Gray-man
vol. 22

D.Gray-man
CHARACTERS

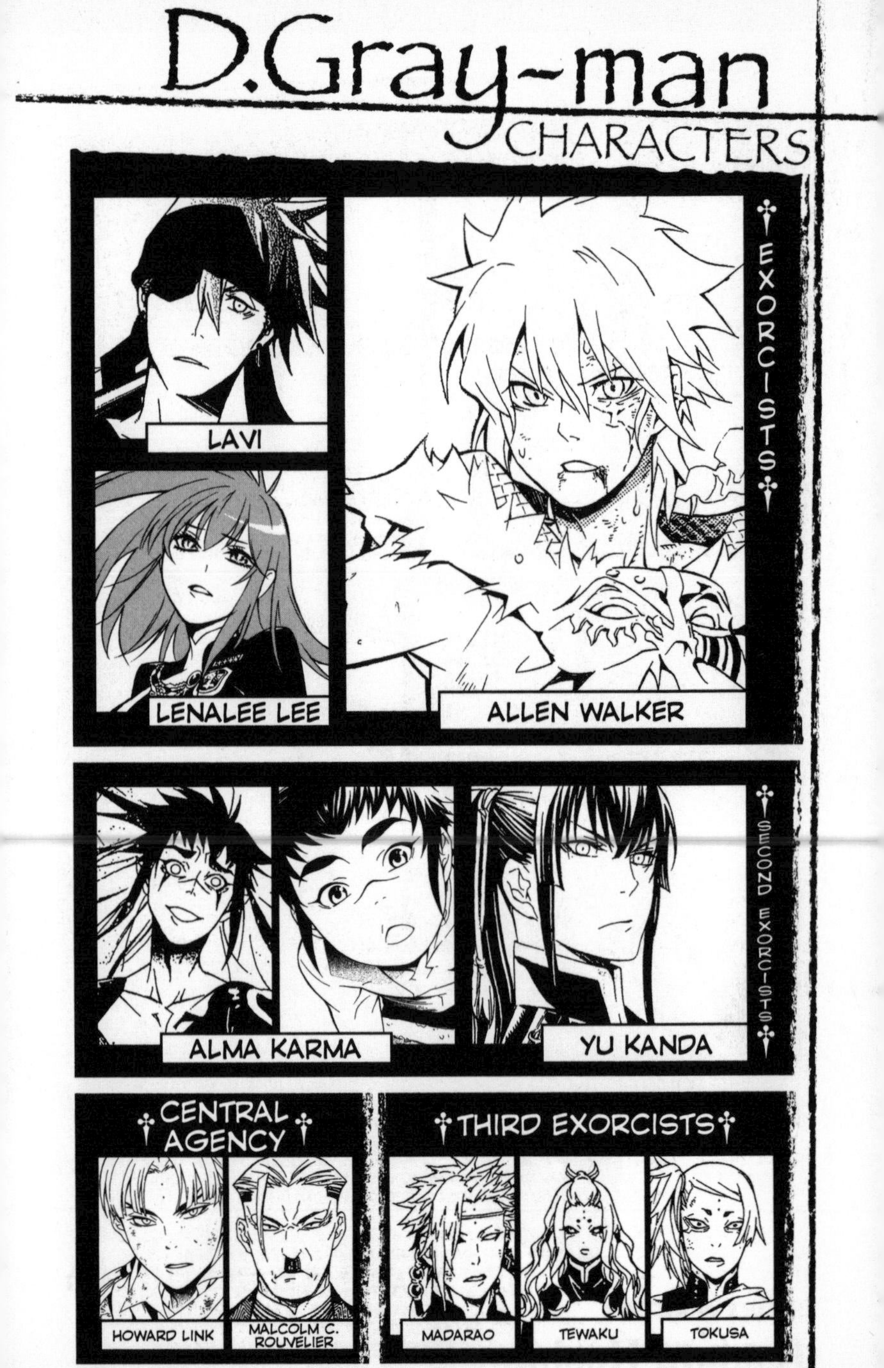
EXORCISTS
ALLEN WALKER
LAVI
LENALEE LEE
SECOND EXORCISTS
YU KANDA
ALMA KARMA
THIRD EXORCISTS
TOKUSA
TEWAKU
MADARAO
CENTRAL AGENCY
MALCOLM C. ROUVELIER
HOWARD LINK

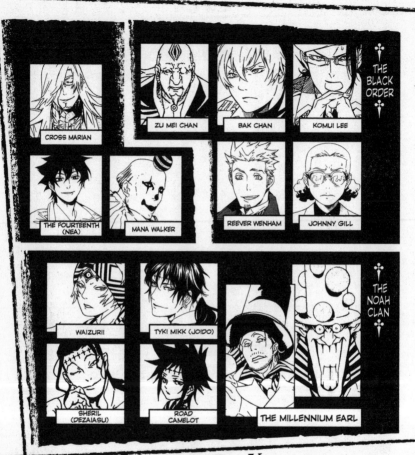

THE BLACK ORDER
KOMUI LEE
BAK CHAN
ZU MEI CHAN
CROSS MARIAN
JOHNNY GILL
REEVER WENHAM
MANA WALKER
THE FOURTEENTH (NEA)
THE NOAH CLAN
THE MILLENNIUM EARL
TYKI MIKK (JOIDO)
WAIZURII
ROAD CAMELOT
SHERIL (DEZAIASU)

STORY

IT ALL BEGAN CENTURIES AGO WITH THE DISCOVERY OF A CUBE CONTAINING AN APOCALYPTIC PROPHECY FROM AN ANCIENT CIVILIZATION AND INSTRUCTIONS IN THE USE OF INNOCENCE, A CRYSTALLINE SUBSTANCE OF WONDROUS SUPERNATURAL POWER. THE CREATORS OF THE CUBE CLAIMED TO HAVE DEFEATED AN EVIL KNOWN AS THE MILLENNIUM EARL BY USING THE INNOCENCE. NEVERTHELESS, THE WORLD WAS DESTROYED BY THE GREAT FLOOD OF THE OLD TESTAMENT. NOW, TO AVERT A SECOND END OF THE WORLD, A GROUP OF EXORCISTS WIELDING WEAPONS MADE OF INNOCENCE MUST BATTLE THE MILLENNIUM EARL AND HIS TERRIBLE MINIONS, THE AKUMA.

THE NOAH CLAN, LED BY THE MILLENNIUM EARL, HAS ATTACKED THE ORDER'S NORTH AMERICA BRANCH AND AWAKENED ALMA KARMA, WHO BECOMES A FEROCIOUS AKUMA AND CLASHES WITH THE FRIEND WHO SLEW HIM, YU KANDA. AND ALLEN—IN WHOM THE MYSTERIOUS NOAH, THE FOURTEENTH, IS SLOWLY AWAKENING—LEARNS OF KANDA AND ALMA'S PAST AND IS GRAVELY INJURED TRYING TO BREAK UP THEIR FIGHT. TO PROTECT THEM, ALLEN SENDS THEM TO A PLACE WHERE NO ONE CAN HARM THEM...

D.GRAY-MAN
Vol. 22

CONTENTS

The 200th Night: Seed of Destruction   9

The 201st Night: Desperate Sinner   41

The 202nd Night: The Changing World   65

The 203rd Night: Fate—Vision   99

The 204th Night: Premonition of Parting   131

The 205th Night: My Home   163

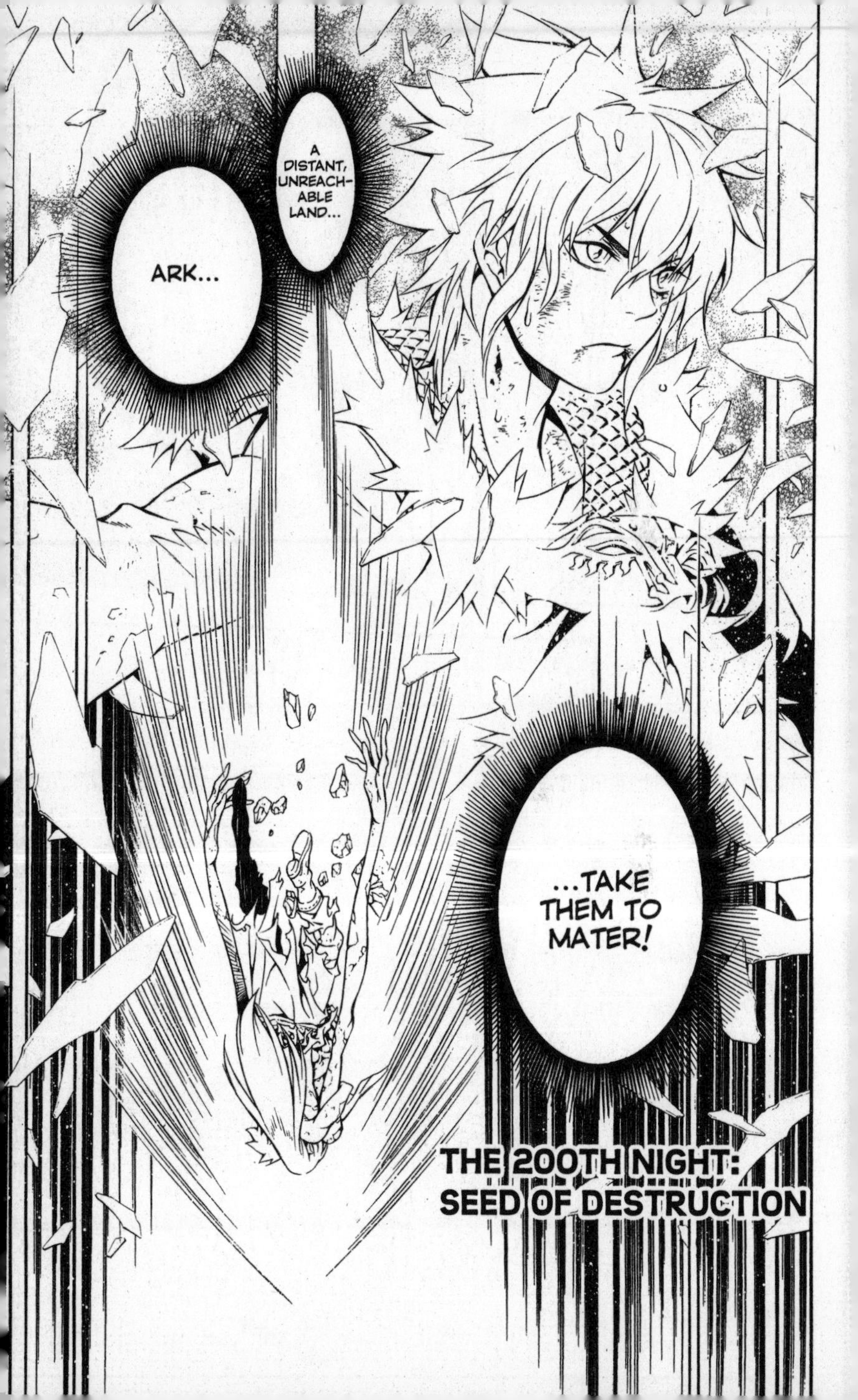
A DISTANT, UNREACHABLE LAND...
ARK...
...TAKE THEM TO MATER!
THE 200TH NIGHT: SEED OF DESTRUCTION

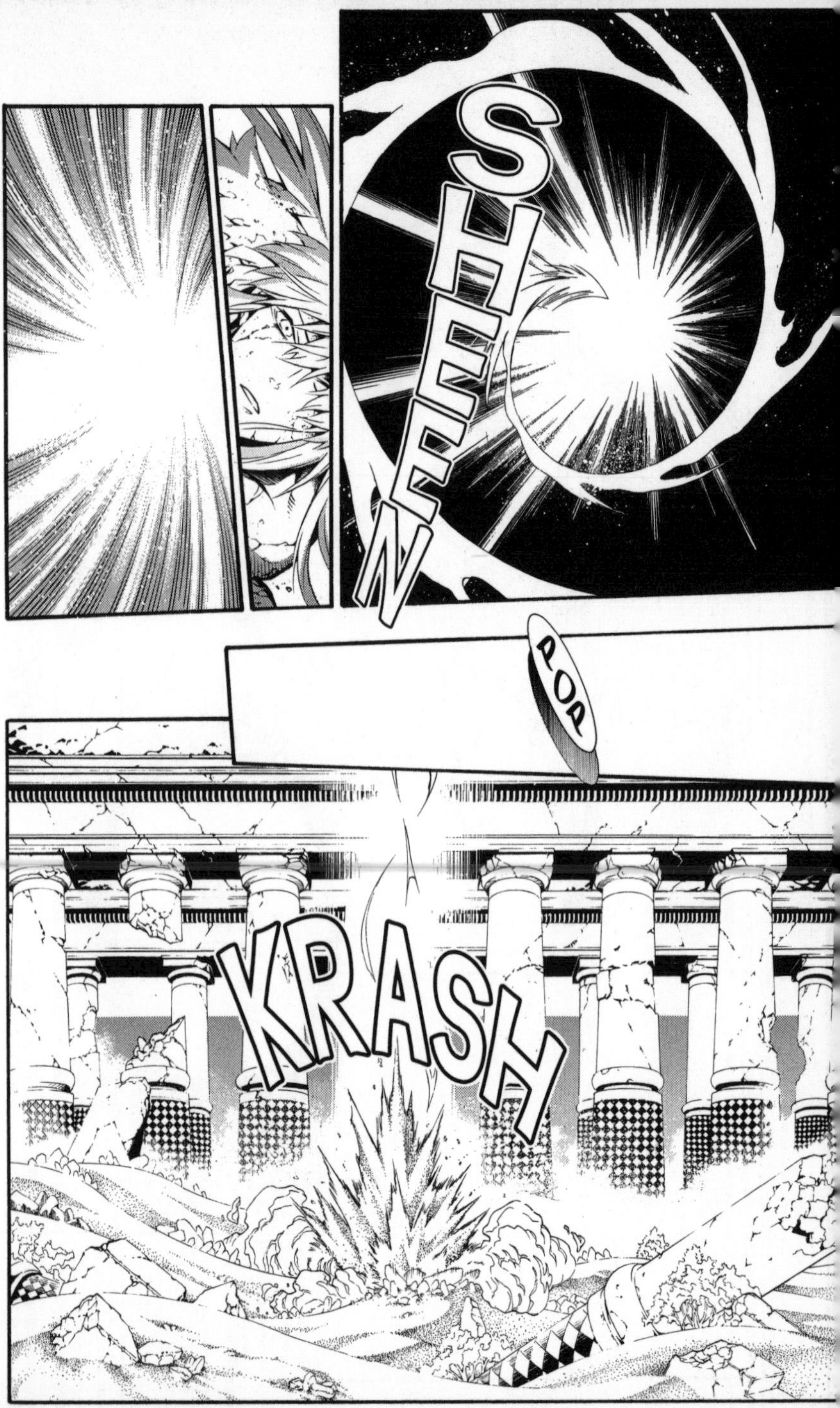
SHEEN
POP
KRASH

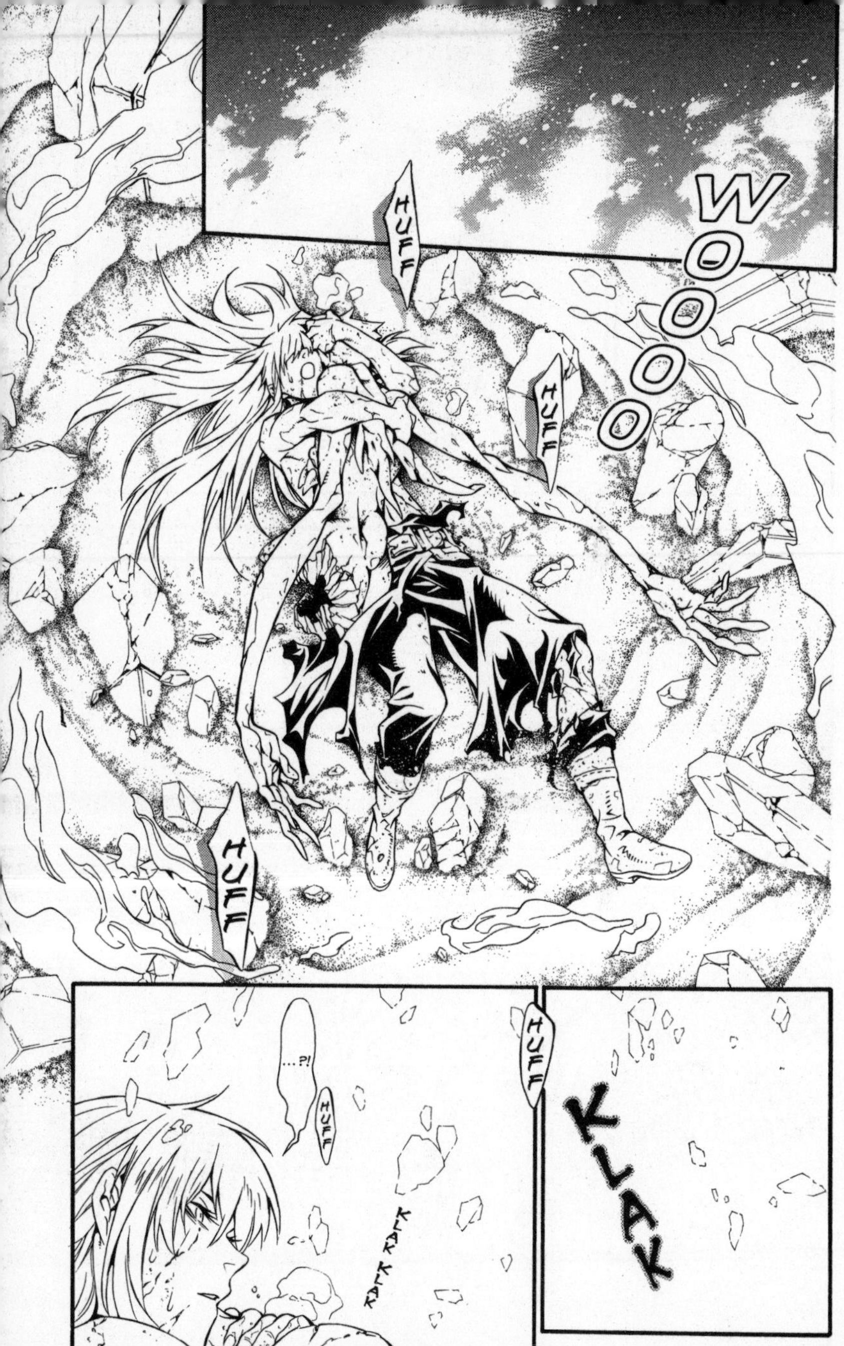
WOOOOO
HUFF
HUFF
HUFF
HUFF
KLAK
...?!
HUFF
KLAK KLAK

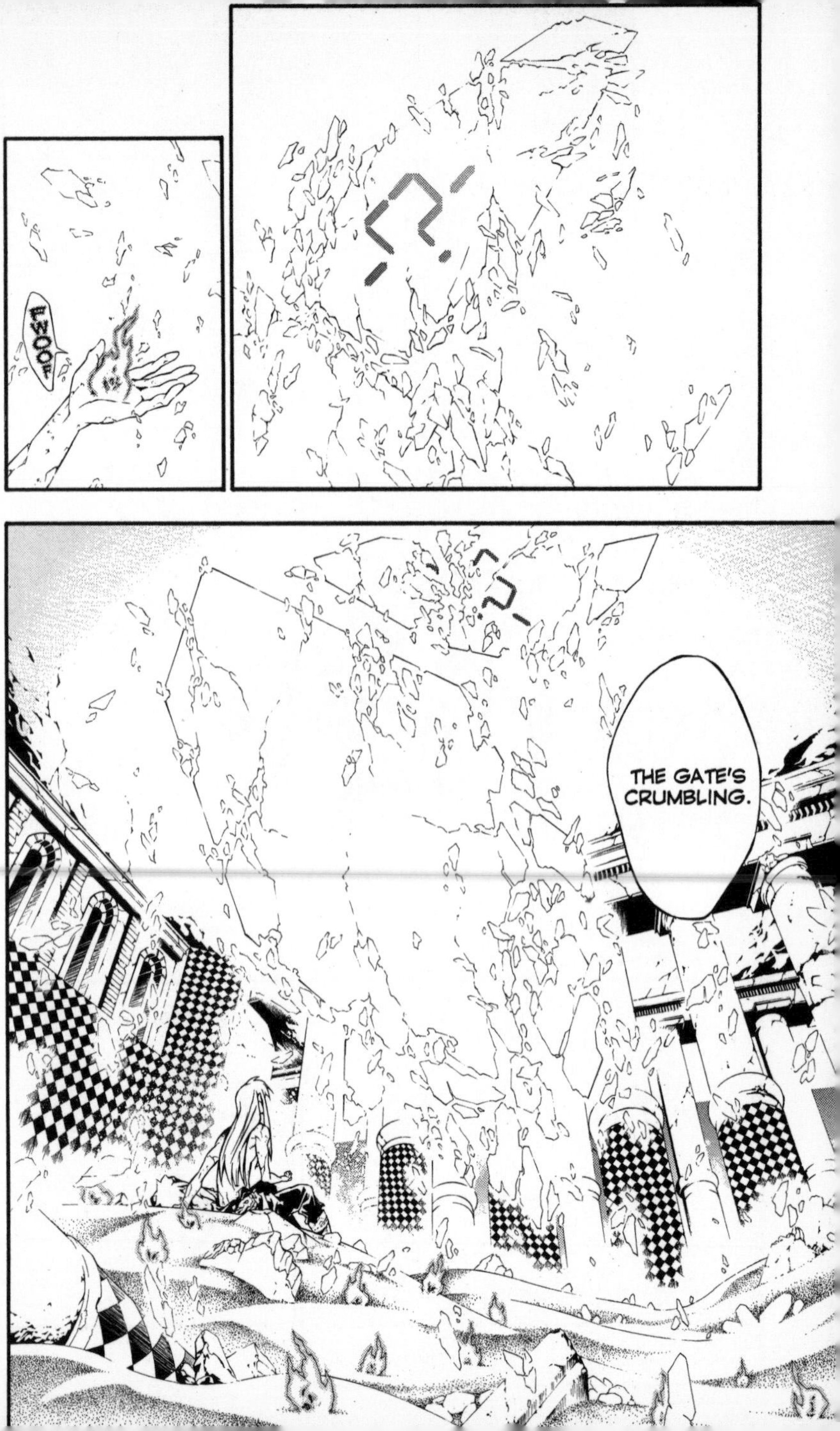
FWOOF
THE GATE'S CRUMBLING.

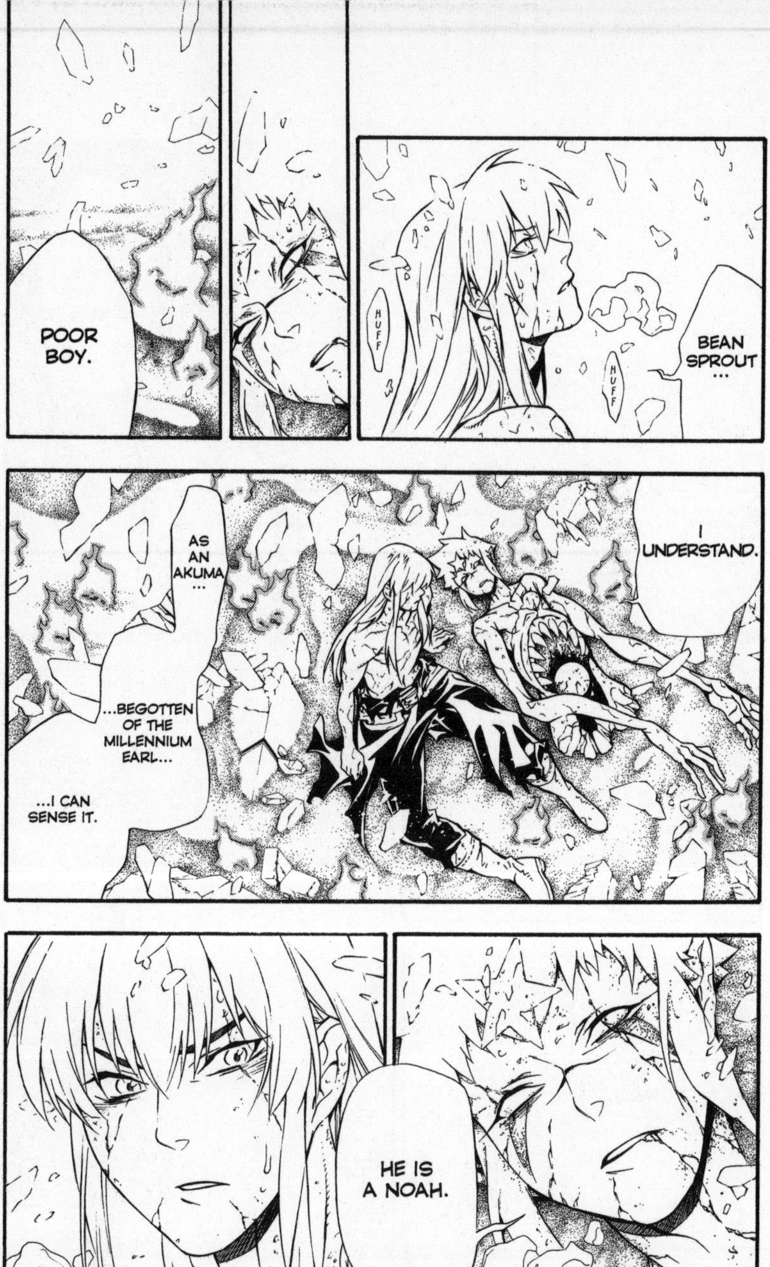
HUFF
HUFF
BEAN SPROUT...
POOR BOY.
I UNDERSTAND.
AS AN AKUMA...
...BEGOTTEN OF THE MILLENNIUM EARL...
...I CAN SENSE IT.
HE IS A NOAH.

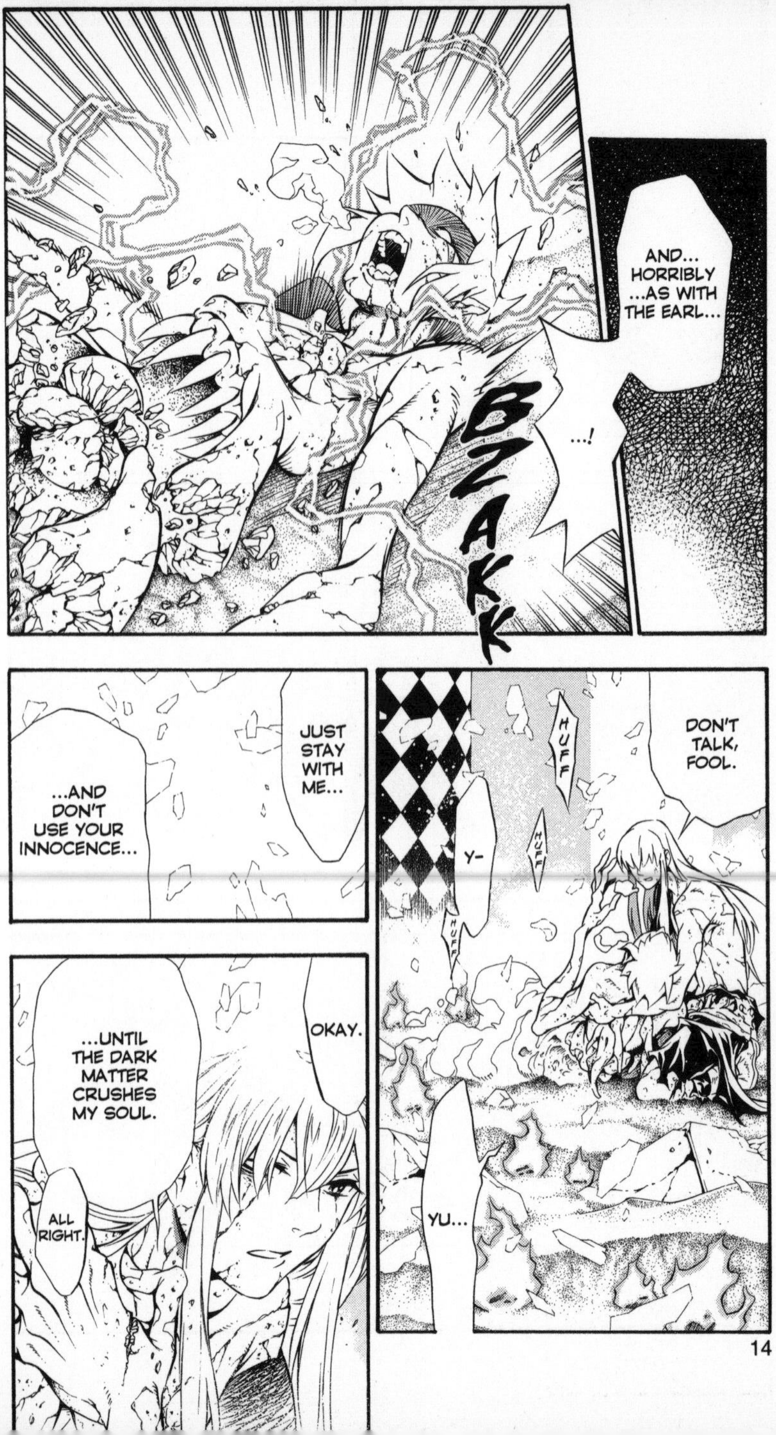
AND... HORRIBLY ...AS WITH THE EARL...
...!
BZAKK
DON'T TALK, FOOL.
HUFF
HUFF
Y-
HUFF
YU...
JUST STAY WITH ME...
...AND DON'T USE YOUR INNOCENCE...
OKAY.
...UNTIL THE DARK MATTER CRUSHES MY SOUL.
ALL RIGHT.

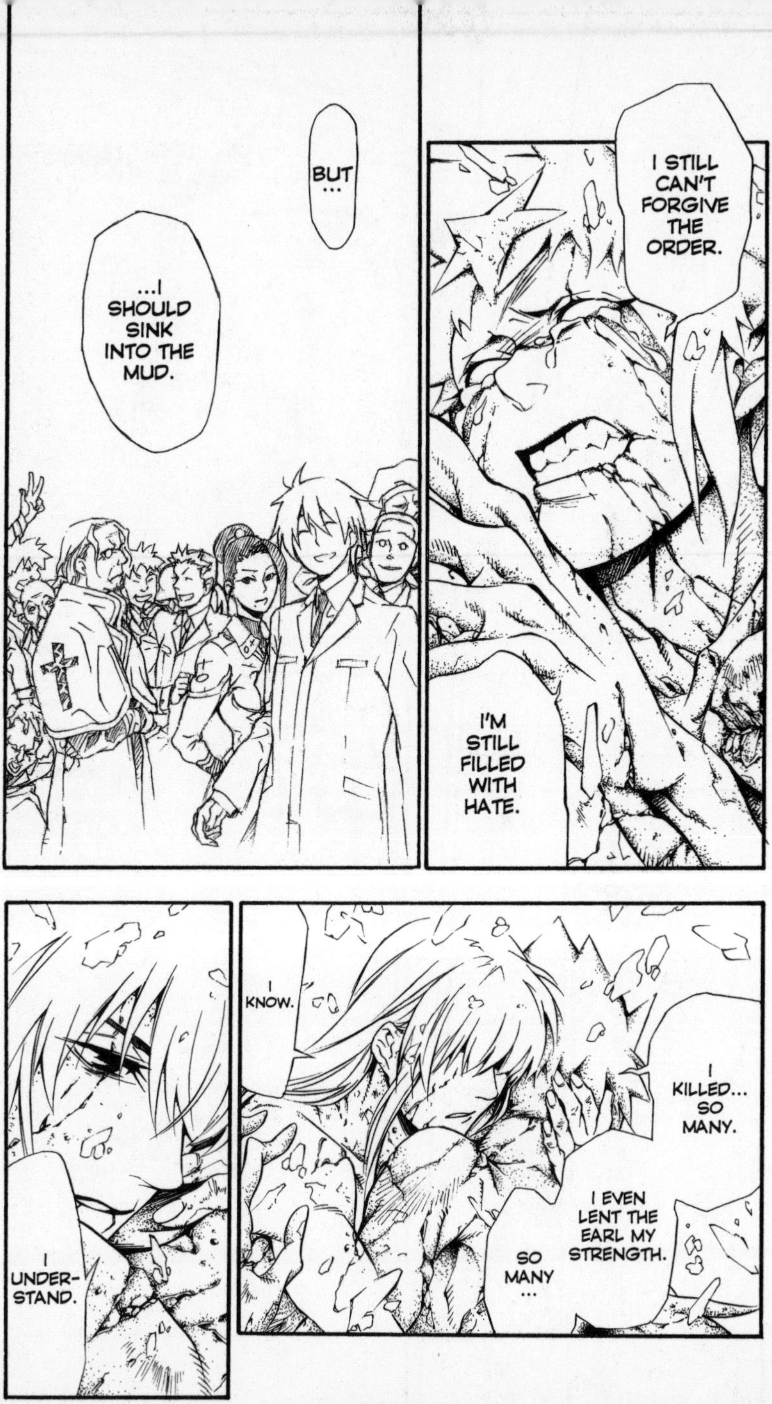
I STILL CAN'T FORGIVE THE ORDER.
I'M STILL FILLED WITH HATE.
BUT ...
...I SHOULD SINK INTO THE MUD.
I KILLED... SO MANY.
I KNOW.
I EVEN LENT THE EARL MY STRENGTH.
SO MANY ...
I UNDER-STAND.

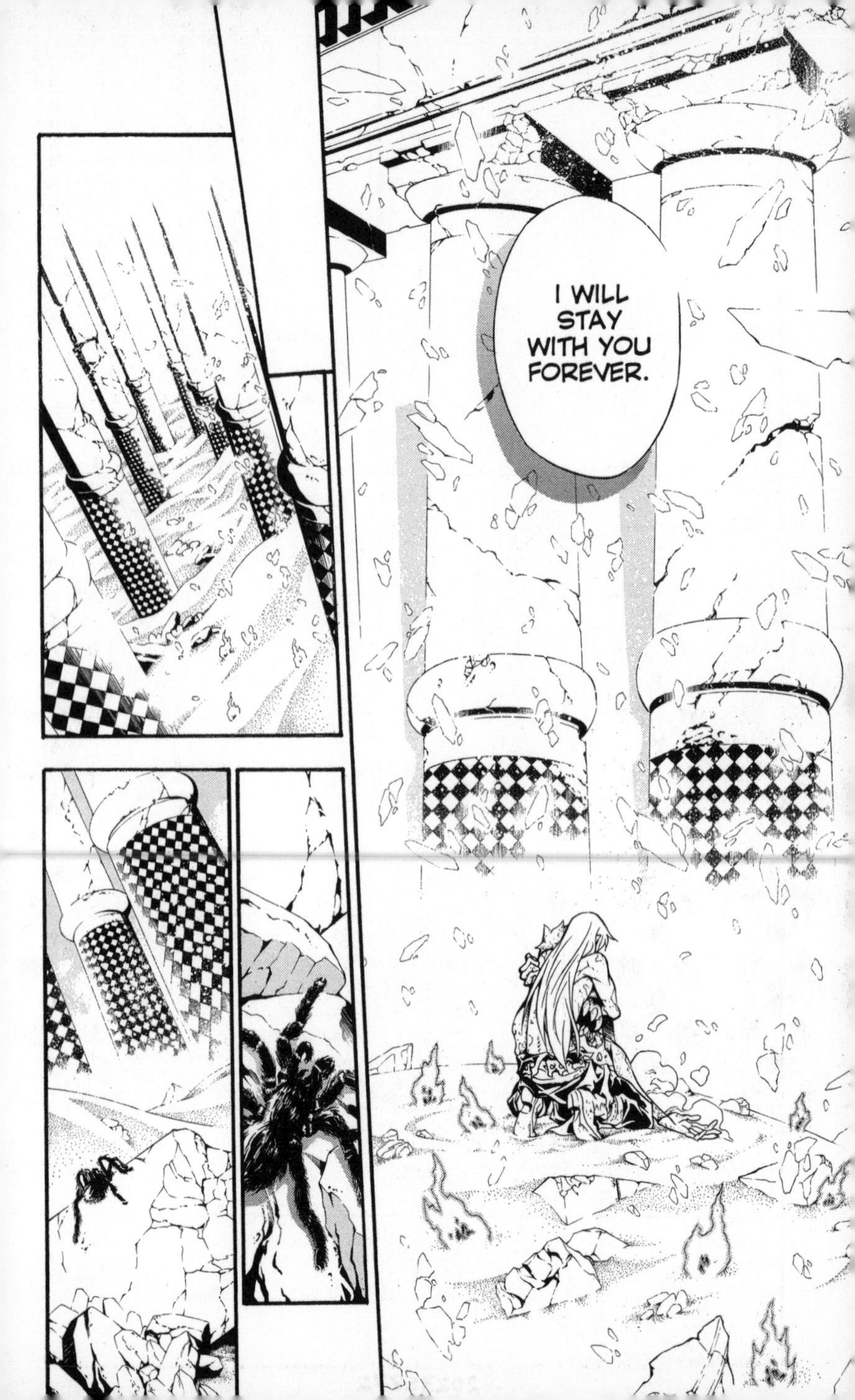
I WILL STAY WITH YOU FOREVER.

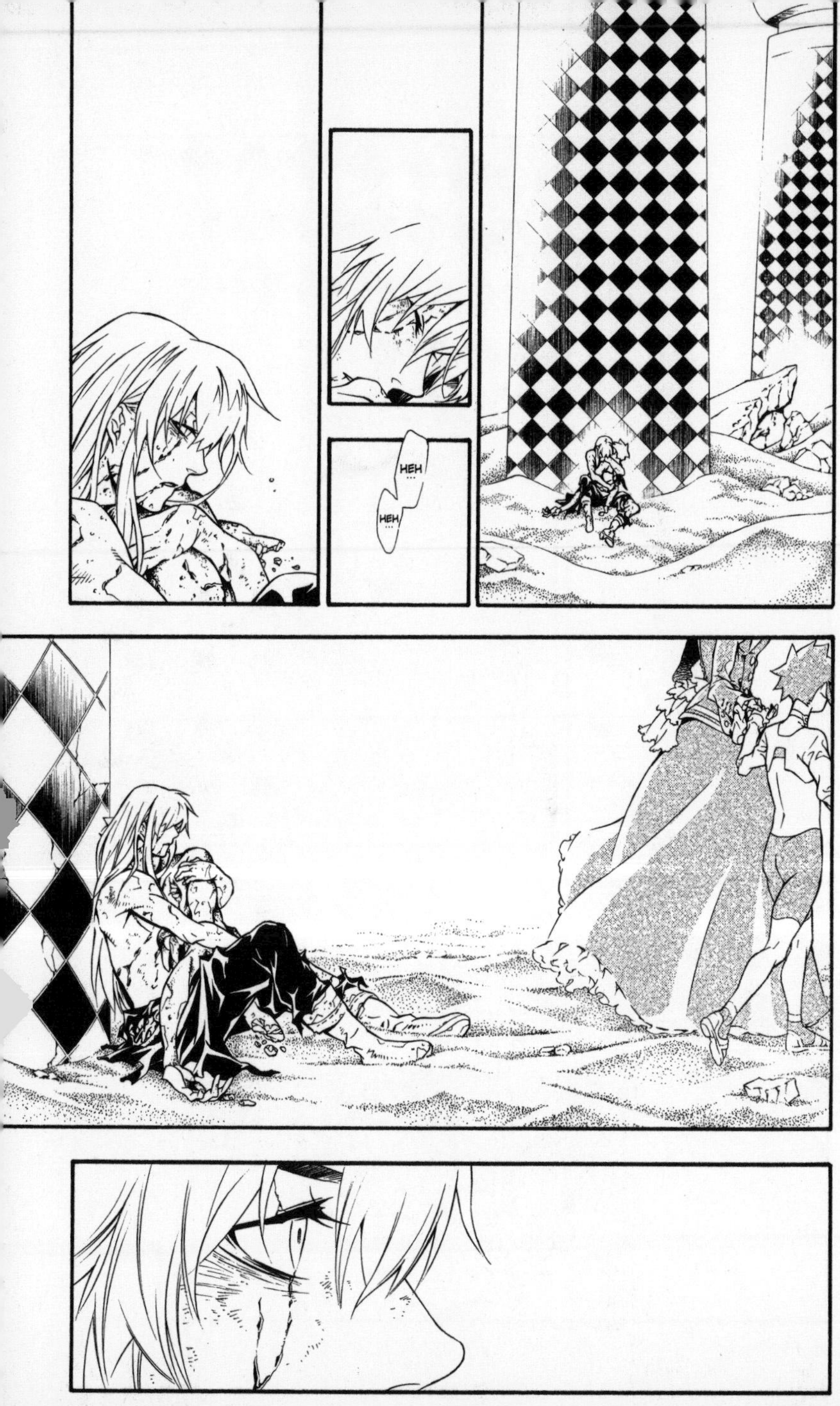
HEH... HEH...

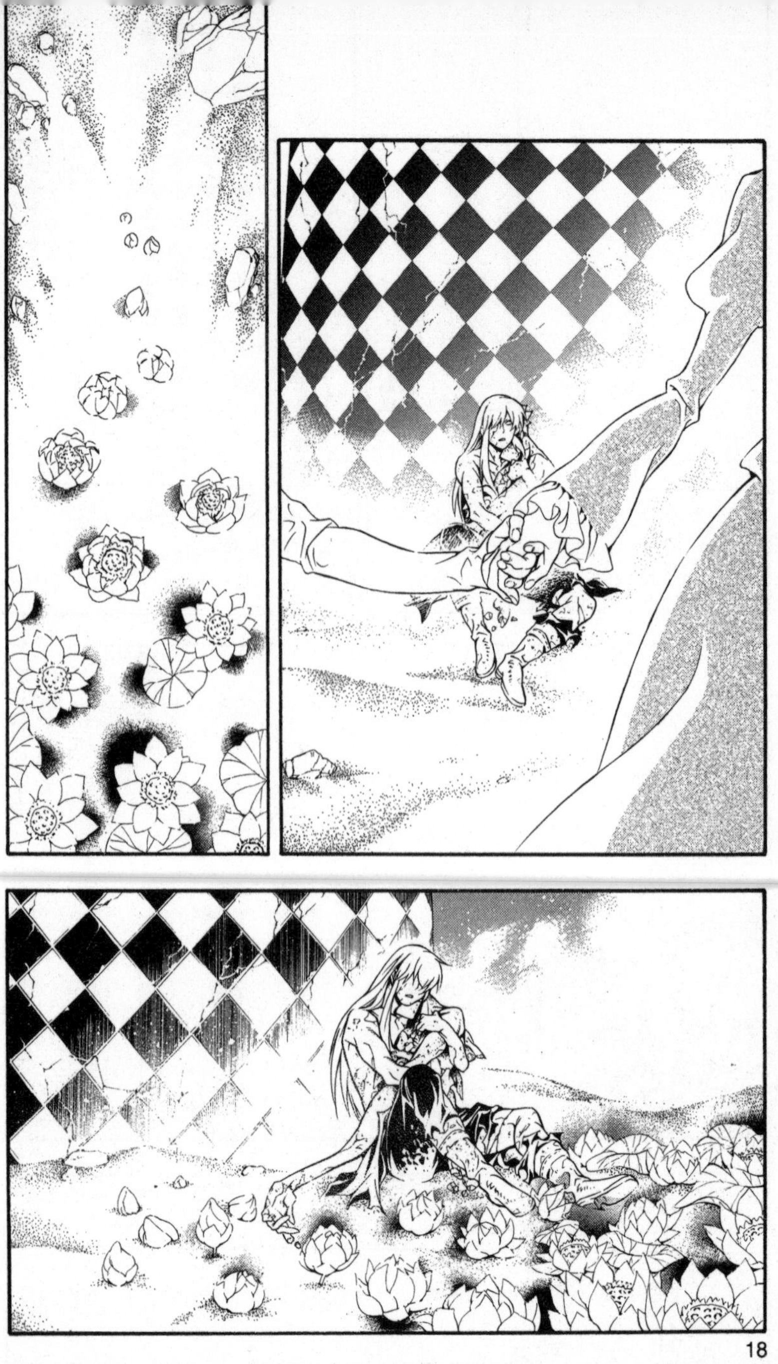

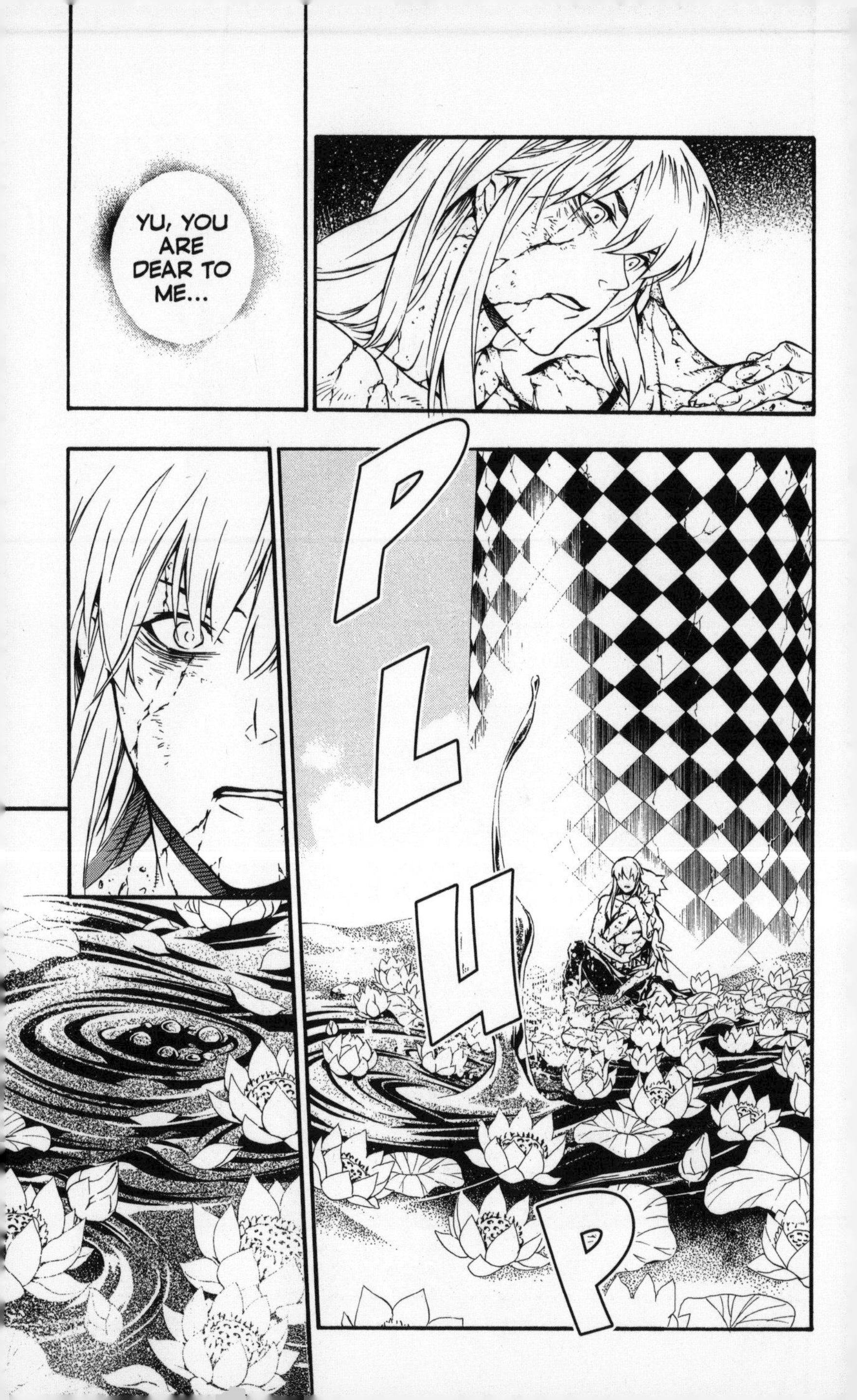
YU, YOU ARE DEAR TO ME...
PLUP

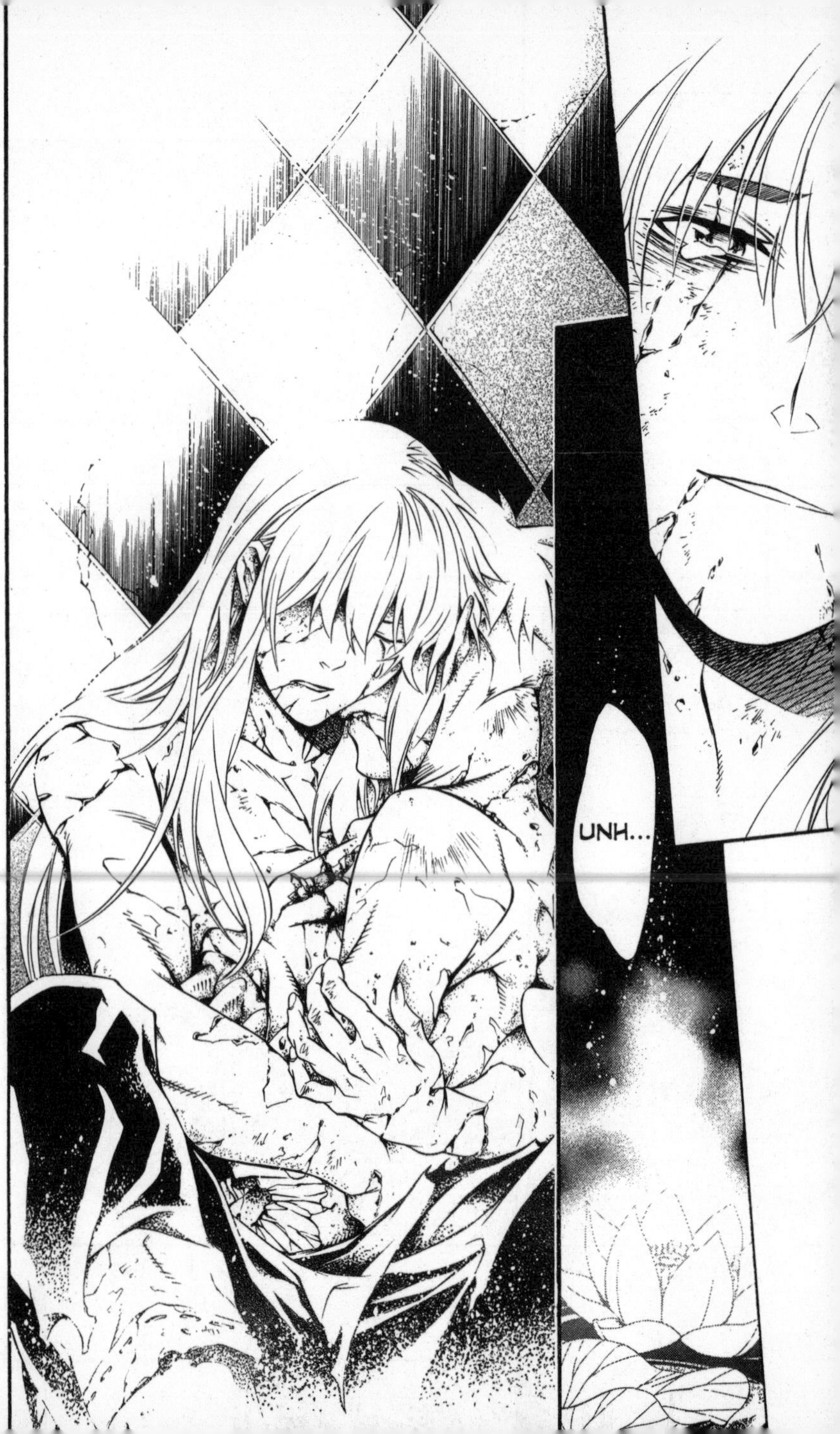
UNH...

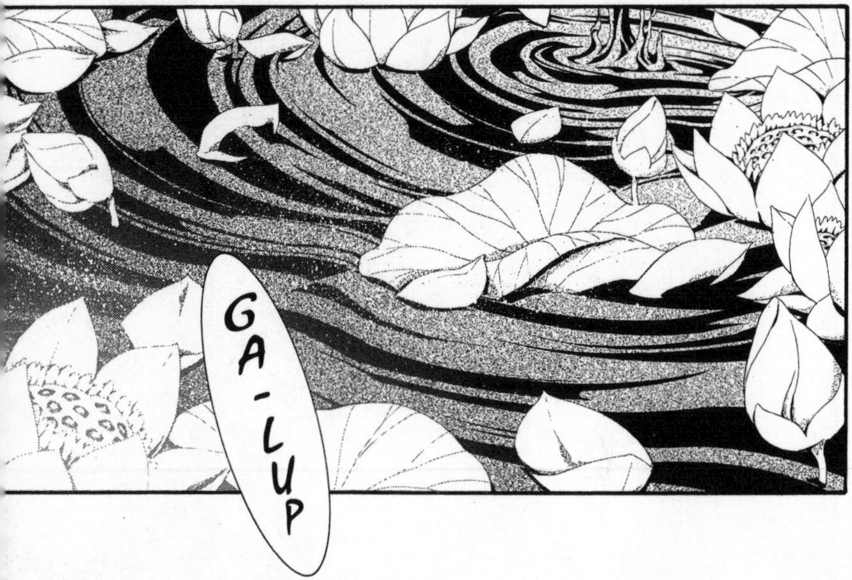
GA-LUP

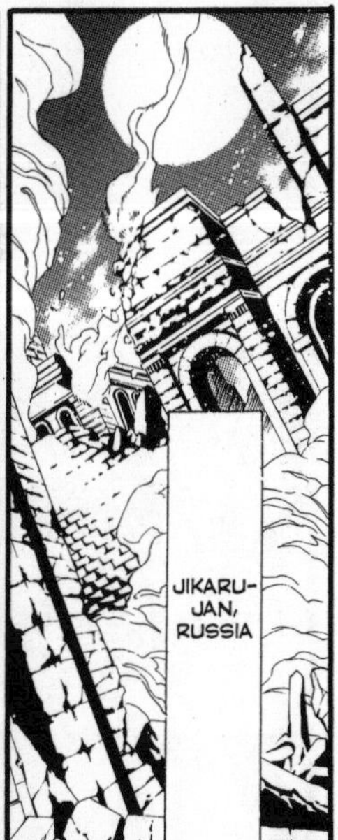
JIKARU-JAN, RUSSIA

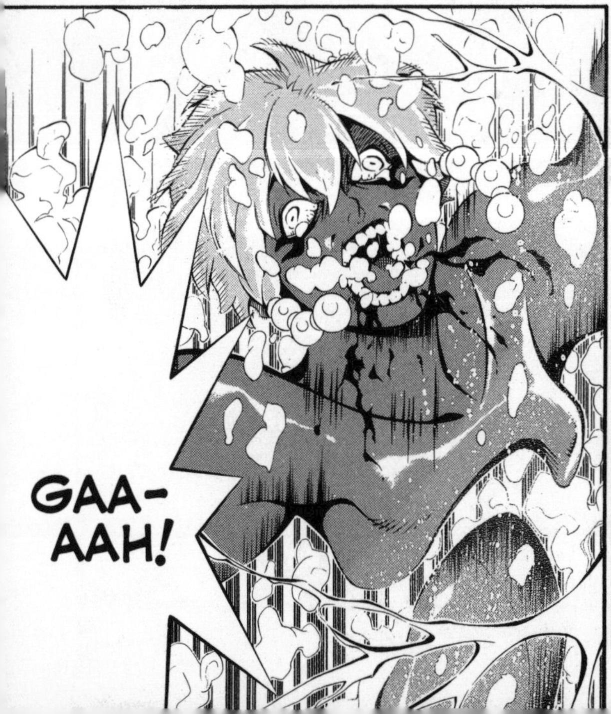
GAA-AAH!

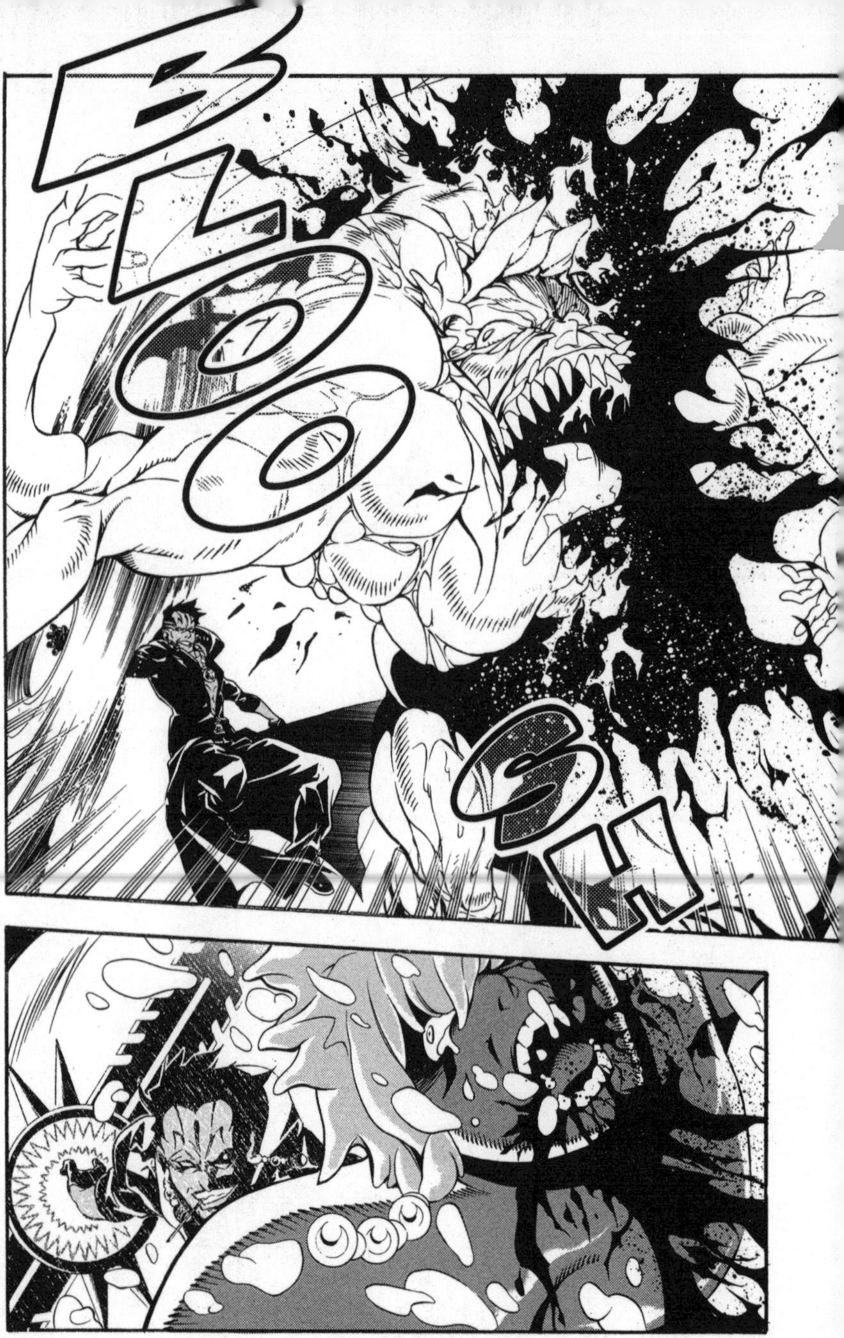
BLOOSH

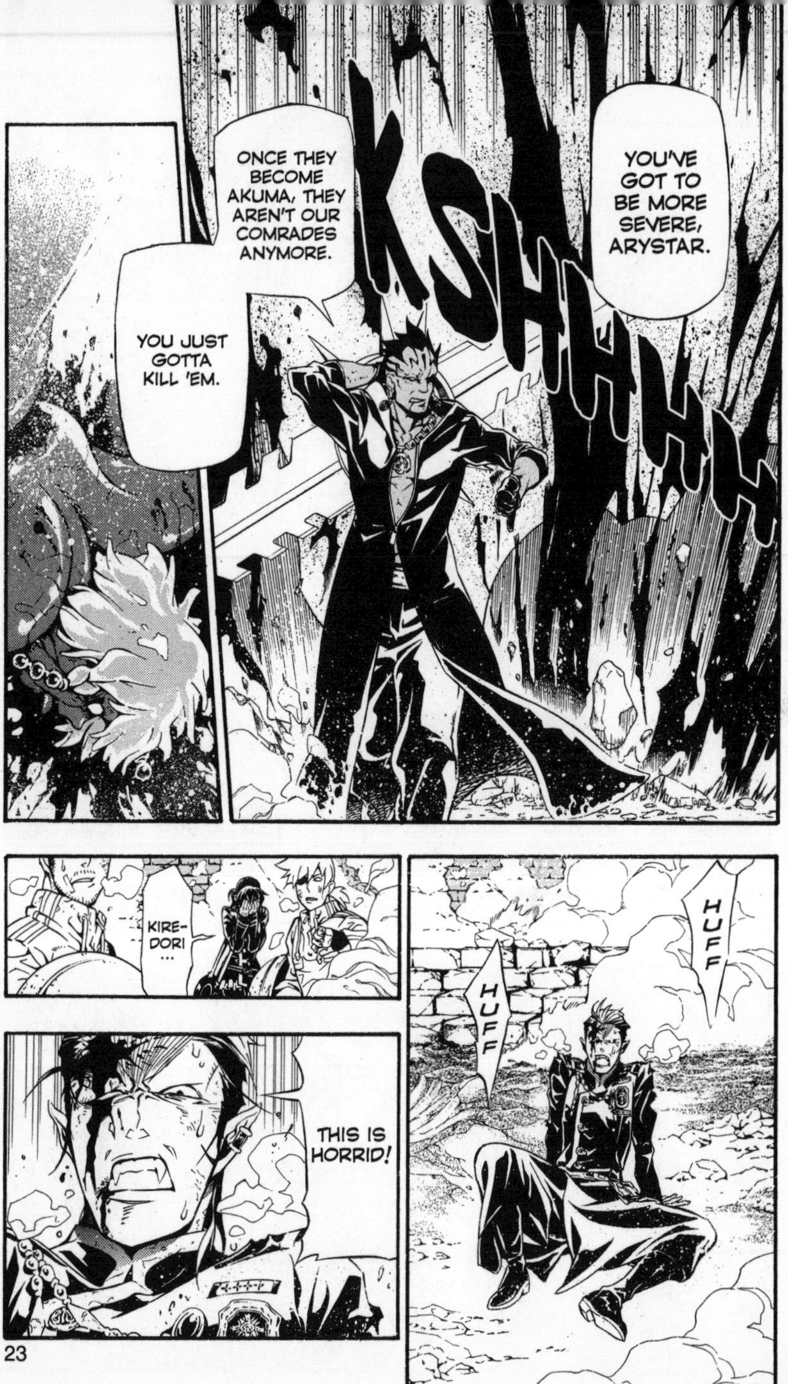
KSHHHHH
YOU'VE GOT TO BE MORE SEVERE, ARYSTAR.
ONCE THEY BECOME AKUMA, THEY AREN'T OUR COMRADES ANYMORE.
YOU JUST GOTTA KILL 'EM.
HUFF
HUFF
HUFF
HUFF
KIRE-DORI...
THIS IS HORRID!

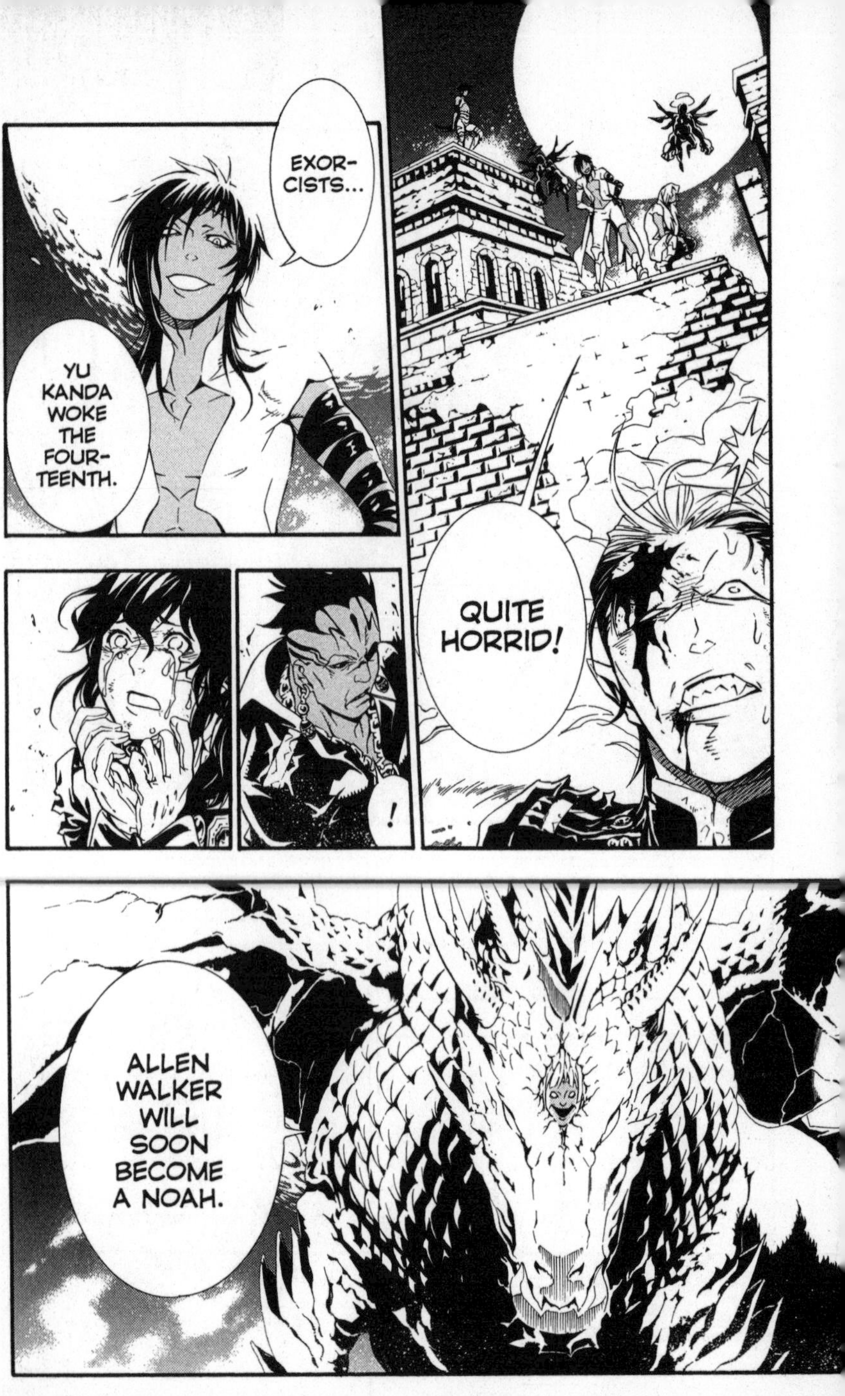
QUITE HORRID!
EXOR-CISTS...
YU KANDA WOKE THE FOUR-TEENTH.
!
ALLEN WALKER WILL SOON BECOME A NOAH.

READ THIS WAY

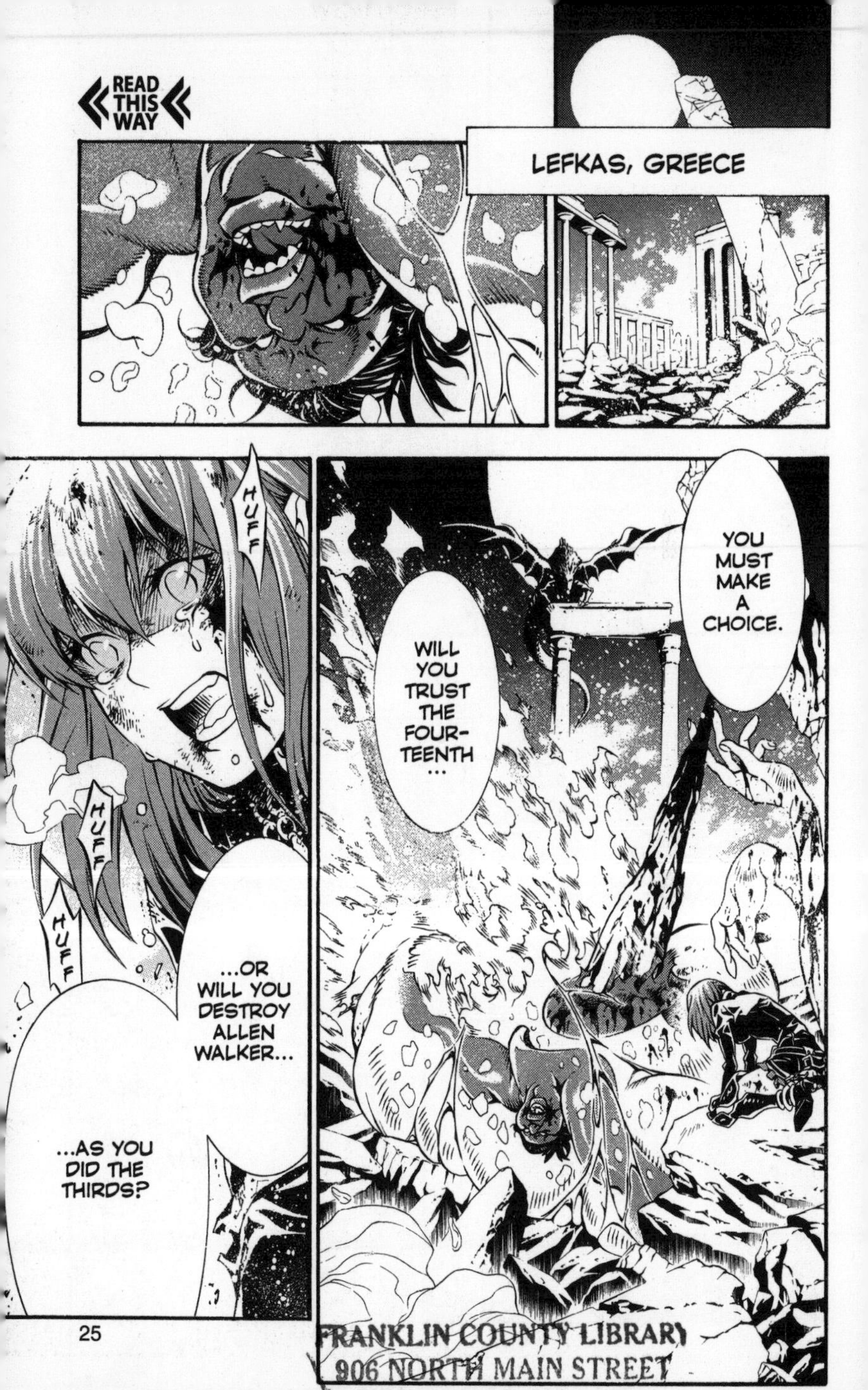
LEFKAS, GREECE
YOU MUST MAKE A CHOICE.
WILL YOU TRUST THE FOURTEENTH...
HUFF
HUFF
HUFF
...OR WILL YOU DESTROY ALLEN WALKER...
...AS YOU DID THE THIRDS?

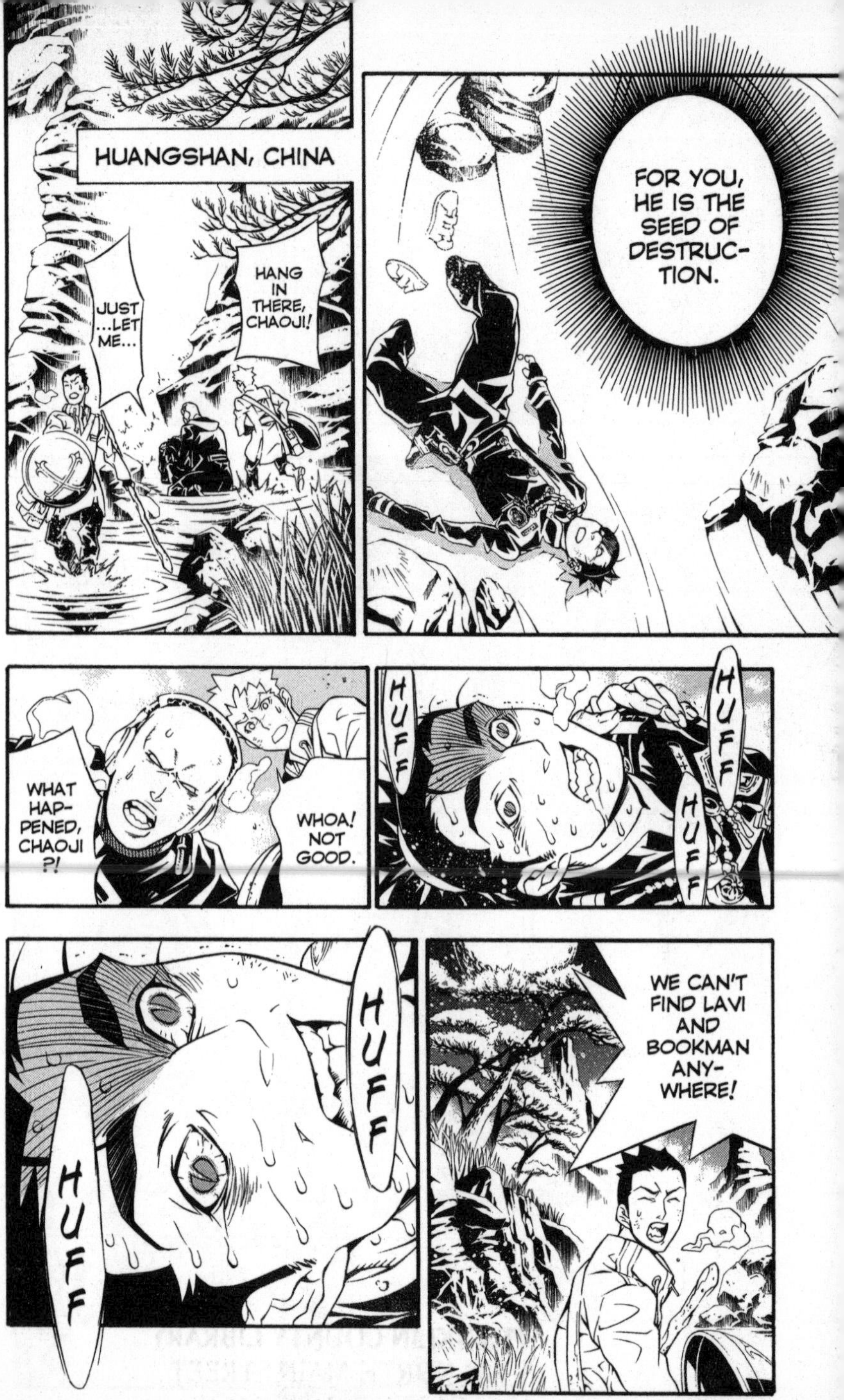
FOR YOU, HE IS THE SEED OF DESTRUCTION.
HUANGSHAN, CHINA
HANG IN THERE, CHAOJI!
JUST ...LET ME...
HUFF
HUFF
HUFF
WHOA! NOT GOOD.
WHAT HAPPENED, CHAOJI?!
WE CAN'T FIND LAVI AND BOOKMAN ANYWHERE!
HUFF
HUFF

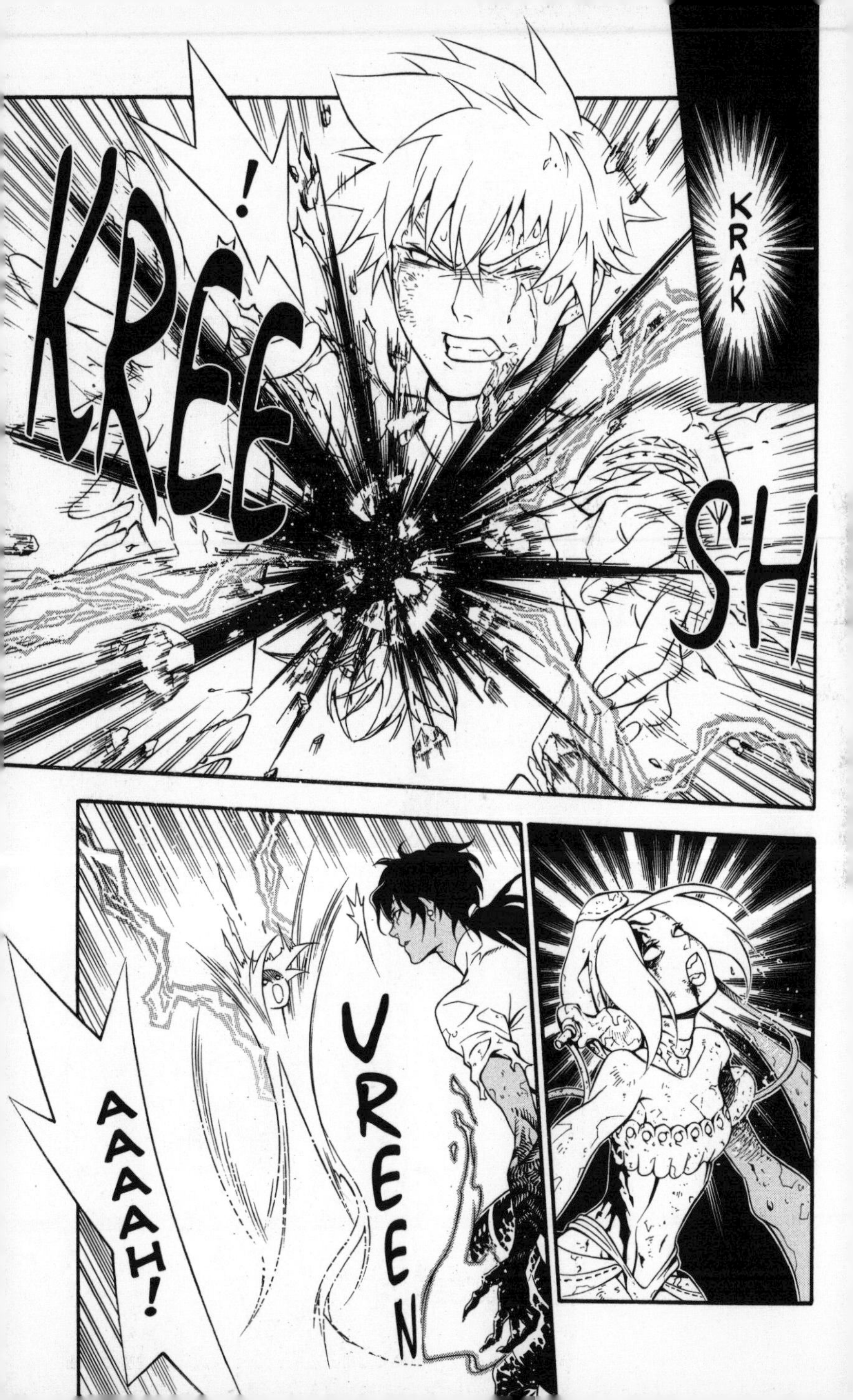
KRAK
!
KREE SH
VREEN
AAAAH!

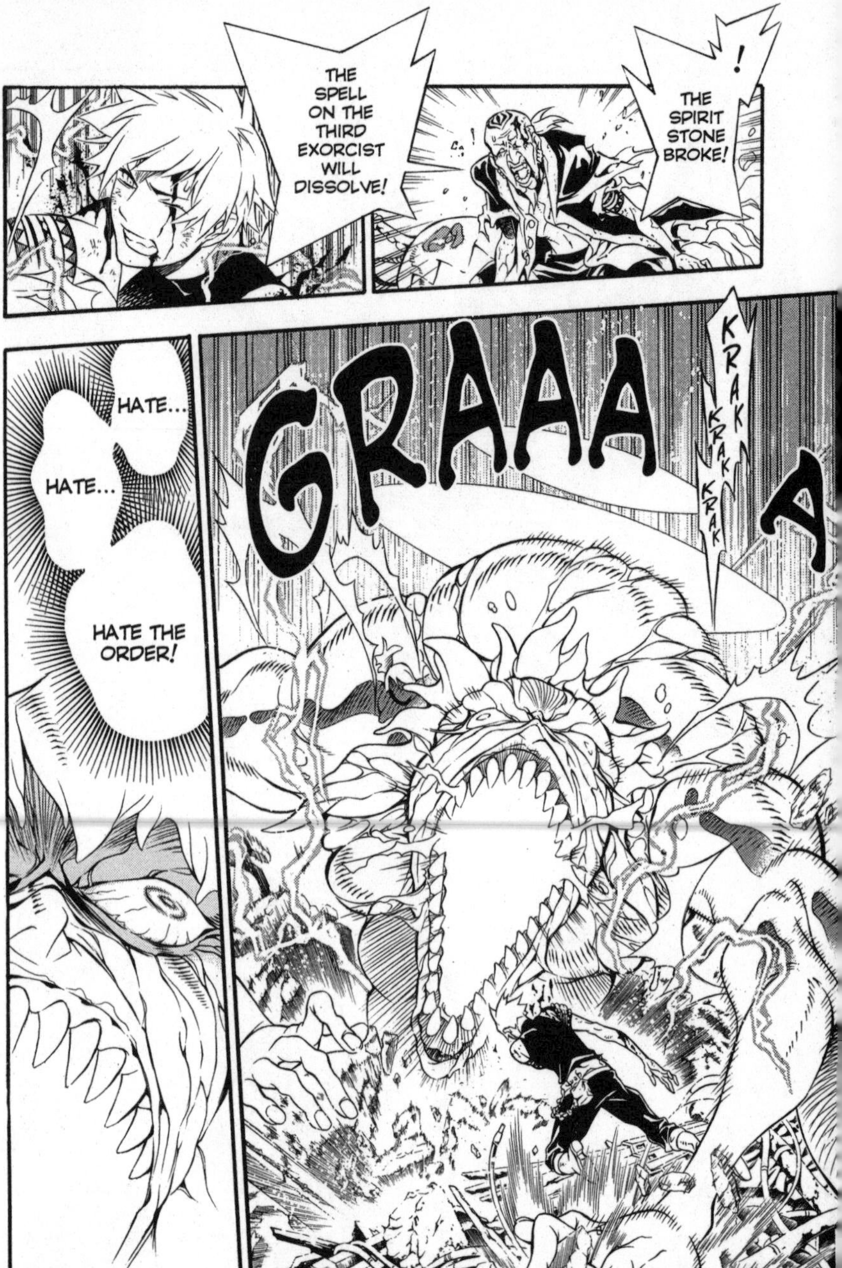
!
THE SPIRIT STONE BROKE!
THE SPELL ON THE THIRD EXORCIST WILL DISSOLVE!
KRAK KRAK KRAK
GRAAAA
HATE...
HATE...
HATE THE ORDER!

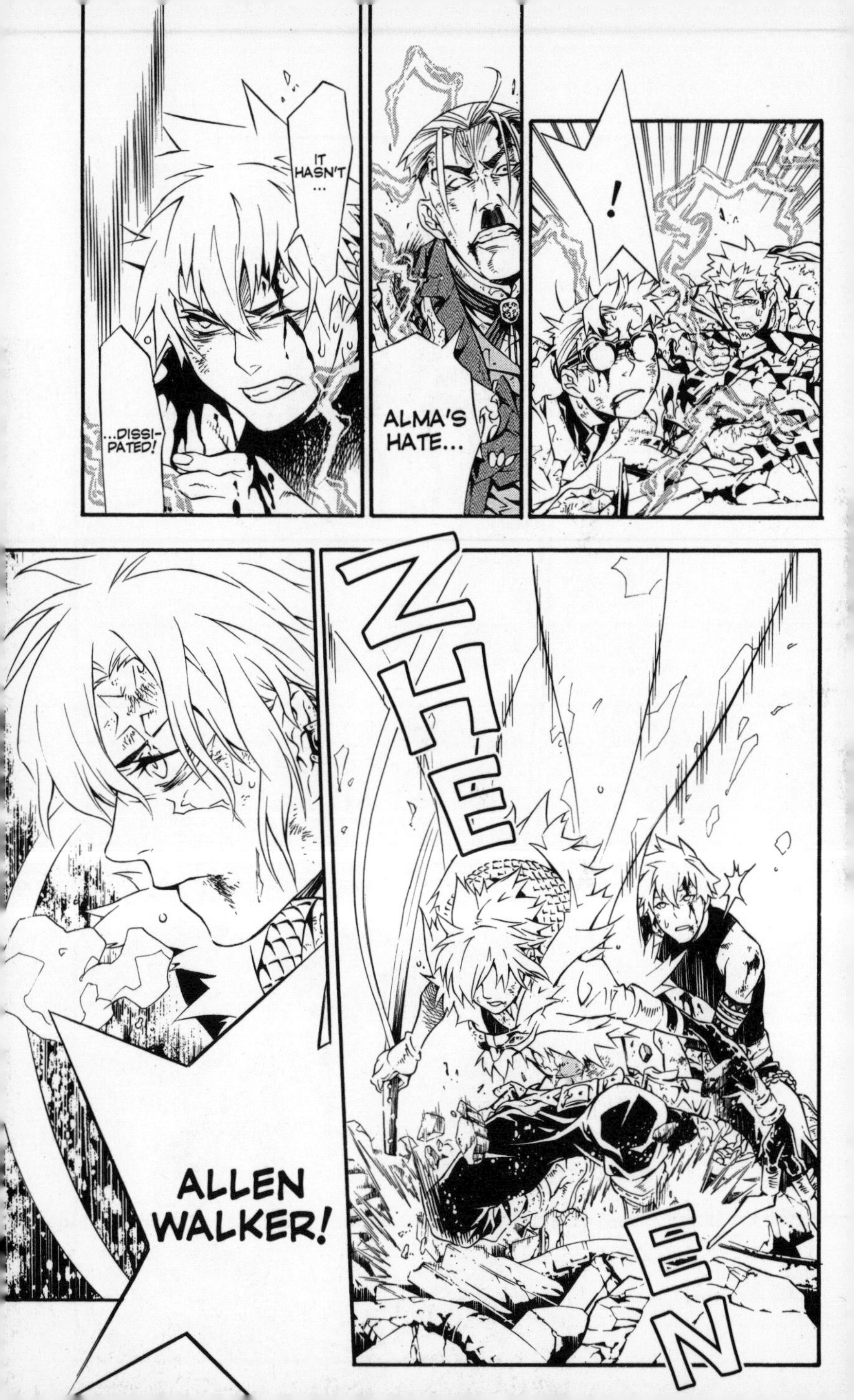
!
ALMA'S HATE...
IT HASN'T ...
...DISSI-PATED!
ZHEEN
ALLEN WALKER!

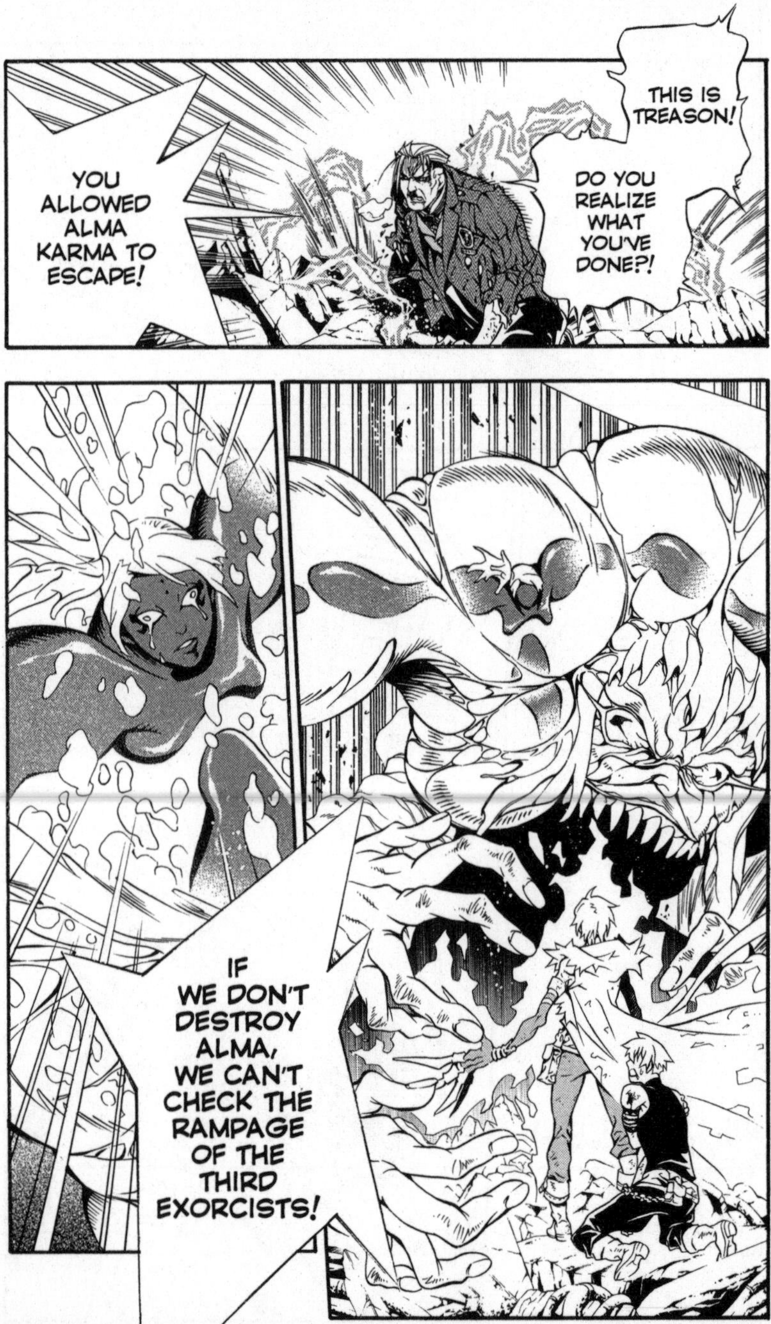
THIS IS TREASON!
DO YOU REALIZE WHAT YOU'VE DONE?!
YOU ALLOWED ALMA KARMA TO ESCAPE!
IF WE DON'T DESTROY ALMA, WE CAN'T CHECK THE RAMPAGE OF THE THIRD EXORCISTS!

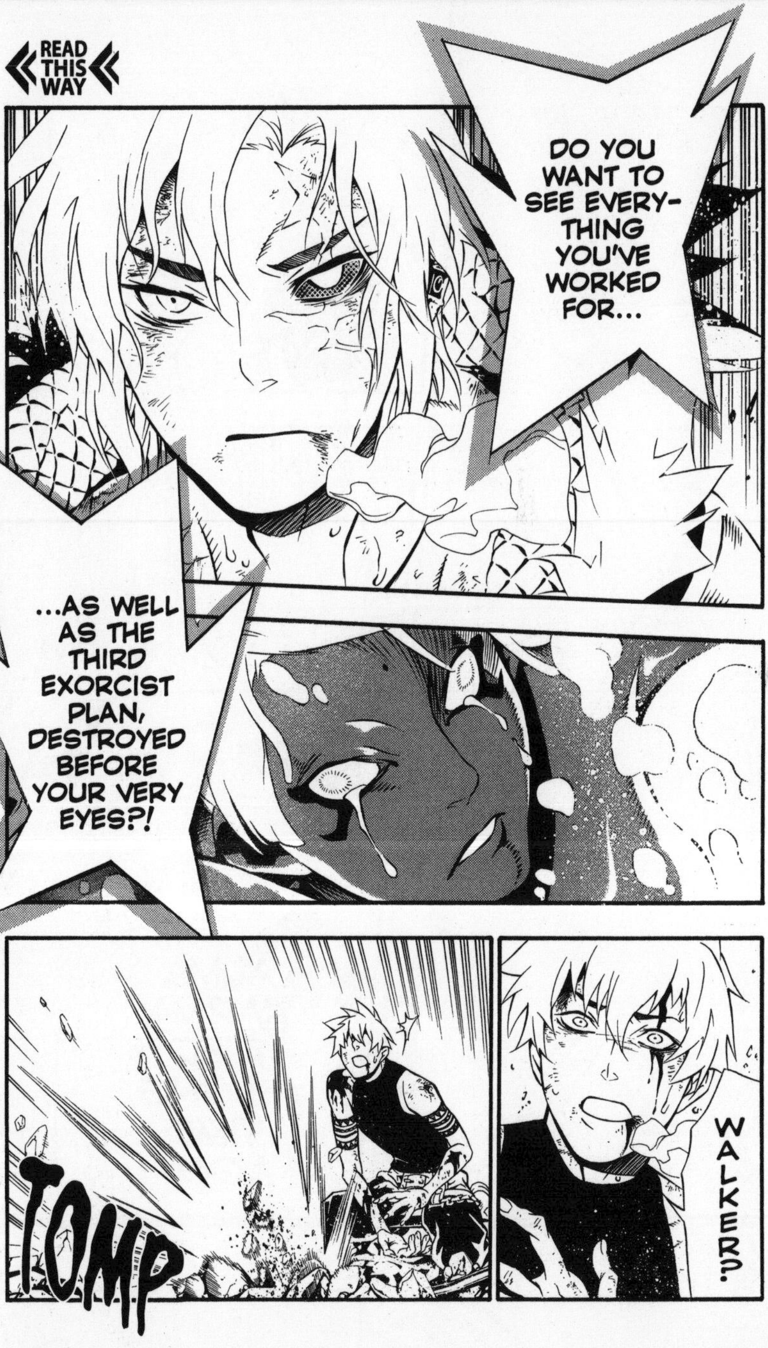
READ THIS WAY
DO YOU WANT TO SEE EVERYTHING YOU'VE WORKED FOR...
...AS WELL AS THE THIRD EXORCIST PLAN, DESTROYED BEFORE YOUR VERY EYES?!
WALKER?
TOMP

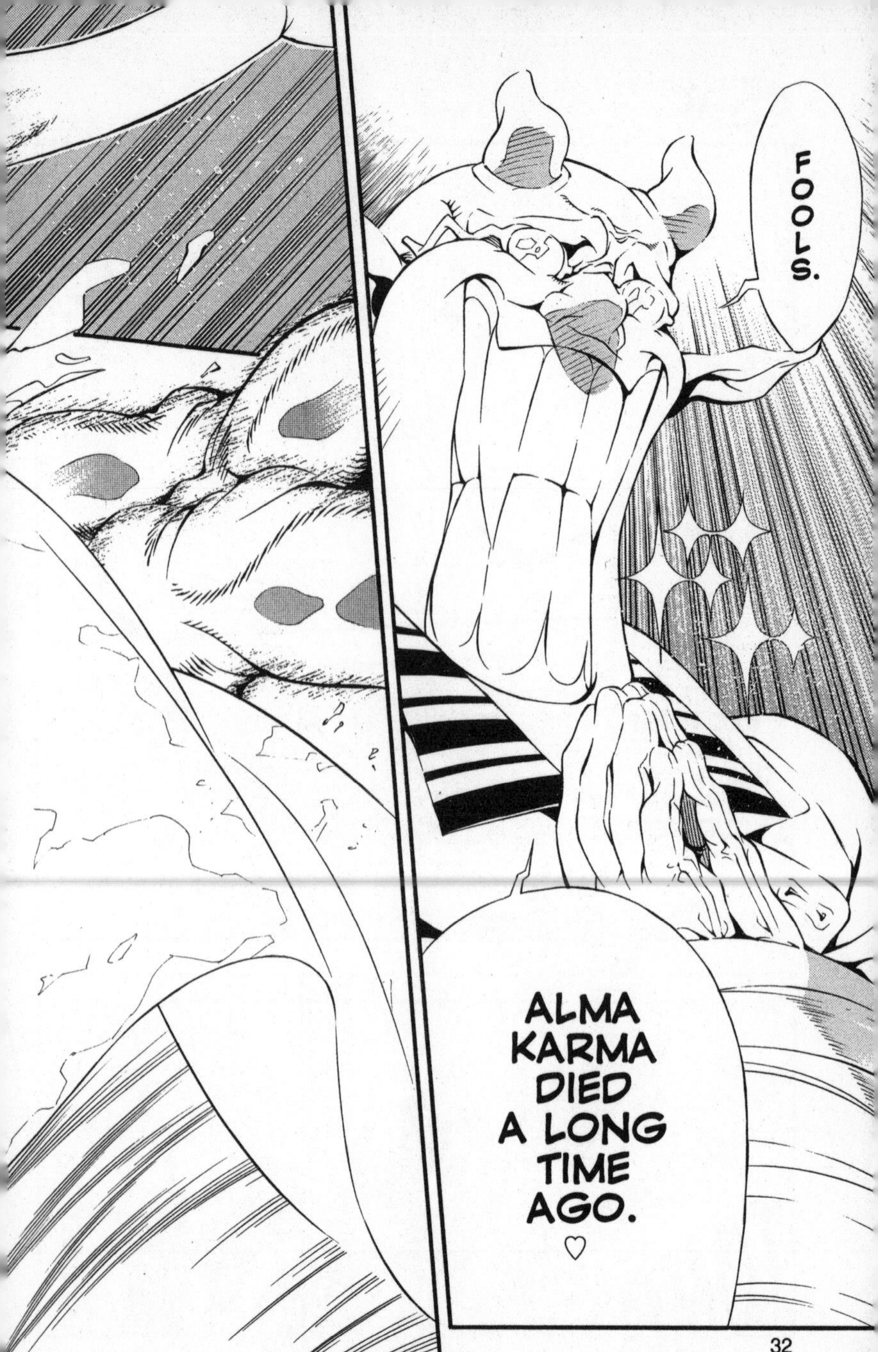
FOOLS.
ALMA KARMA DIED A LONG TIME AGO. ♡

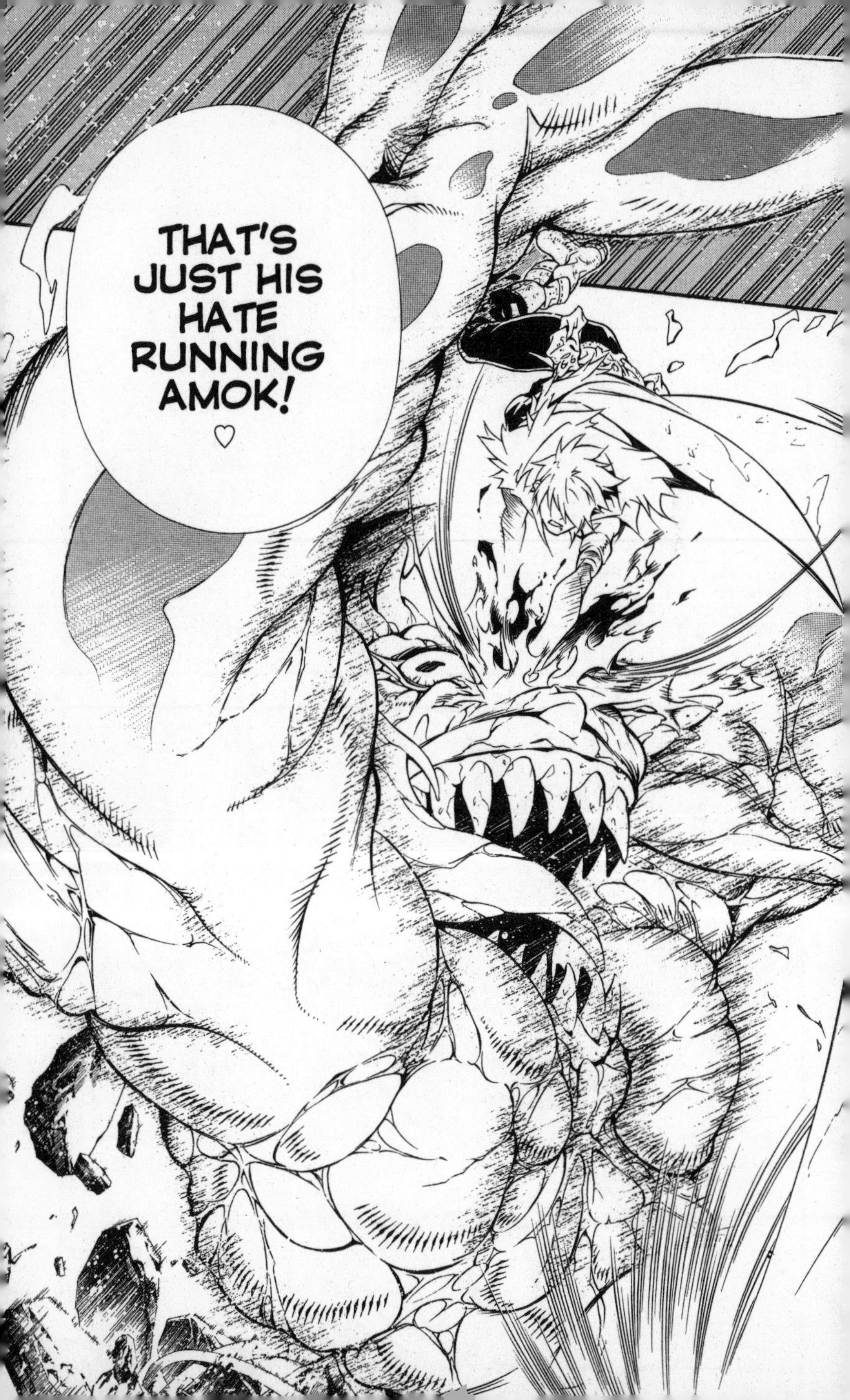
THAT'S JUST HIS HATE RUNNING AMOK! ♡

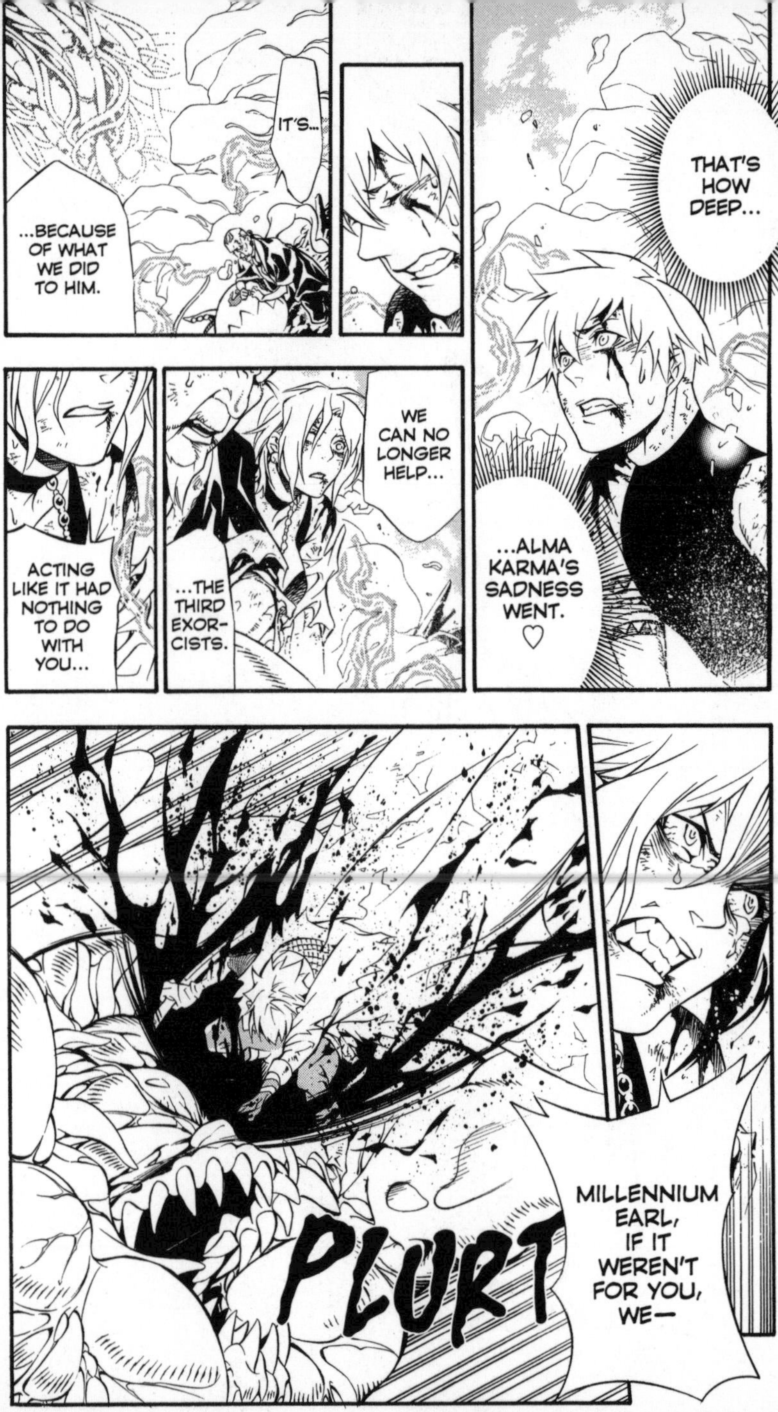
THAT'S HOW DEEP...
...ALMA KARMA'S SADNESS WENT. ♡
IT'S...
...BECAUSE OF WHAT WE DID TO HIM.
WE CAN NO LONGER HELP...
...THE THIRD EXORCISTS.
ACTING LIKE IT HAD NOTHING TO DO WITH YOU...
MILLENNIUM EARL, IF IT WEREN'T FOR YOU, WE—
PLURT

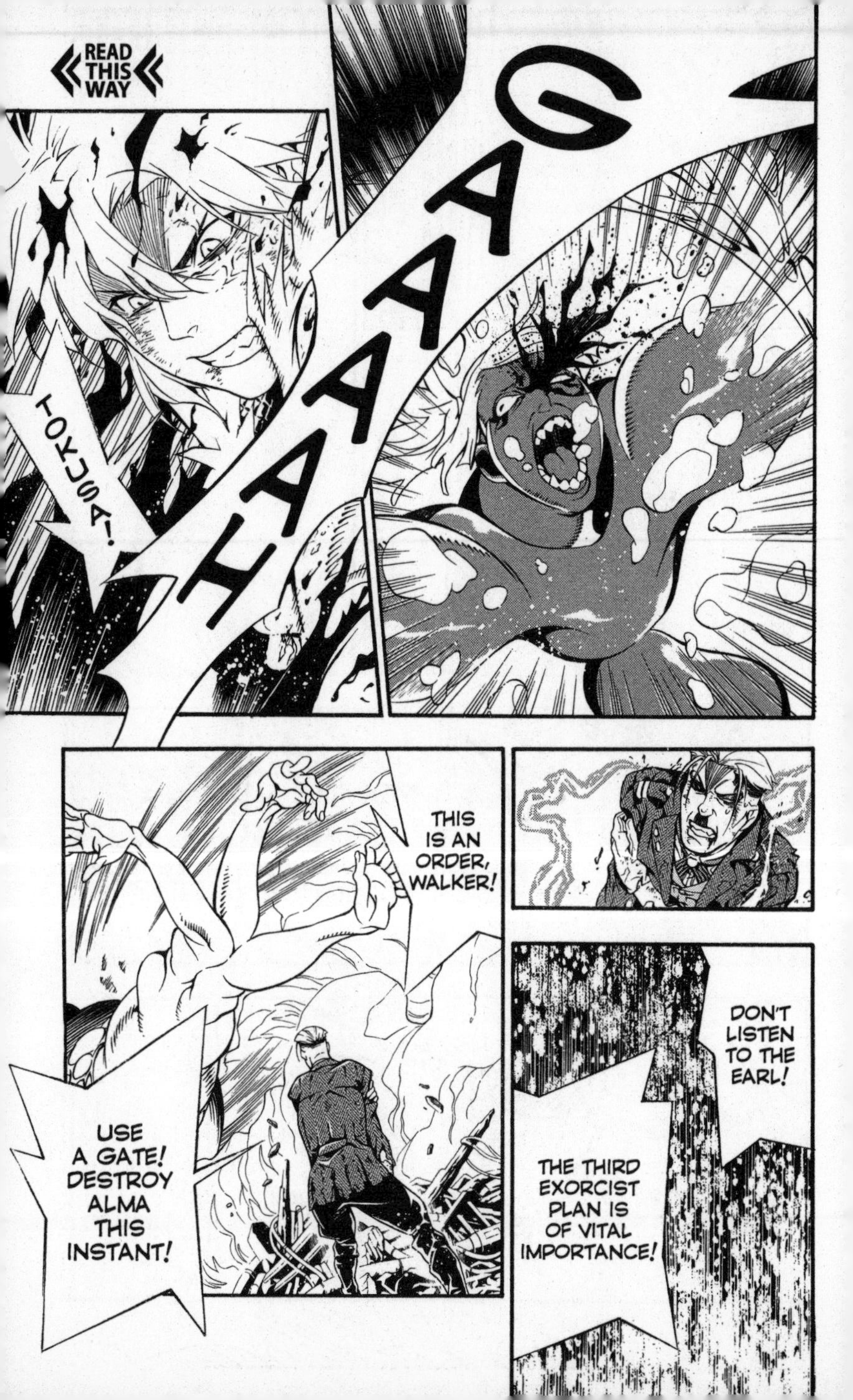
READ THIS WAY
GAAAAH
TOKUSA!
THIS IS AN ORDER, WALKER!
USE A GATE! DESTROY ALMA THIS INSTANT!
DON'T LISTEN TO THE EARL!
THE THIRD EXORCIST PLAN IS OF VITAL IMPORTANCE!

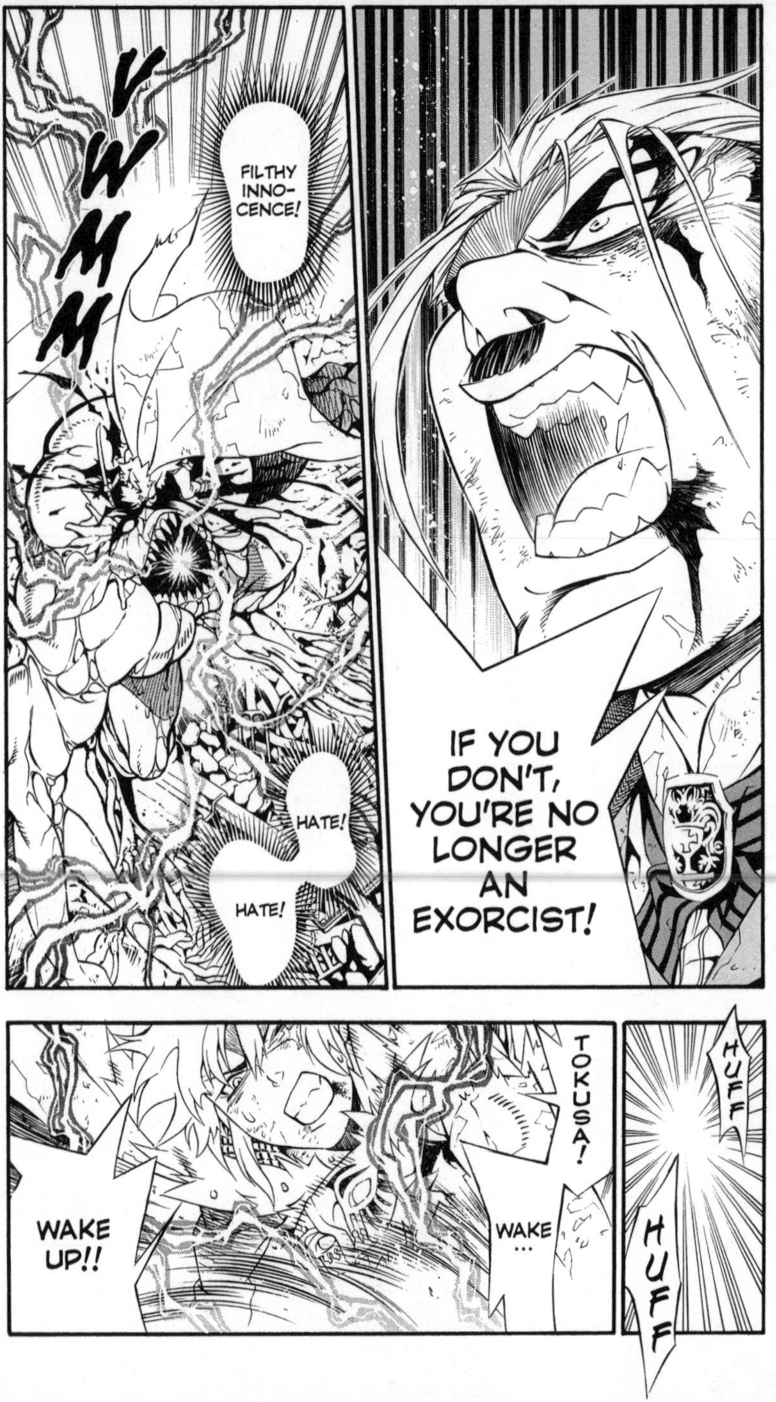
IF YOU DON'T, YOU'RE NO LONGER AN EXORCIST!
VWMMM
FILTHY INNOCENCE!
HATE!
HATE!
HUFF
HUFF
TOKUSA!
WAKE ...
WAKE UP!!

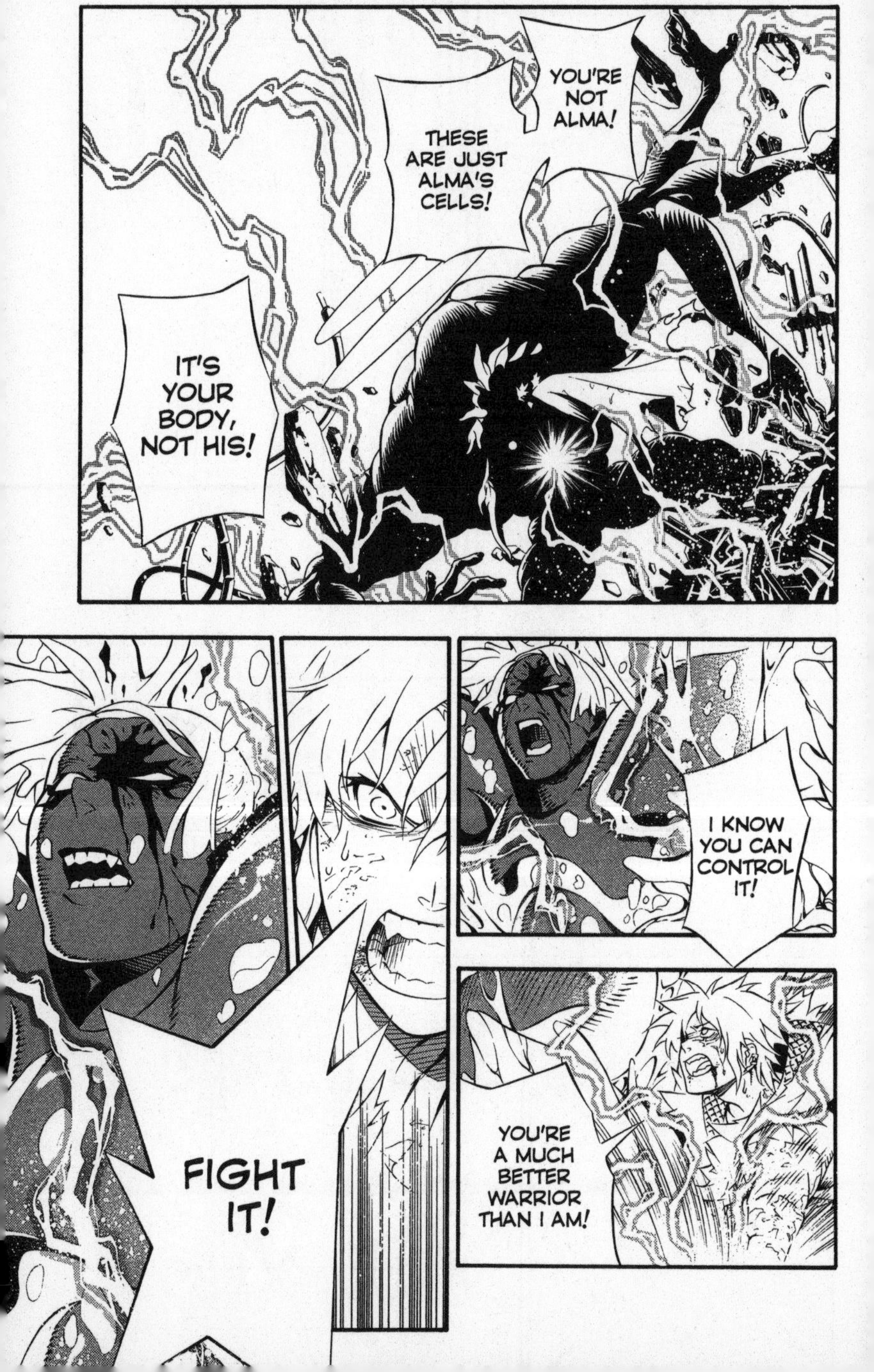
YOU'RE NOT ALMA!
THESE ARE JUST ALMA'S CELLS!
IT'S YOUR BODY, NOT HIS!
I KNOW YOU CAN CONTROL IT!
YOU'RE A MUCH BETTER WARRIOR THAN I AM!
FIGHT IT!

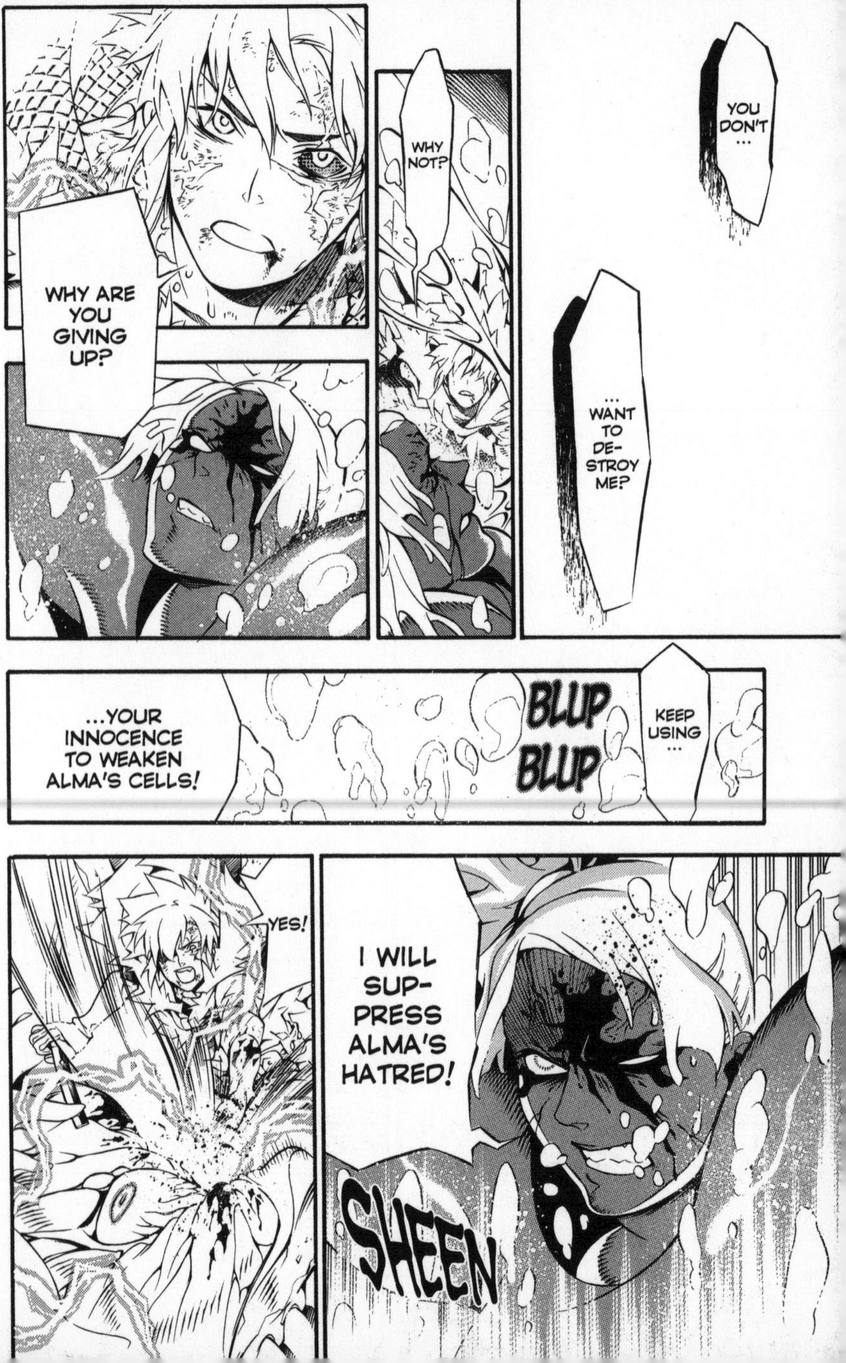
YOU DON'T ...
... WANT TO DE-STROY ME?
WHY NOT?
WHY ARE YOU GIVING UP?
KEEP USING ...
BLUP BLUP
...YOUR INNOCENCE TO WEAKEN ALMA'S CELLS!
I WILL SUP-PRESS ALMA'S HATRED!
SHEEN
YES!

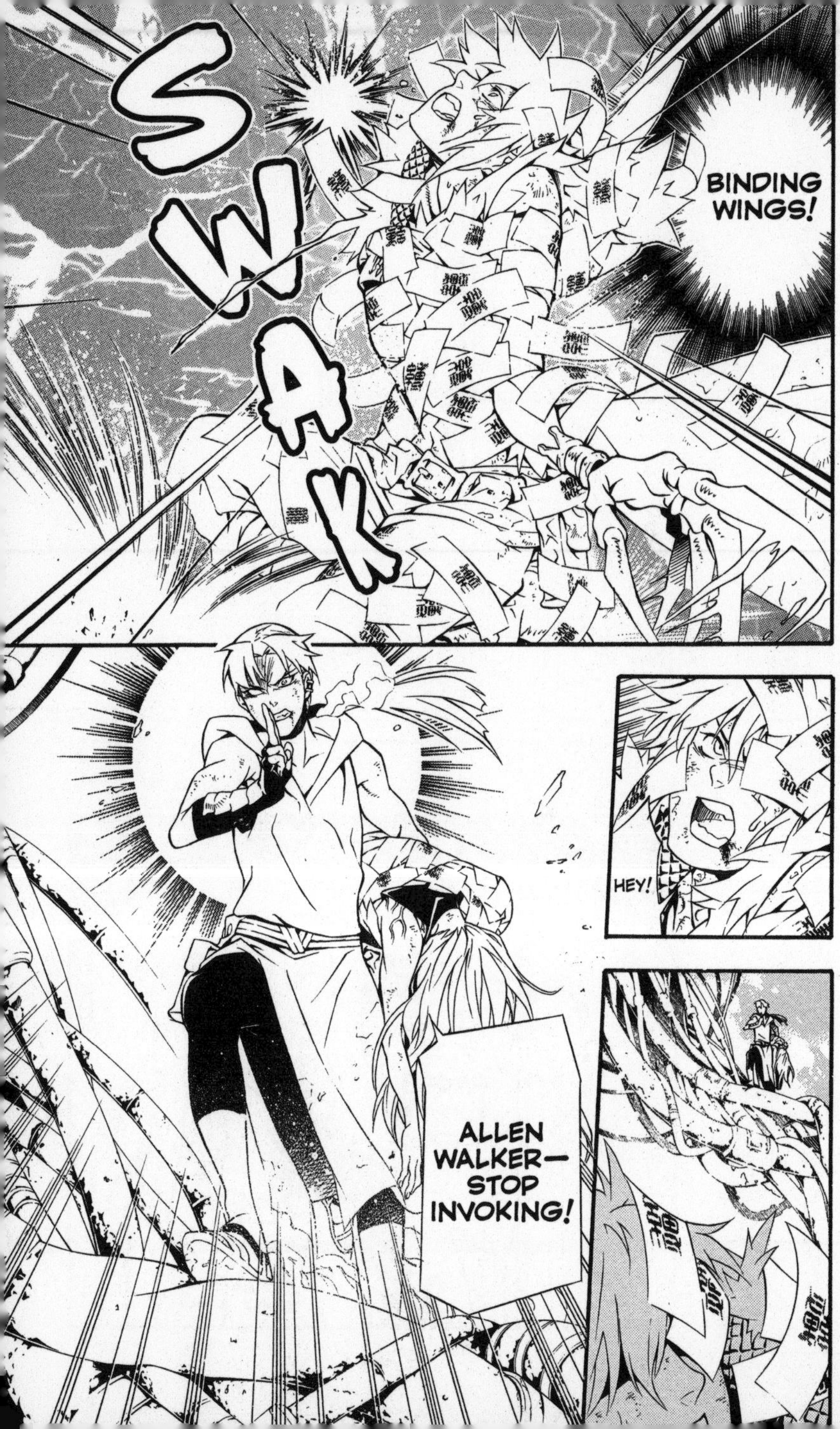
BINDING WINGS!
SWAK
HEY!
ALLEN WALKER—STOP INVOKING!

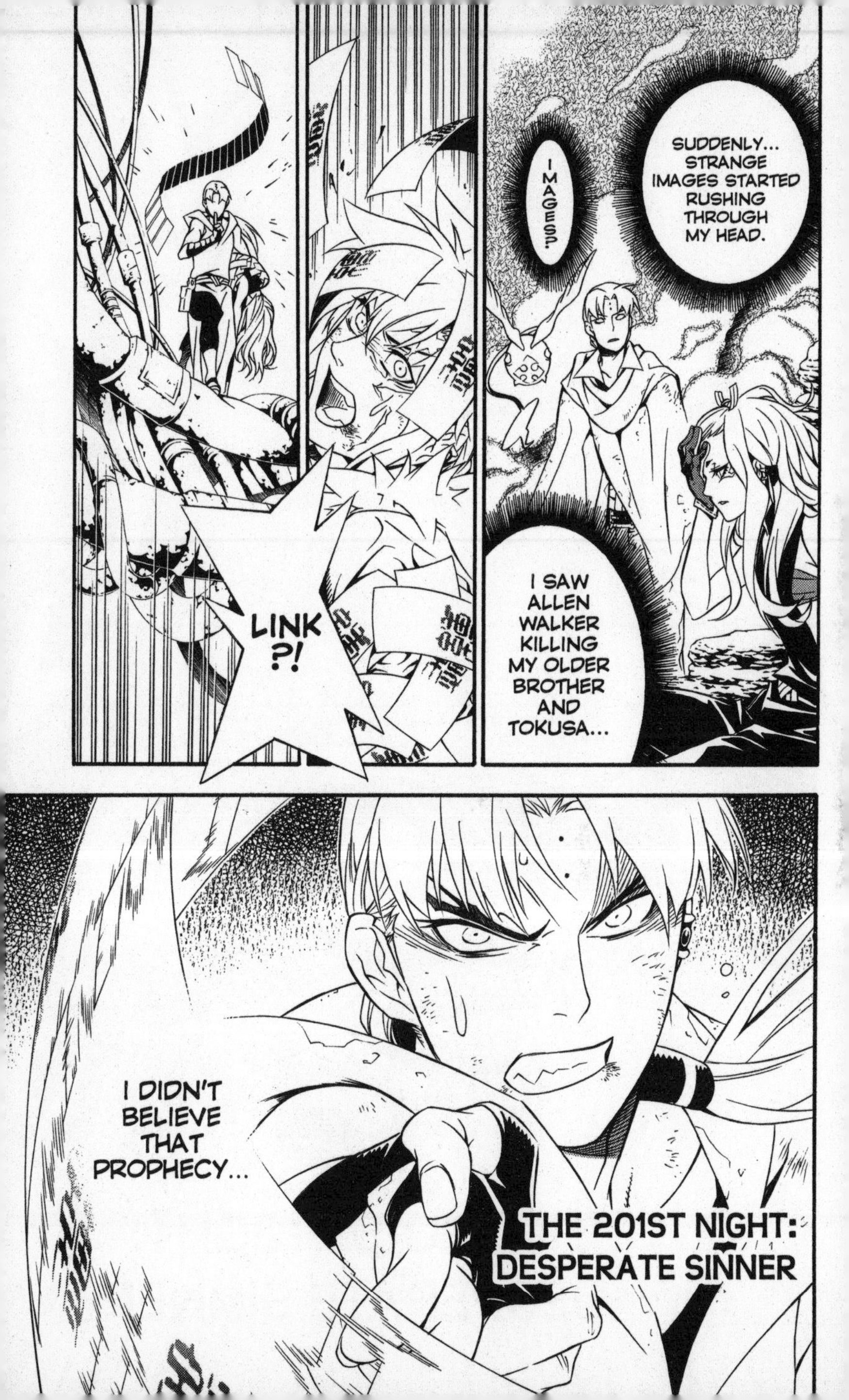
SUDDENLY... STRANGE IMAGES STARTED RUSHING THROUGH MY HEAD.
IMAGES?
I SAW ALLEN WALKER KILLING MY OLDER BROTHER AND TOKUSA...
LINK ?!
I DIDN'T BELIEVE THAT PROPHECY...
THE 201ST NIGHT: DESPERATE SINNER

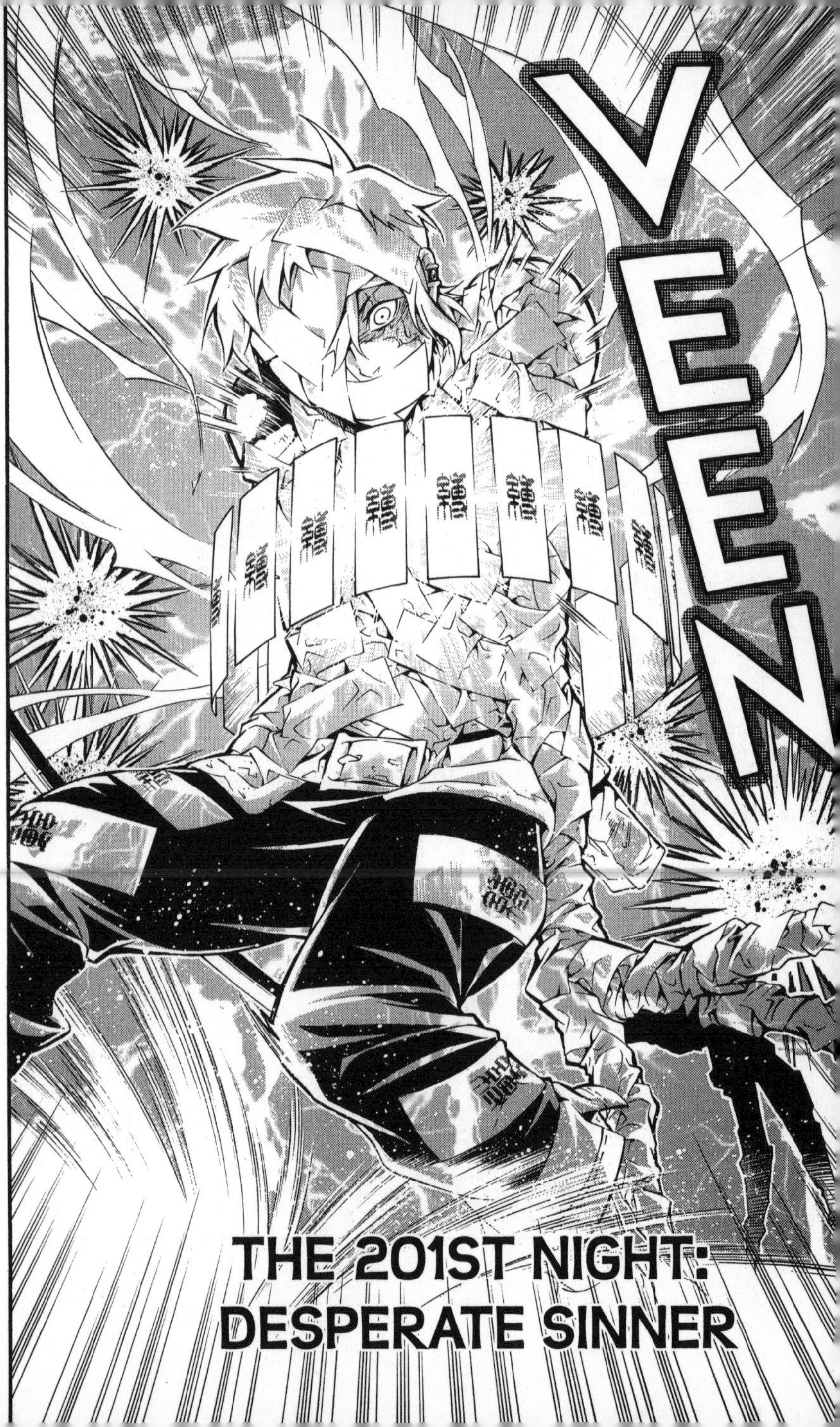
VEEN

THE 201ST NIGHT: DESPERATE SINNER

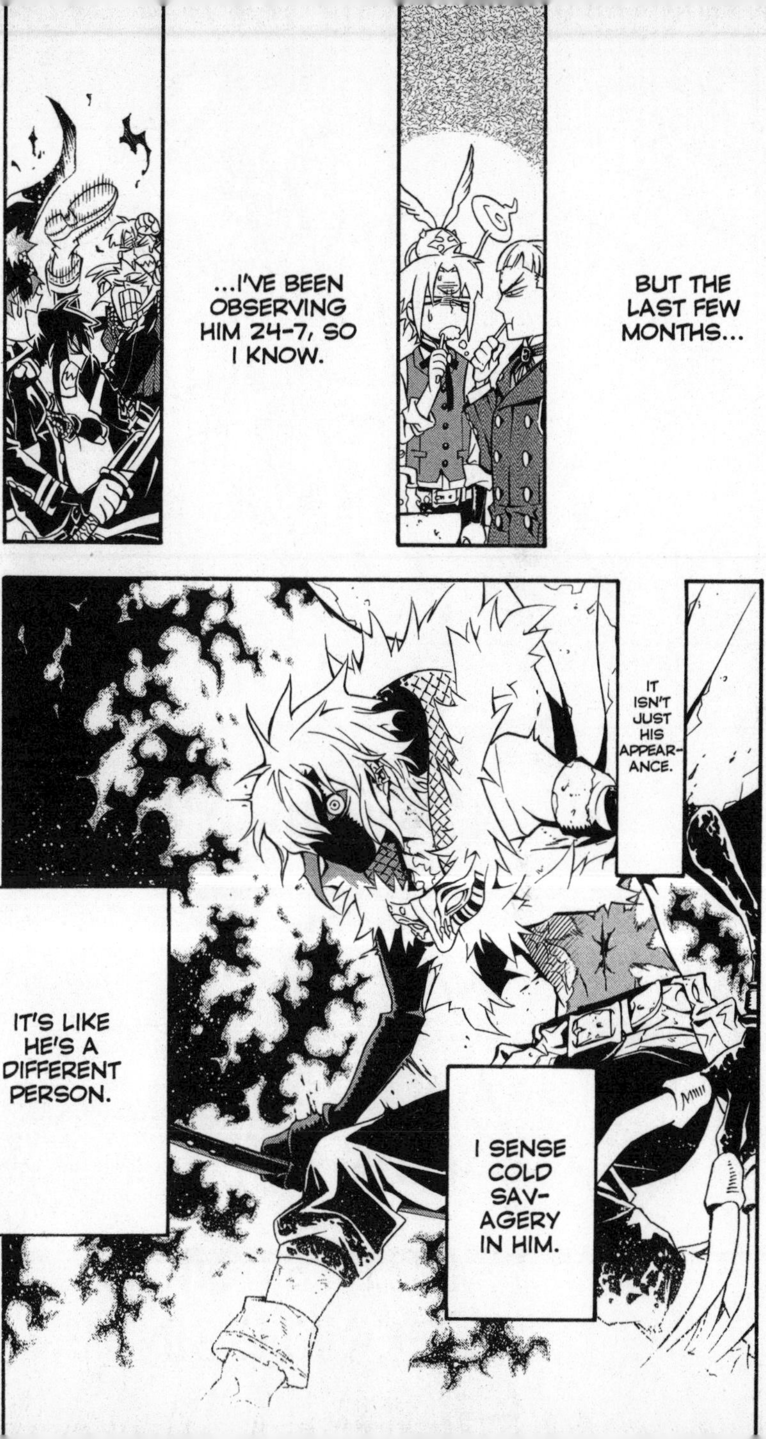
BUT THE LAST FEW MONTHS...
...I'VE BEEN OBSERVING HIM 24-7, SO I KNOW.
IT ISN'T JUST HIS APPEAR-ANCE.
I SENSE COLD SAV-AGERY IN HIM.
IT'S LIKE HE'S A DIFFERENT PERSON.

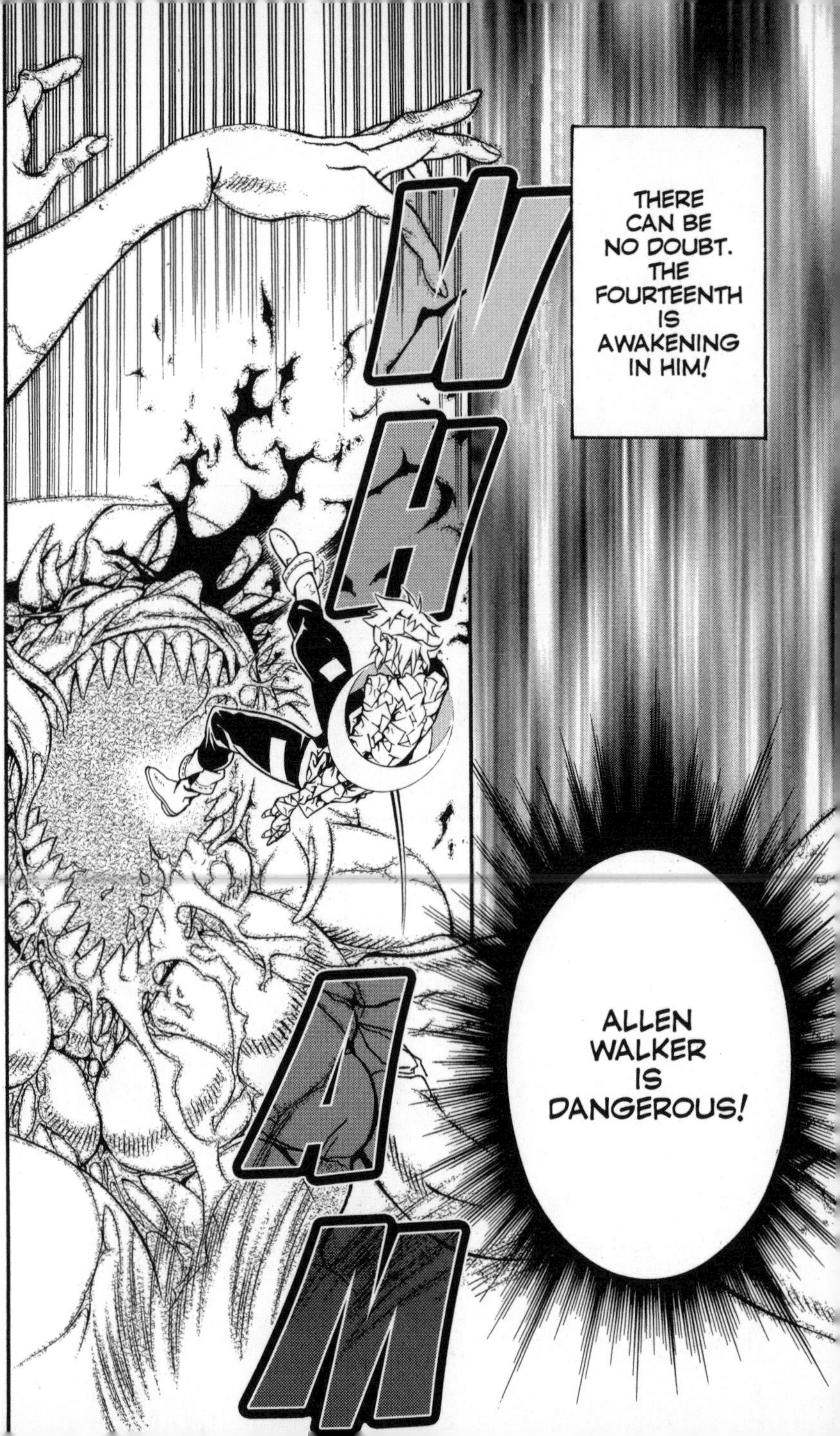
THERE CAN BE NO DOUBT. THE FOURTEENTH IS AWAKENING IN HIM!
WHAM
ALLEN WALKER IS DANGEROUS!

READ THIS WAY

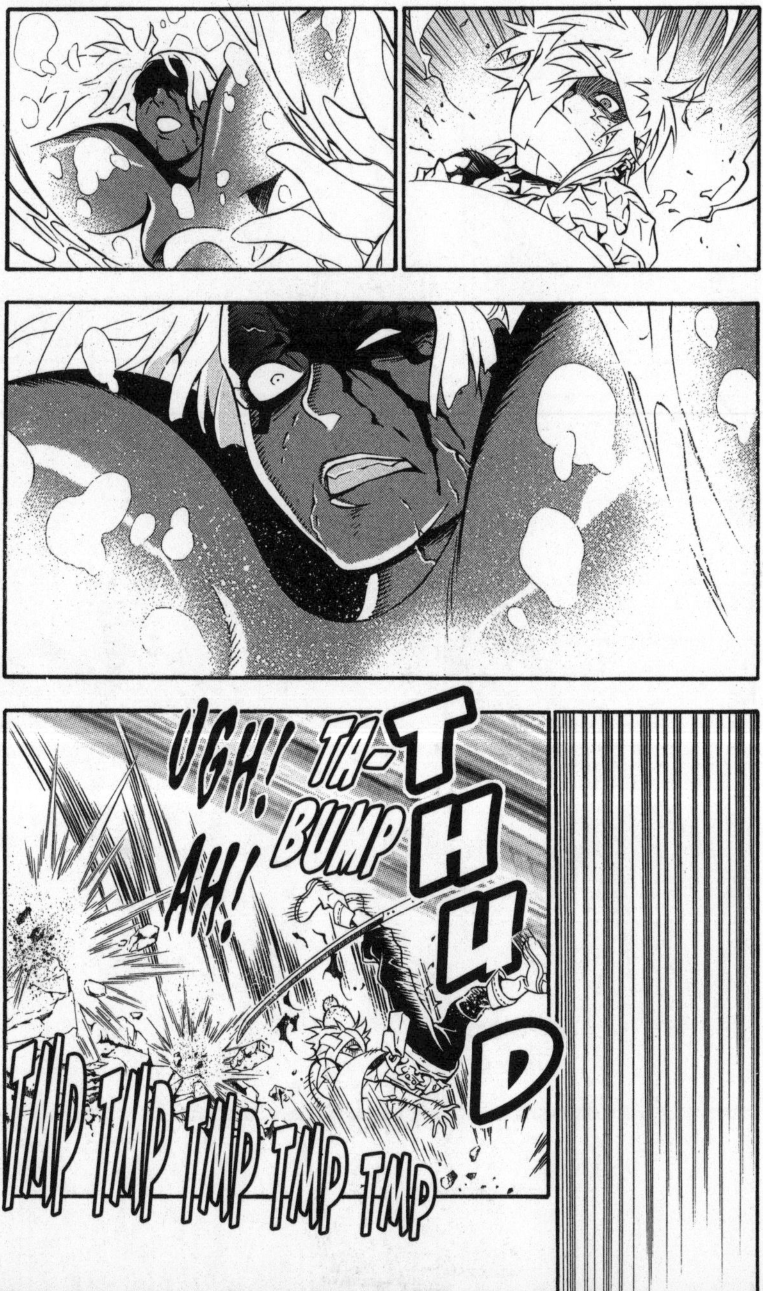
THUD
TA-BUMP
UGH! AH!
TMP TMP TMP TMP TMP

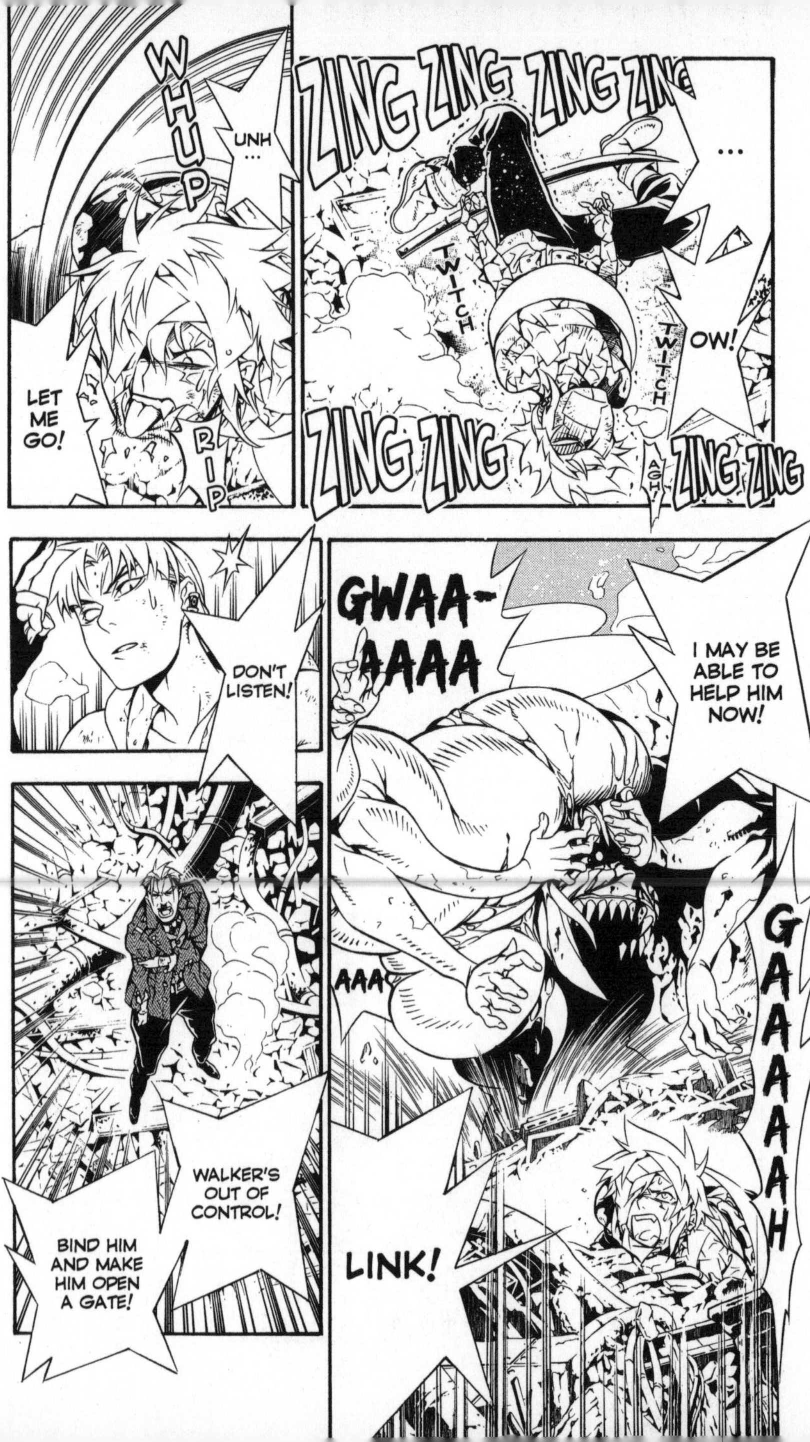
ZING ZING ZING ZING
...
TWITCH
TWITCH
OW!
ZING ZING
AGH!
ZING ZING
WHUP
UNH ...
LET ME GO!
RIP
I MAY BE ABLE TO HELP HIM NOW!
GWAA-AAAA
GAAAAAAH
AAA
LINK!
DON'T LISTEN!
WALKER'S OUT OF CONTROL!
BIND HIM AND MAKE HIM OPEN A GATE!

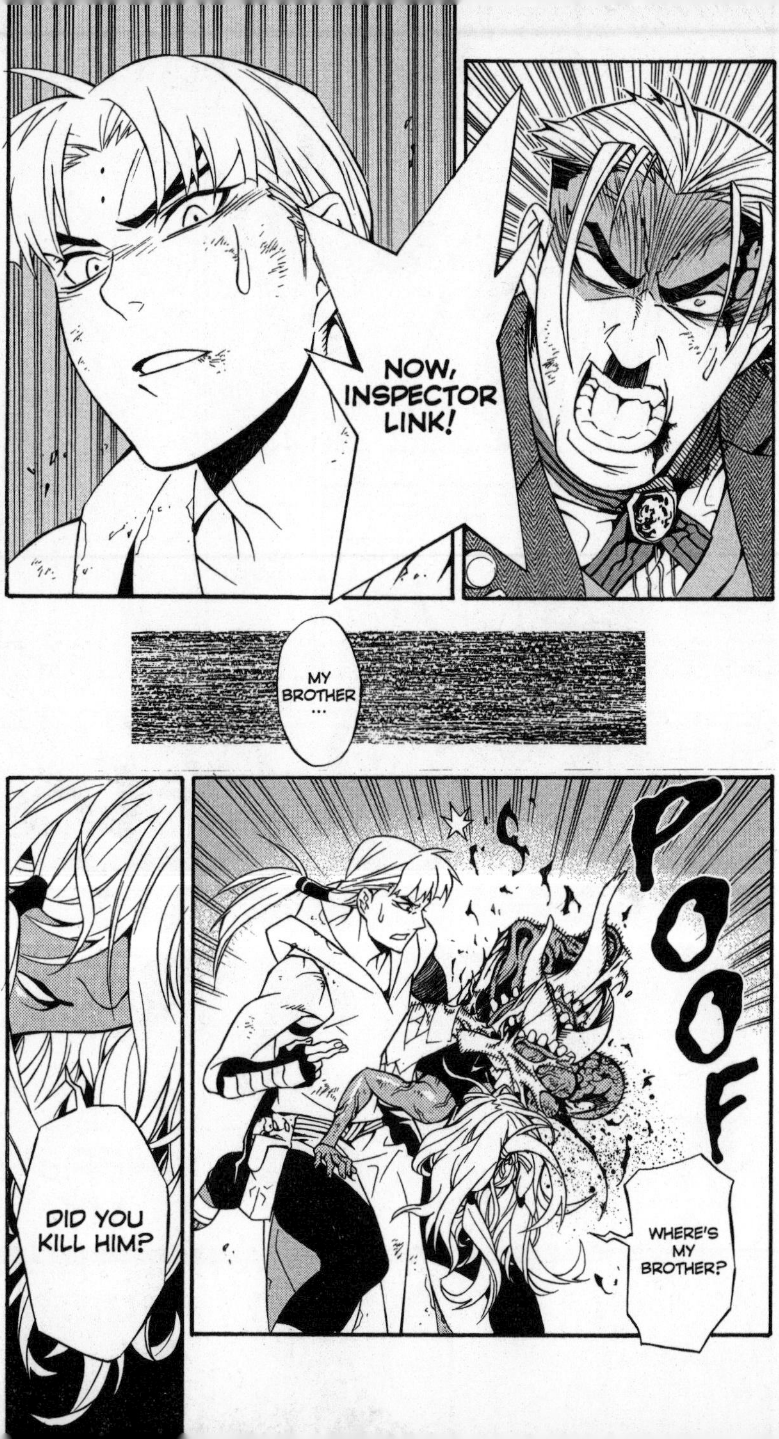
NOW, INSPECTOR LINK!
MY BROTHER ...
POOF
WHERE'S MY BROTHER?
DID YOU KILL HIM?

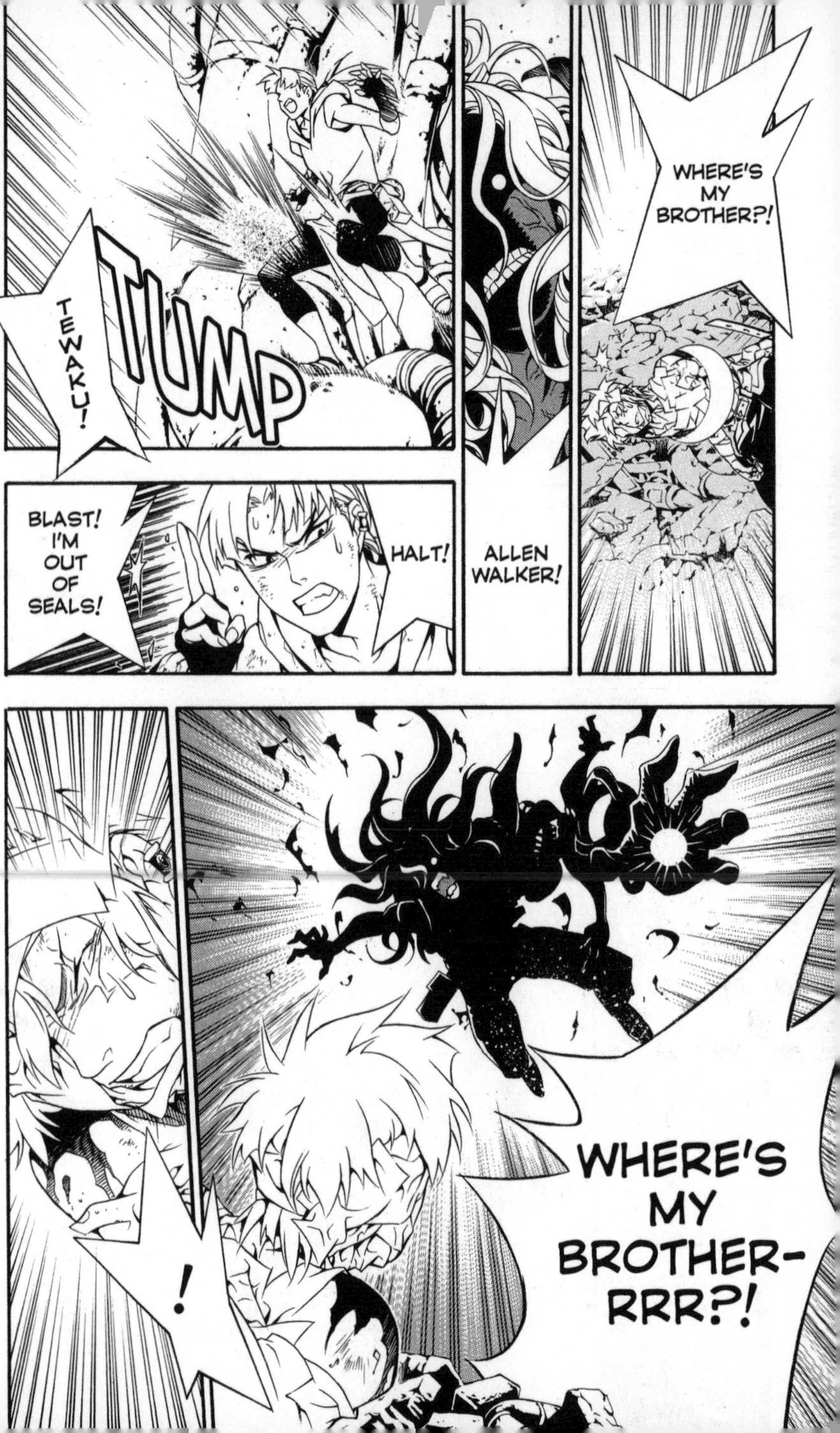
WHERE'S MY BROTHER?!
ALLEN WALKER!
TUMP
TEWAKU!
HALT!
BLAST! I'M OUT OF SEALS!
WHERE'S MY BROTHER-RRR?!
!

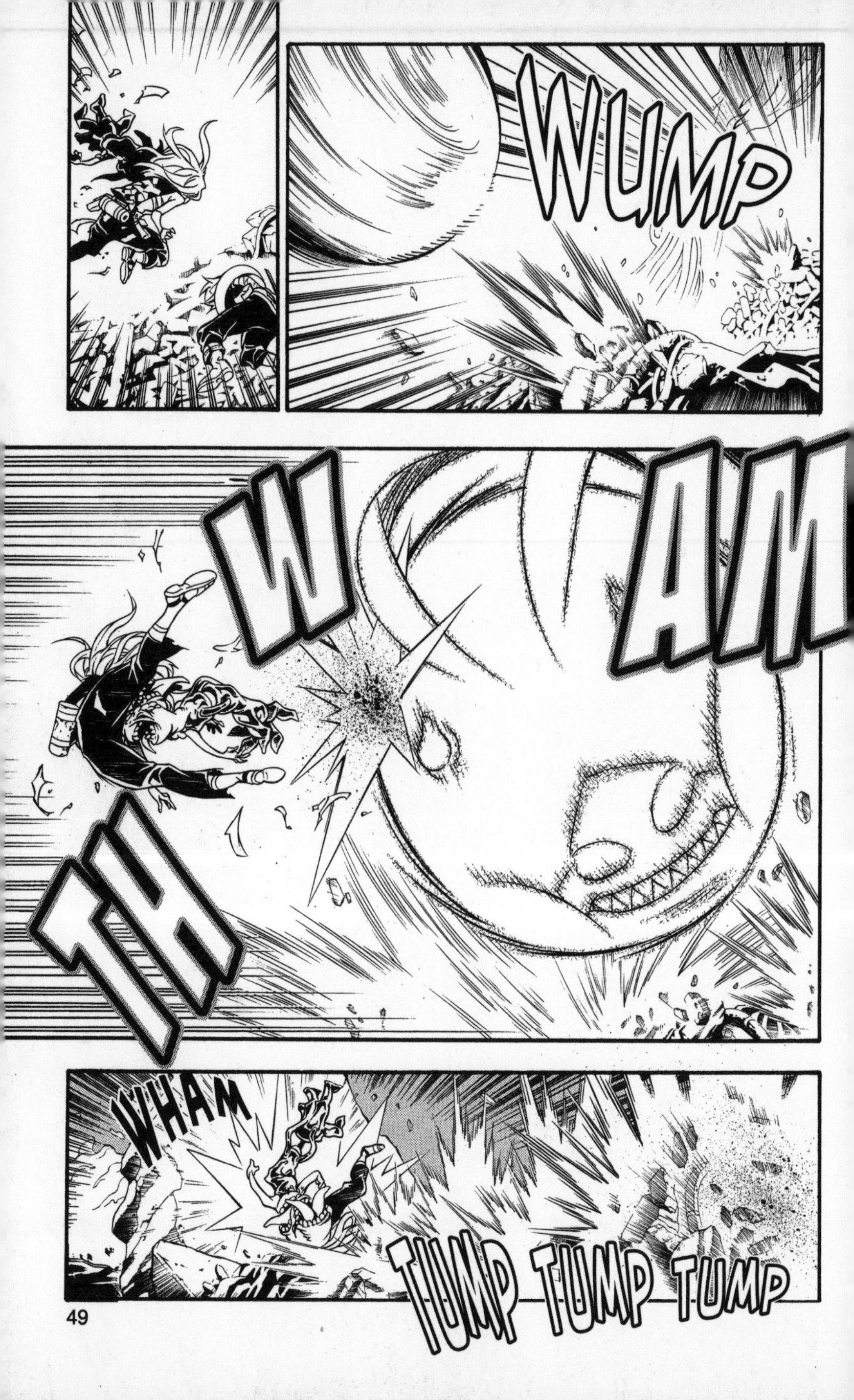
WUMP
THWAM
WHAM
TUMP TUMP TUMP

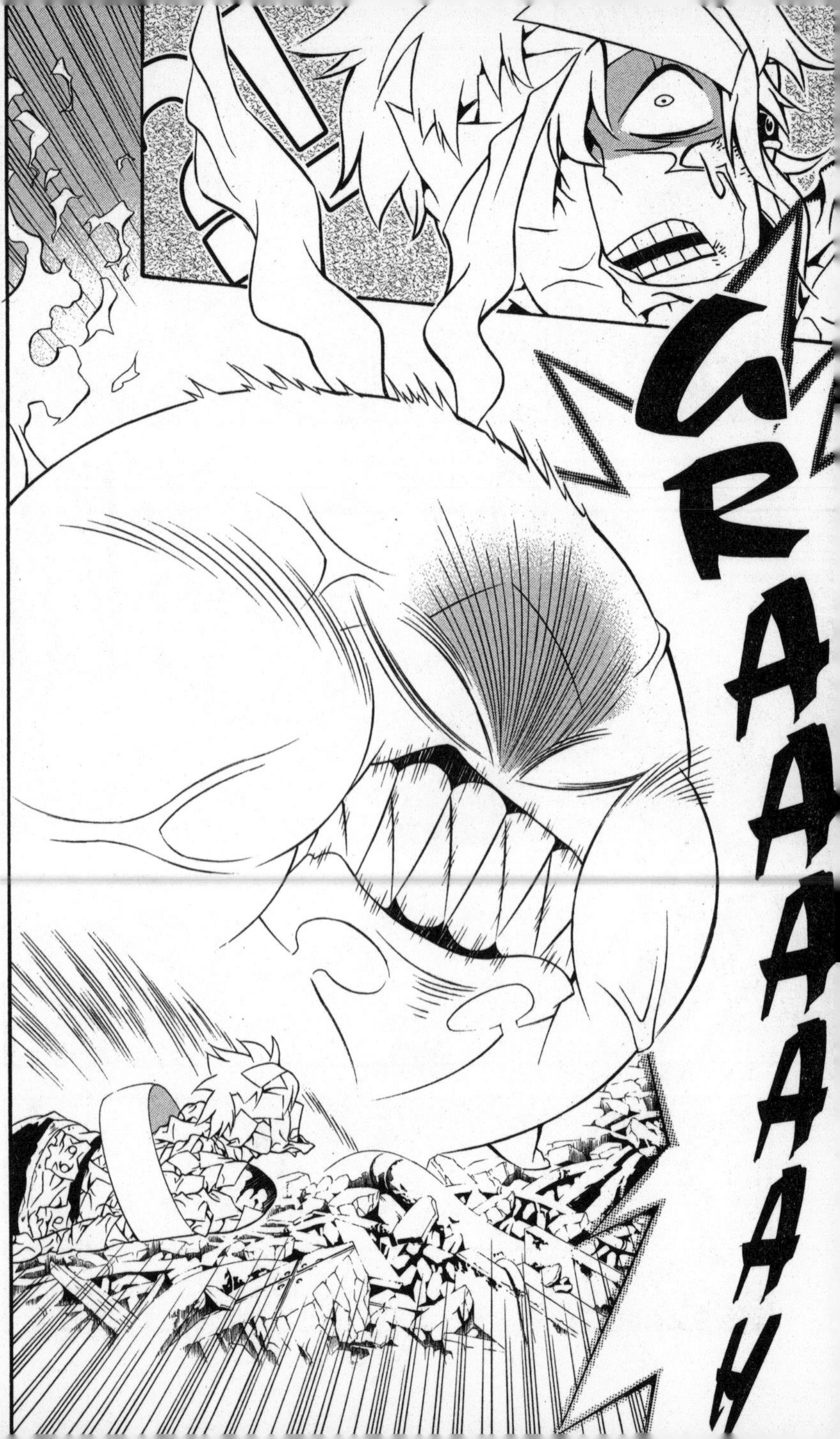
CRAAAAAH

READ THIS WAY

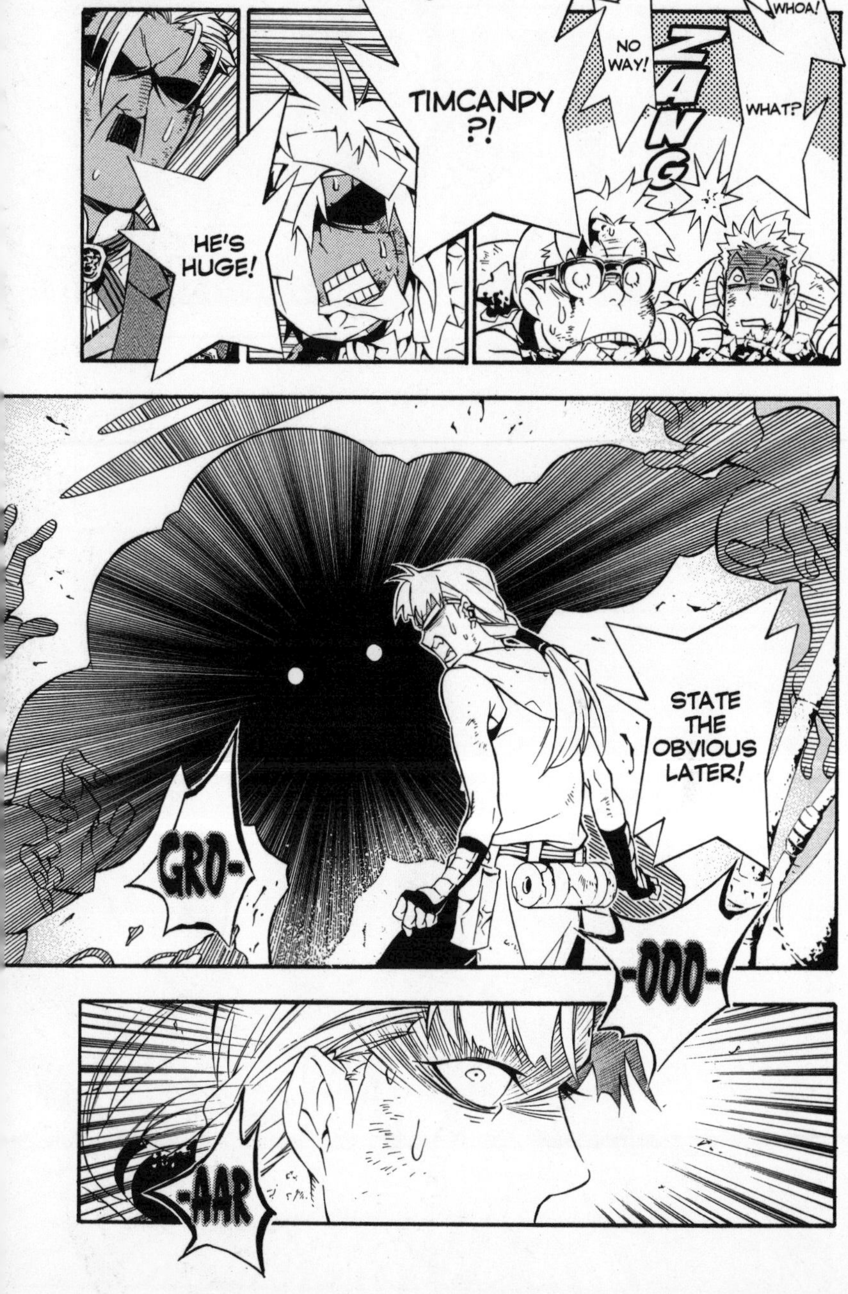

WHOA!
WHAT?
NO WAY!
ZANG
TIMCANPY ?!
HE'S HUGE!
STATE THE OBVIOUS LATER!
GRO-
-OOO-
-AAR

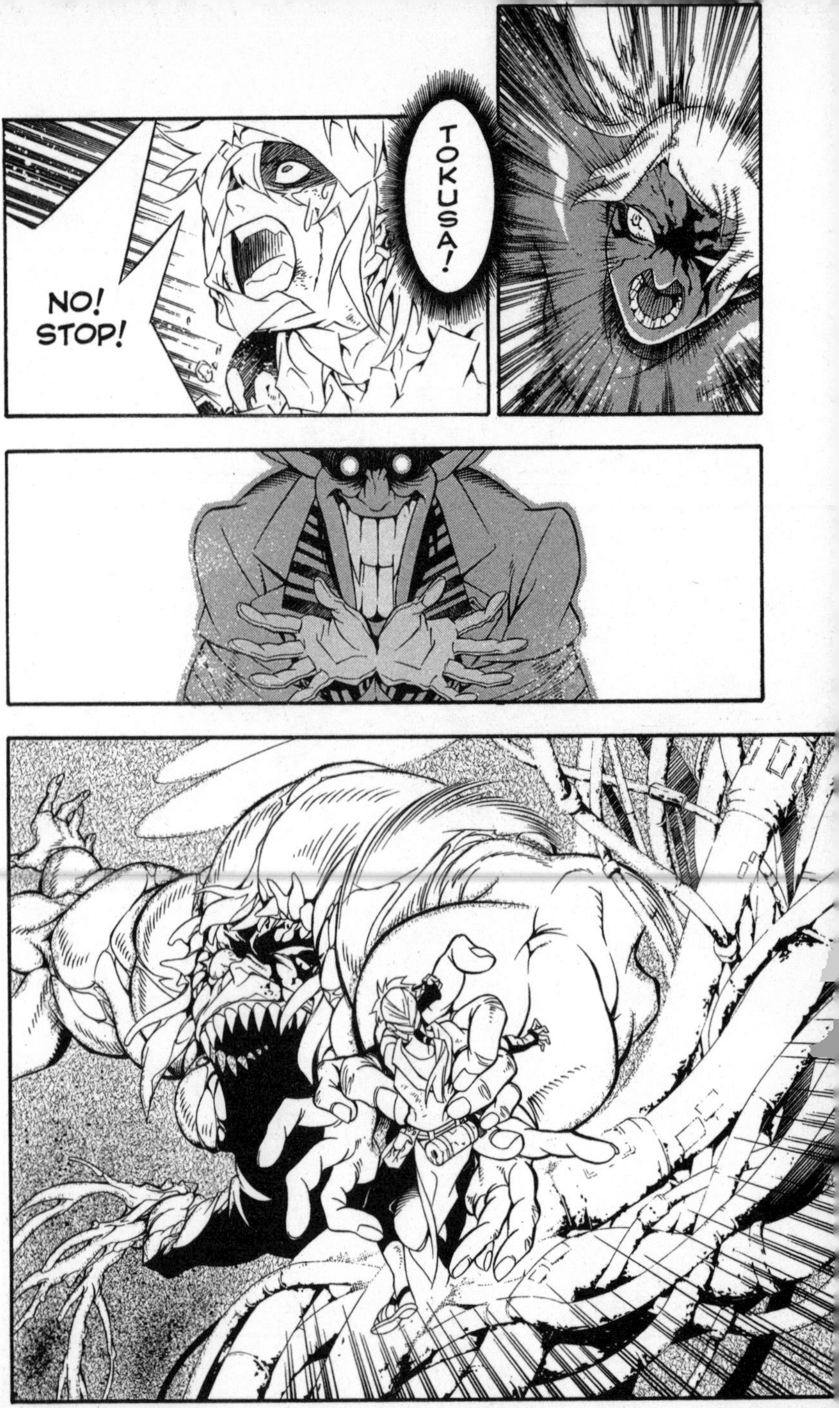
TOKUSA!
NO! STOP!

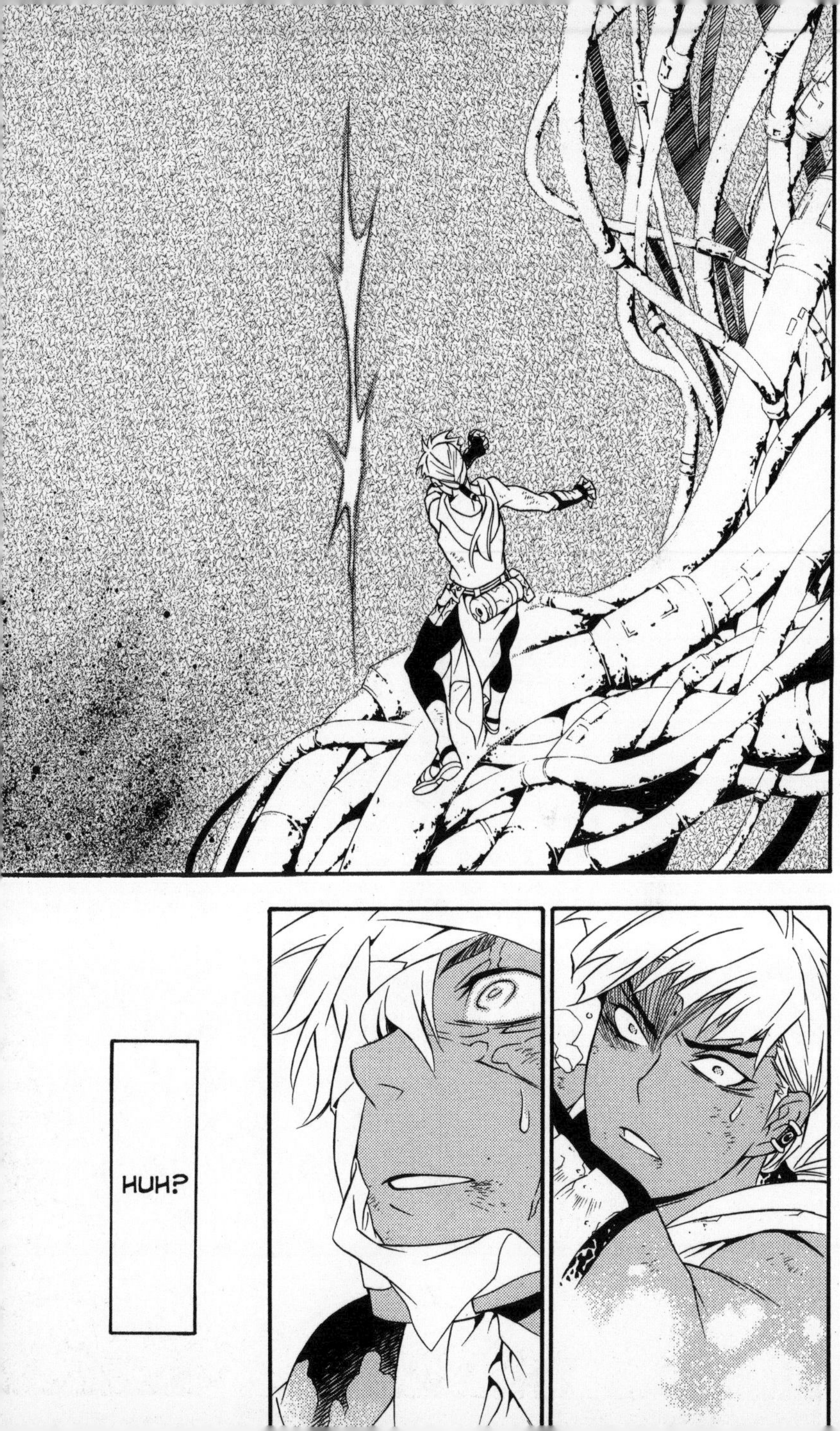
HUH?

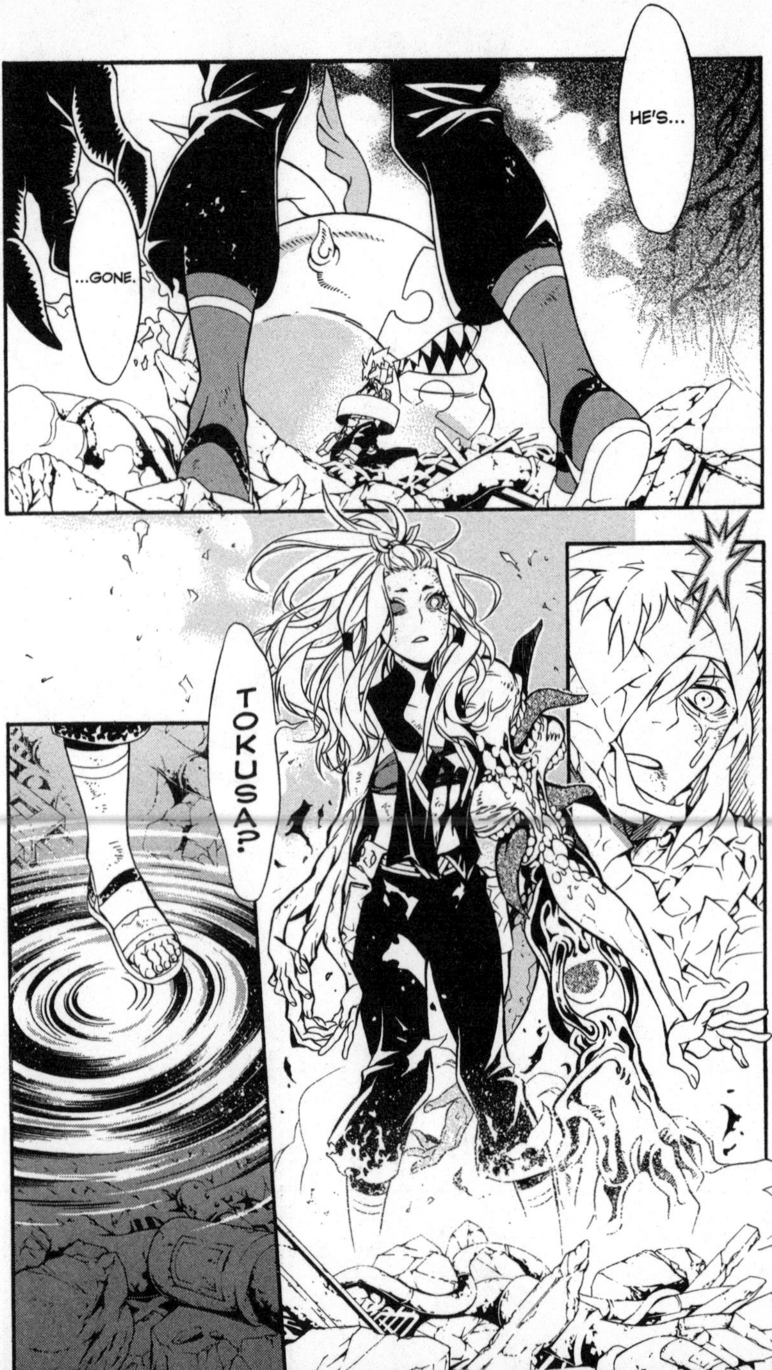
HE'S...
...GONE.
TOKUSA?

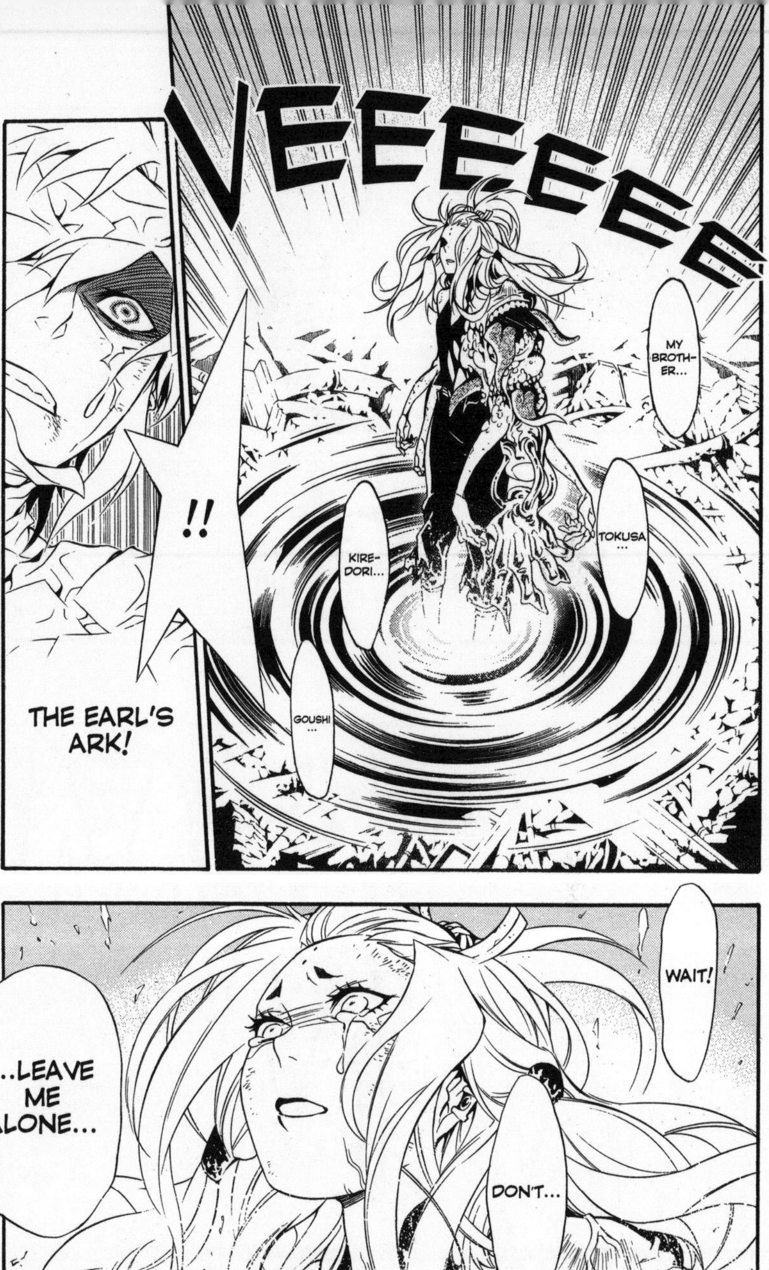
VEEEEEEE
MY BROTHER-ER...
TOKUSA...
KIRE-DORI...
GOUSHI...
!!
THE EARL'S ARK!
WAIT!
DON'T...
...LEAVE ME ALONE...

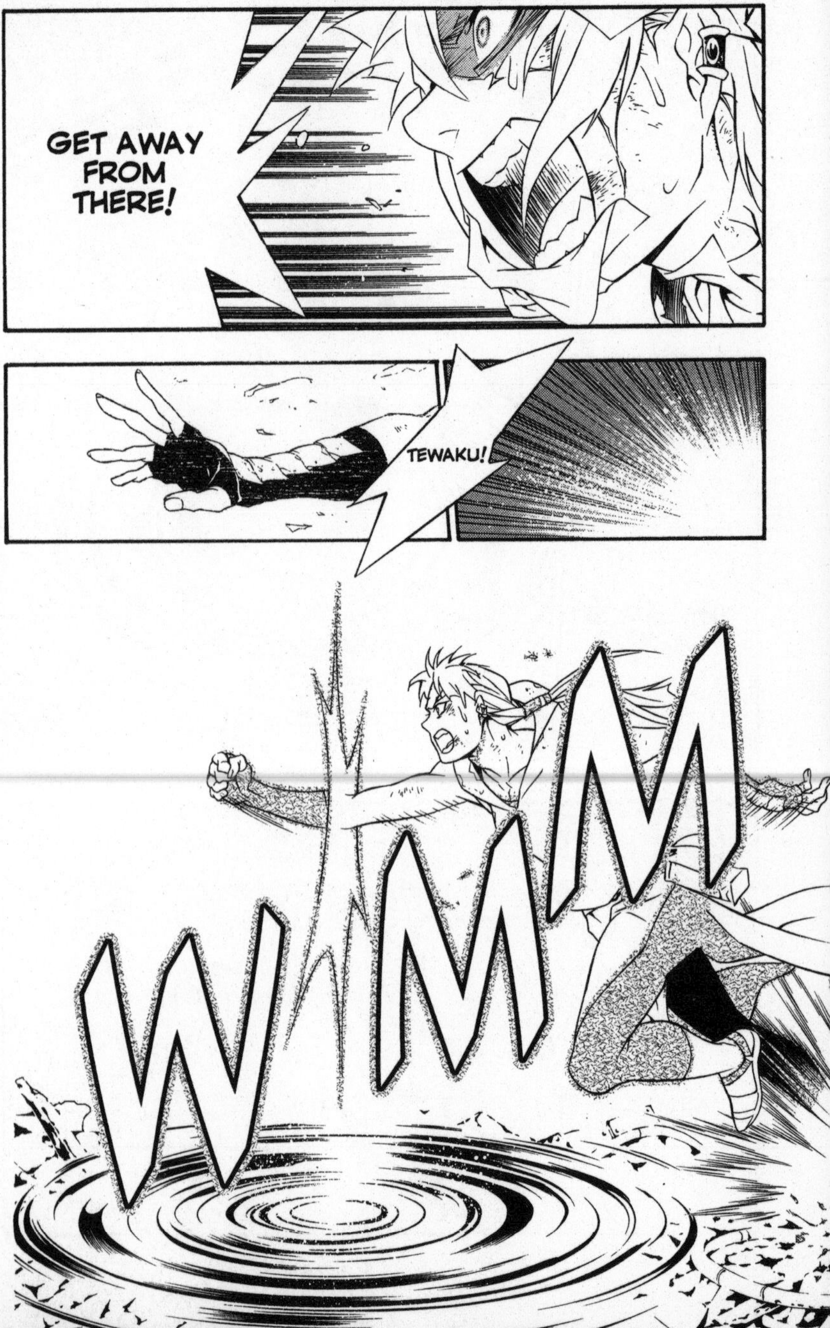
GET AWAY FROM THERE!
TEWAKU!
WMMM

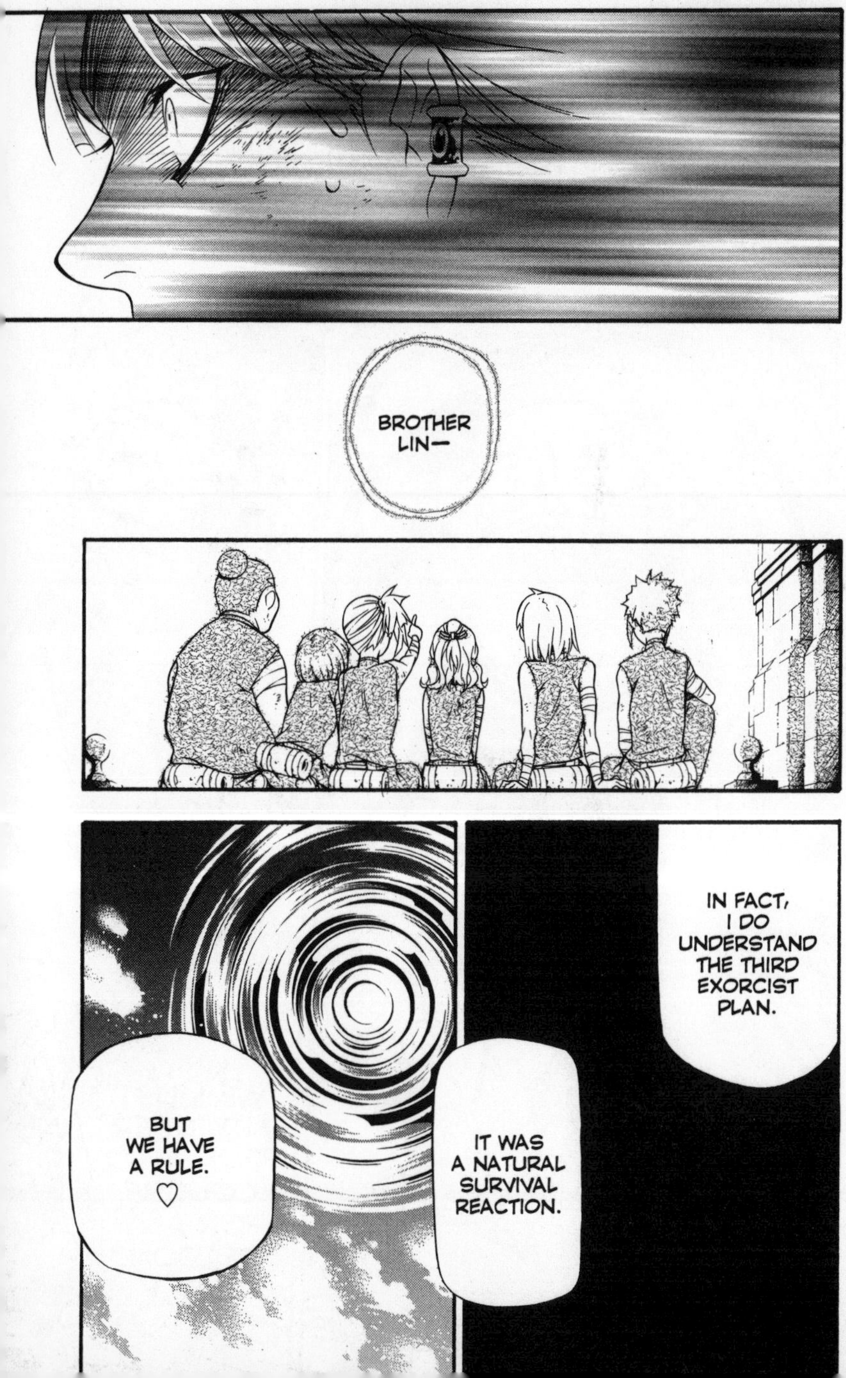
BROTHER LIN—
IN FACT, I DO UNDERSTAND THE THIRD EXORCIST PLAN.
IT WAS A NATURAL SURVIVAL REACTION.
BUT WE HAVE A RULE. ♡

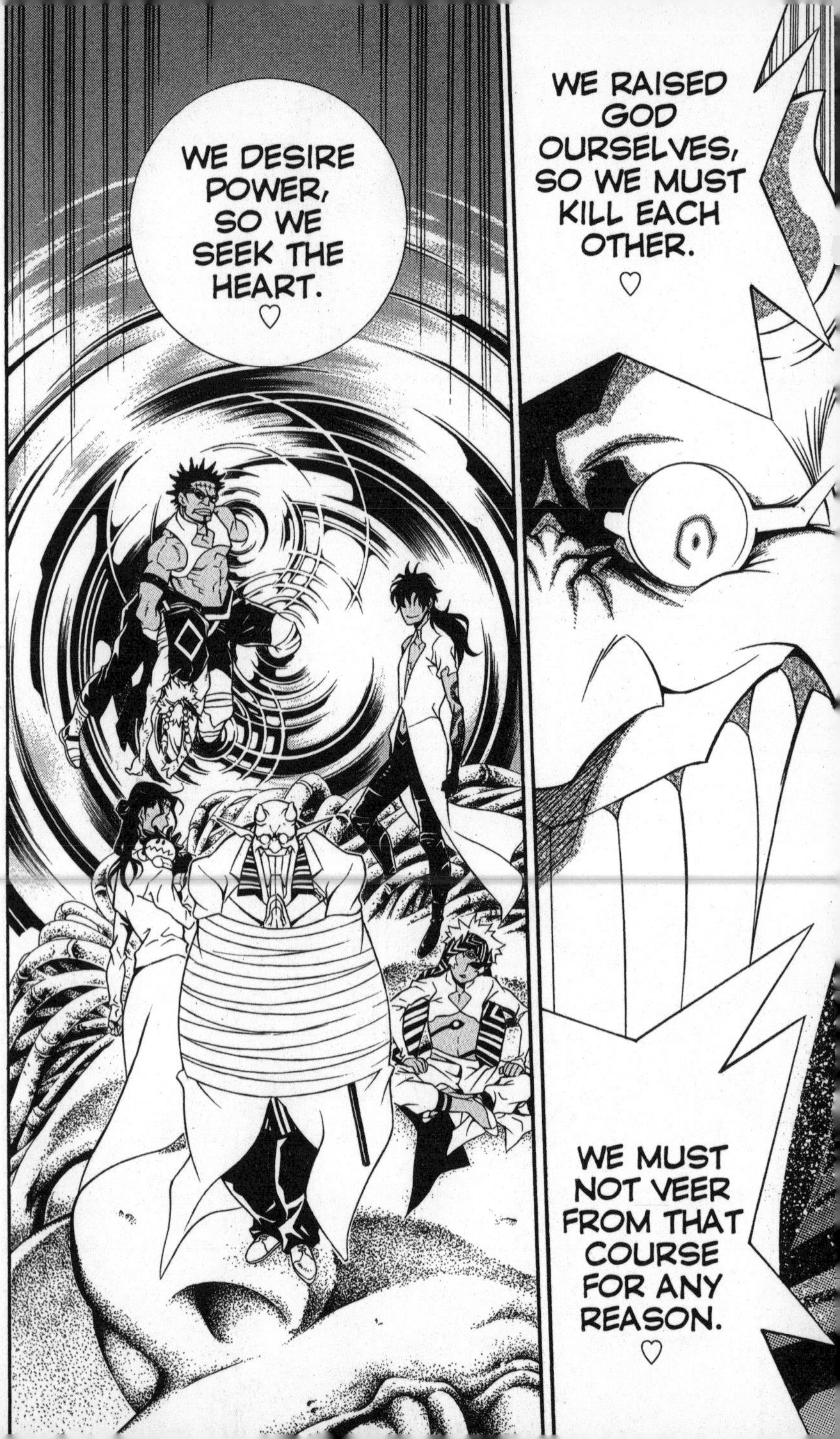
WE RAISED GOD OURSELVES, SO WE MUST KILL EACH OTHER. ♡
WE MUST NOT VEER FROM THAT COURSE FOR ANY REASON. ♡
WE DESIRE POWER, SO WE SEEK THE HEART. ♡

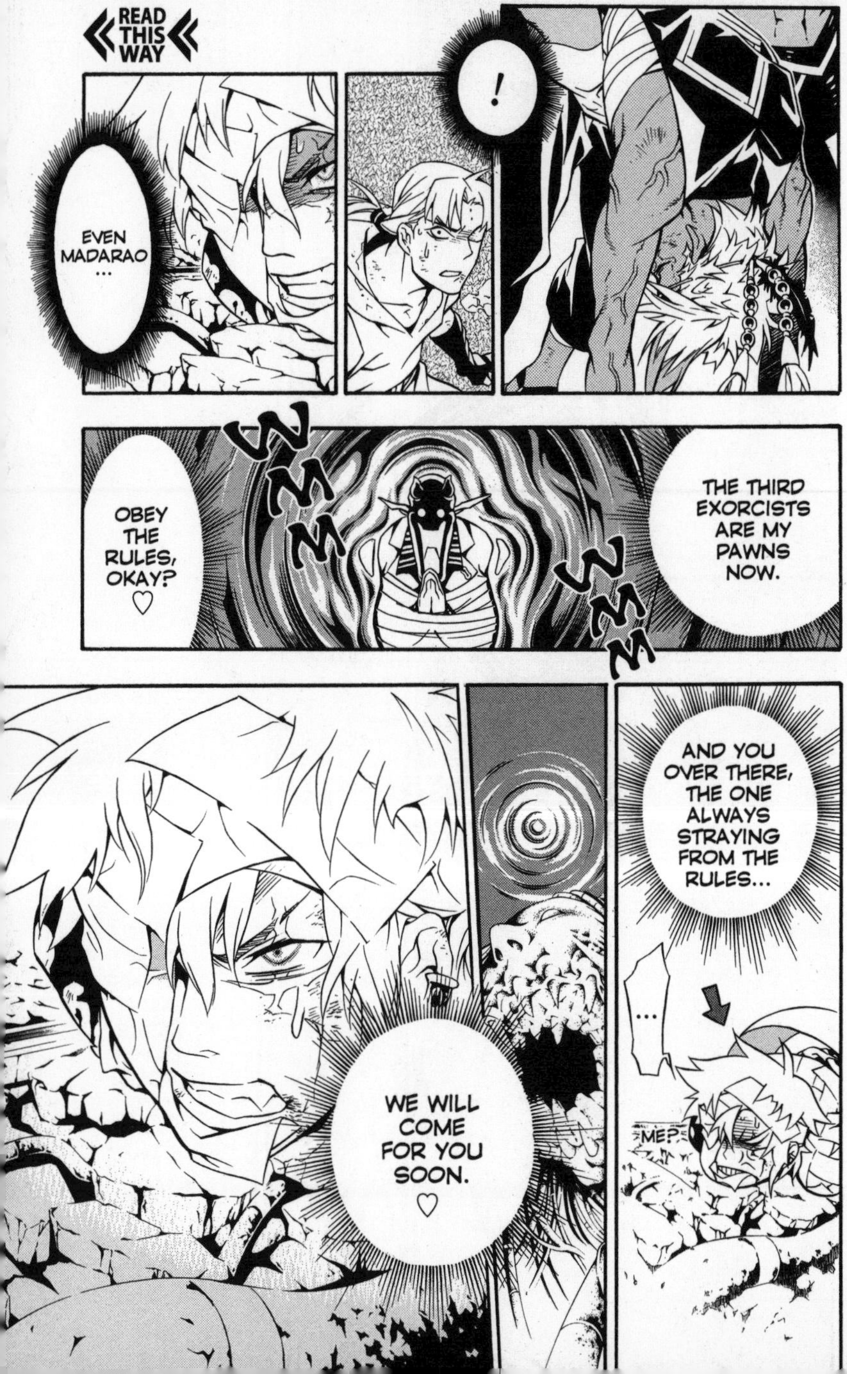

READ THIS WAY
!
EVEN MADARAO ...
THE THIRD EXORCISTS ARE MY PAWNS NOW.
WMM
WMM
OBEY THE RULES, OKAY? ♡
AND YOU OVER THERE, THE ONE ALWAYS STRAYING FROM THE RULES...
...
ME?
WE WILL COME FOR YOU SOON. ♡

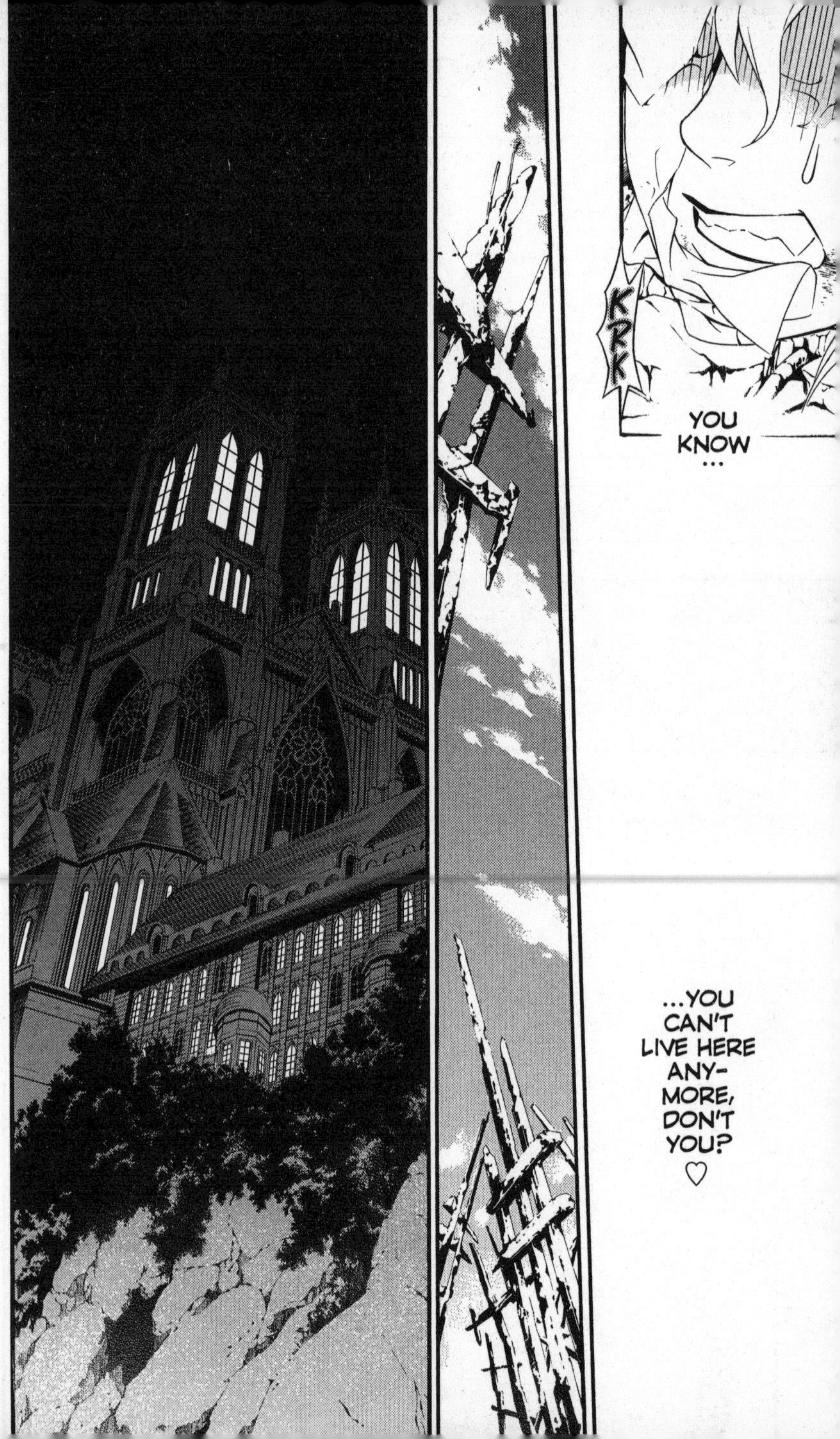
KRK
YOU KNOW...
...YOU CAN'T LIVE HERE ANY-MORE, DON'T YOU? ♡

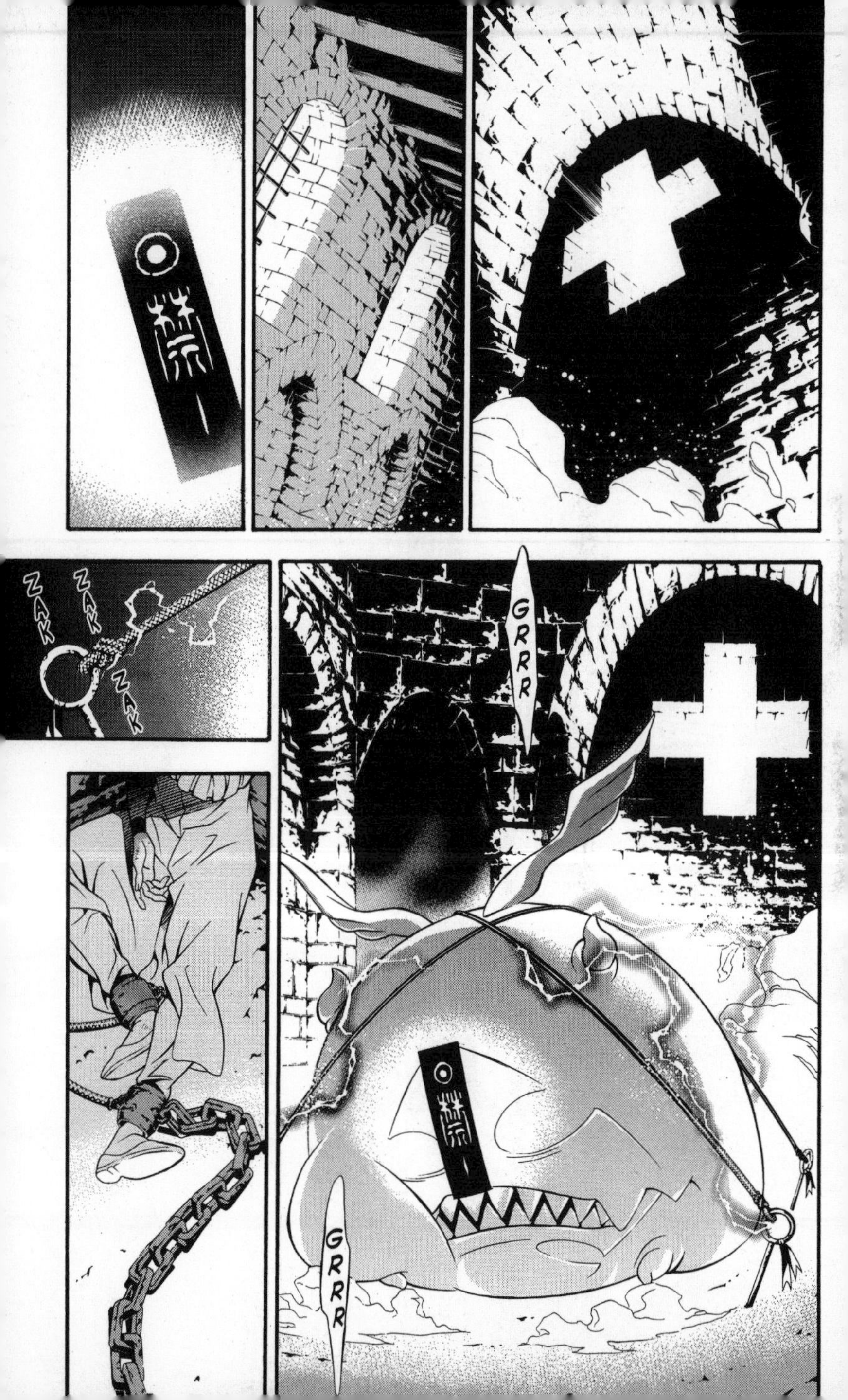

禁
GRRR
禁
GRRR
ZAK ZAK ZAK

禁
禁
禁
禁

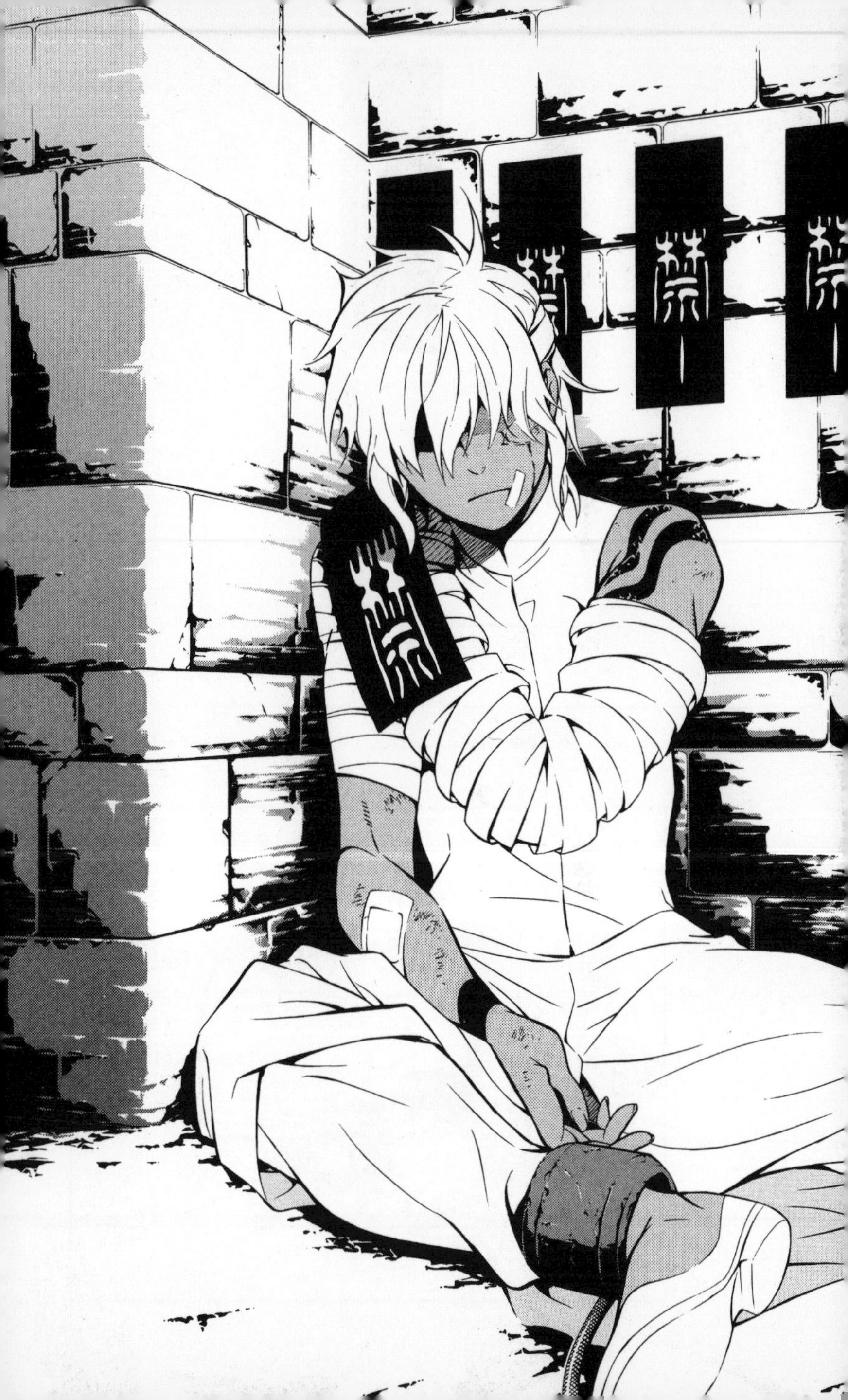
禁
禁
禁
禁

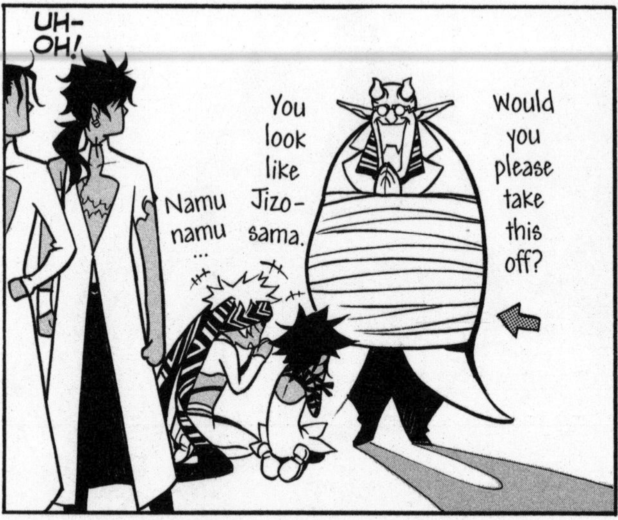
Would you please take this off?
You look like Jizo-sama.
Namu namu ...
UH-OH!

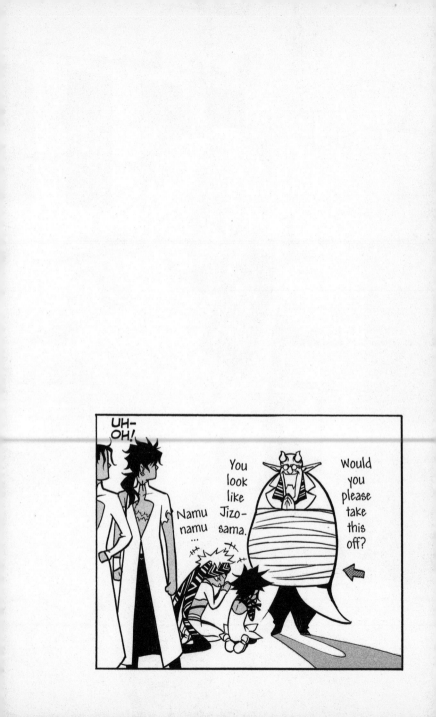

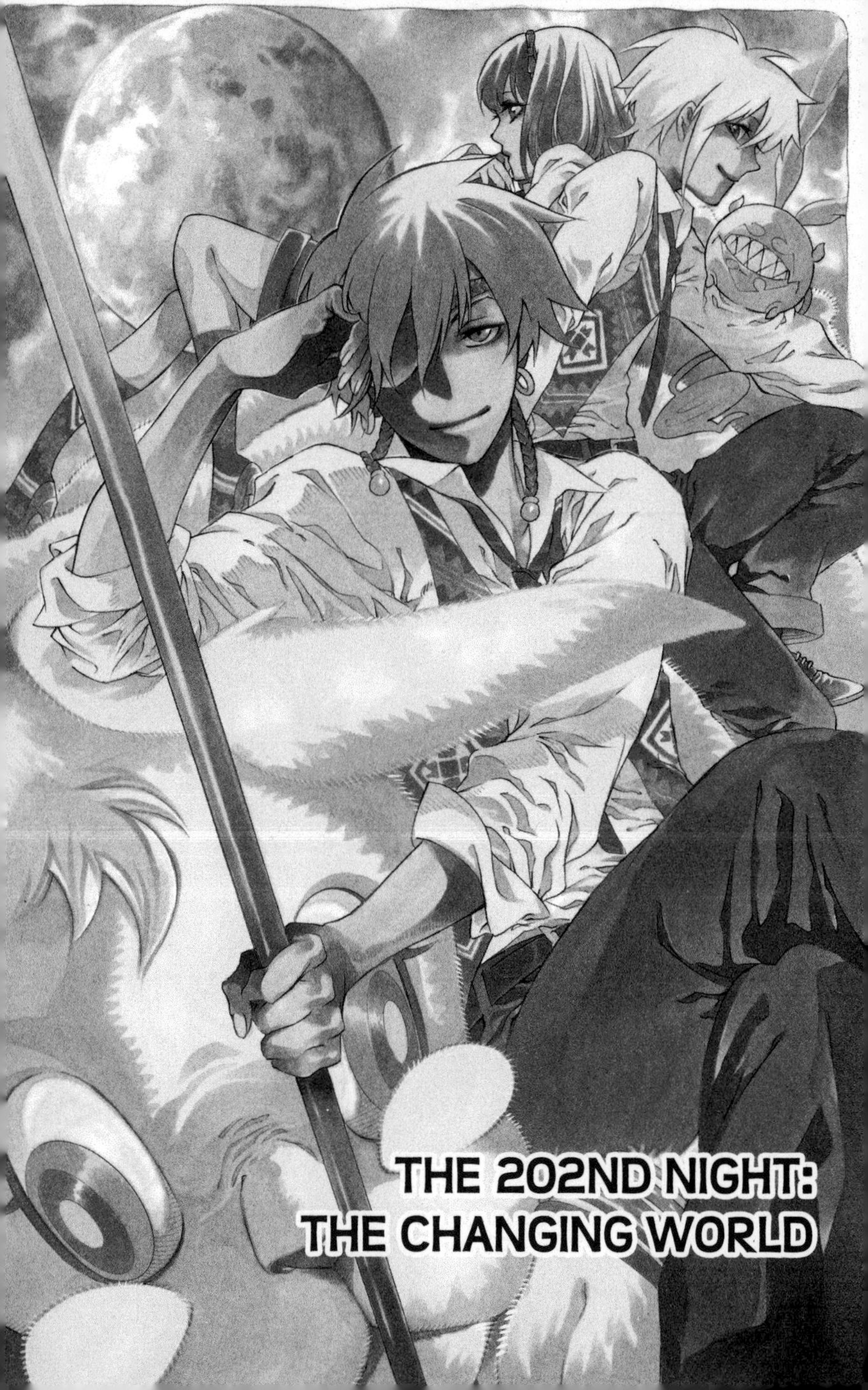
THE 202ND NIGHT:
THE CHANGING WORLD

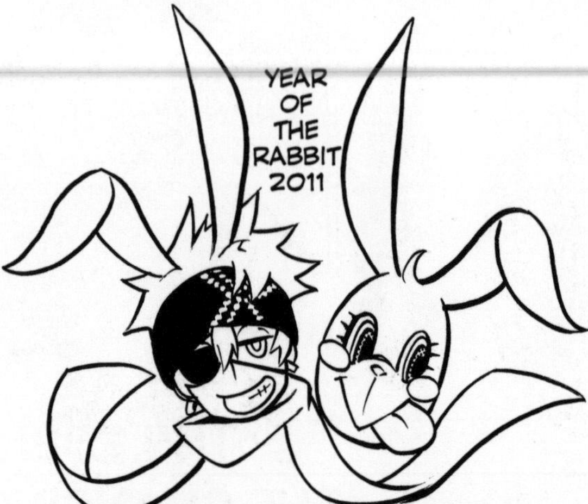
YEAR
OF
THE
RABBIT
2011

THANKS FOR ALL THE NEW
YEAR'S CARDS AGAIN THIS YEAR!

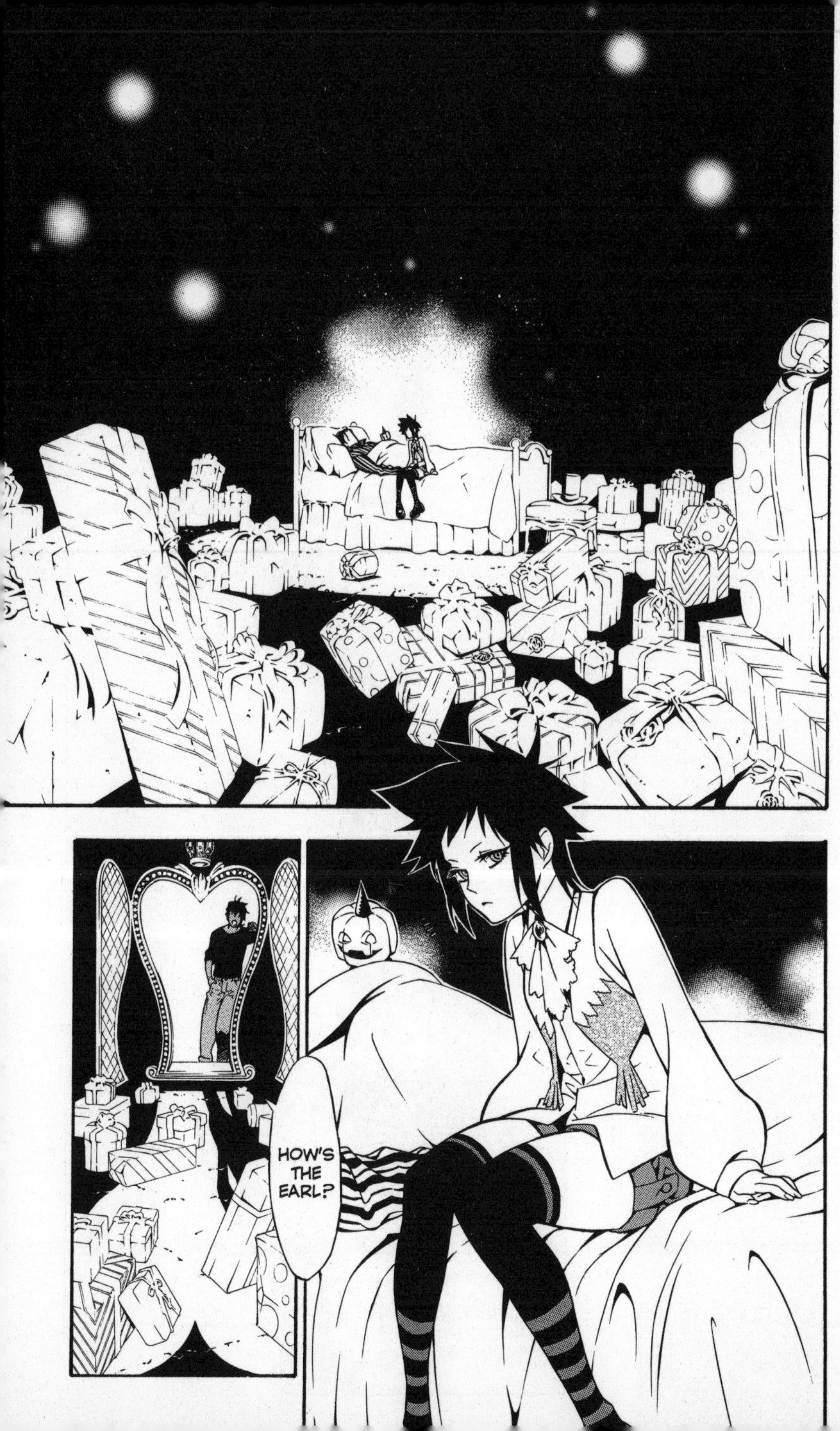
HOW'S THE EARL?

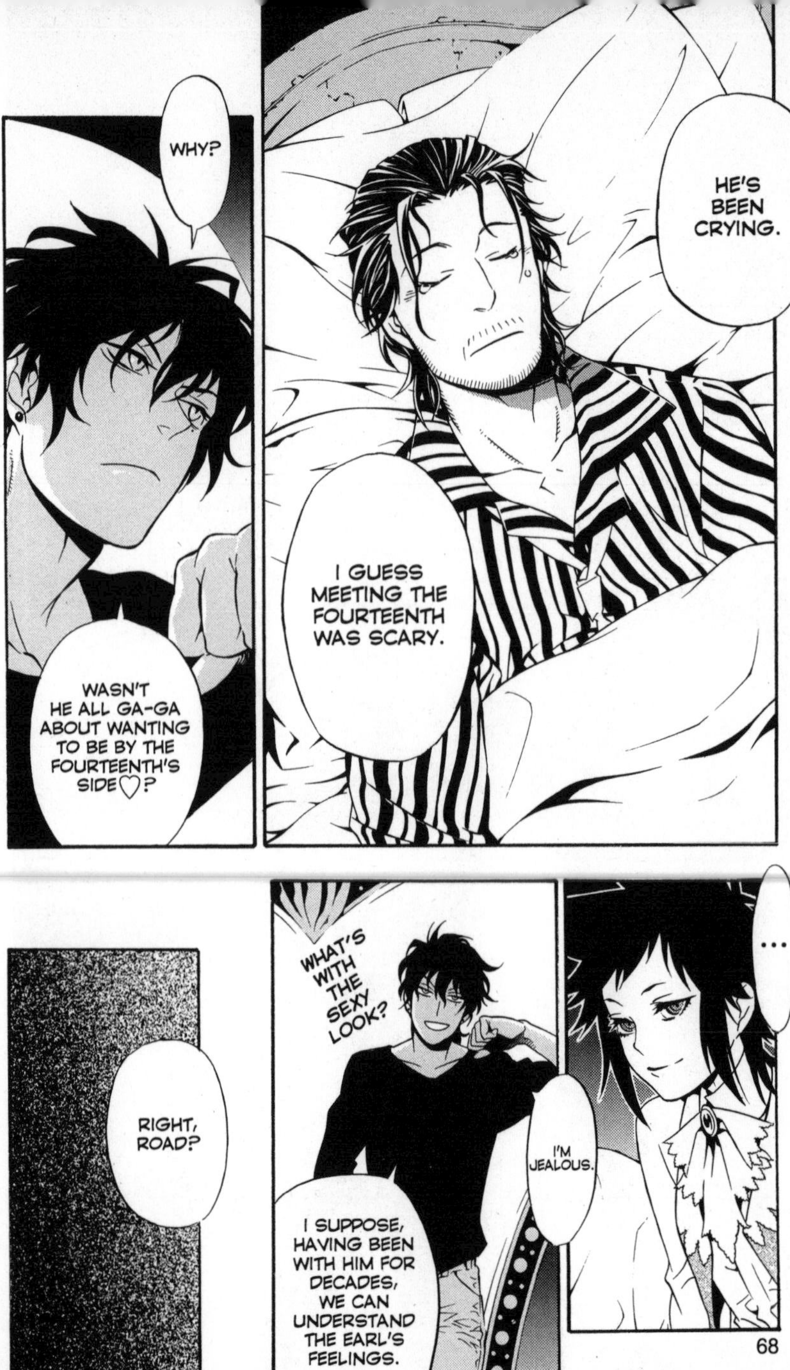

HE'S BEEN CRYING.
I GUESS MEETING THE FOURTEENTH WAS SCARY.
WHY?
WASN'T HE ALL GA-GA ABOUT WANTING TO BE BY THE FOURTEENTH'S SIDE♡?
...
I'M JEALOUS.
WHAT'S WITH THE SEXY LOOK?
I SUPPOSE, HAVING BEEN WITH HIM FOR DECADES, WE CAN UNDERSTAND THE EARL'S FEELINGS.
RIGHT, ROAD?

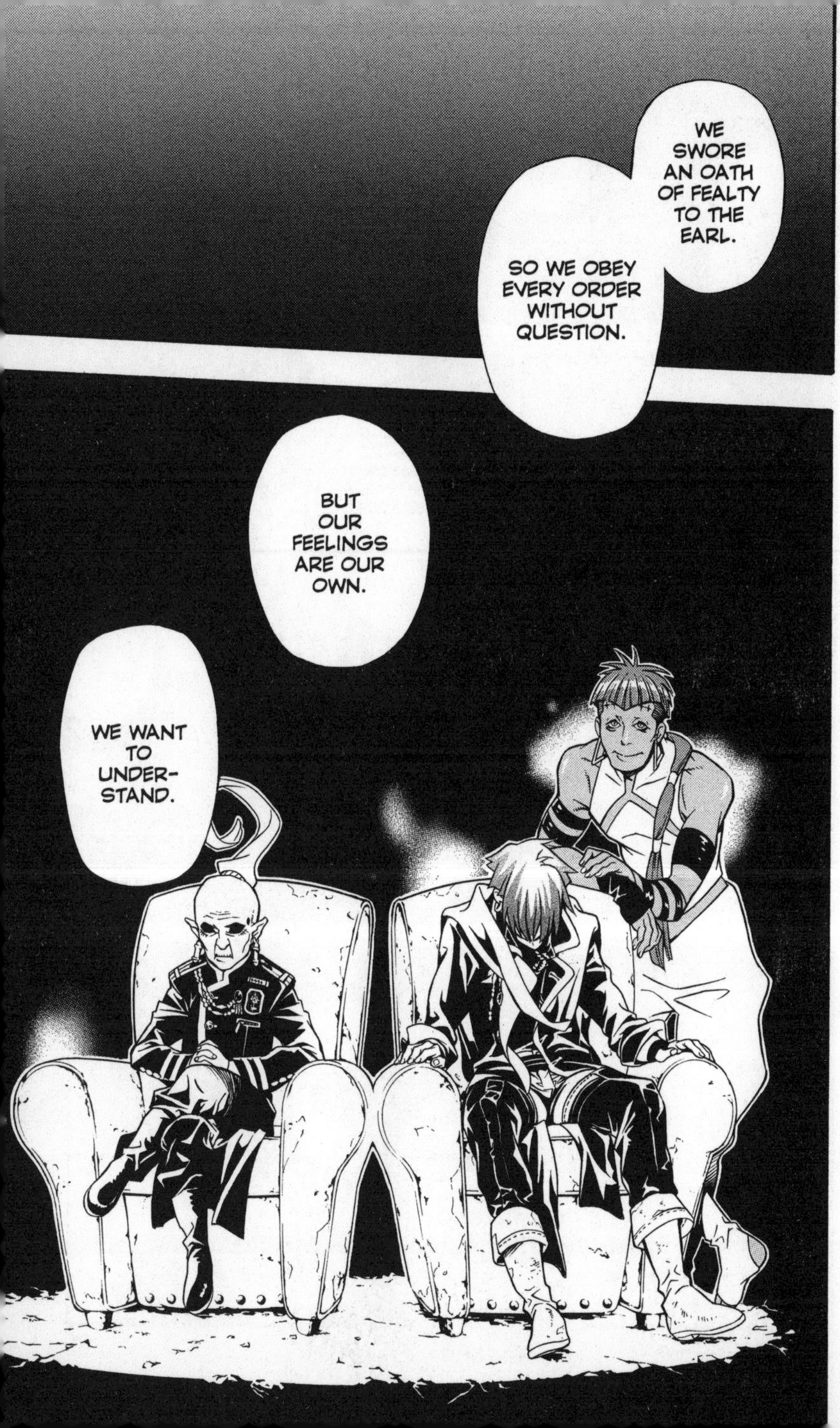
WE SWORE AN OATH OF FEALTY TO THE EARL.
SO WE OBEY EVERY ORDER WITHOUT QUESTION.
BUT OUR FEELINGS ARE OUR OWN.
WE WANT TO UNDER-STAND.

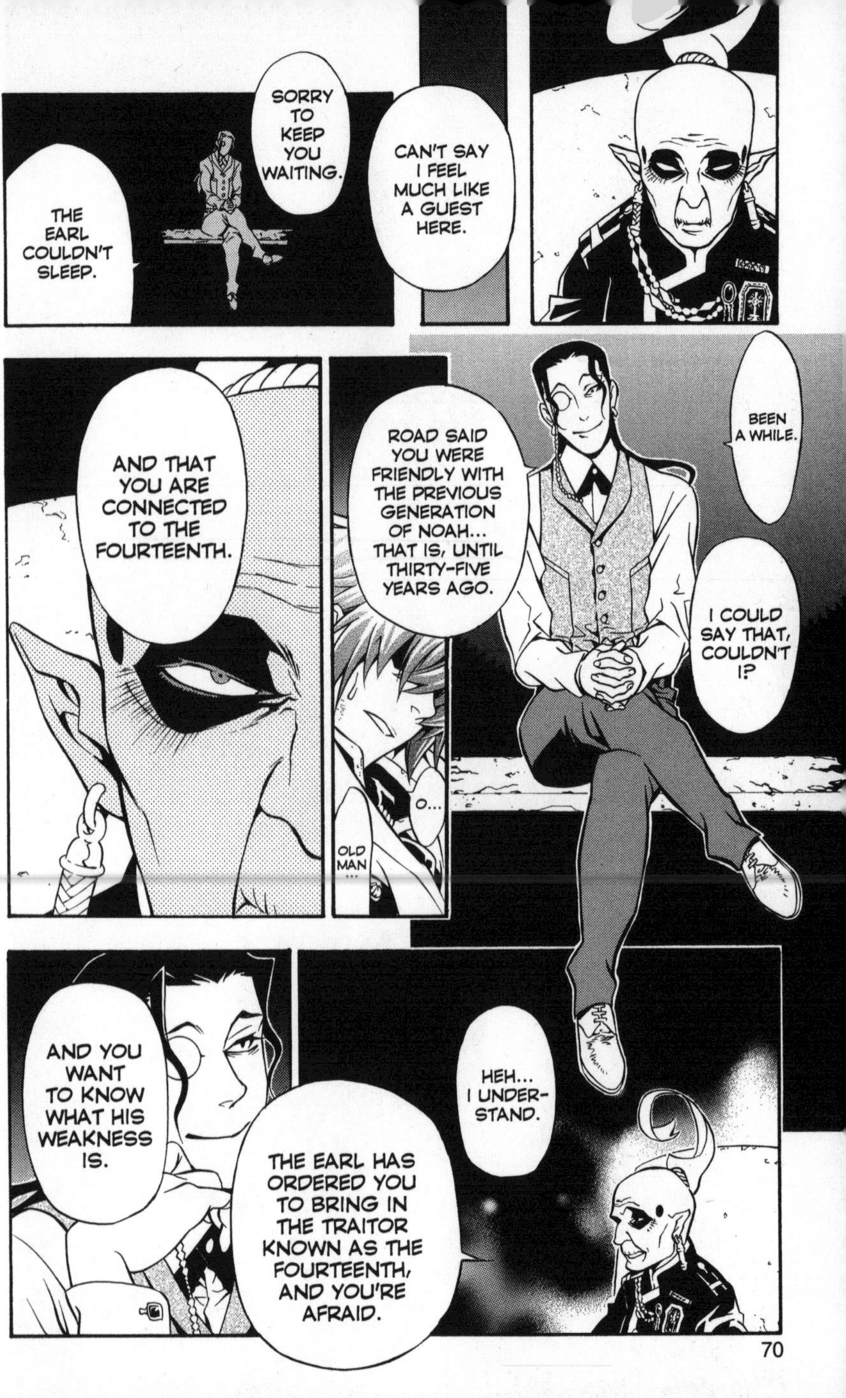
SORRY TO KEEP YOU WAITING.
CAN'T SAY I FEEL MUCH LIKE A GUEST HERE.
THE EARL COULDN'T SLEEP.
BEEN A WHILE.
I COULD SAY THAT, COULDN'T I?
ROAD SAID YOU WERE FRIENDLY WITH THE PREVIOUS GENERATION OF NOAH... THAT IS, UNTIL THIRTY-FIVE YEARS AGO.
O...
OLD MAN...
AND THAT YOU ARE CONNECTED TO THE FOURTEENTH.
HEH... I UNDERSTAND.
THE EARL HAS ORDERED YOU TO BRING IN THE TRAITOR KNOWN AS THE FOURTEENTH, AND YOU'RE AFRAID.
AND YOU WANT TO KNOW WHAT HIS WEAKNESS IS.

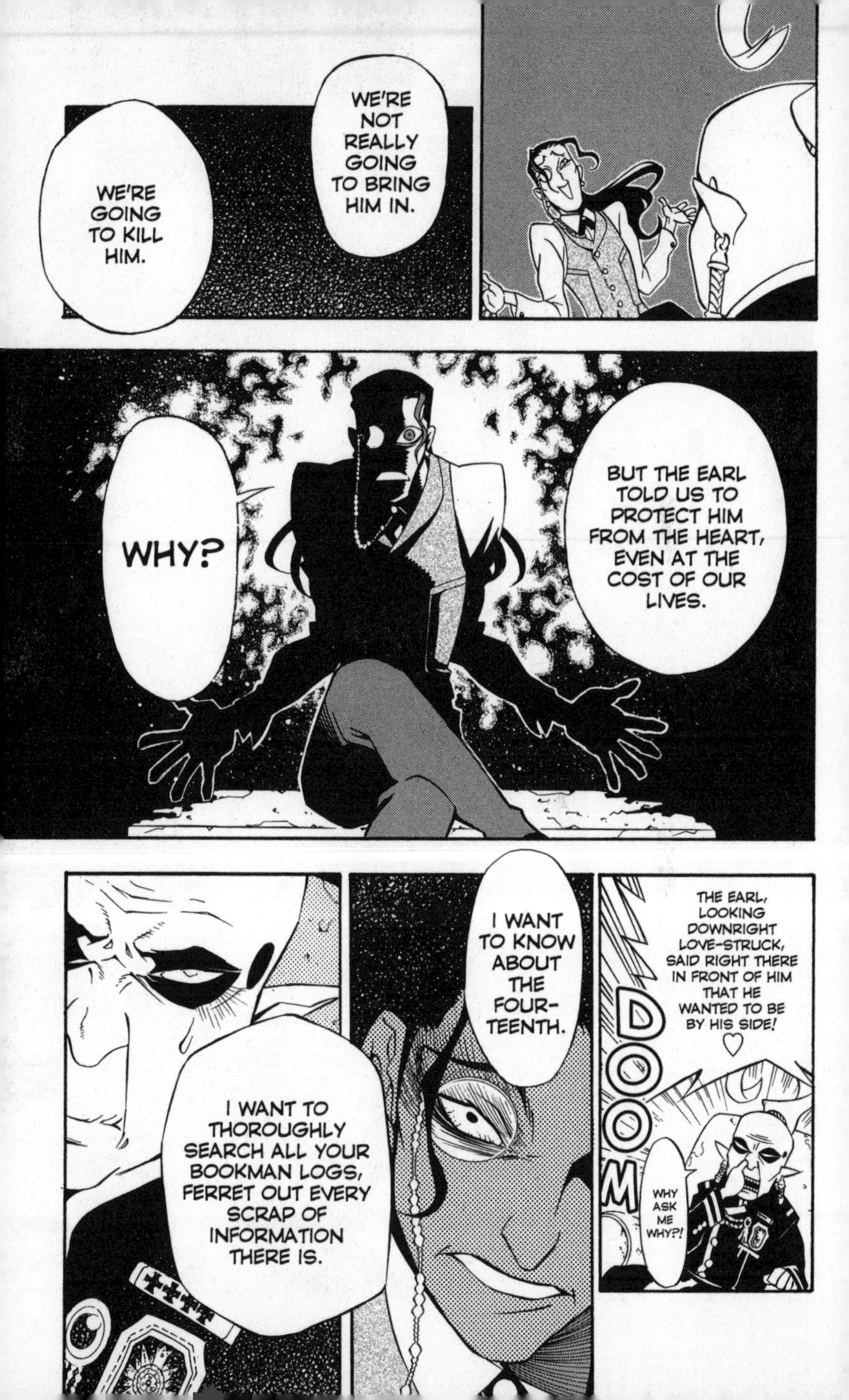
WE'RE NOT REALLY GOING TO BRING HIM IN.
WE'RE GOING TO KILL HIM.
BUT THE EARL TOLD US TO PROTECT HIM FROM THE HEART, EVEN AT THE COST OF OUR LIVES.
WHY?
THE EARL, LOOKING DOWNRIGHT LOVE-STRUCK, SAID RIGHT THERE IN FRONT OF HIM THAT HE WANTED TO BE BY HIS SIDE! ♡
DOOM
WHY ASK ME WHY?!
I WANT TO KNOW ABOUT THE FOUR-TEENTH.
I WANT TO THOROUGHLY SEARCH ALL YOUR BOOKMAN LOGS, FERRET OUT EVERY SCRAP OF INFORMATION THERE IS.

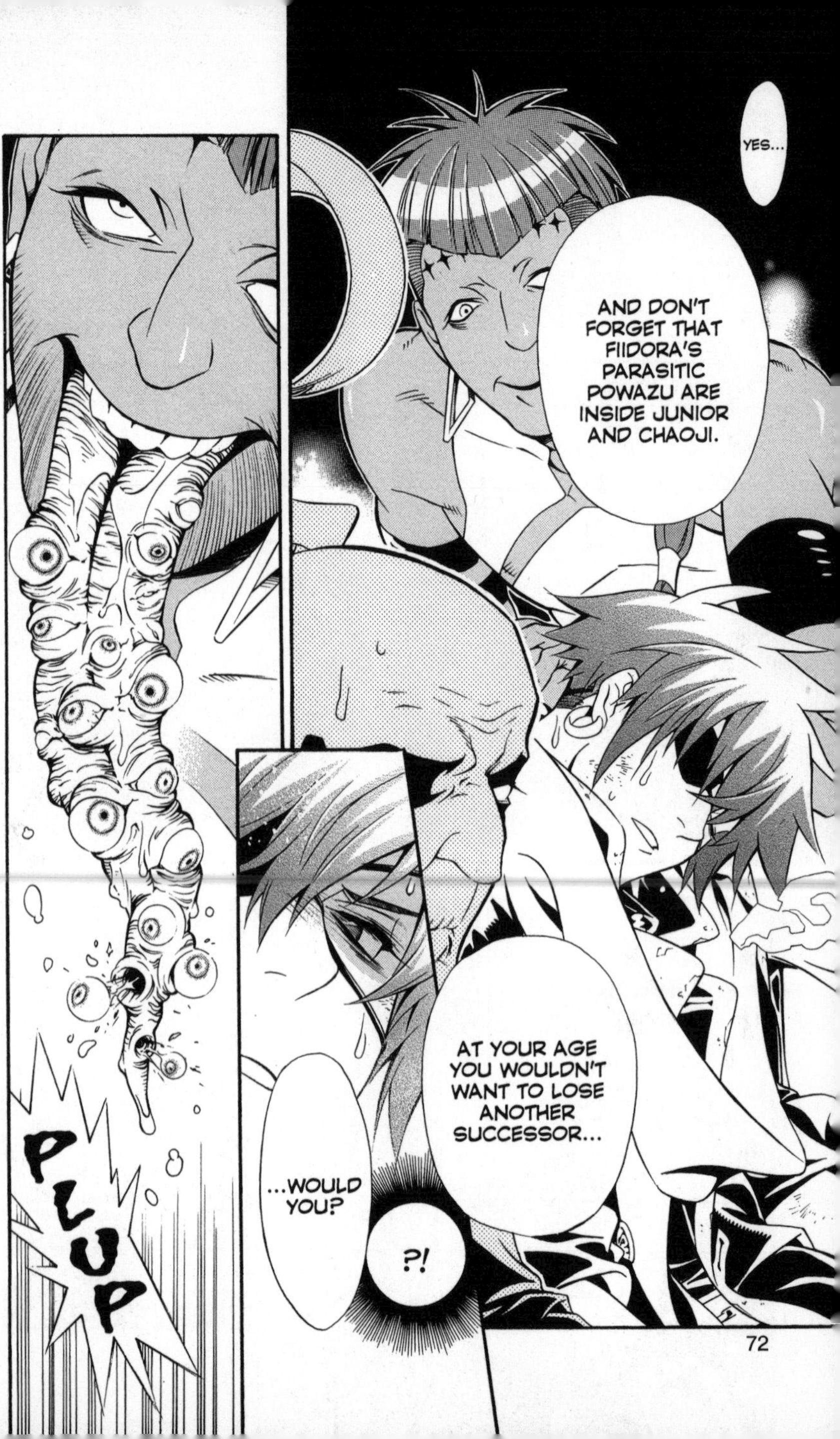
YES...
AND DON'T FORGET THAT FIIDORA'S PARASITIC POWAZU ARE INSIDE JUNIOR AND CHAOJI.
AT YOUR AGE YOU WOULDN'T WANT TO LOSE ANOTHER SUCCESSOR...
...WOULD YOU?
?!
PLUP

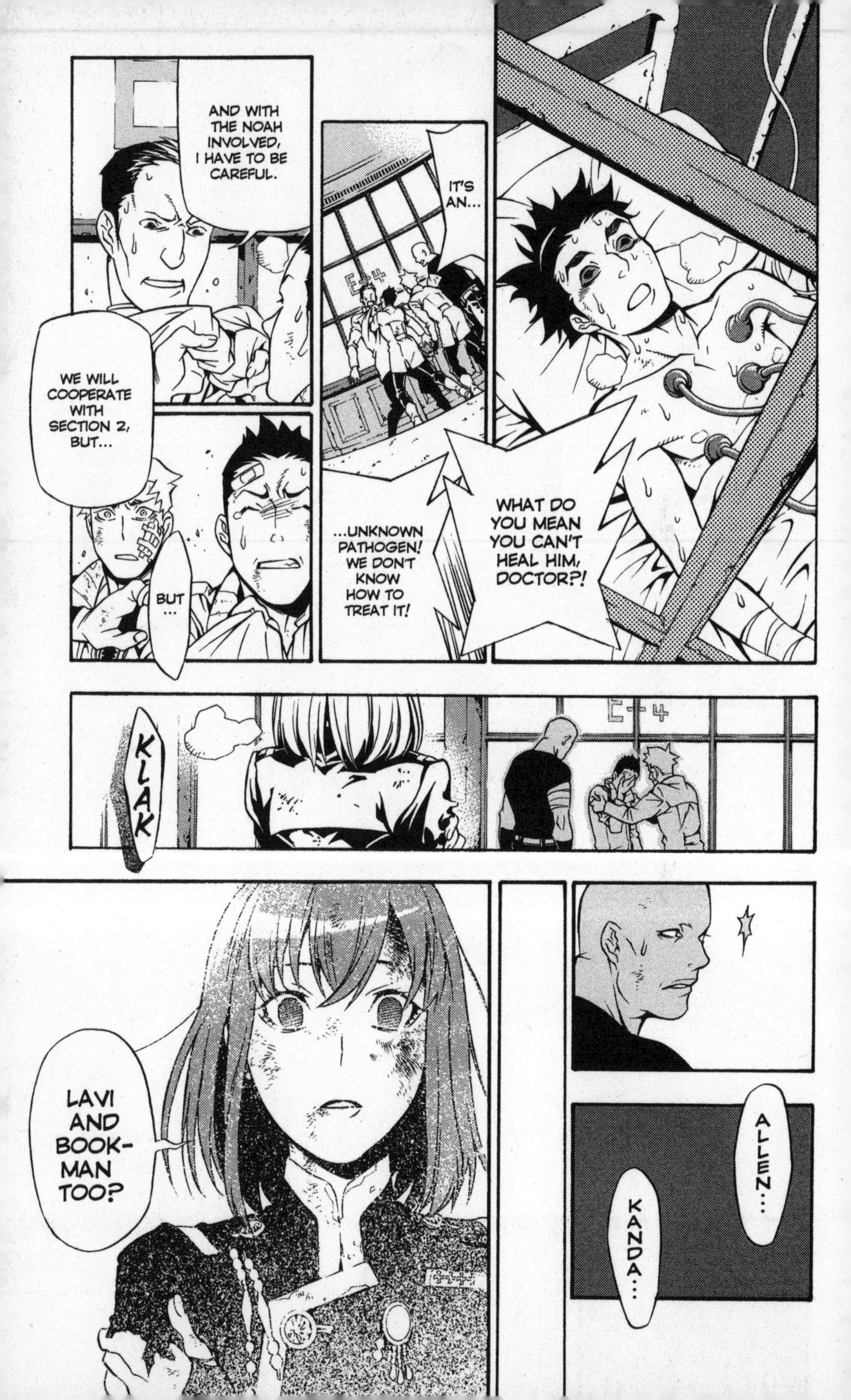
WHAT DO YOU MEAN YOU CAN'T HEAL HIM, DOCTOR?!
IT'S AN...
...UNKNOWN PATHOGEN! WE DON'T KNOW HOW TO TREAT IT!
AND WITH THE NOAH INVOLVED, I HAVE TO BE CAREFUL.
WE WILL COOPERATE WITH SECTION 2, BUT...
BUT...
KLAK
ALLEN...
KANDA...
LAVI AND BOOKMAN TOO?

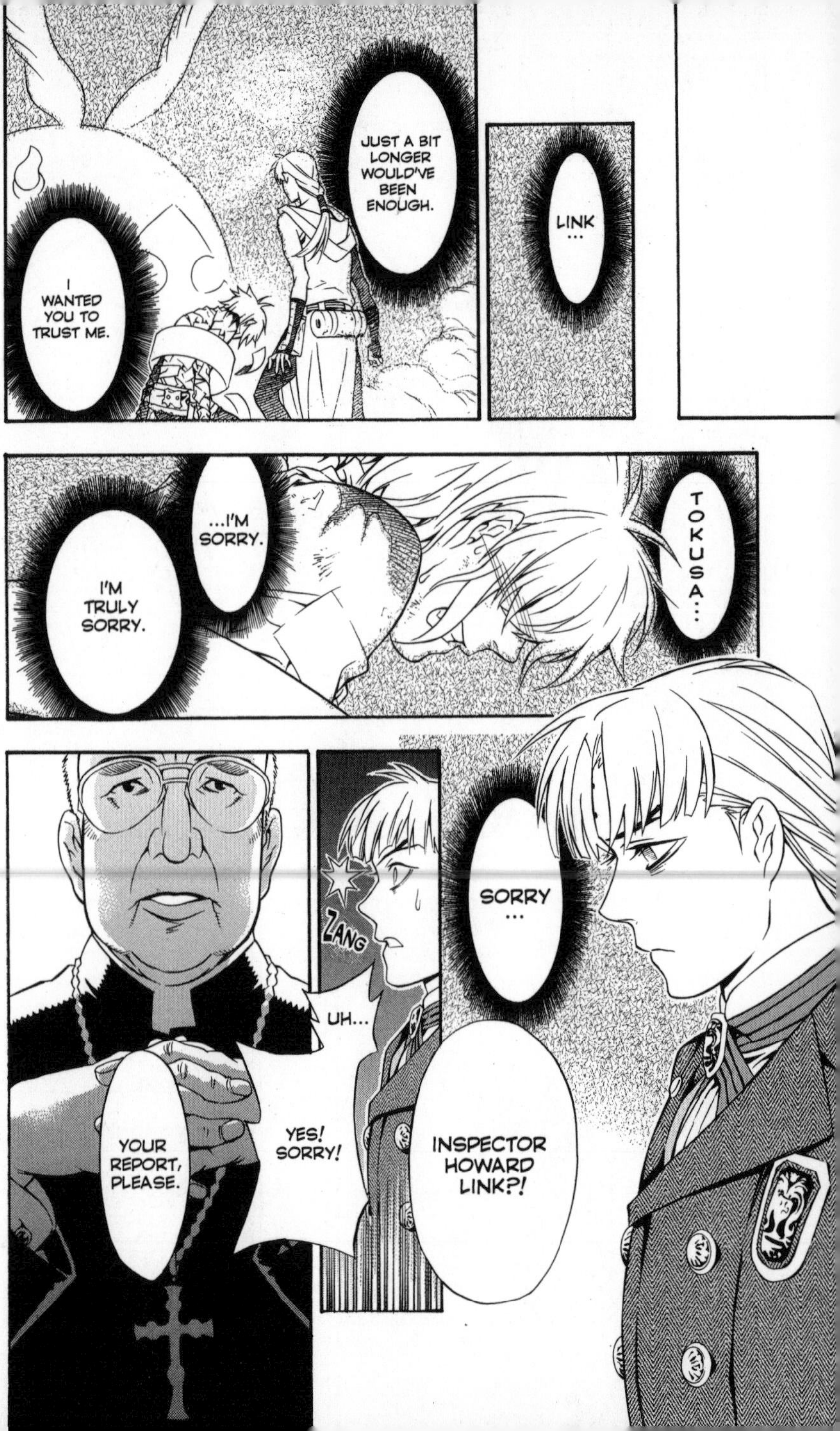

LINK ...
JUST A BIT LONGER WOULD'VE BEEN ENOUGH.
I WANTED YOU TO TRUST ME.
TOKUSA...
...I'M SORRY.
I'M TRULY SORRY.
SORRY ...
INSPECTOR HOWARD LINK?!
ZANG
UH...
YES! SORRY!
YOUR REPORT, PLEASE.

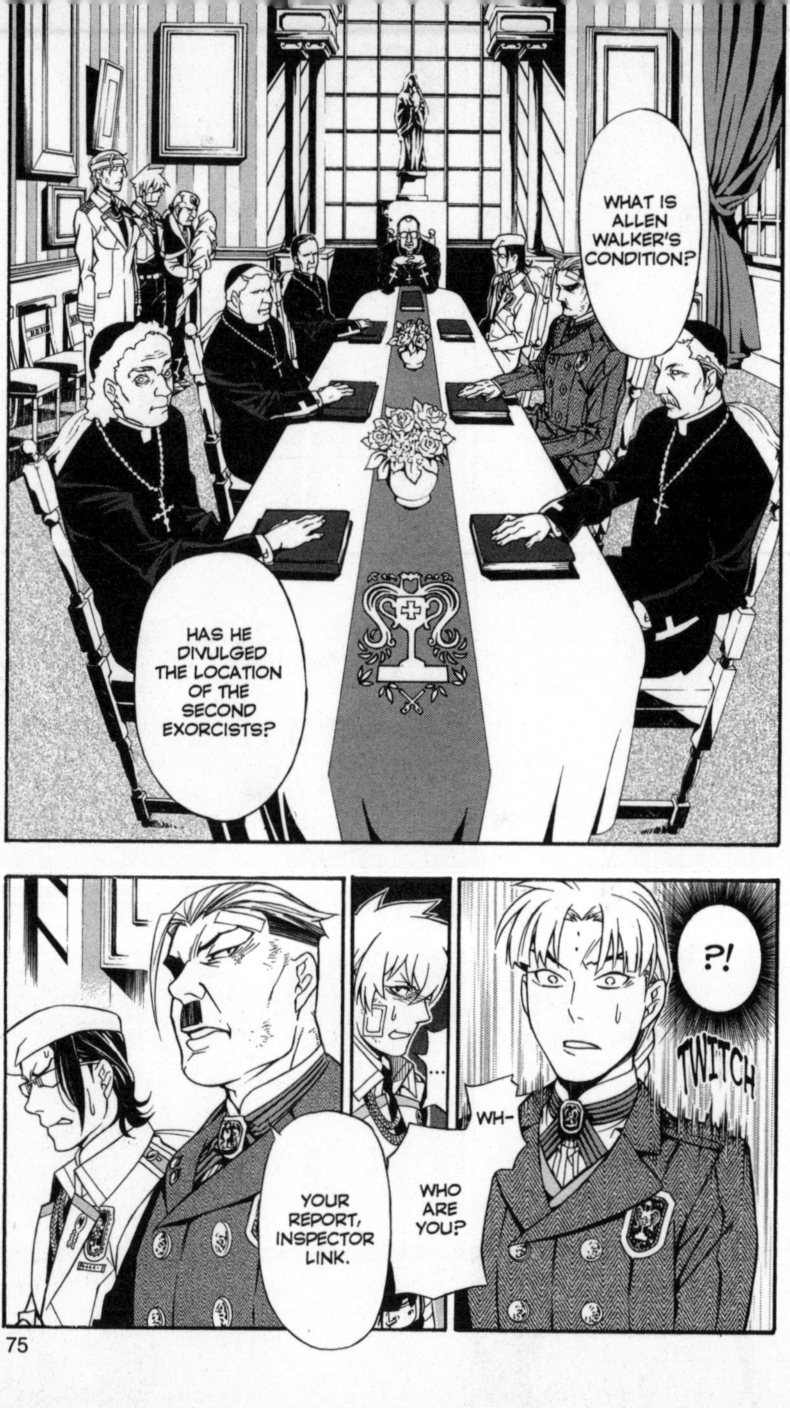
WHAT IS ALLEN WALKER'S CONDITION?
HAS HE DIVULGED THE LOCATION OF THE SECOND EXORCISTS?
?!
TWITCH
WH-
WHO ARE YOU?
...
YOUR REPORT, INSPECTOR LINK.

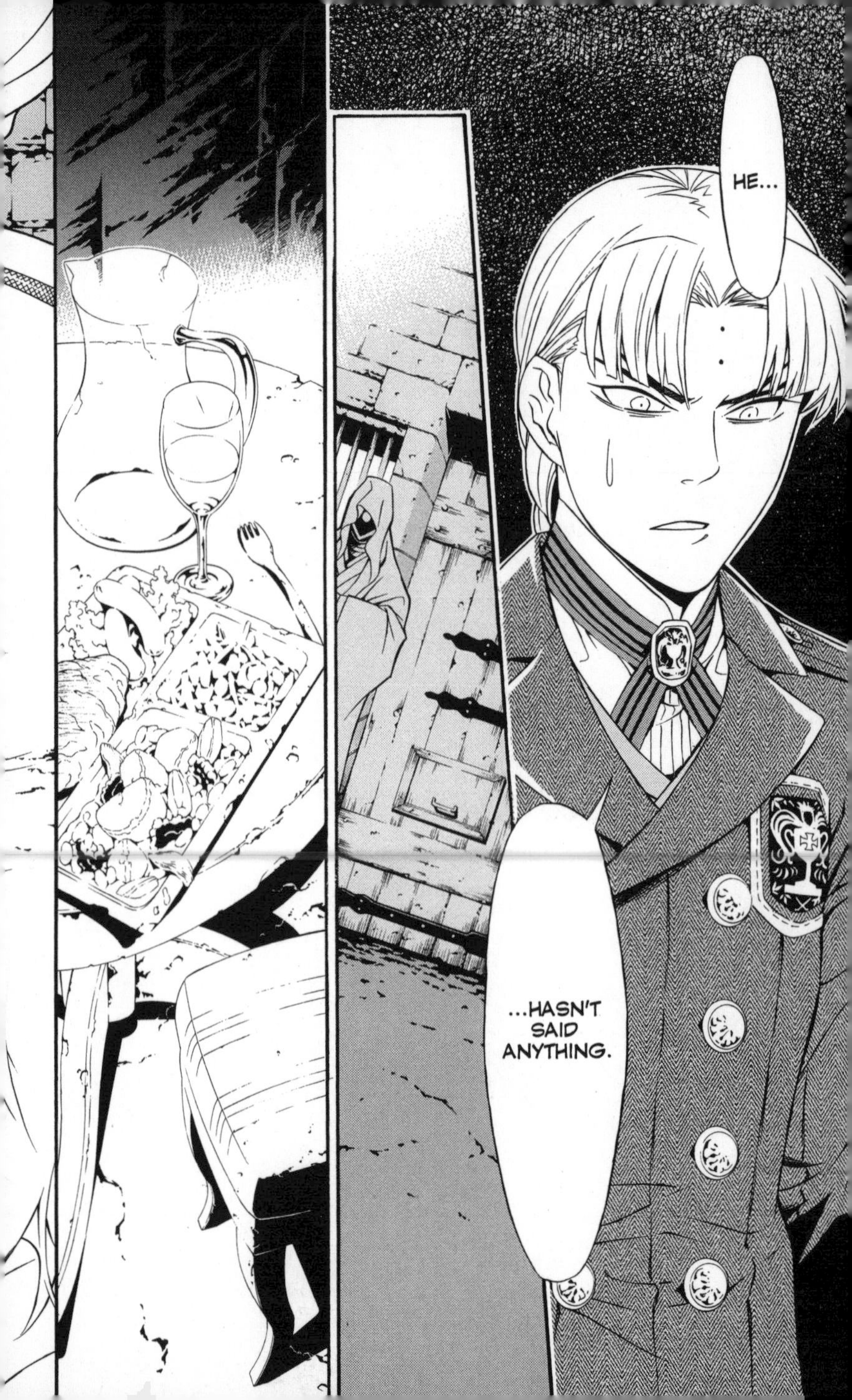
HE...
...HASN'T SAID ANYTHING.

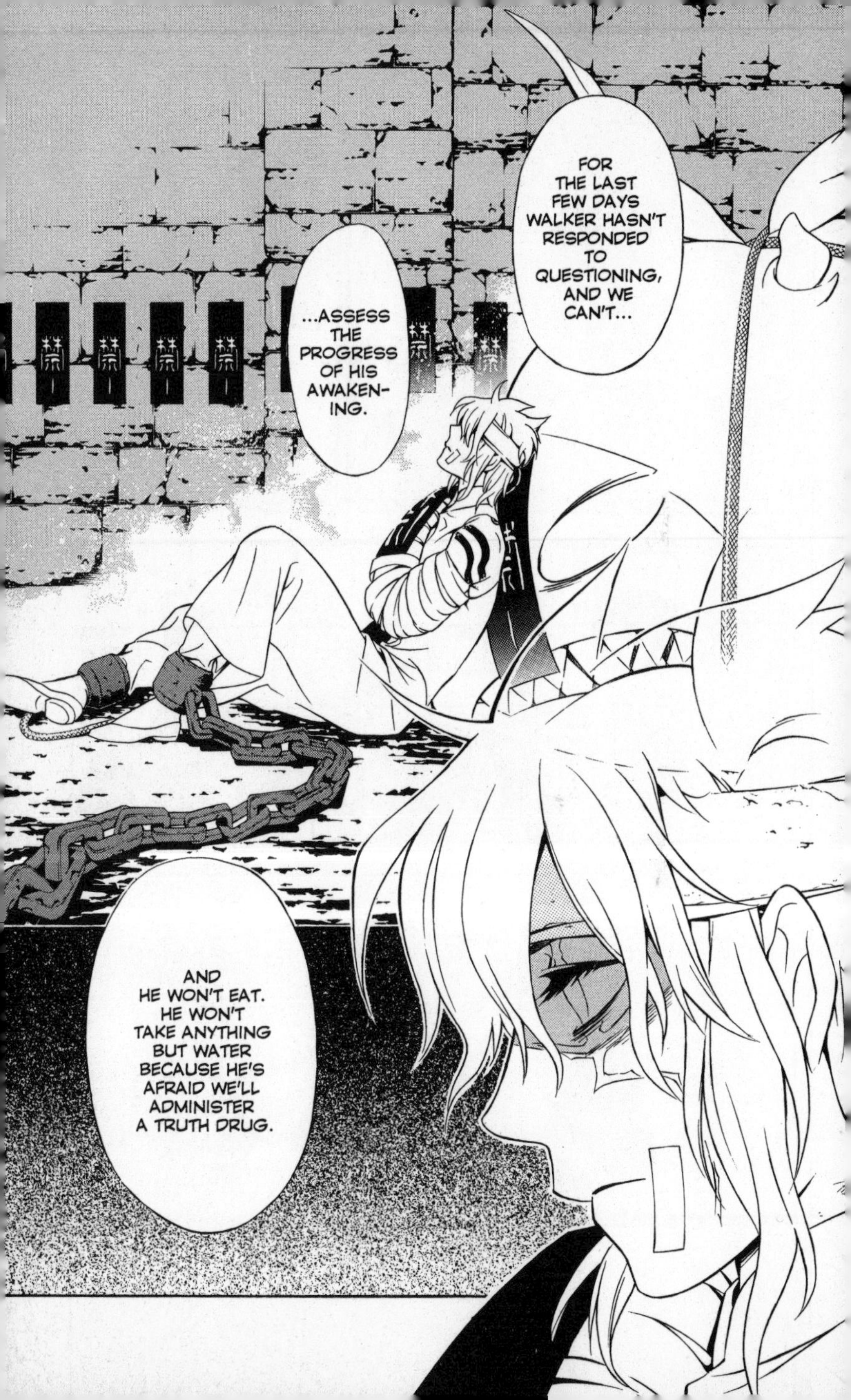
FOR THE LAST FEW DAYS WALKER HASN'T RESPONDED TO QUESTIONING, AND WE CAN'T...
...ASSESS THE PROGRESS OF HIS AWAKEN-ING.
AND HE WON'T EAT. HE WON'T TAKE ANYTHING BUT WATER BECAUSE HE'S AFRAID WE'LL ADMINISTER A TRUTH DRUG.

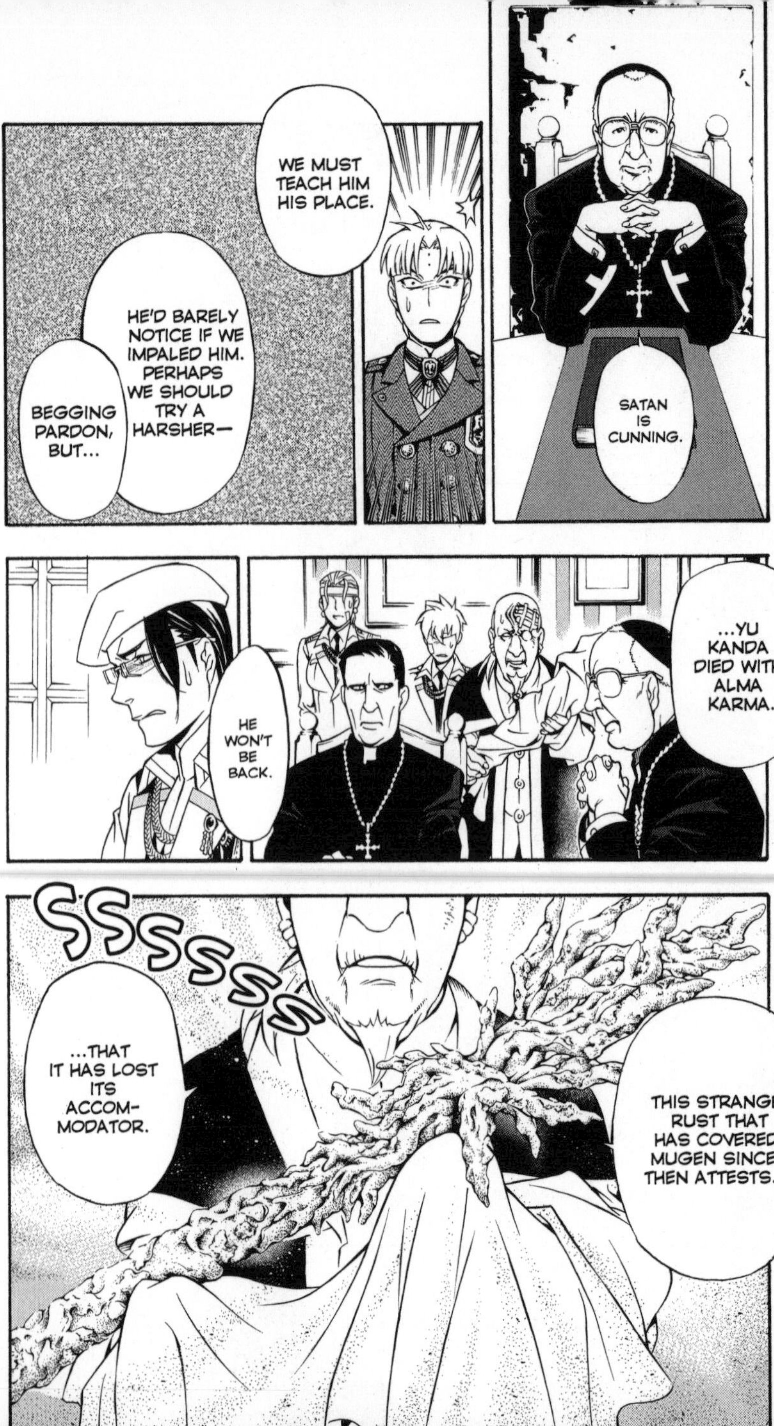
SATAN IS CUNNING.
WE MUST TEACH HIM HIS PLACE.
BEGGING PARDON, BUT…
HE'D BARELY NOTICE IF WE IMPALED HIM. PERHAPS WE SHOULD TRY A HARSHER—
…YU KANDA DIED WITH ALMA KARMA.
HE WON'T BE BACK.
SSSSSS
THIS STRANGE RUST THAT HAS COVERED MUGEN SINCE THEN ATTESTS…
…THAT IT HAS LOST ITS ACCOM-MODATOR.

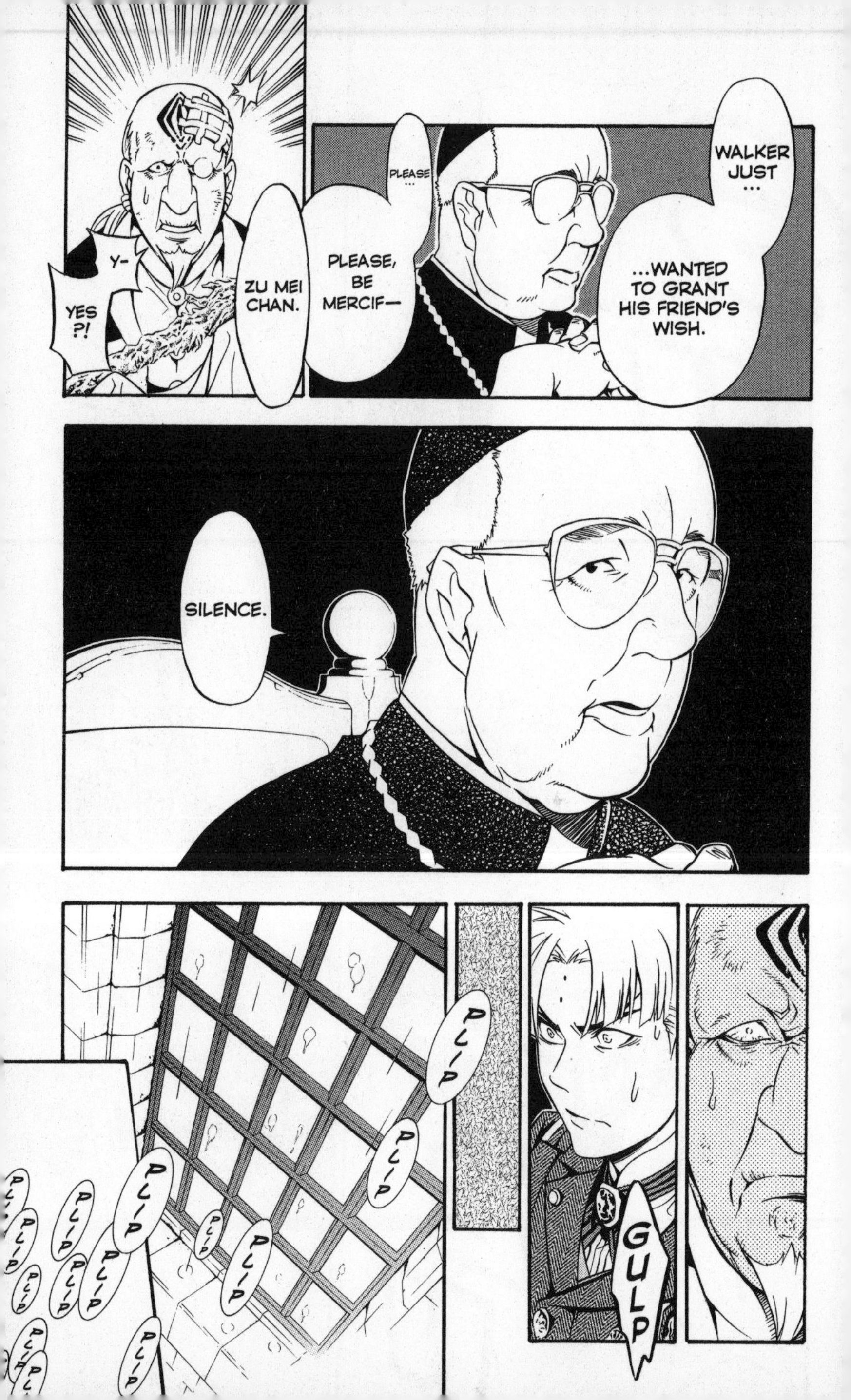
WALKER JUST ...
...WANTED TO GRANT HIS FRIEND'S WISH.
PLEASE ...
PLEASE, BE MERCIF—
ZU MEI CHAN.
Y-
YES ?!
SILENCE.
GULP
PLIP
PLIP
PLIP
PLIP
PLIP
PLIP
PLIP
PLIP

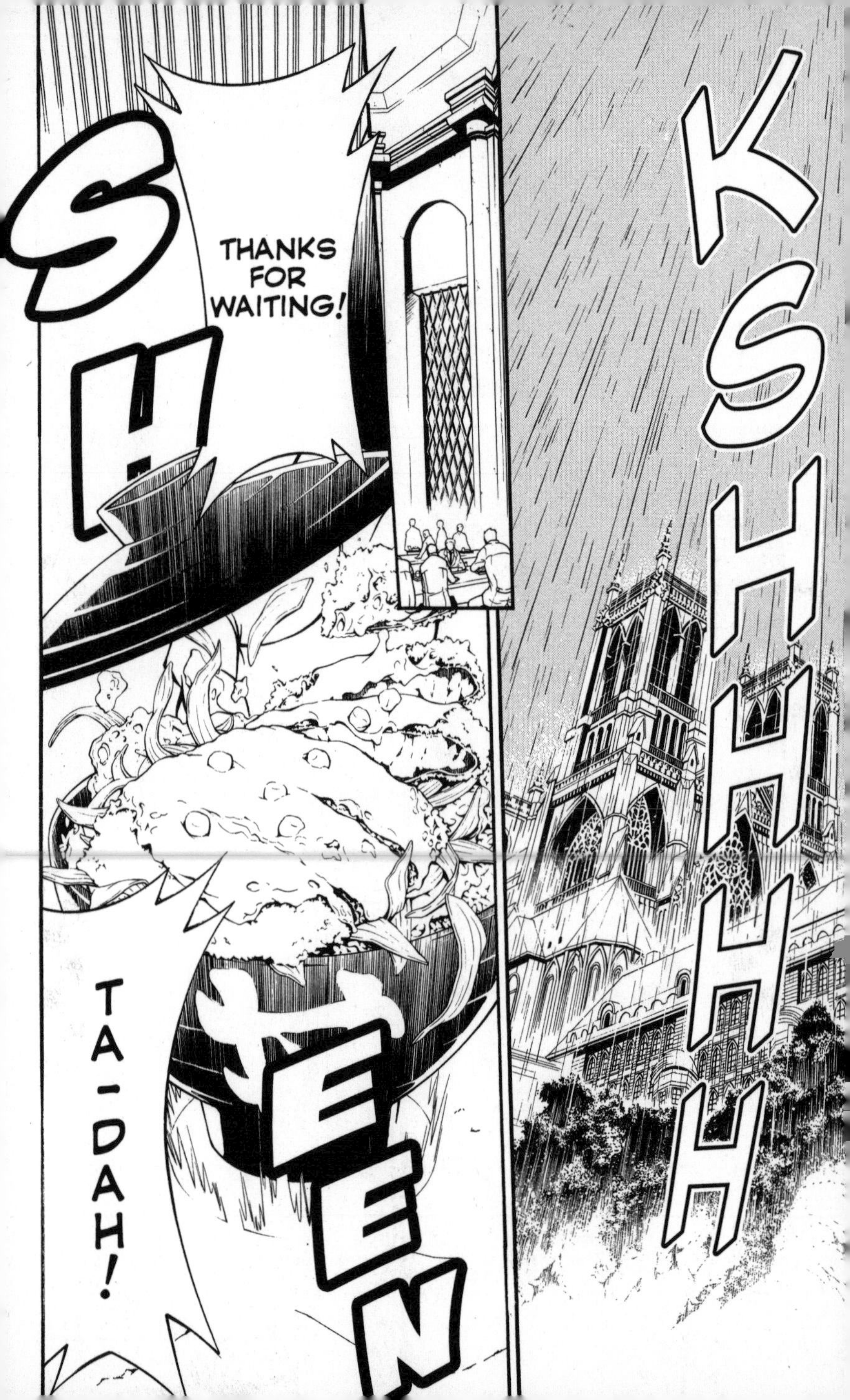
KSHHHH
THANKS FOR WAITING!
SH!
TA-DAH!
EEN

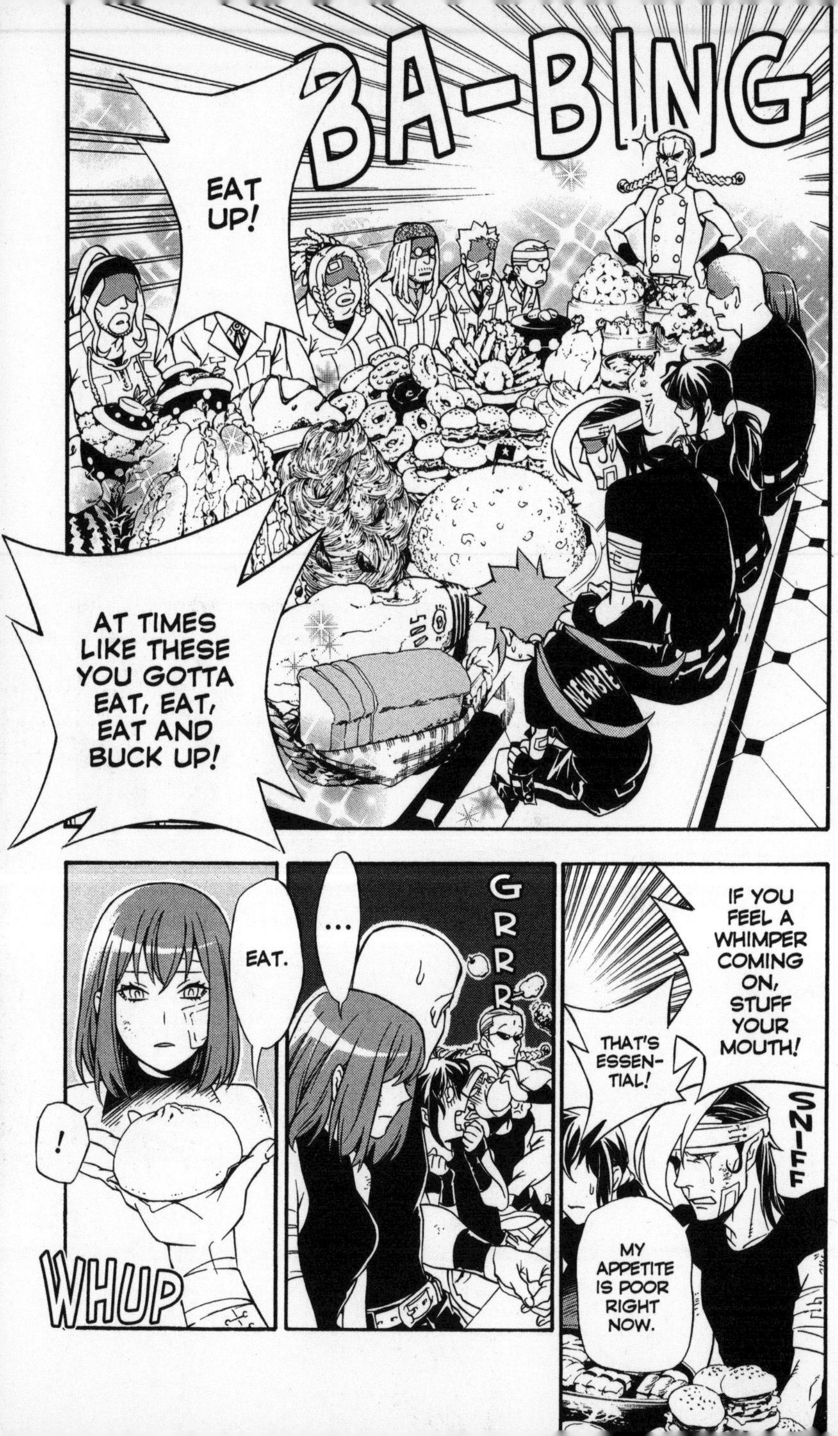
BA-BING
EAT UP!
AT TIMES LIKE THESE YOU GOTTA EAT, EAT, EAT AND BUCK UP!
IF YOU FEEL A WHIMPER COMING ON, STUFF YOUR MOUTH!
THAT'S ESSEN-TIAL!
SNIFF
MY APPETITE IS POOR RIGHT NOW.
GRRR
...
EAT.
!
WHUP

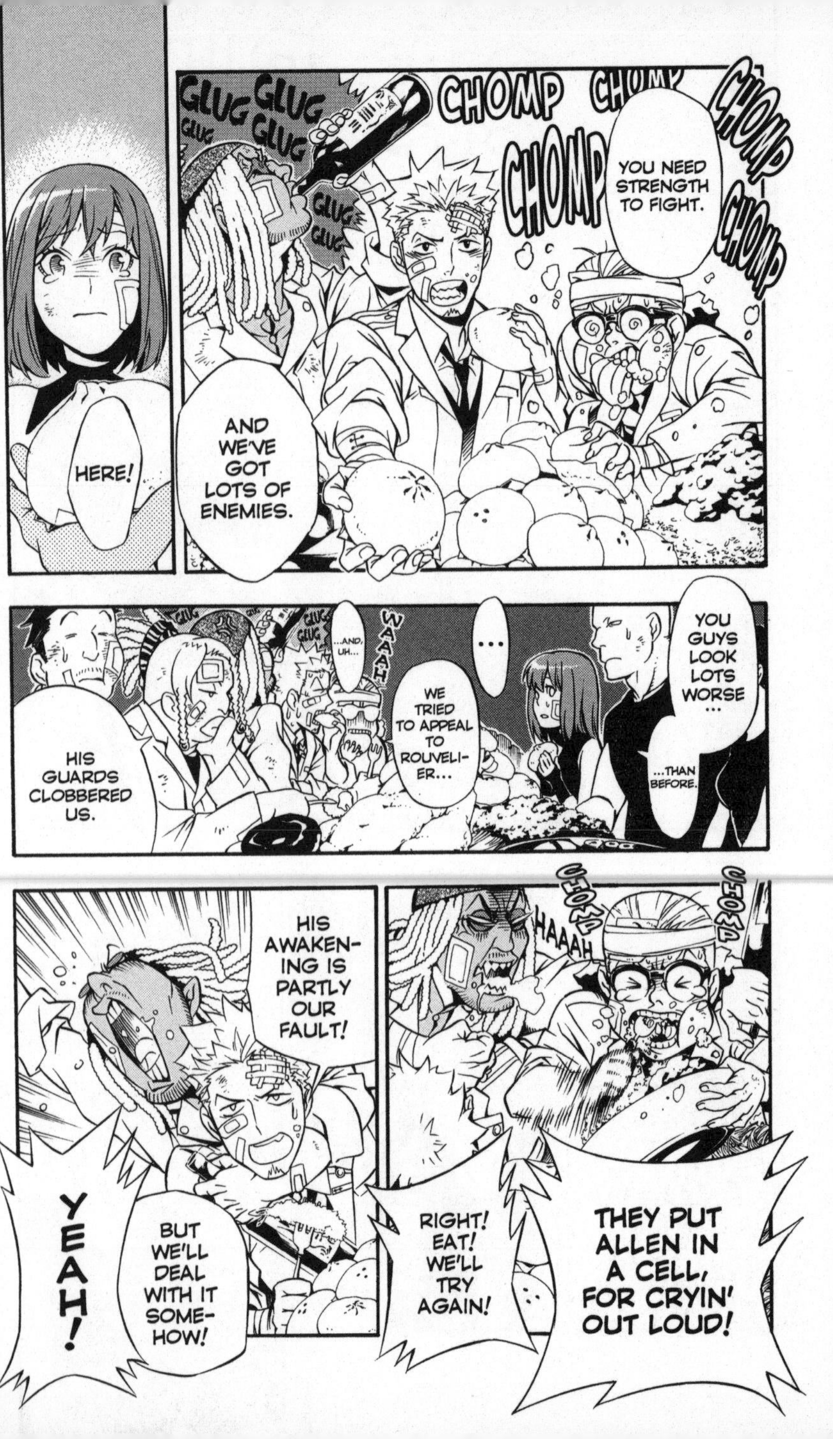

CHOMP CHOMP
CHOMP
CHOMP
CHOMP
YOU NEED STRENGTH TO FIGHT.
GLUG GLUG GLUG GLUG
GLUG GLUG
AND WE'VE GOT LOTS OF ENEMIES.
HERE!
YOU GUYS LOOK LOTS WORSE...
...THAN BEFORE.
...
WE TRIED TO APPEAL TO ROUVELIER...
WAAAAH
...AND, UH...
GLUG GLUG
GLUG
HIS GUARDS CLOBBERED US.
CHOMP
CHOMP
HAAAAH
THEY PUT ALLEN IN A CELL, FOR CRYIN' OUT LOUD!
RIGHT! EAT! WE'LL TRY AGAIN!
HIS AWAKENING IS PARTLY OUR FAULT!
BUT WE'LL DEAL WITH IT SOMEHOW!
YEAH!

READ THIS WAY

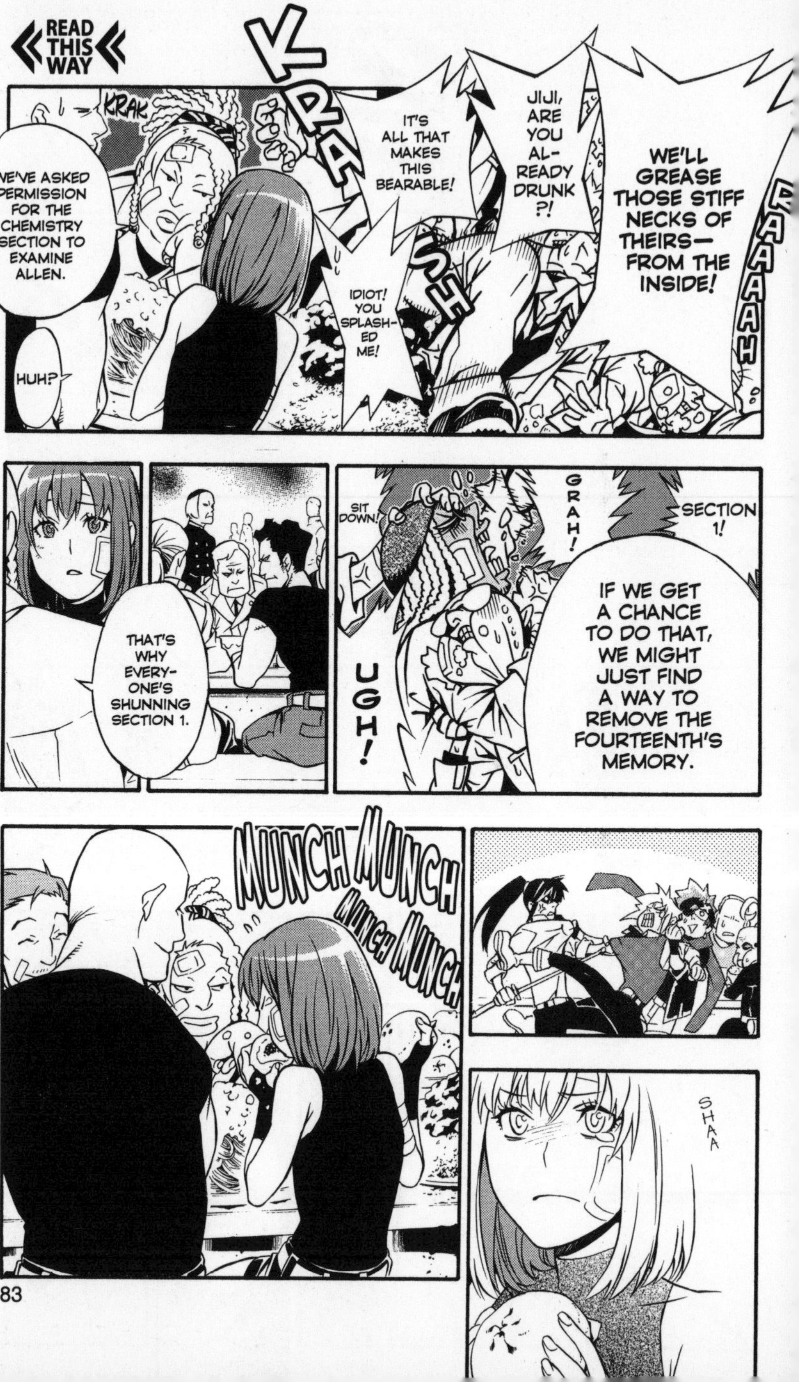
RAAAAAH
WE'LL GREASE THOSE STIFF NECKS OF THEIRS—FROM THE INSIDE!
JIJI, ARE YOU AL-READY DRUNK?!
IT'S ALL THAT MAKES THIS BEARABLE!
KRASH
IDIOT! YOU SPLASH-ED ME!
KRAK
WE'VE ASKED PERMISSION FOR THE CHEMISTRY SECTION TO EXAMINE ALLEN.
HUH?
SECTION 1!
GRAH!
IF WE GET A CHANCE TO DO THAT, WE MIGHT JUST FIND A WAY TO REMOVE THE FOURTEENTH'S MEMORY.
SIT DOWN!
UGH!
THAT'S WHY EVERY-ONE'S SHUNNING SECTION 1.
SHAA
MUNCH MUNCH
MUNCH MUNCH

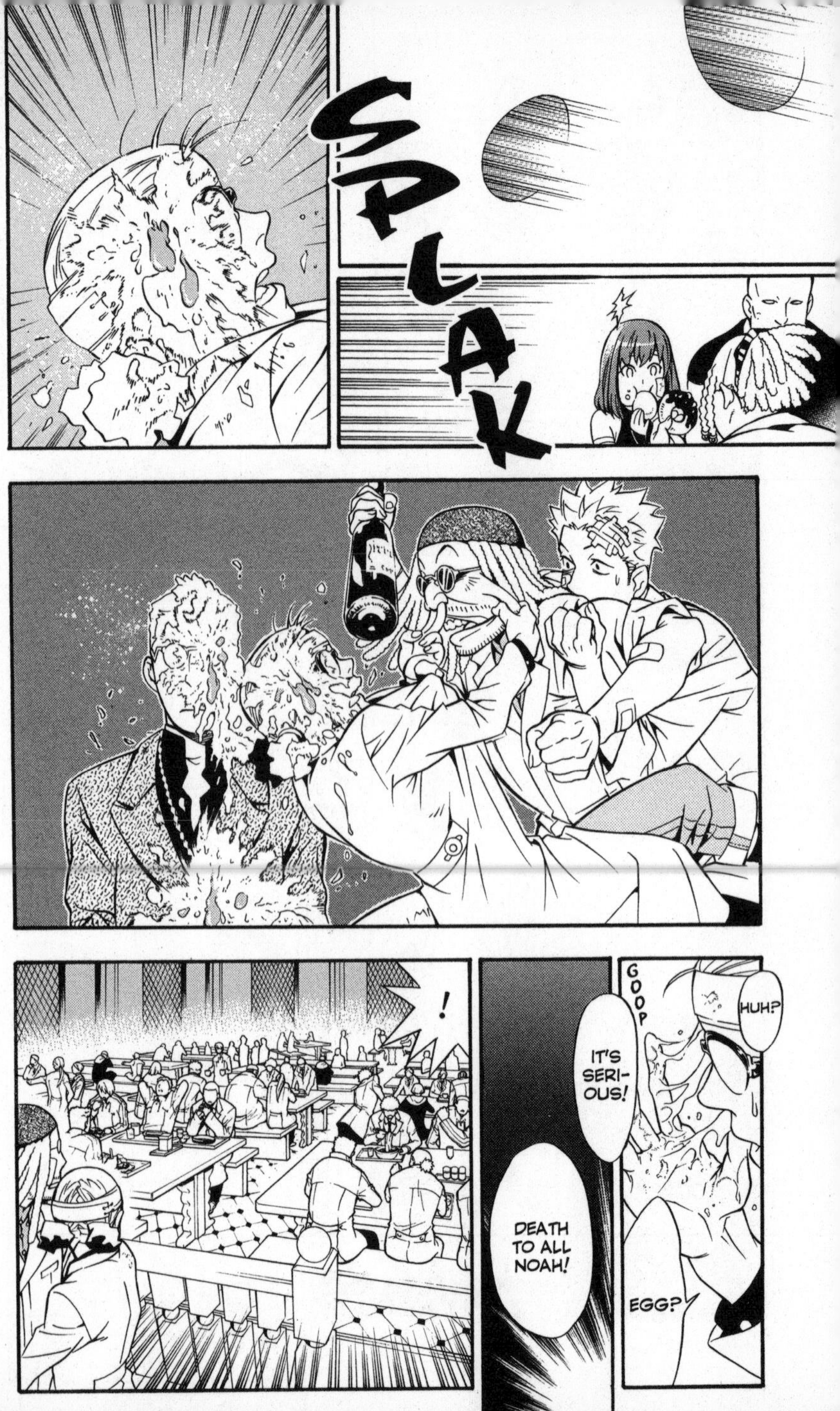
SPLAK
GOOP
HUH?
EGG?
IT'S SERI-OUS!
DEATH TO ALL NOAH!
!

READ THIS WAY

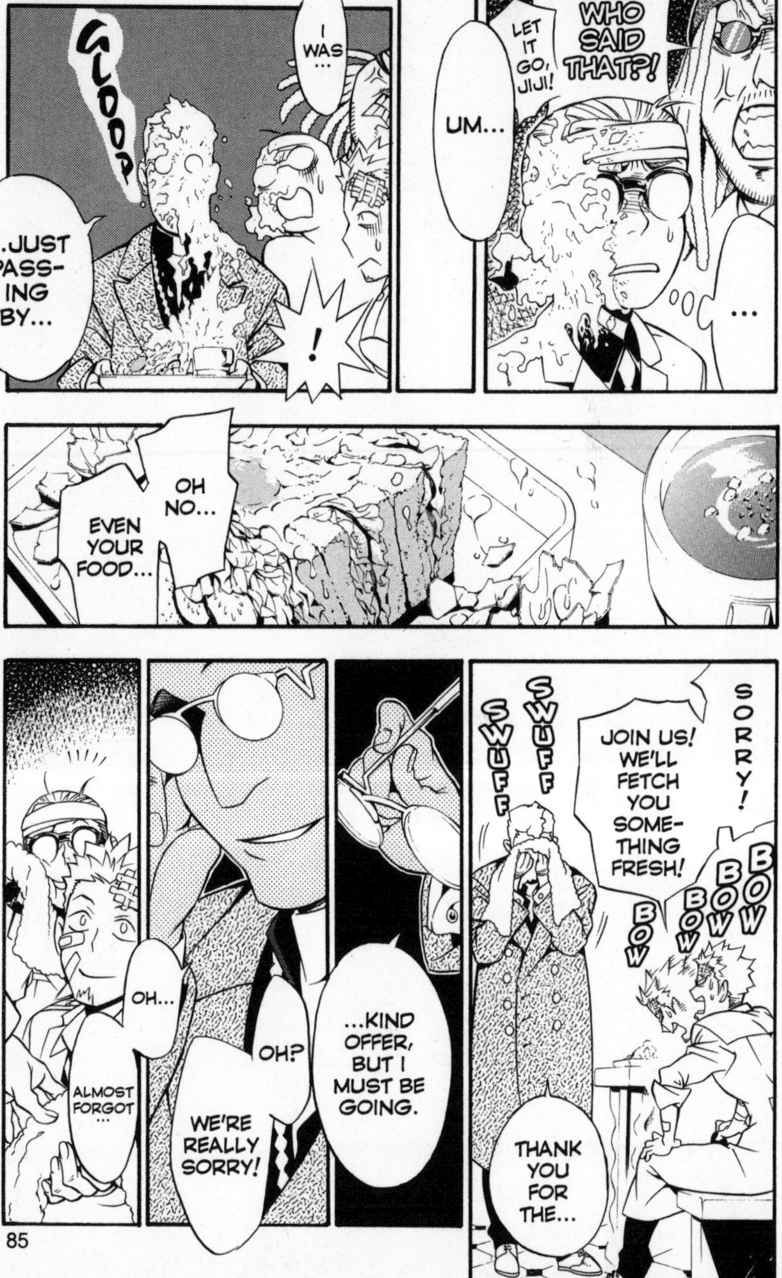
HEY, WHO SAID THAT?!
LET IT GO, JIJI!
...
UM...
I WAS...
...JUST PASSING-ING BY...
GLOOP
!
OH NO...
EVEN YOUR FOOD...
SORRY!
JOIN US! WE'LL FETCH YOU SOME-THING FRESH!
BOW
BOW
BOW
BOW
SWUFF
SWUFF
THANK YOU FOR THE...
...KIND OFFER, BUT I MUST BE GOING.
OH?
WE'RE REALLY SORRY!
OH...
ALMOST FORGOT...

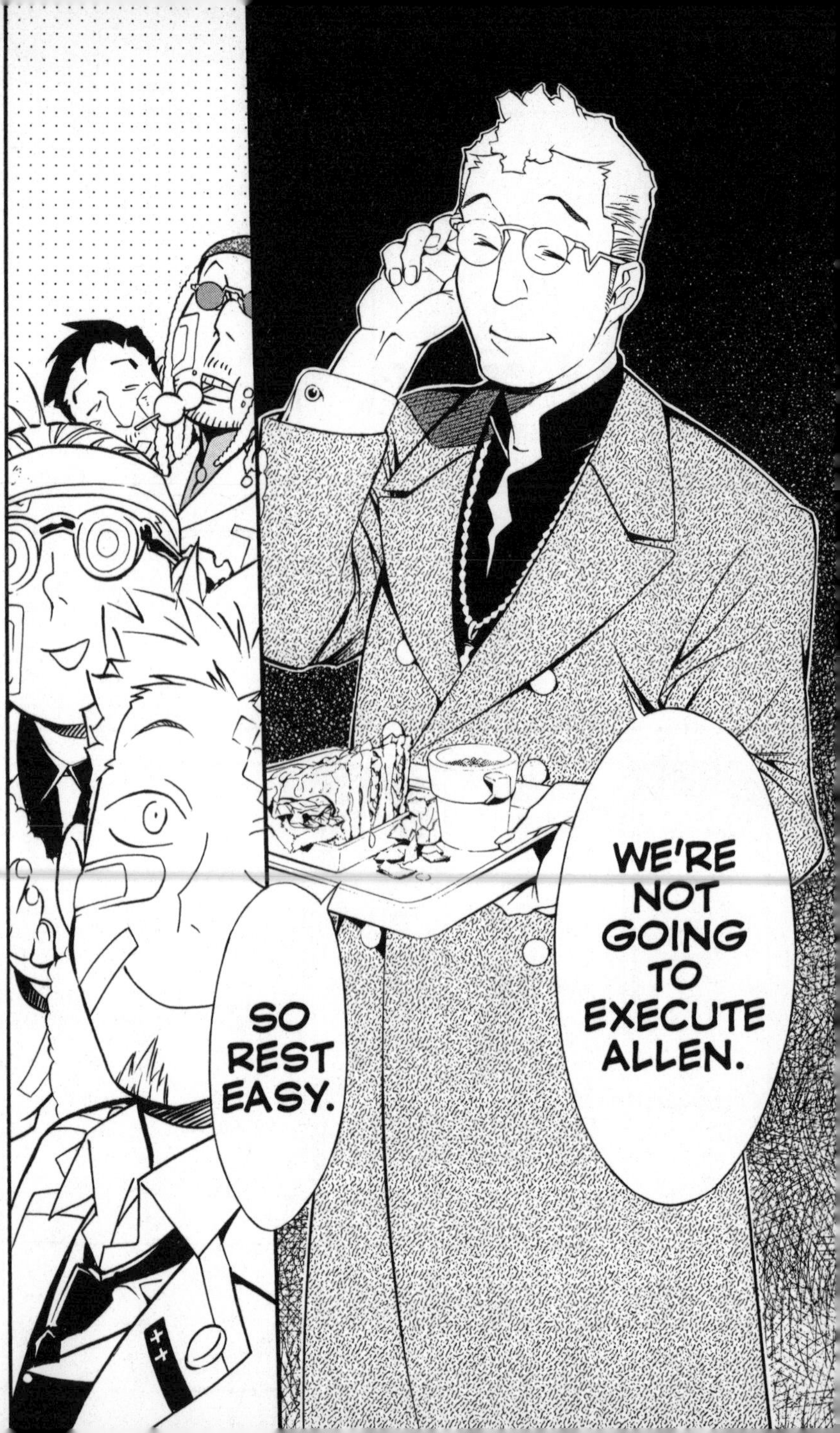
WE'RE NOT GOING TO EXECUTE ALLEN.
SO REST EASY.

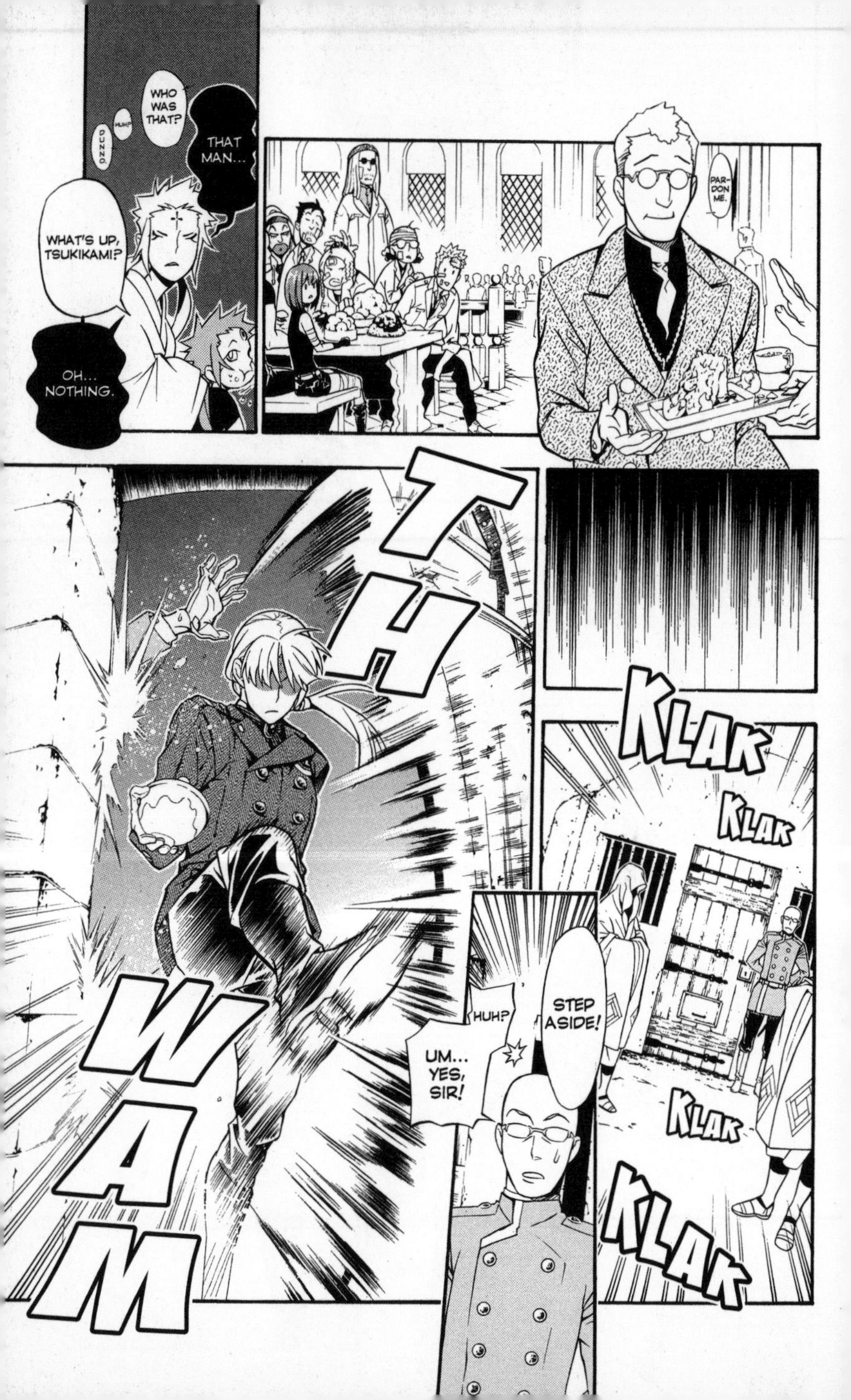
PARDON ME.
THAT MAN...
WHO WAS THAT?
HUH?
DUNNO.
WHAT'S UP, TSUKIKAMI?
OH... NOTHING.
KLAK
KLAK
KLAK
KLAK
STEP ASIDE!
HUH?
UM... YES, SIR!
THWAM

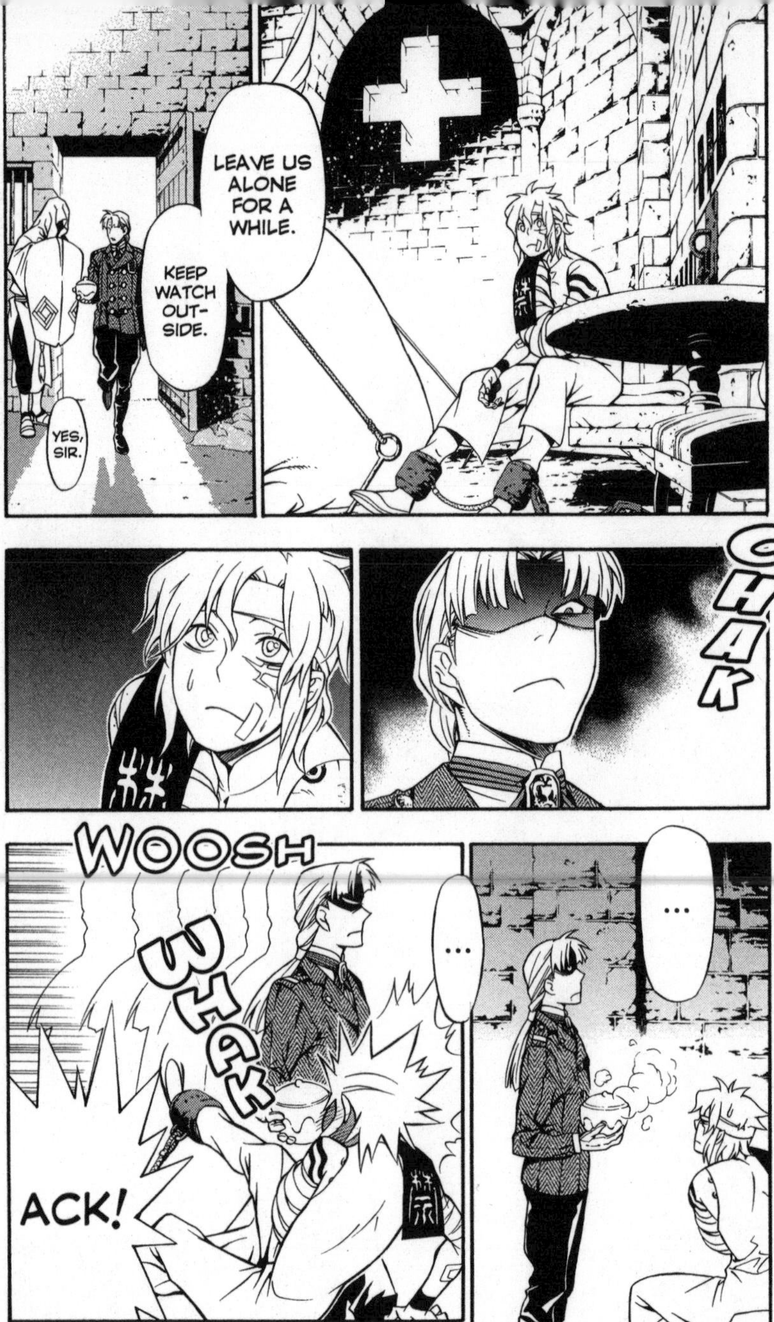
LEAVE US ALONE FOR A WHILE.
KEEP WATCH OUT-SIDE.
YES, SIR.
CHAK
...
...
WOOSH
WHAK
ACK!

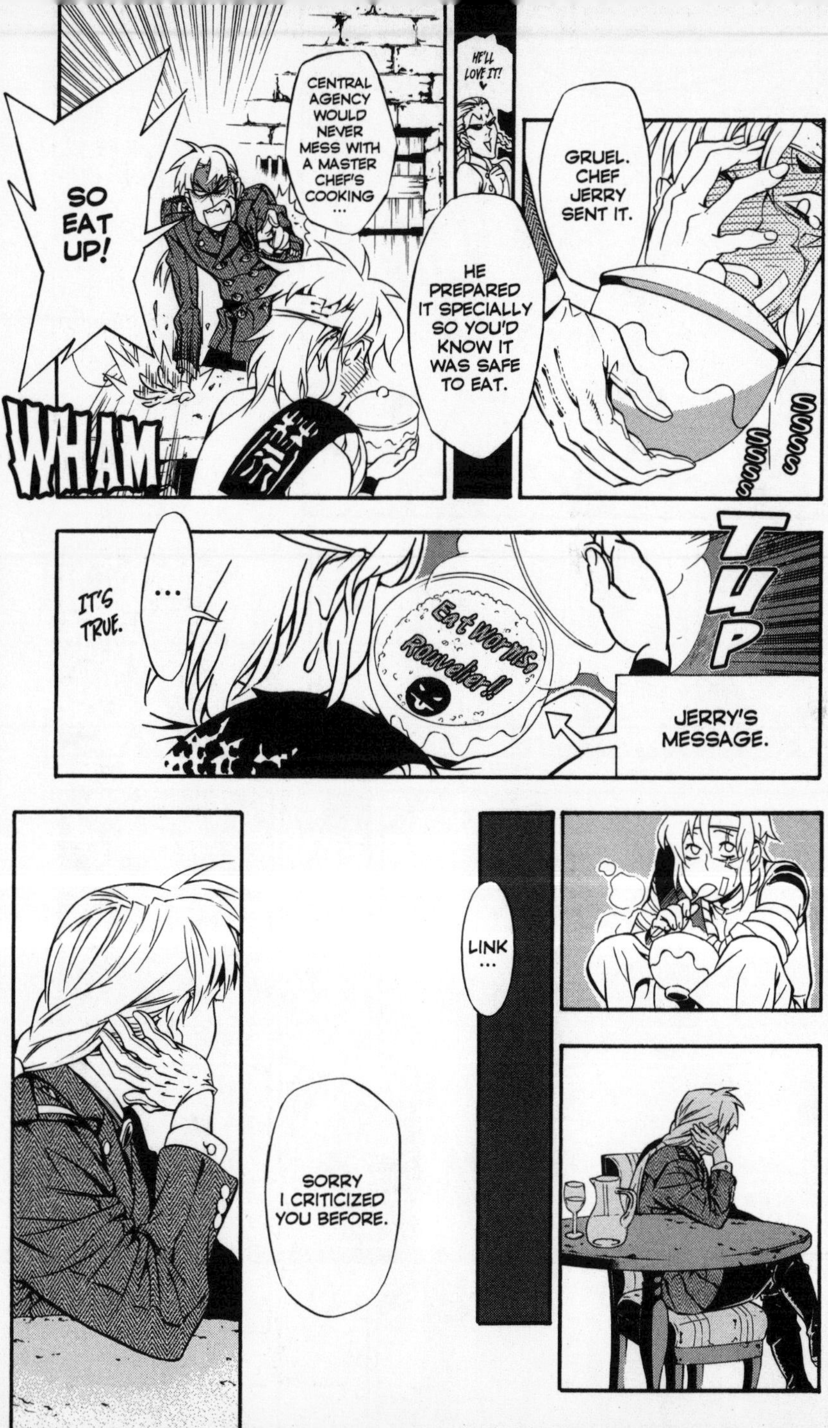

GRUEL. CHEF JERRY SENT IT.
HE PREPARED IT SPECIALLY SO YOU'D KNOW IT WAS SAFE TO EAT.
SSSSS
SSSSS
HE'LL LOVE IT!
CENTRAL AGENCY WOULD NEVER MESS WITH A MASTER CHEF'S COOKING...
SO EAT UP!
WHAM
THUP
Eat Worms, Rouvelier!!
JERRY'S MESSAGE.
...
IT'S TRUE.
LINK...
SORRY I CRITICIZED YOU BEFORE.

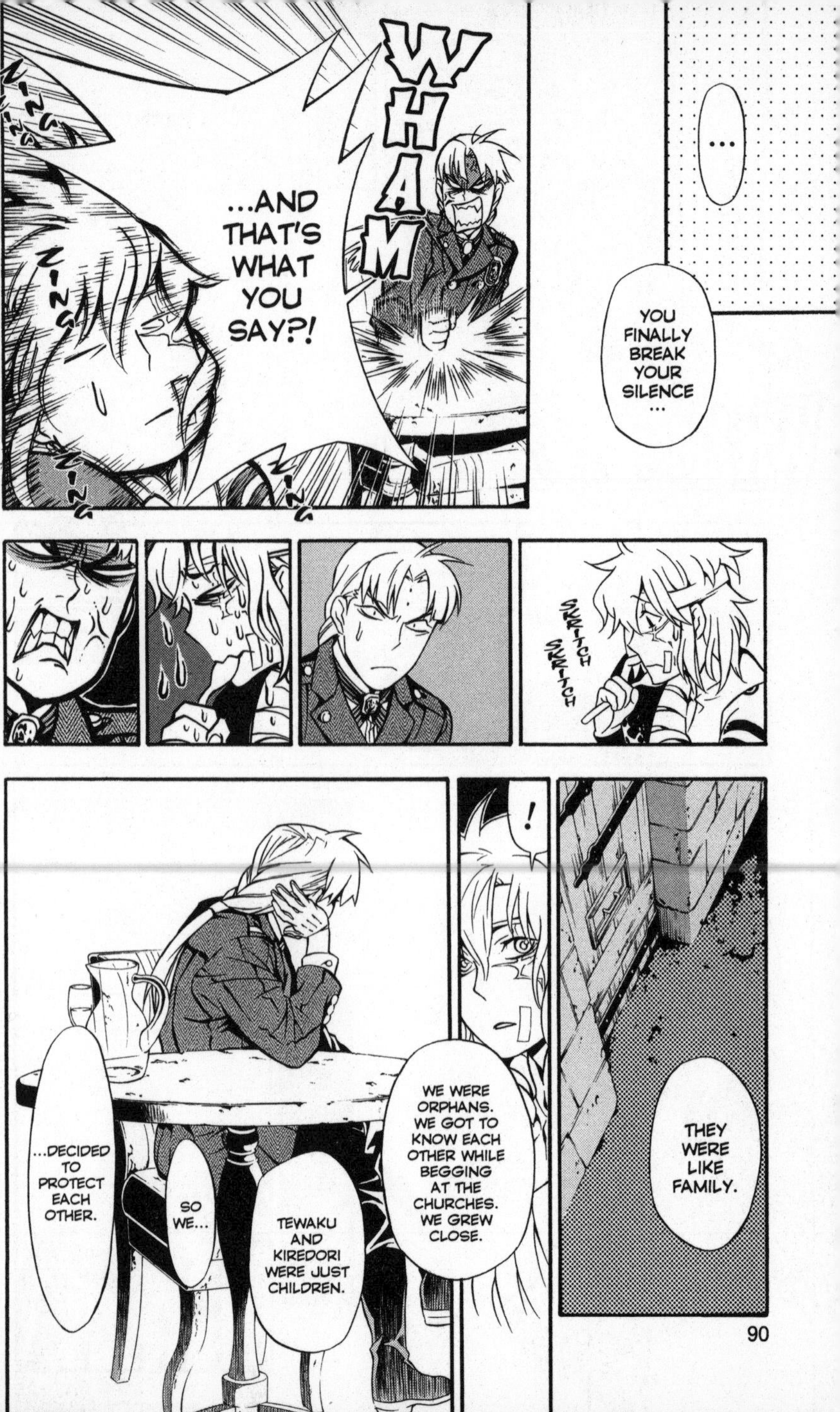
...
YOU FINALLY BREAK YOUR SILENCE ...
WHAM
...AND THAT'S WHAT YOU SAY?!
ZING ZING
ZING
ZING
ZING
SKRITCH SKRITCH
THEY WERE LIKE FAMILY.
!
WE WERE ORPHANS. WE GOT TO KNOW EACH OTHER WHILE BEGGING AT THE CHURCHES. WE GREW CLOSE.
TEWAKU AND KIREDORI WERE JUST CHILDREN.
SO WE...
...DECIDED TO PROTECT EACH OTHER.

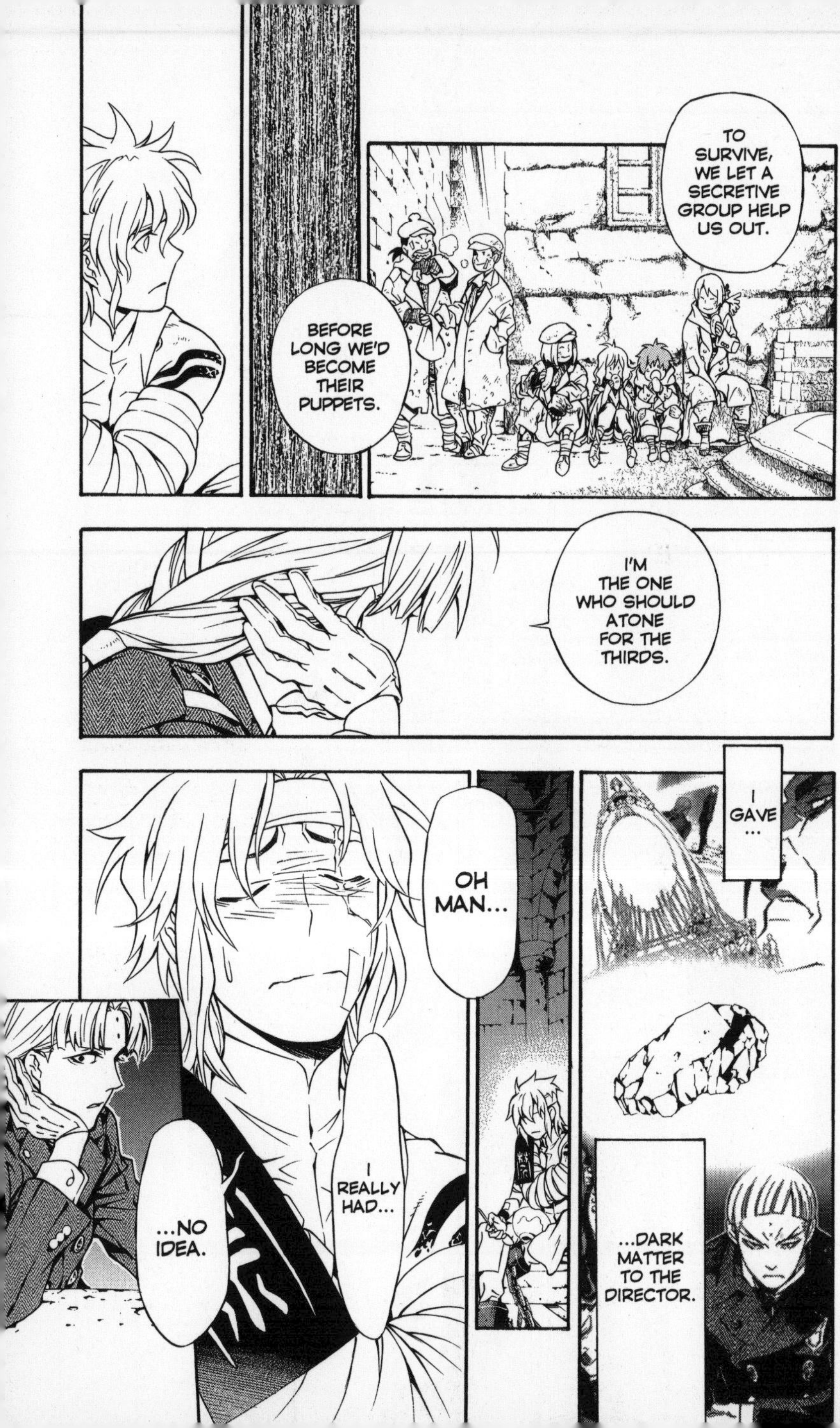
TO SURVIVE, WE LET A SECRETIVE GROUP HELP US OUT.
BEFORE LONG WE'D BECOME THEIR PUPPETS.
I'M THE ONE WHO SHOULD ATONE FOR THE THIRDS.
I GAVE...
...DARK MATTER TO THE DIRECTOR.
OH MAN...
I REALLY HAD...
...NO IDEA.

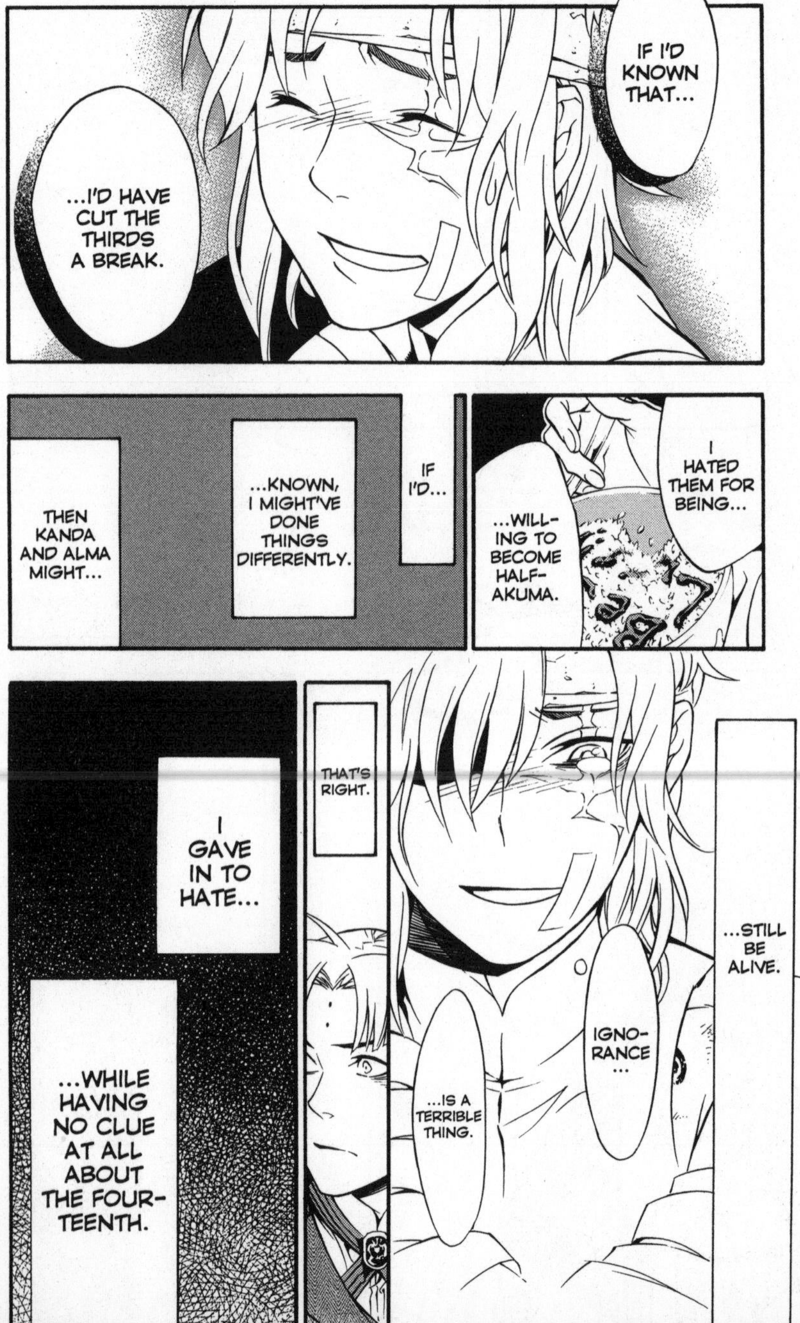
IF I'D KNOWN THAT...
...I'D HAVE CUT THE THIRDS A BREAK.
I HATED THEM FOR BEING...
...WILLING TO BECOME HALF-AKUMA.
IF I'D...
...KNOWN, I MIGHT'VE DONE THINGS DIFFERENTLY.
THEN KANDA AND ALMA MIGHT...
...STILL BE ALIVE.
IGNORANCE...
...IS A TERRIBLE THING.
THAT'S RIGHT.
I GAVE IN TO HATE...
...WHILE HAVING NO CLUE AT ALL ABOUT THE FOURTEENTH.

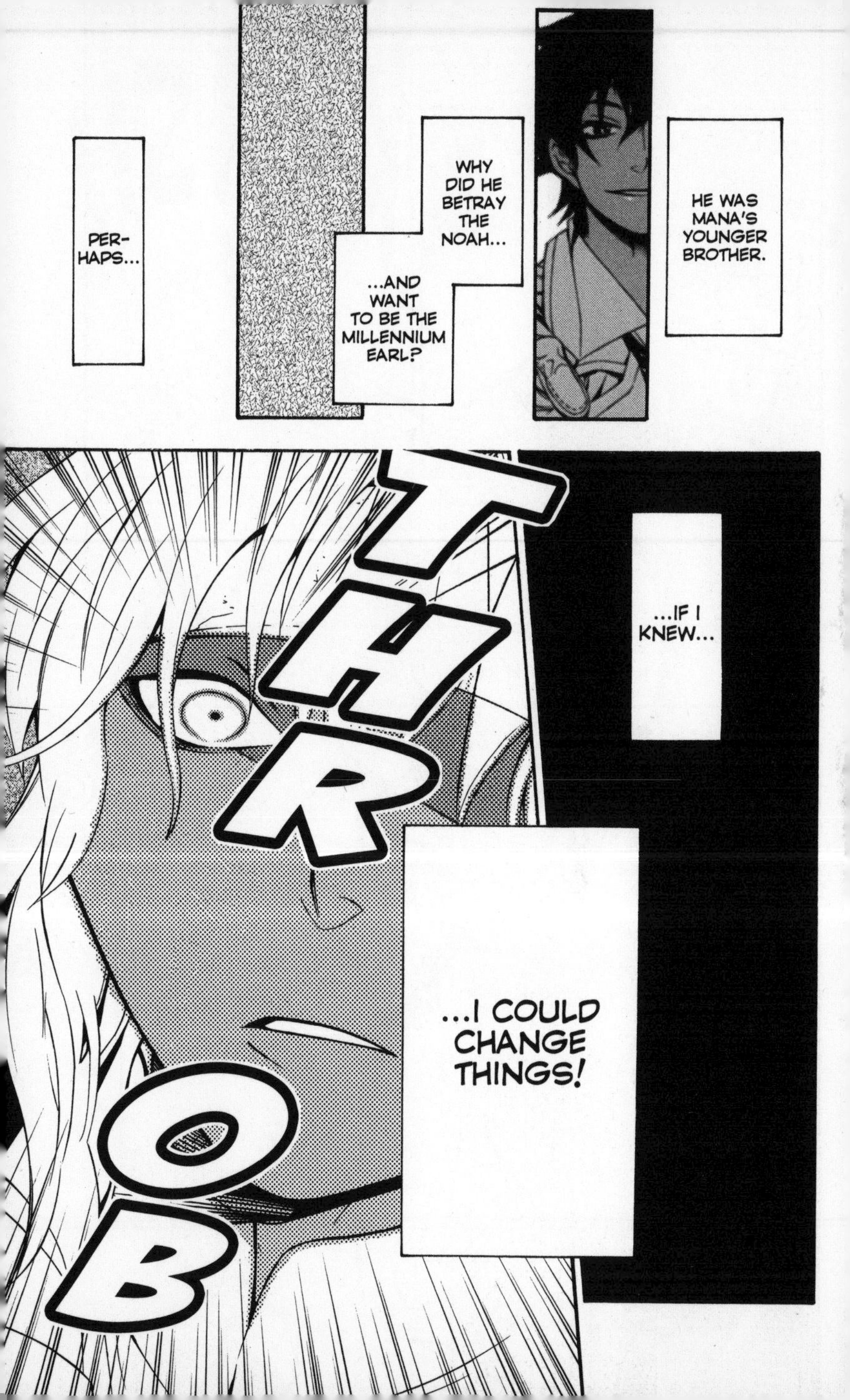
HE WAS MANA'S YOUNGER BROTHER.
WHY DID HE BETRAY THE NOAH...
...AND WANT TO BE THE MILLENNIUM EARL?
PER-HAPS...
...IF I KNEW...
THROB
...I COULD CHANGE THINGS!

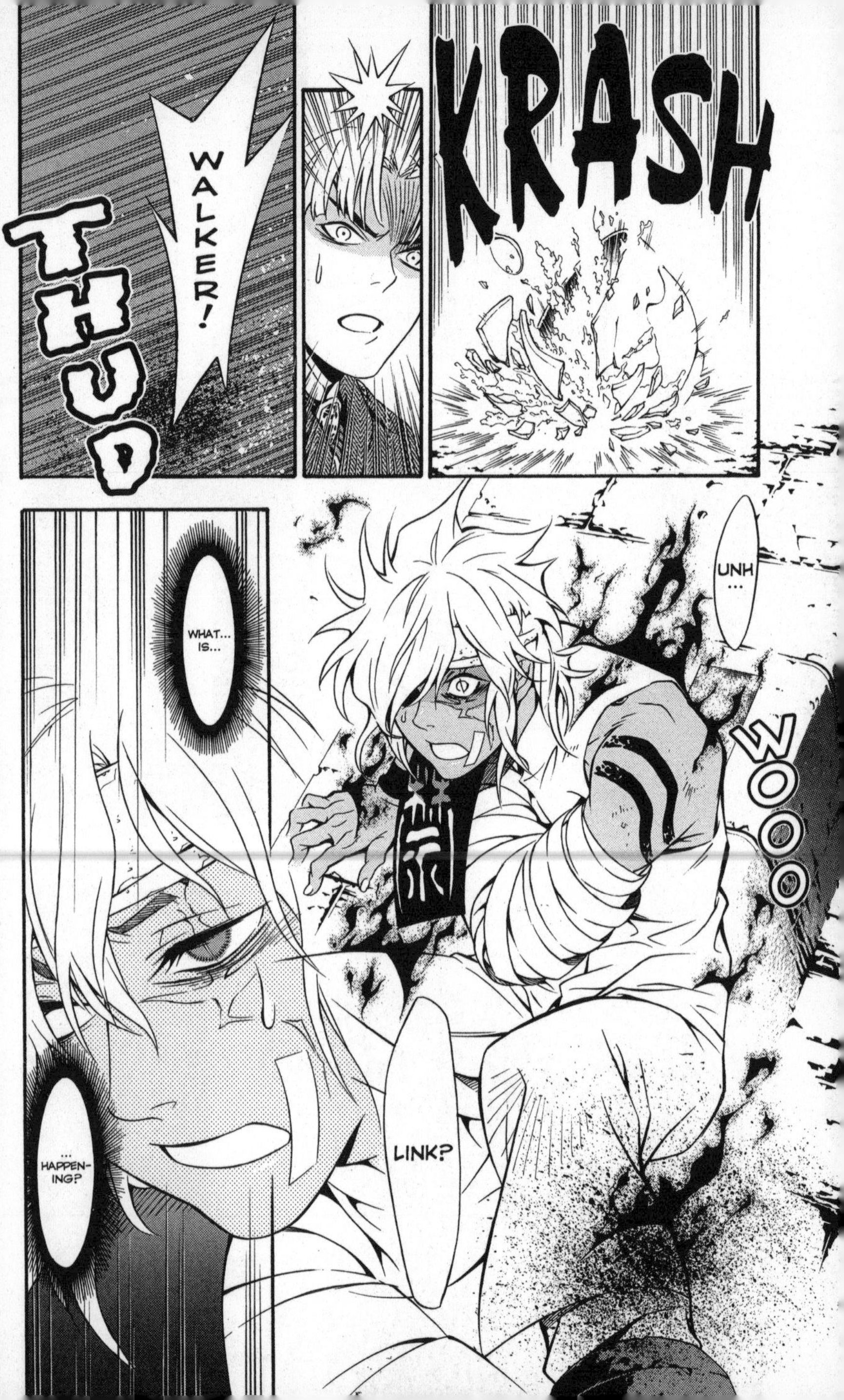
KRASH
WALKER!
THUD
UNH...
WOOO
WHAT... IS...
LINK?
...HAPPEN-ING?

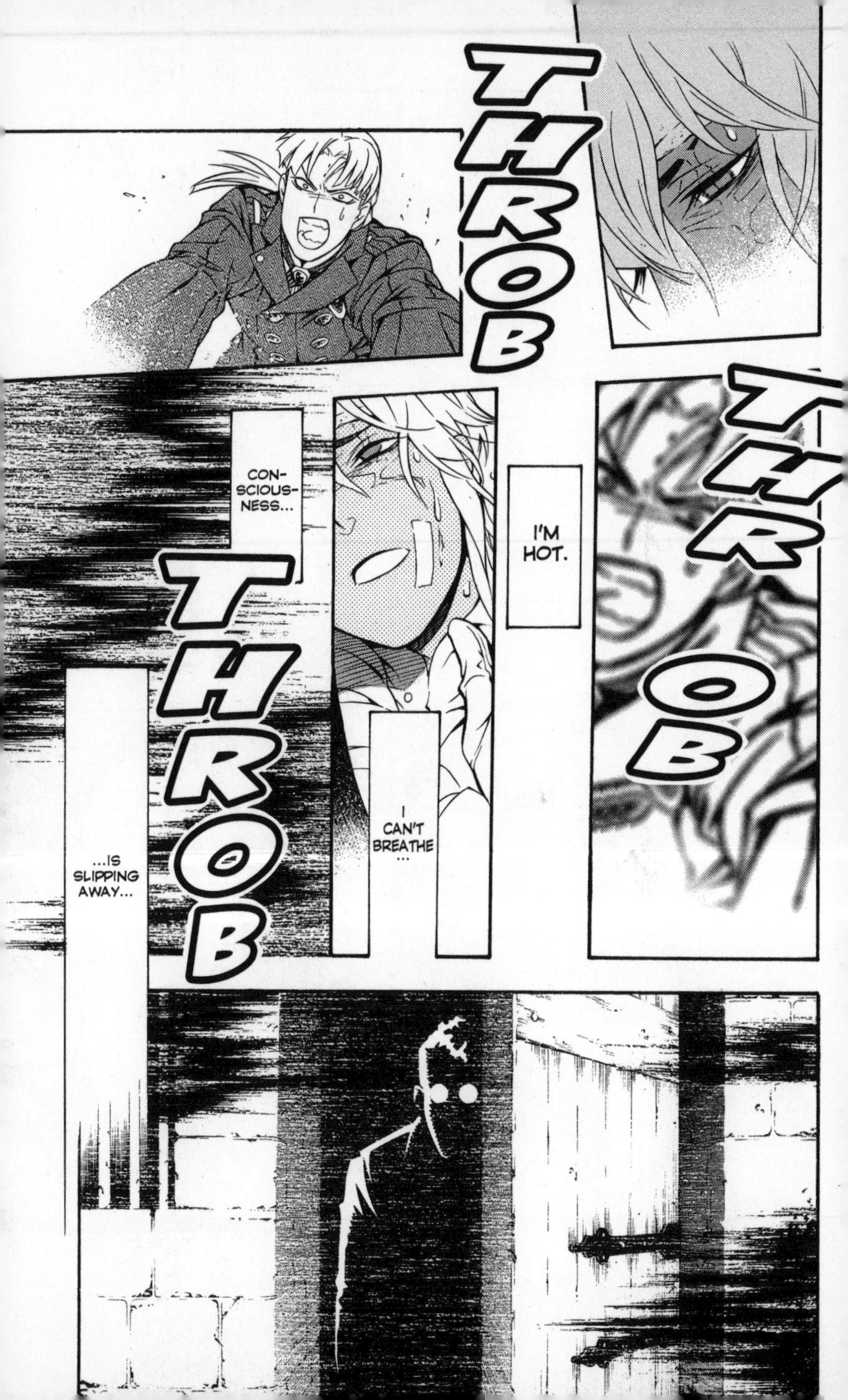

THROB
THROB
I'M HOT.
I CAN'T BREATHE...
CON-SCIOUSNESS...
THROB
...IS SLIPPING AWAY...

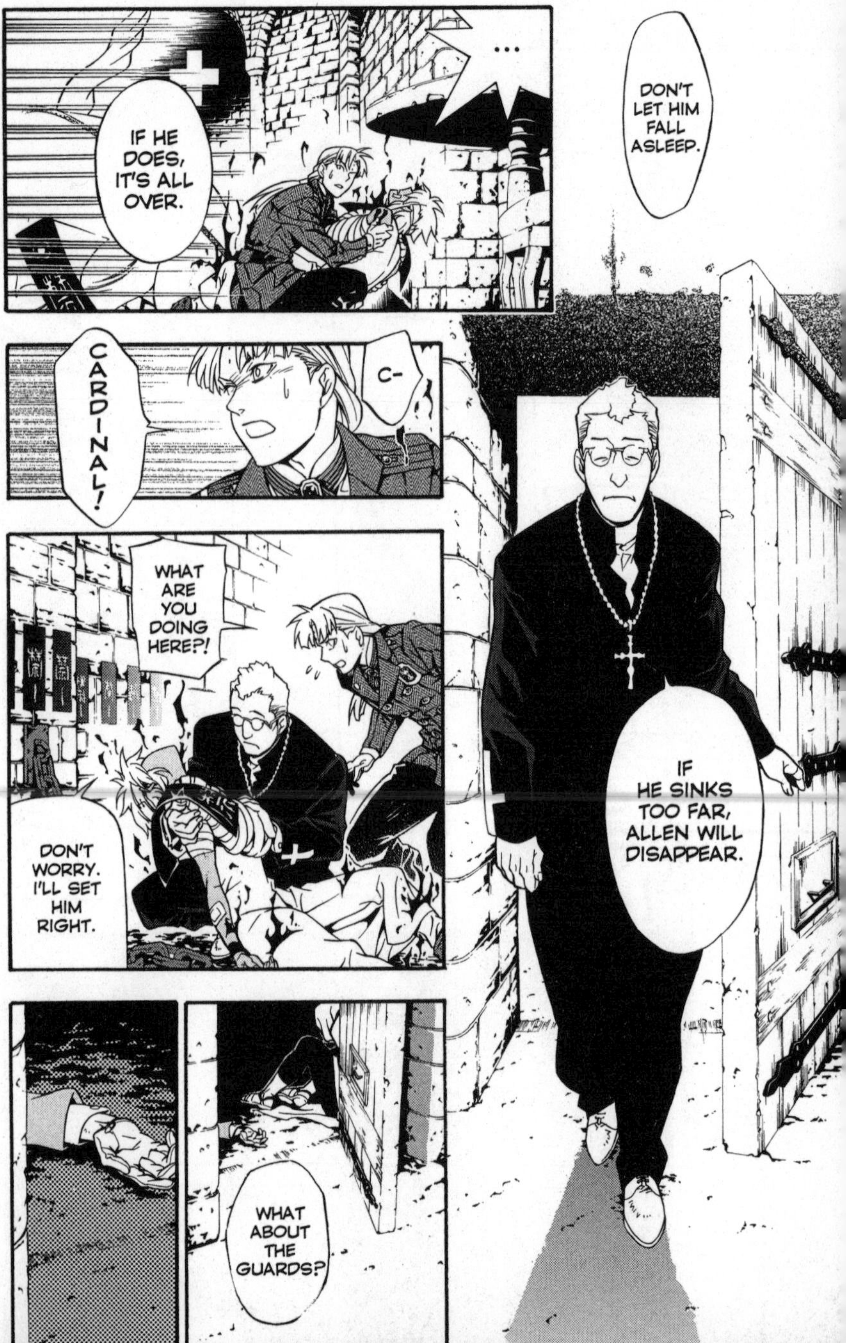
DON'T LET HIM FALL ASLEEP.
...
IF HE DOES, IT'S ALL OVER.
IF HE SINKS TOO FAR, ALLEN WILL DISAPPEAR.
C-
CARDINAL!
WHAT ARE YOU DOING HERE?!
DON'T WORRY. I'LL SET HIM RIGHT.
WHAT ABOUT THE GUARDS?

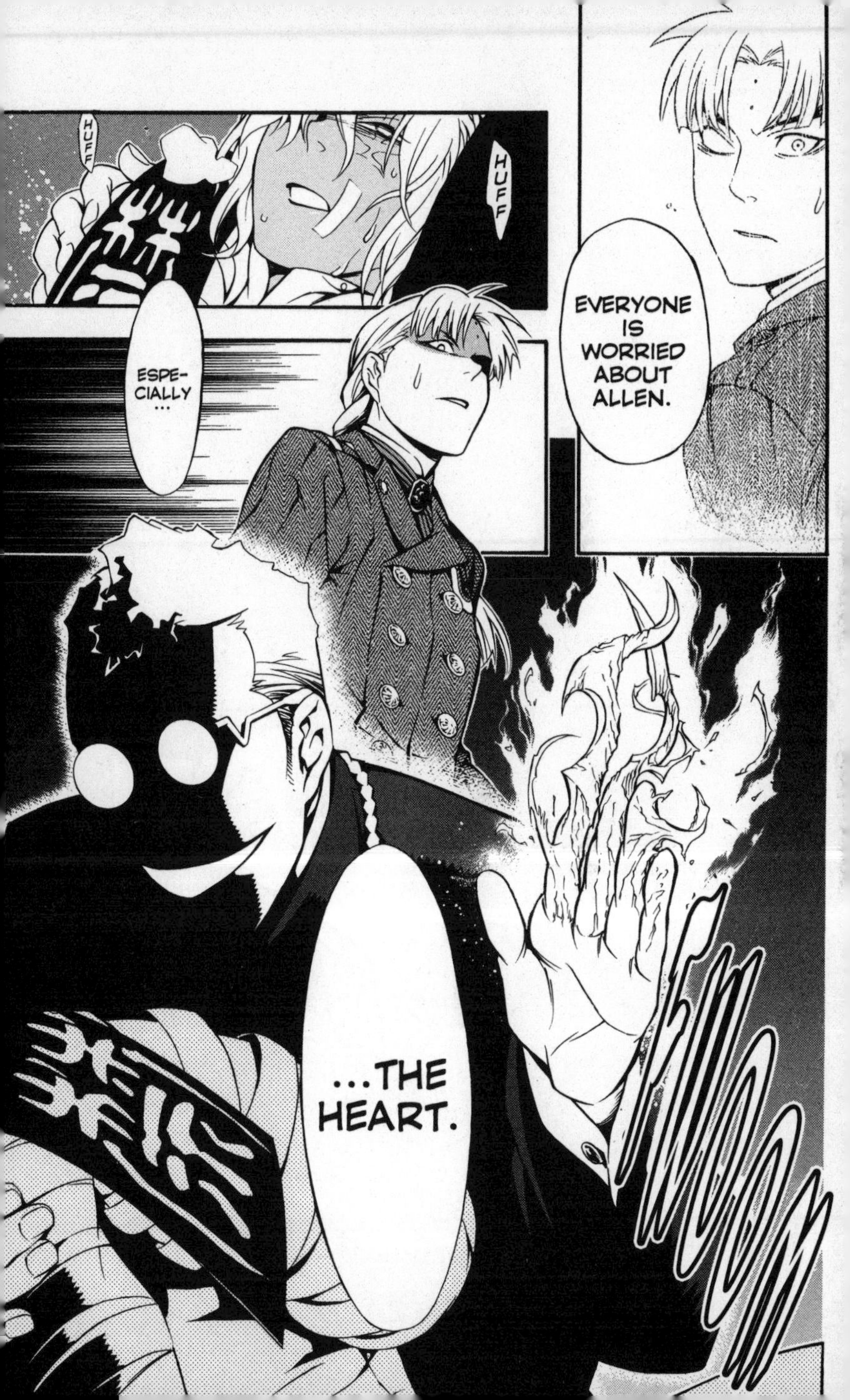
EVERYONE IS WORRIED ABOUT ALLEN.
HUFF
HUFF
ESPE-CIALLY...
...THE HEART.

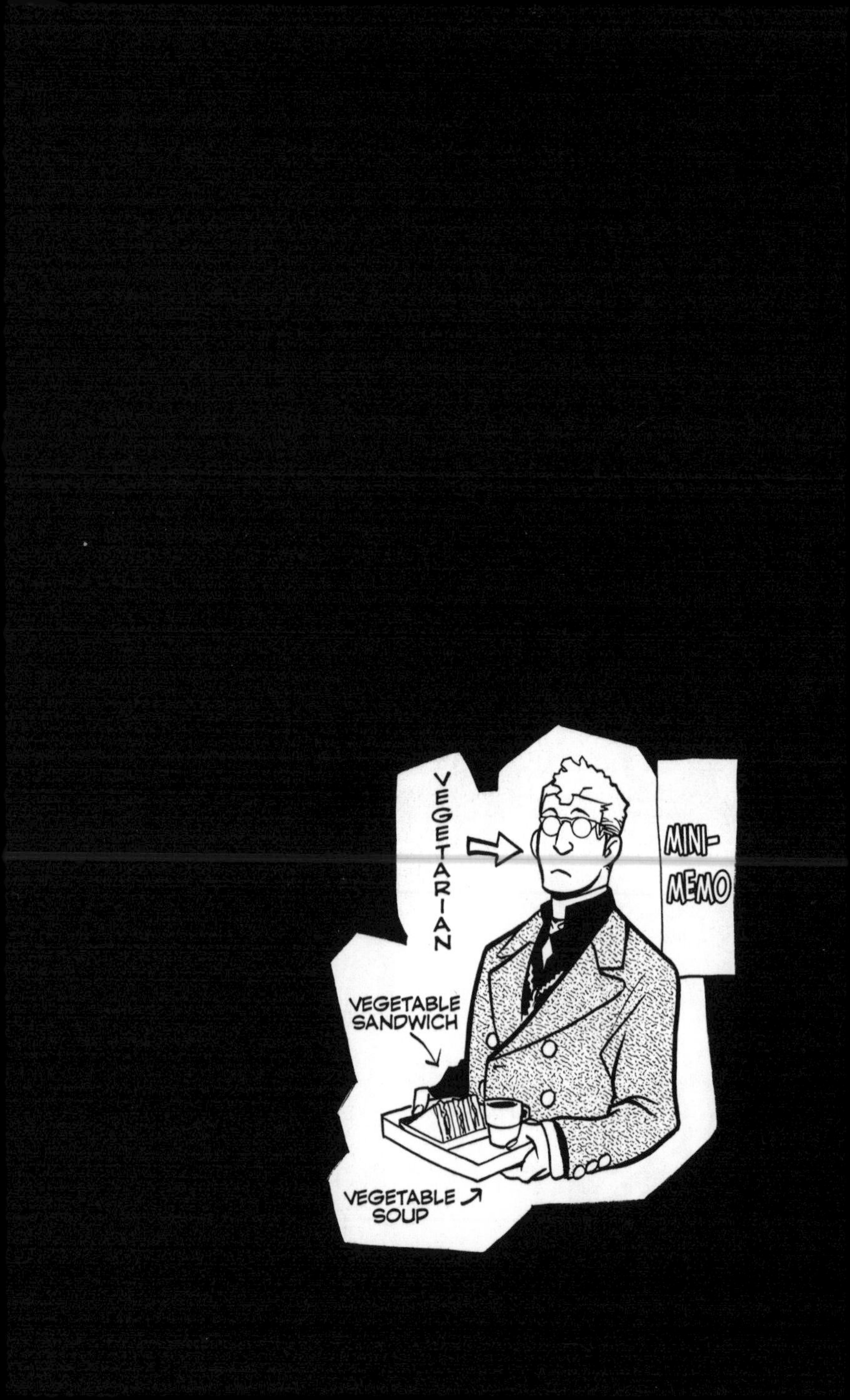
MINI-MEMO
VEGETARIAN
VEGETABLE SANDWICH
VEGETABLE SOUP

THE 203RD NIGHT: FATE-VISION

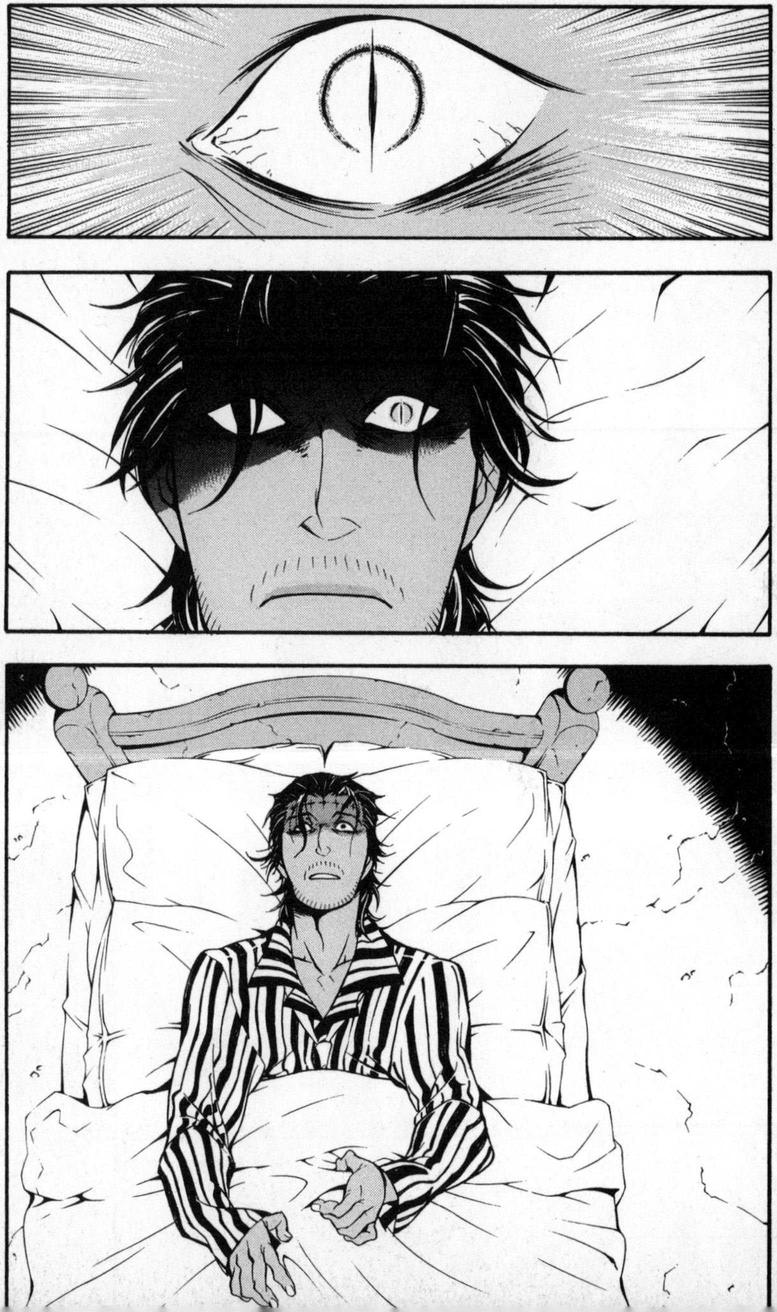

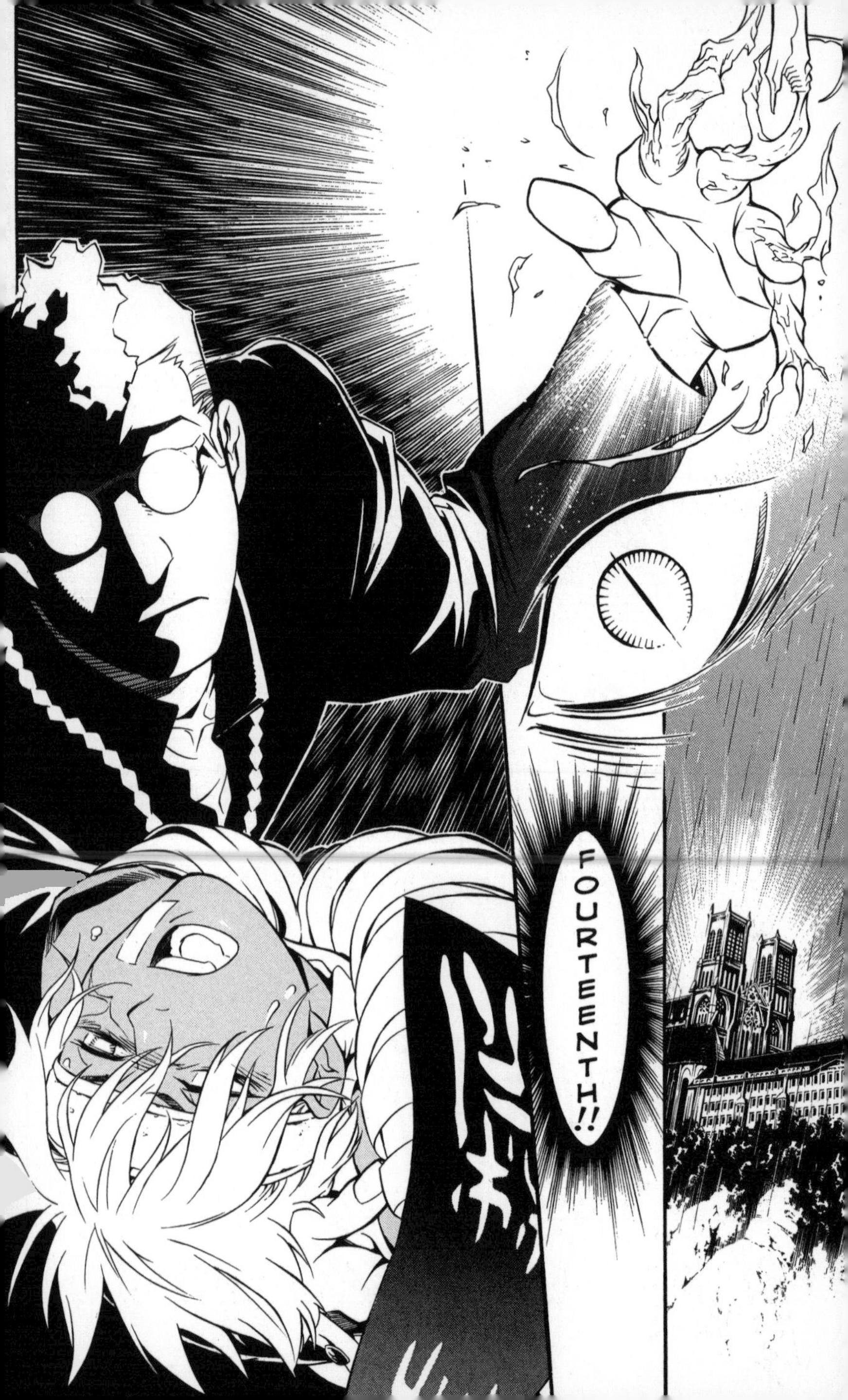
FOURTEENTH!!

READ THIS WAY

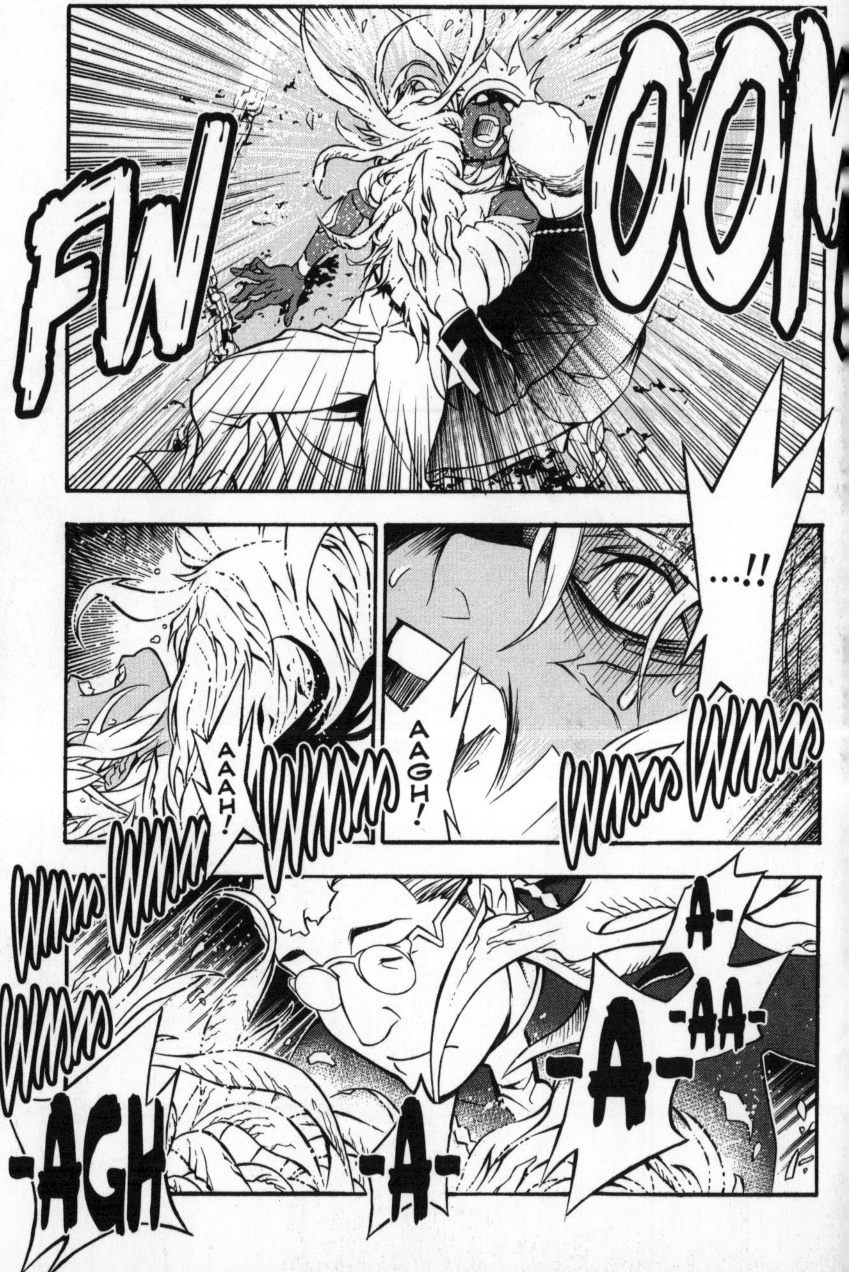
FWOOM
...!!
AAGH!
AAAH!
A-
-AA-
-A-
-A-
-AGH

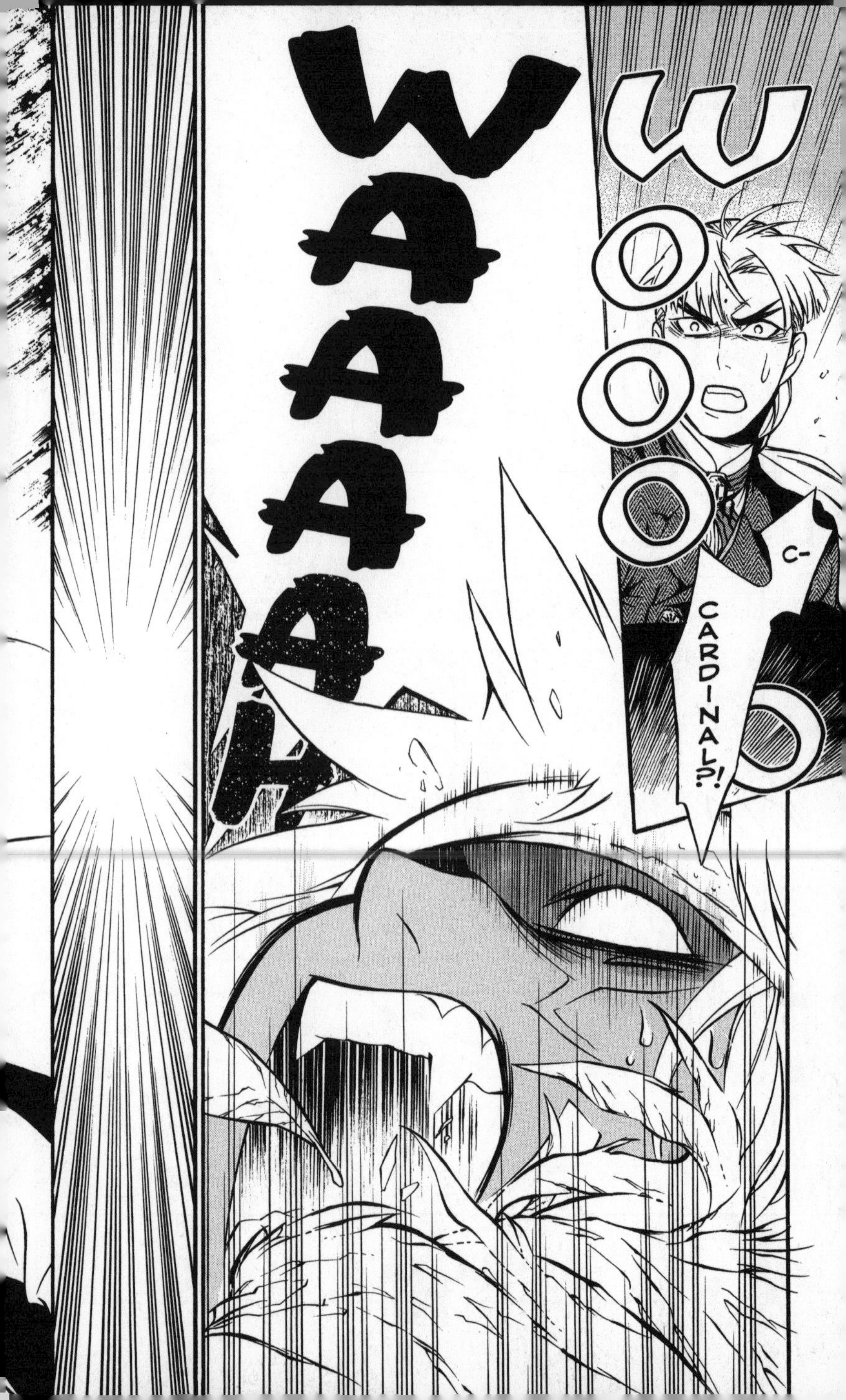
WOOOO
C- CARDINAL?!
WAAAAAH

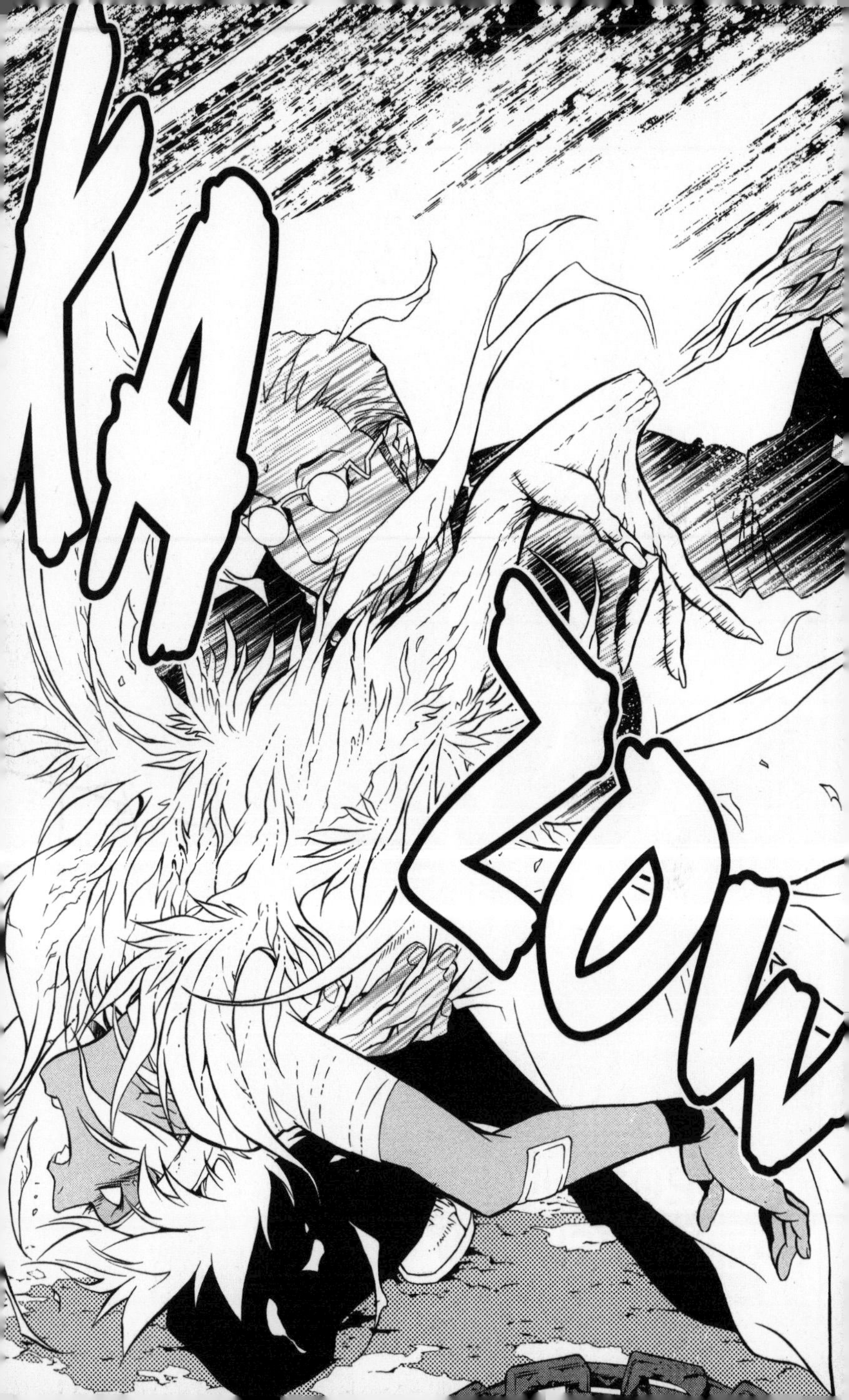
KA
LOW

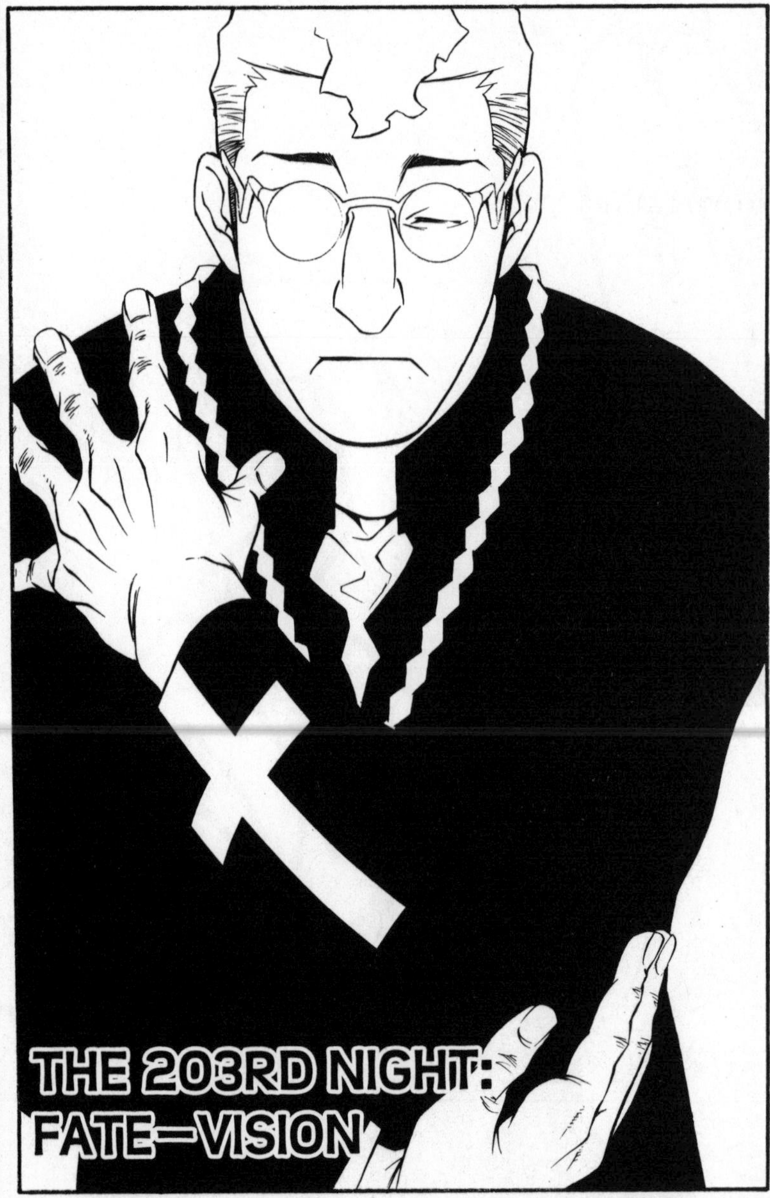
THE 203RD NIGHT:
FATE—VISION

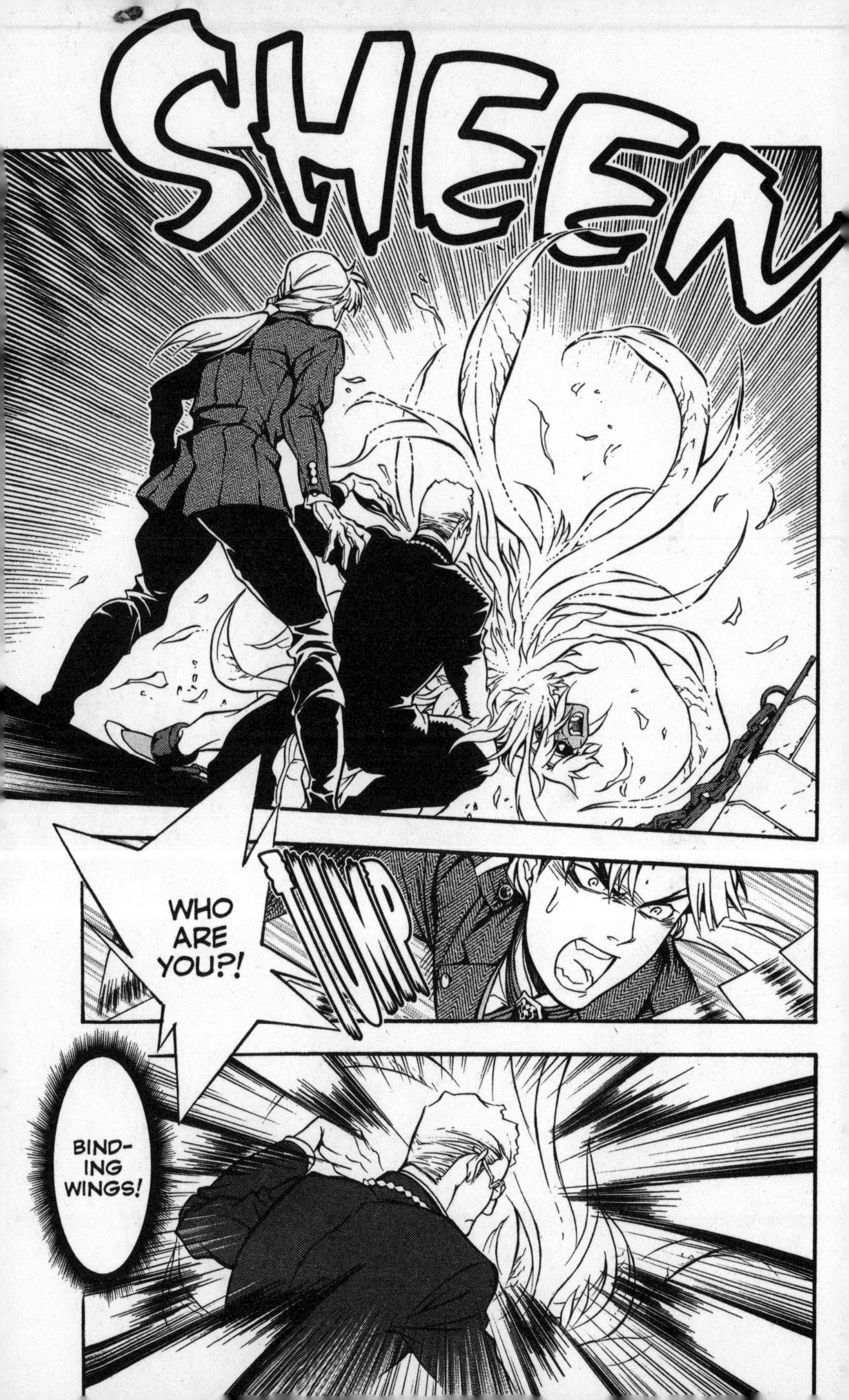
SHEEN
THMP
WHO ARE YOU?!
BIND-ING WINGS!

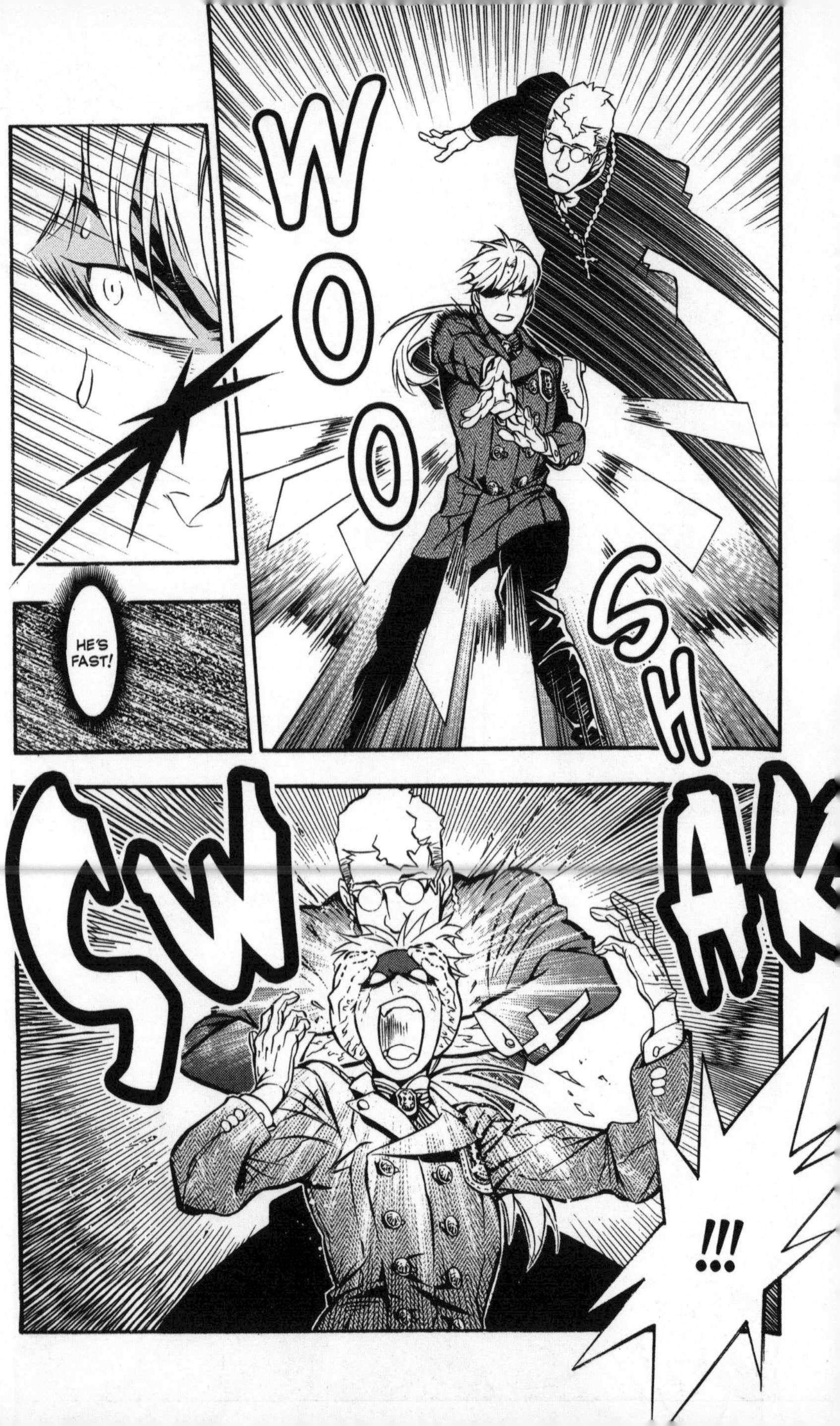
WOOOSH
HE'S FAST!
SWAK
!!!

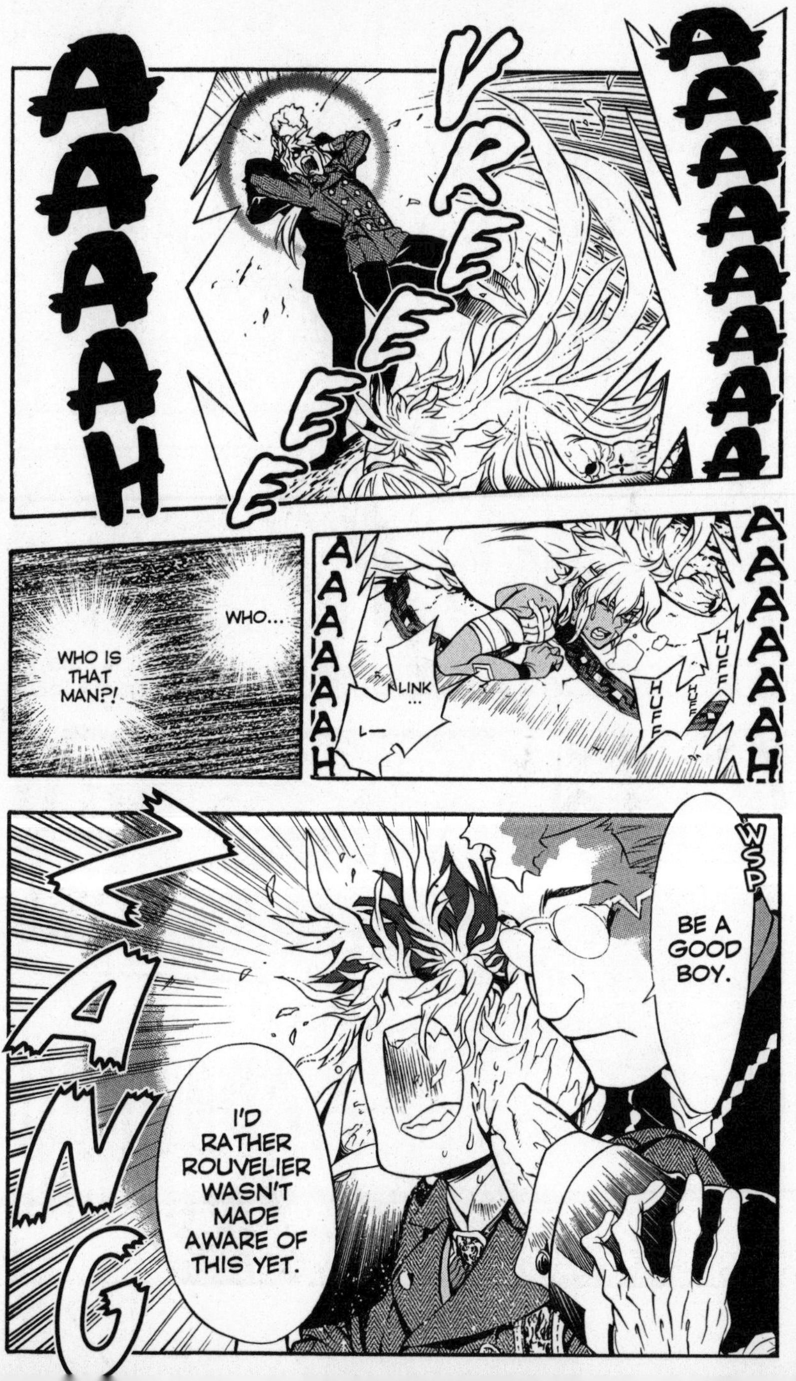
AAAAAAAAA
VREEEE
AAAAAH
AAAAAAAH.
HUFF
HUFF
HUFF
HUFF
LINK...
L—
AAAAAAAH
WHO...
WHO IS THAT MAN?!
WSP
BE A GOOD BOY.
I'D RATHER ROUVELIER WASN'T MADE AWARE OF THIS YET.
ZANG

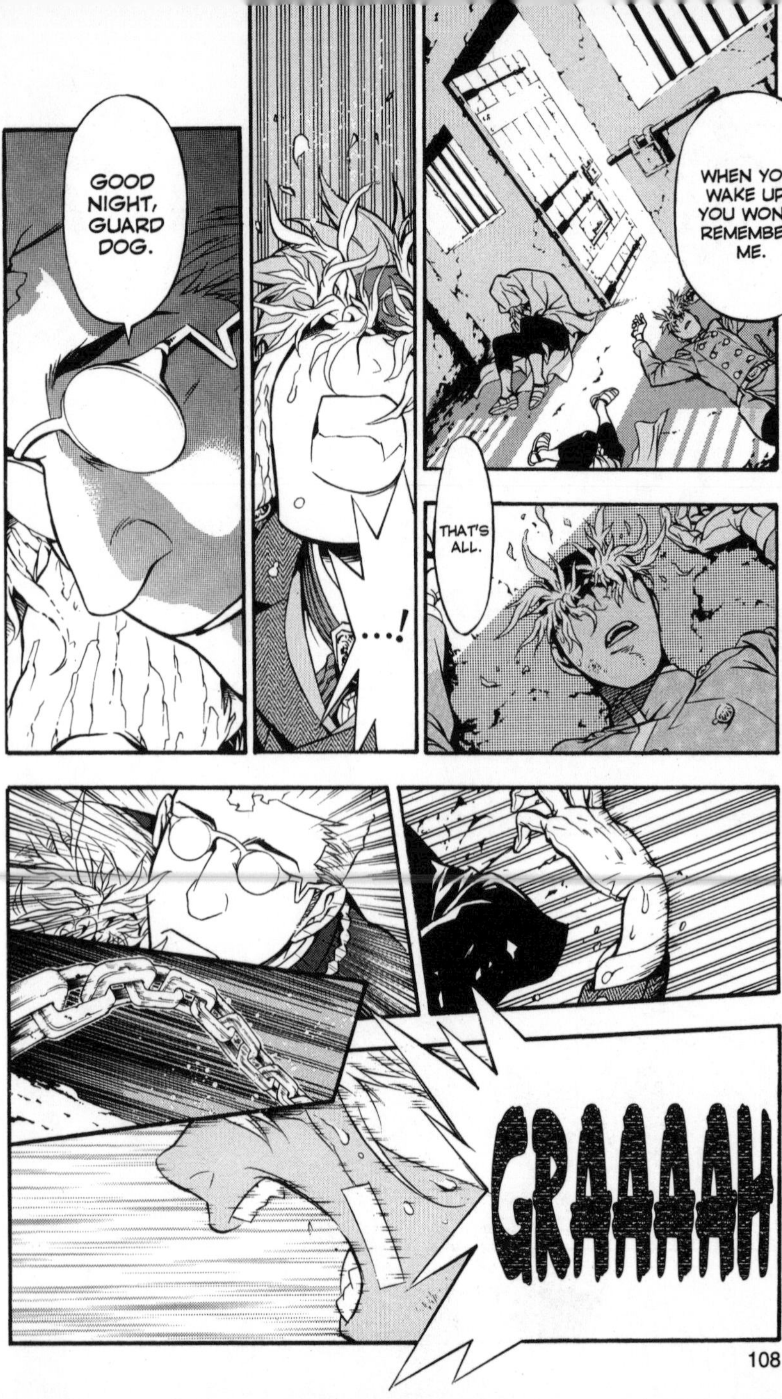
WHEN YOU WAKE UP, YOU WON'T REMEMBER ME.
THAT'S ALL.
...!
GOOD NIGHT, GUARD DOG.
GRAAAAH

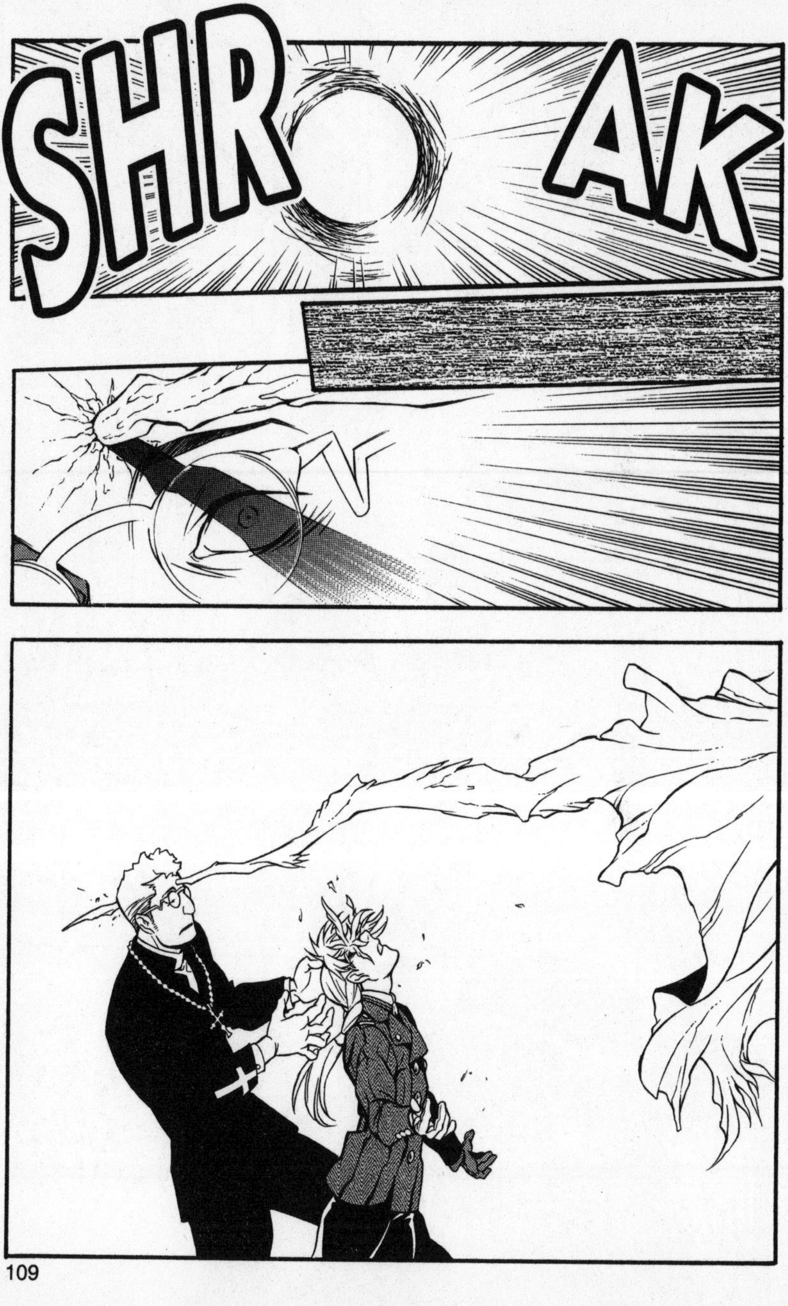
SHROAK

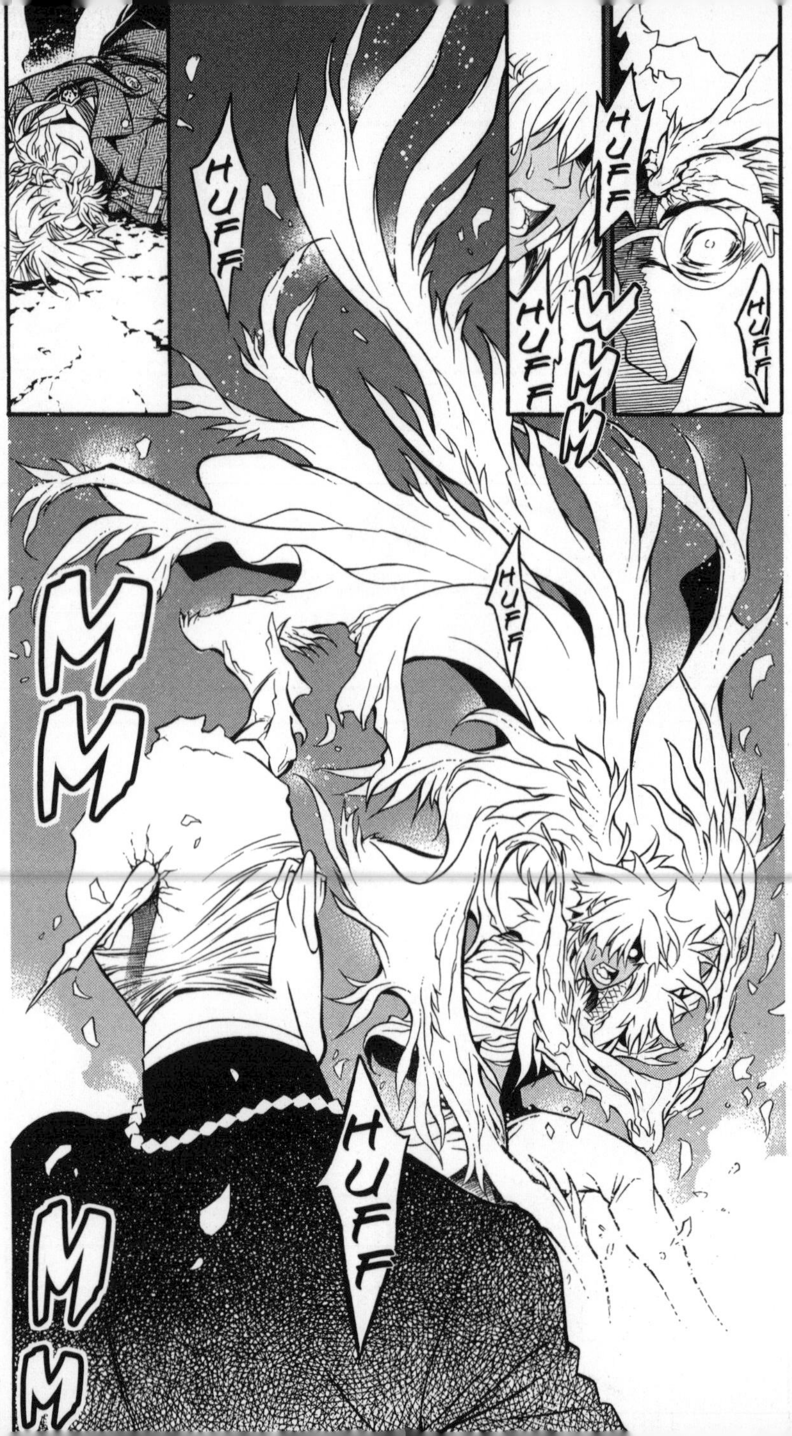
HUFF
HUFF
HUFF
WMMM
HUFF
HUFF
HUFF
MM
HUFF
MM

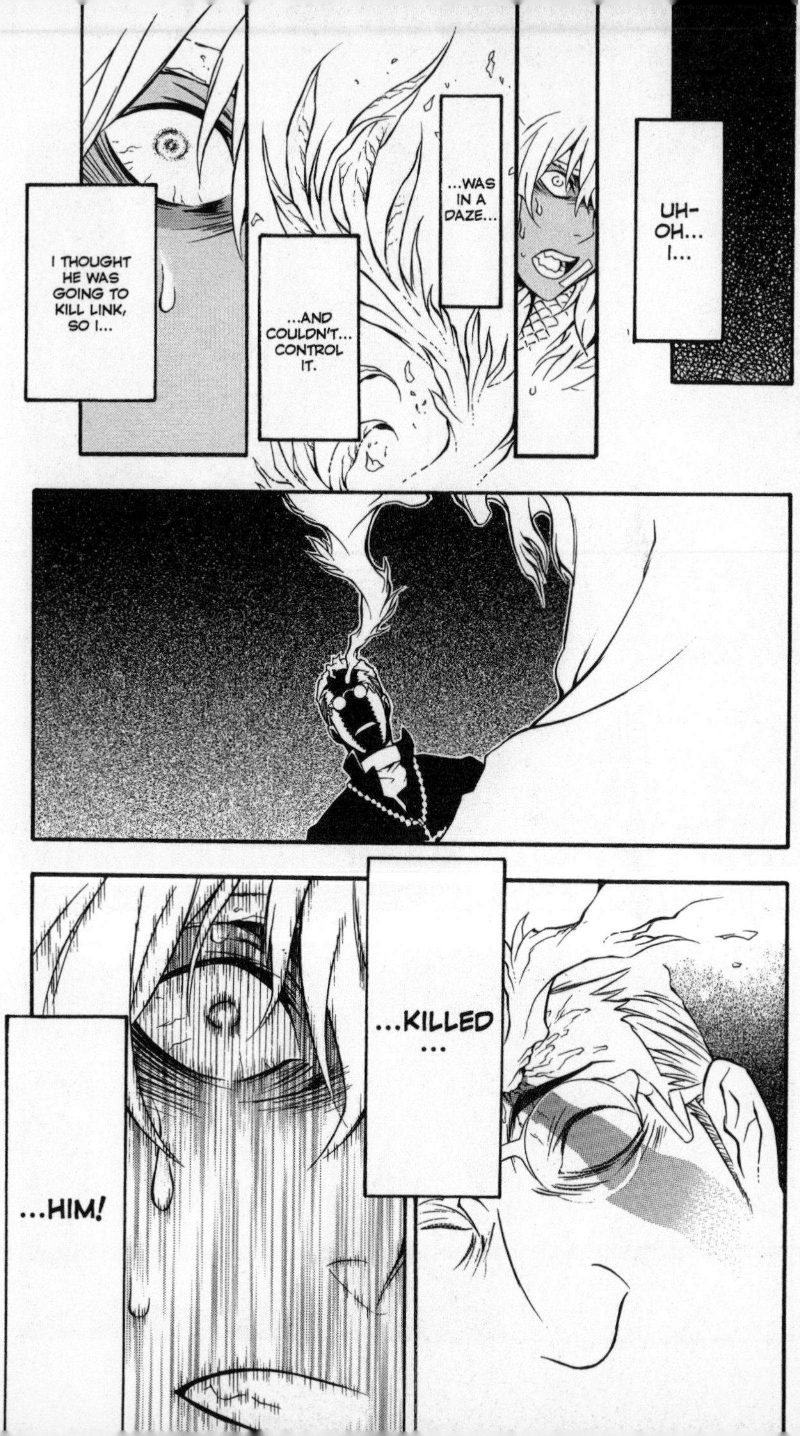
UH-OH... I...
...WAS IN A DAZE...
...AND COULDN'T... CONTROL IT.
I THOUGHT HE WAS GOING TO KILL LINK, SO I...
...KILLED ...
...HIM!

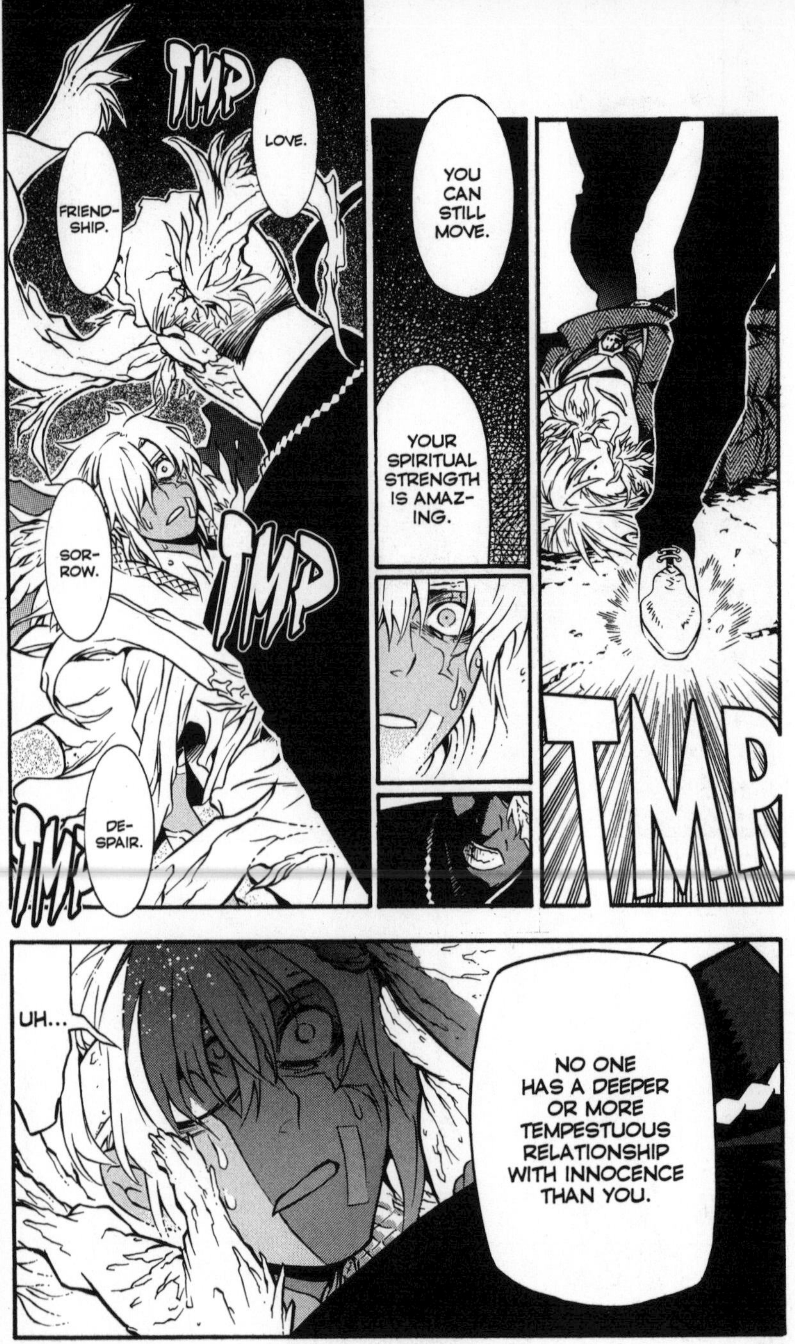
TMP
YOU CAN STILL MOVE.
YOUR SPIRITUAL STRENGTH IS AMAZ-ING.
TMP
LOVE.
FRIEND-SHIP.
TMP
SOR-ROW.
DE-SPAIR.
TMP
NO ONE HAS A DEEPER OR MORE TEMPESTUOUS RELATIONSHIP WITH INNOCENCE THAN YOU.
UH...

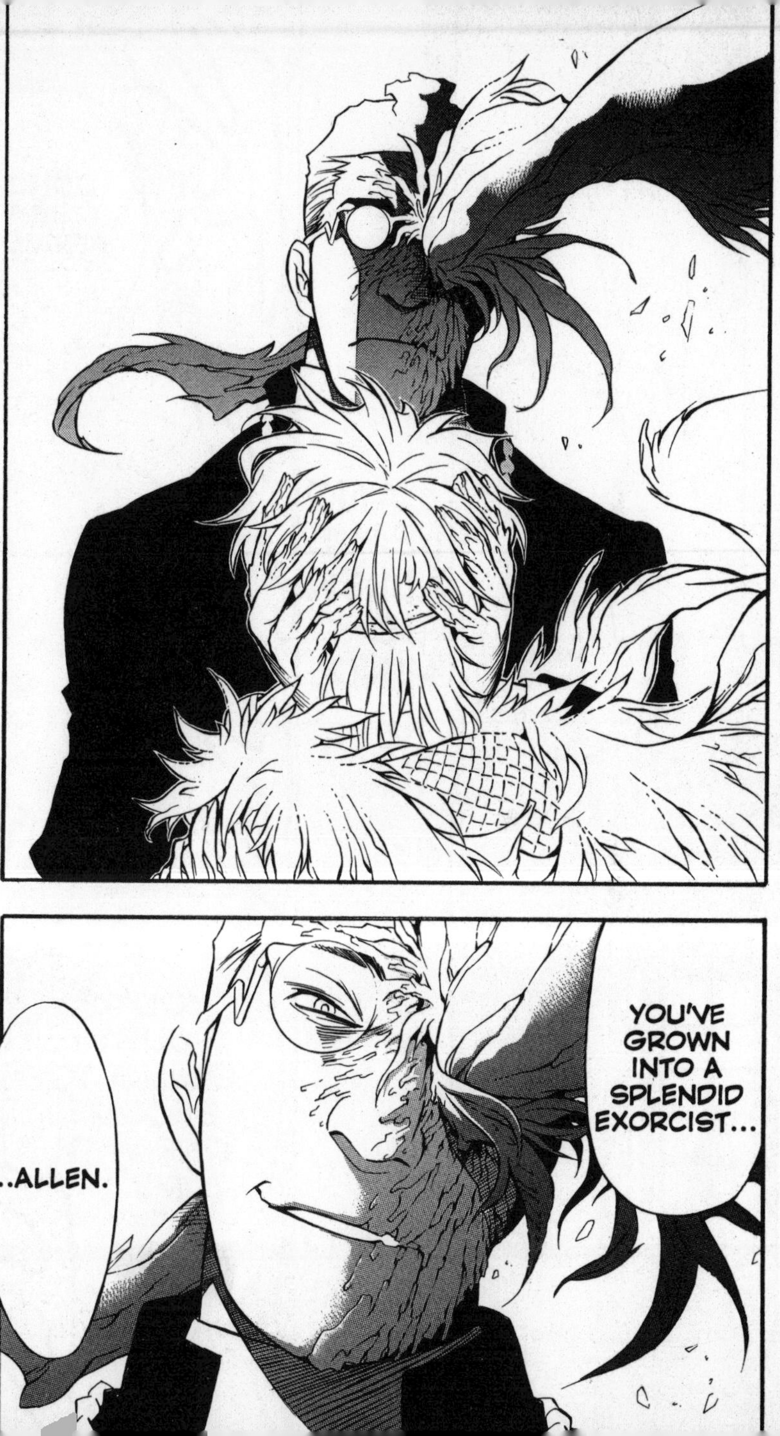
YOU'VE GROWN INTO A SPLENDID EXORCIST...
...ALLEN.

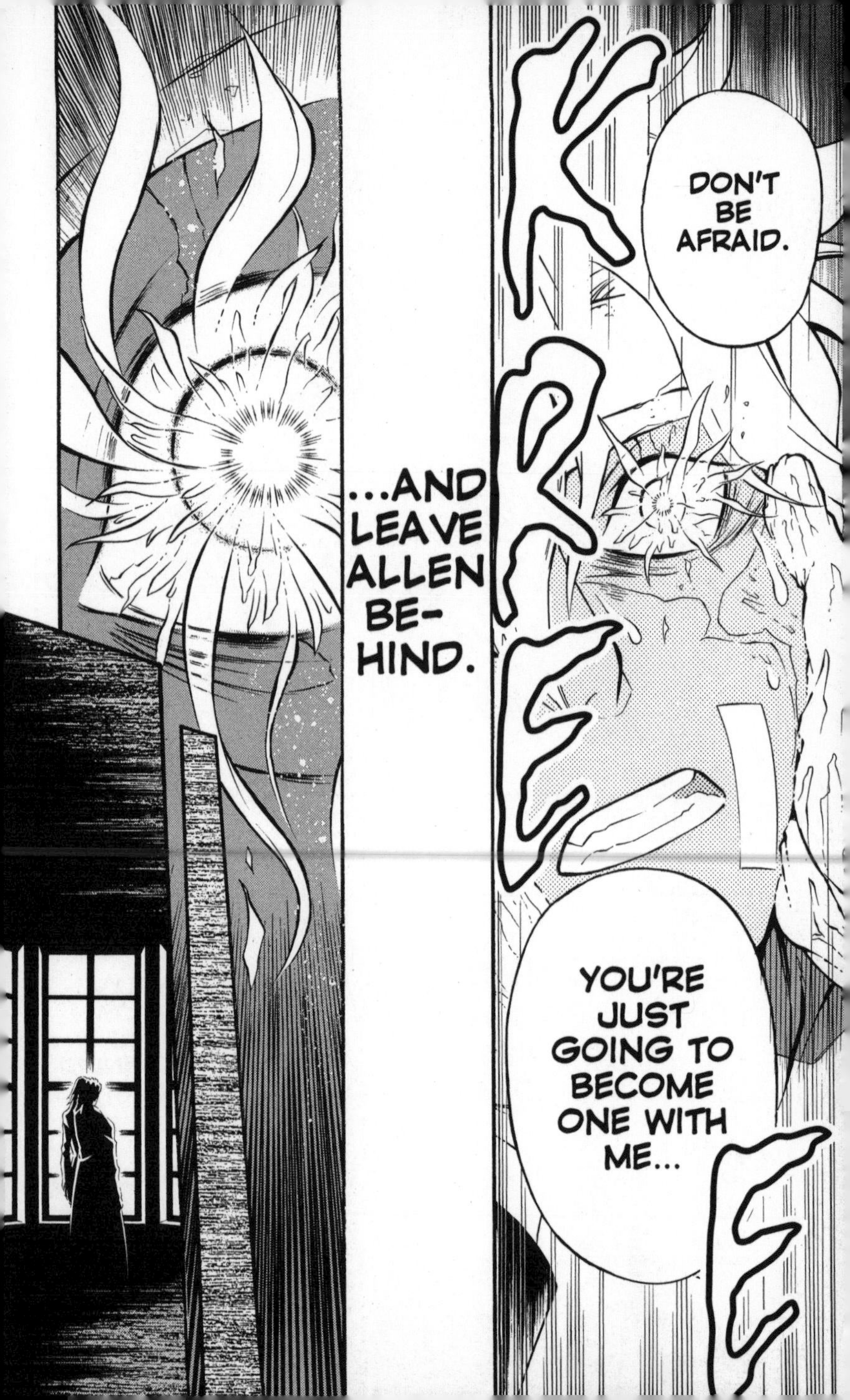
DON'T BE AFRAID.
KREE
YOU'RE JUST GOING TO BECOME ONE WITH ME...
...AND LEAVE ALLEN BE-HIND.

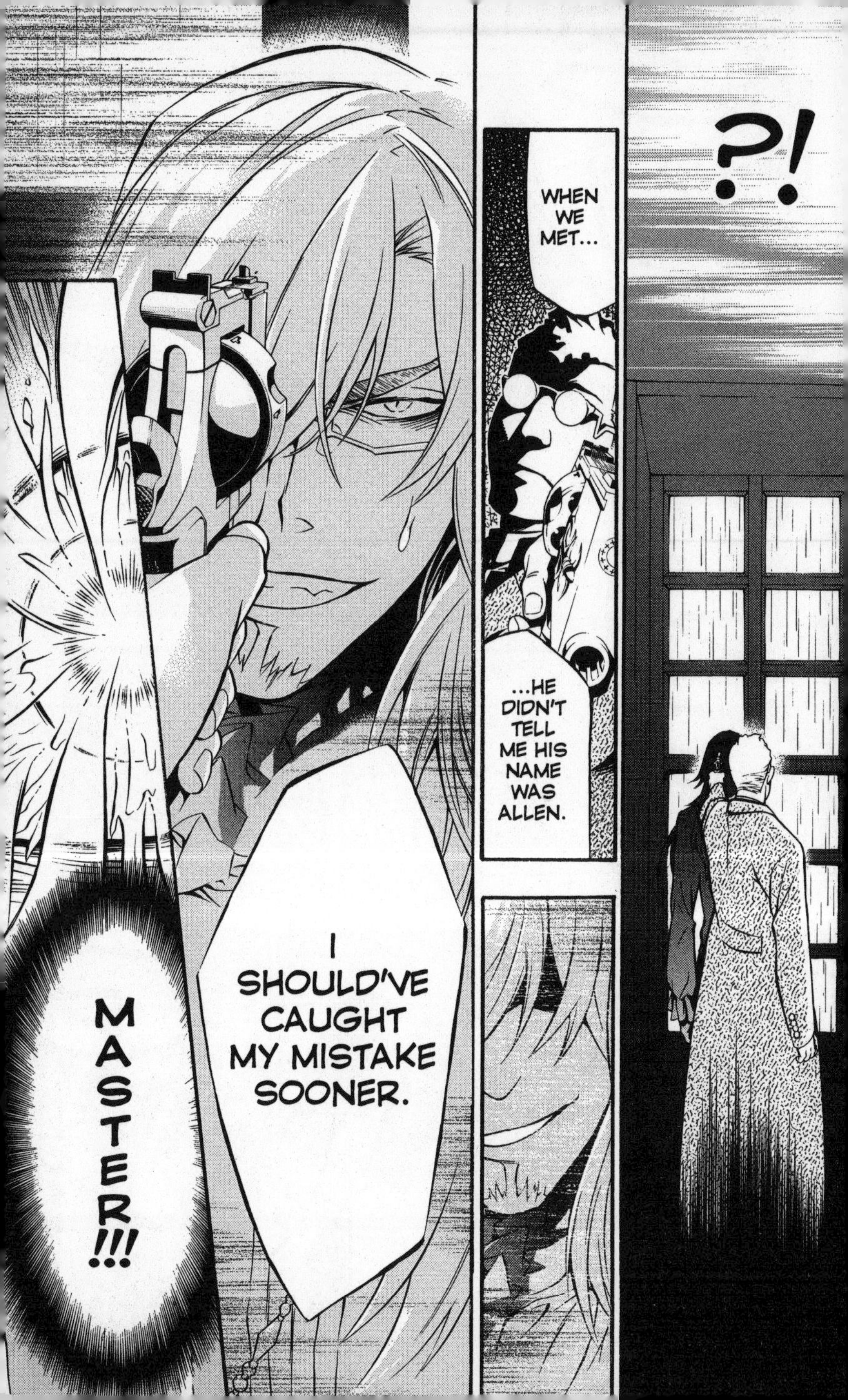
?!
WHEN WE MET...
...HE DIDN'T TELL ME HIS NAME WAS ALLEN.
I SHOULD'VE CAUGHT MY MISTAKE SOONER.
MASTER!!!

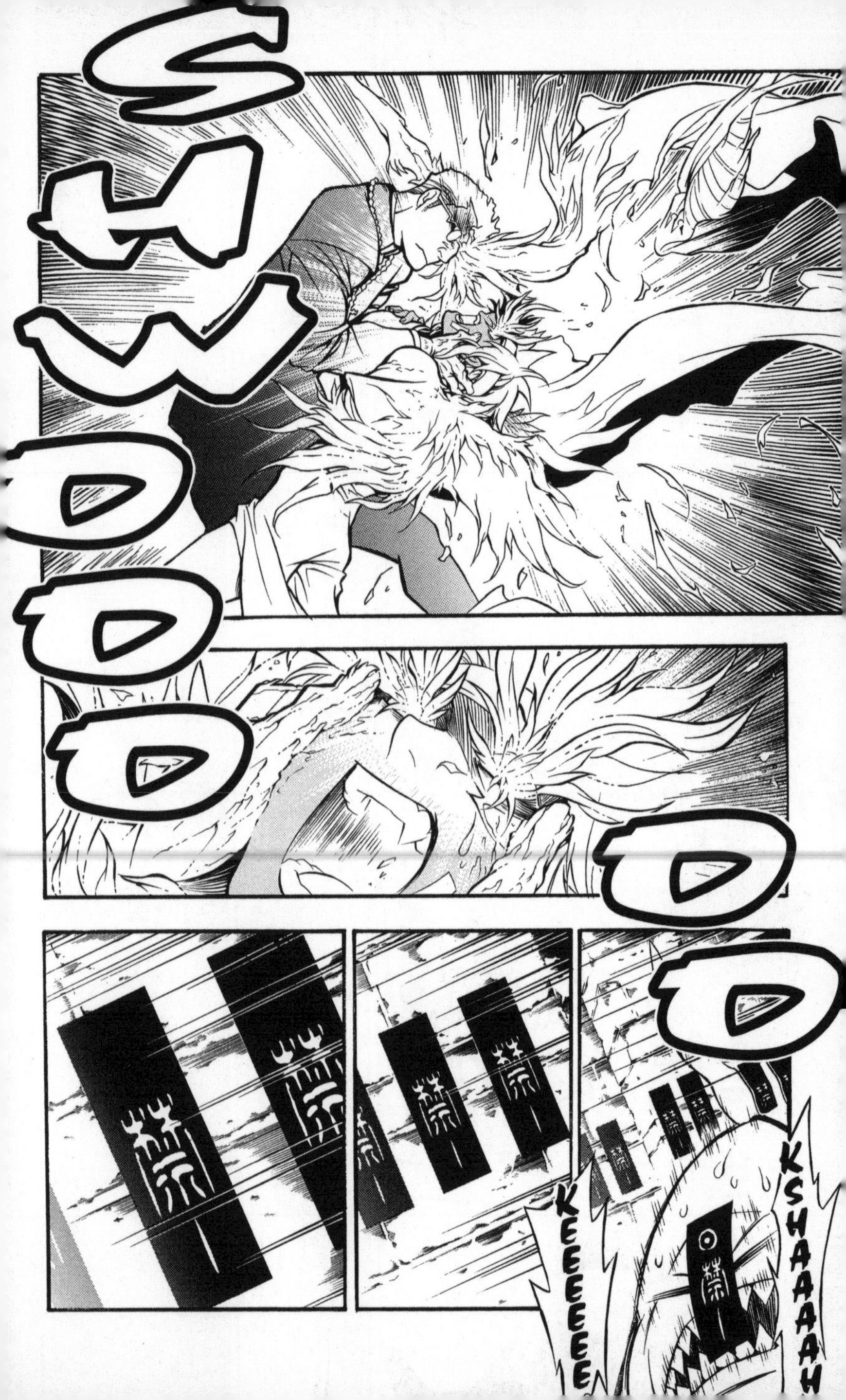
禁
禁
禁
KSHAAAAH
KEEEEEEE

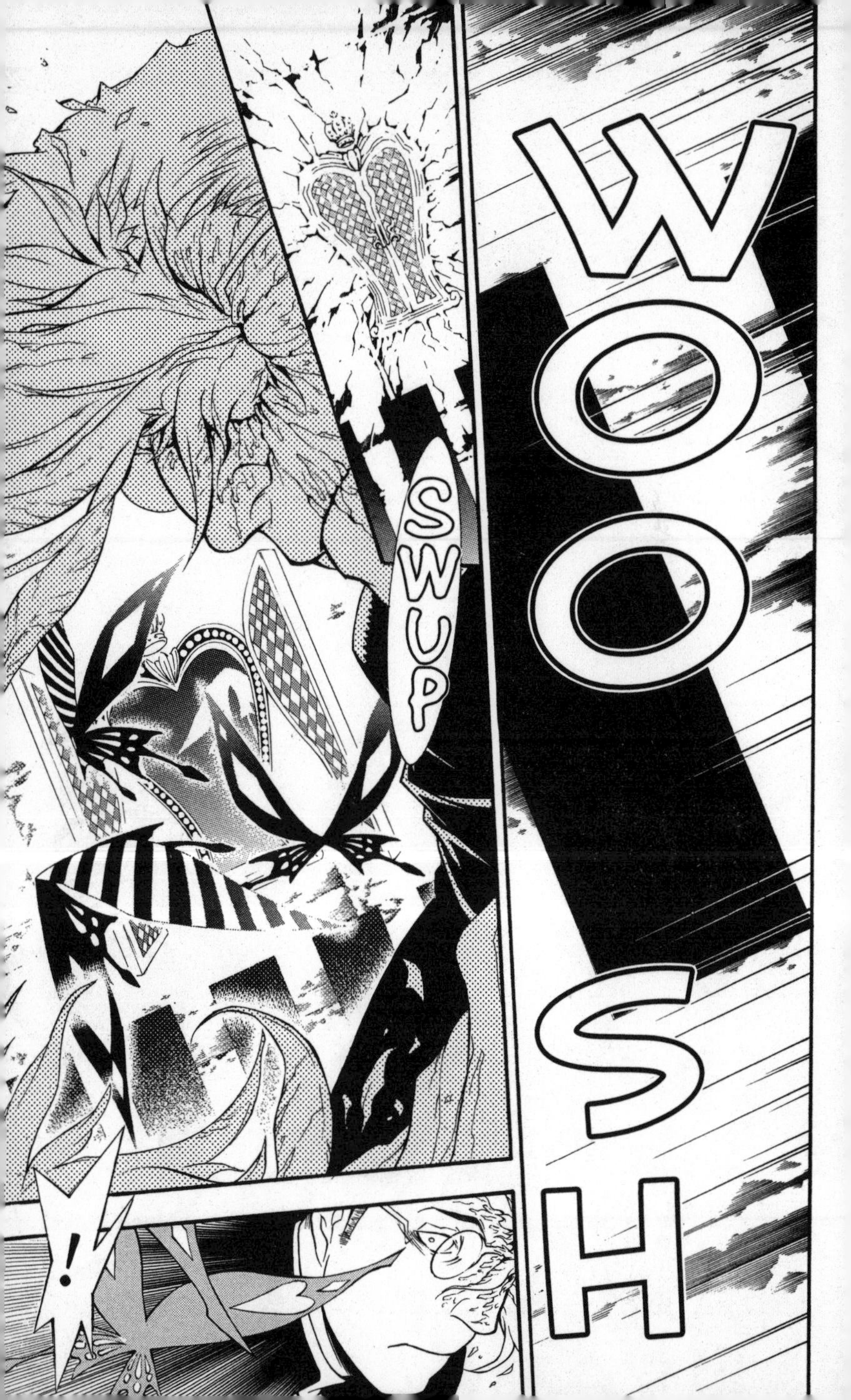
WOOSH
SWUP
!

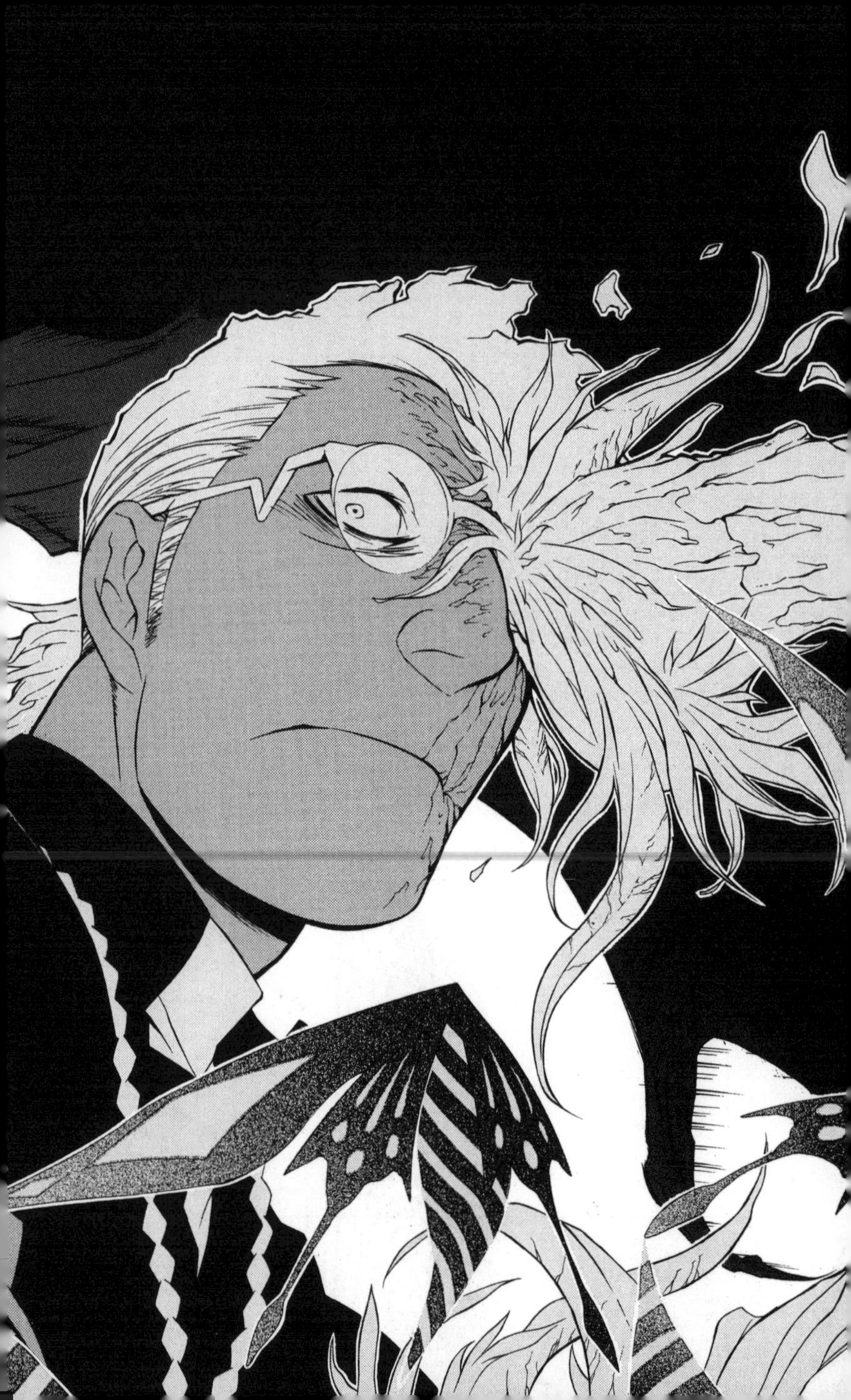

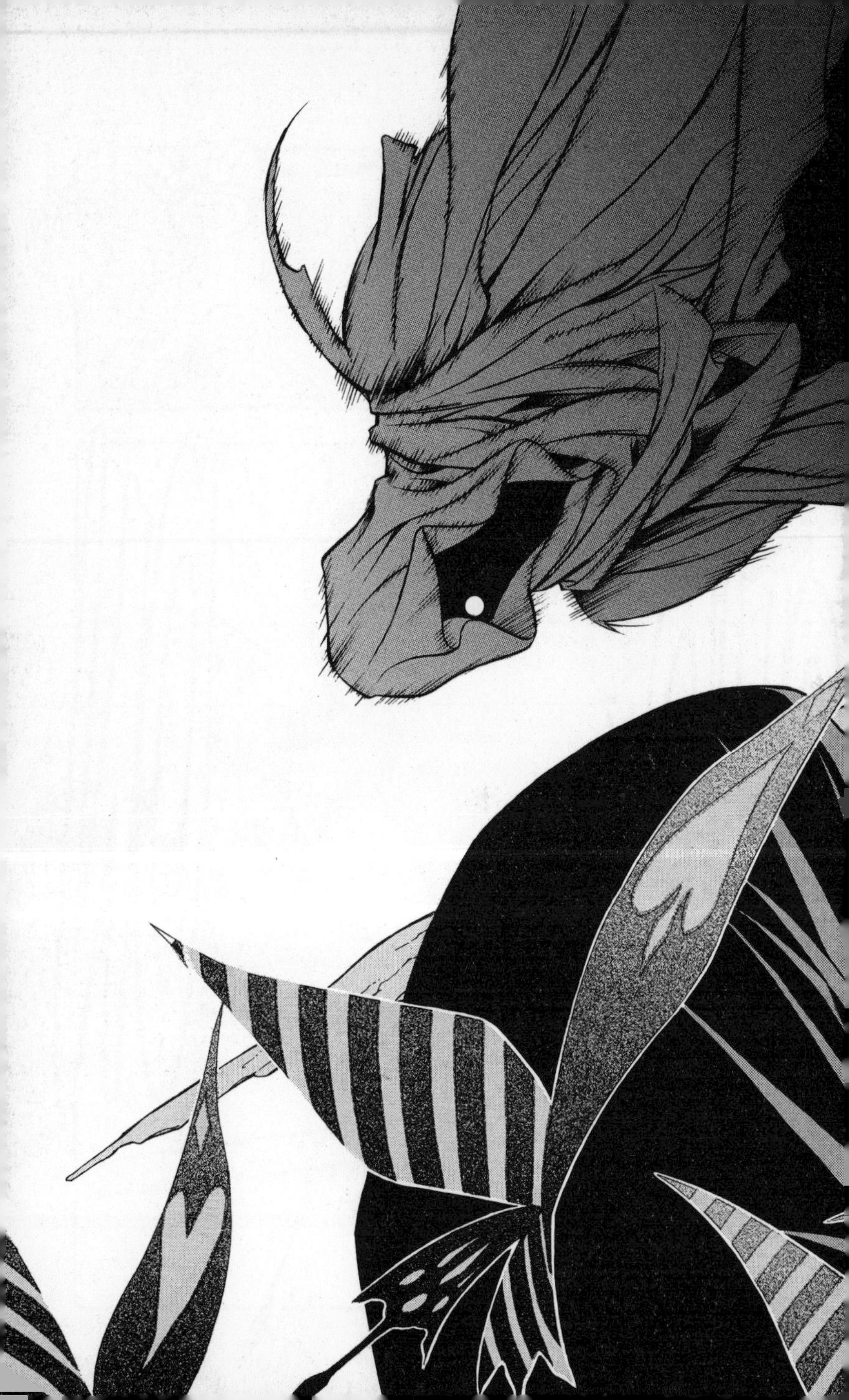

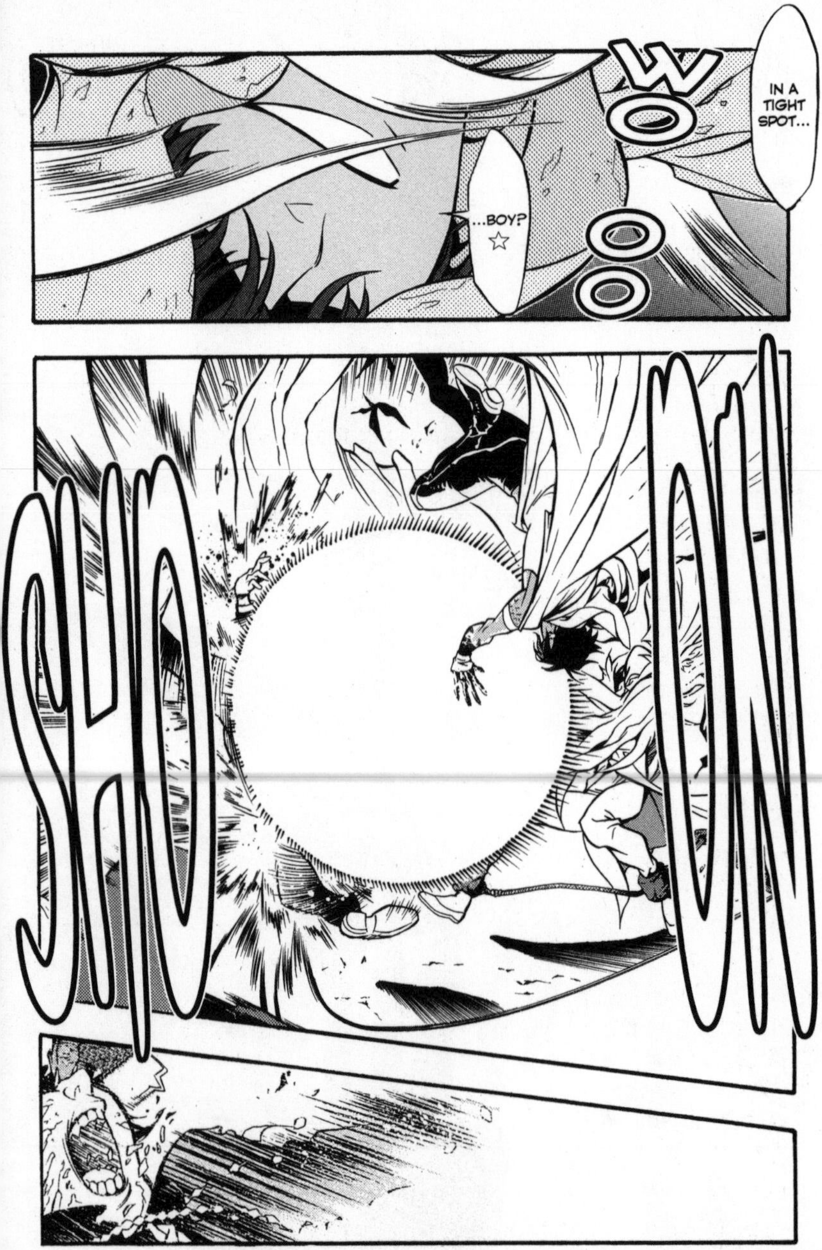
WOOO
IN A TIGHT SPOT...
...BOY? ☆

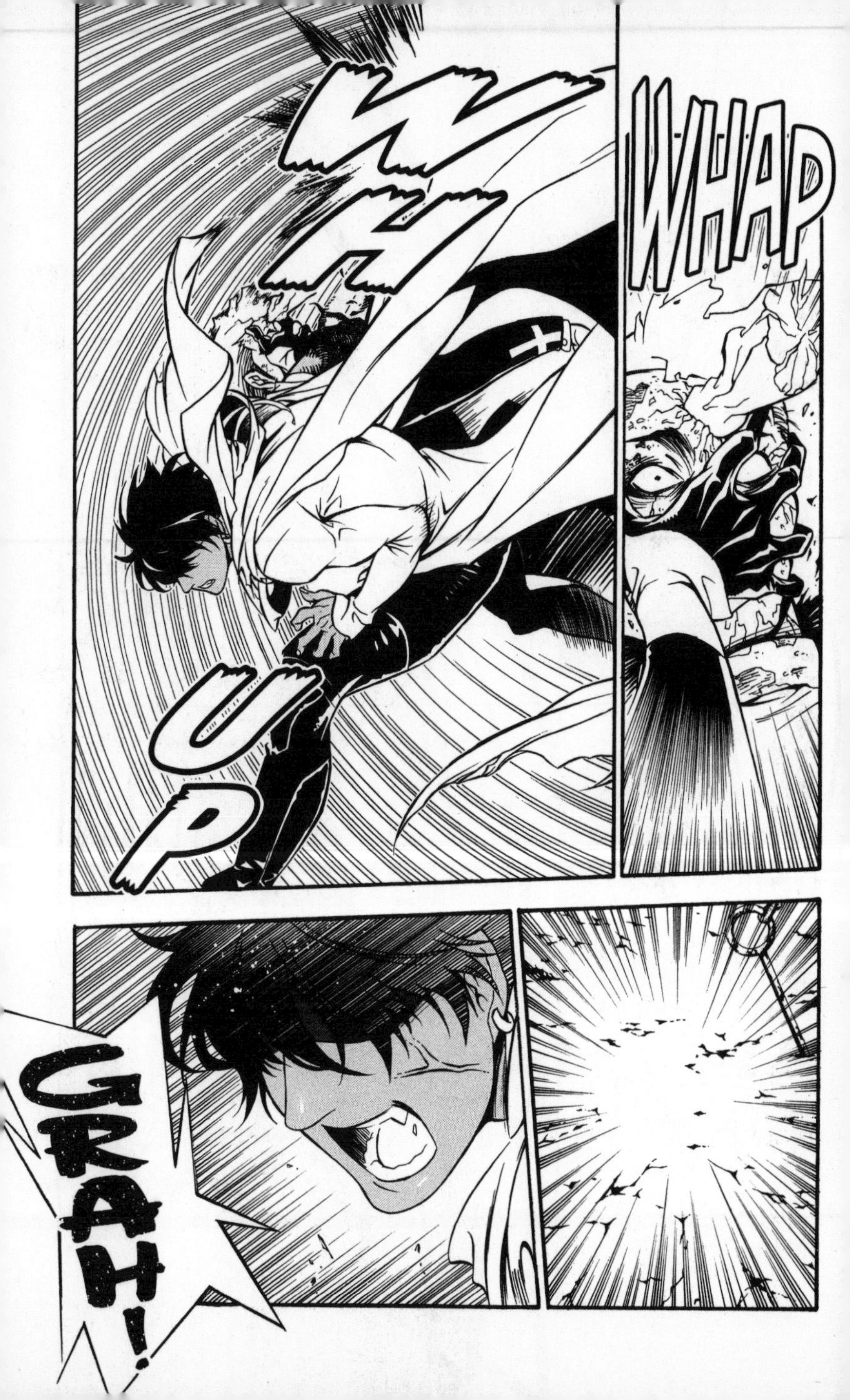
WHAP
WHUP
GRAH!

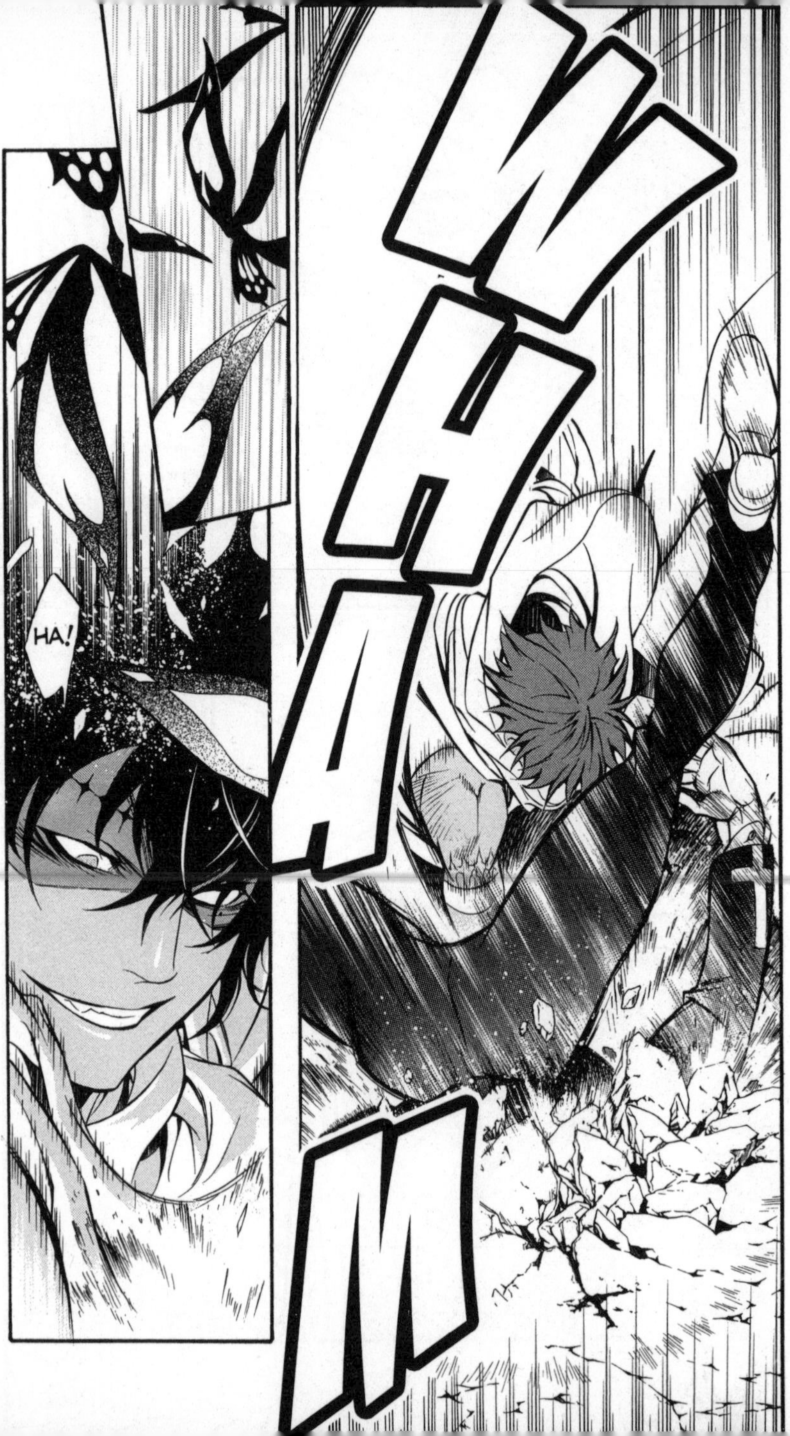
WHAAM
HA!

READ THIS WAY

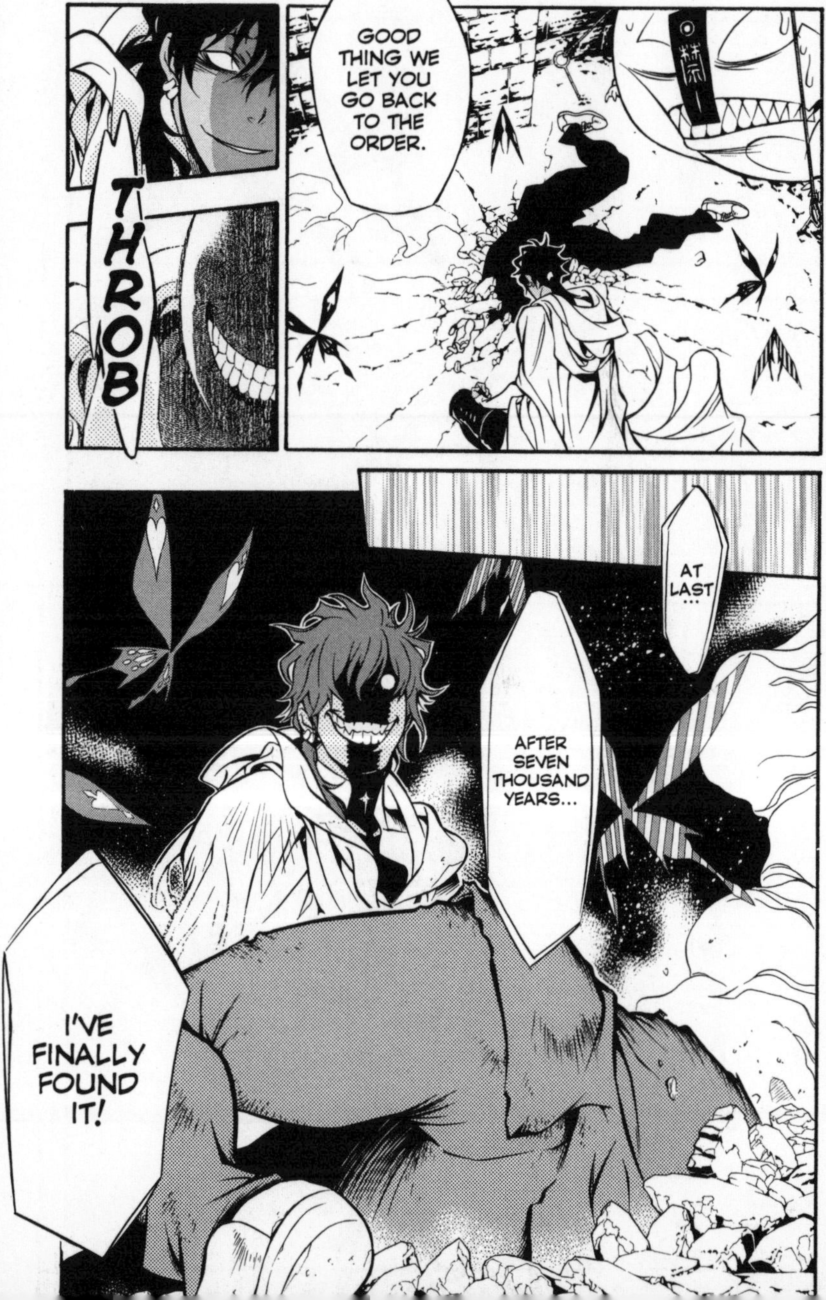
GOOD THING WE LET YOU GO BACK TO THE ORDER.
THROB
AT LAST...
AFTER SEVEN THOUSAND YEARS...
I'VE FINALLY FOUND IT!

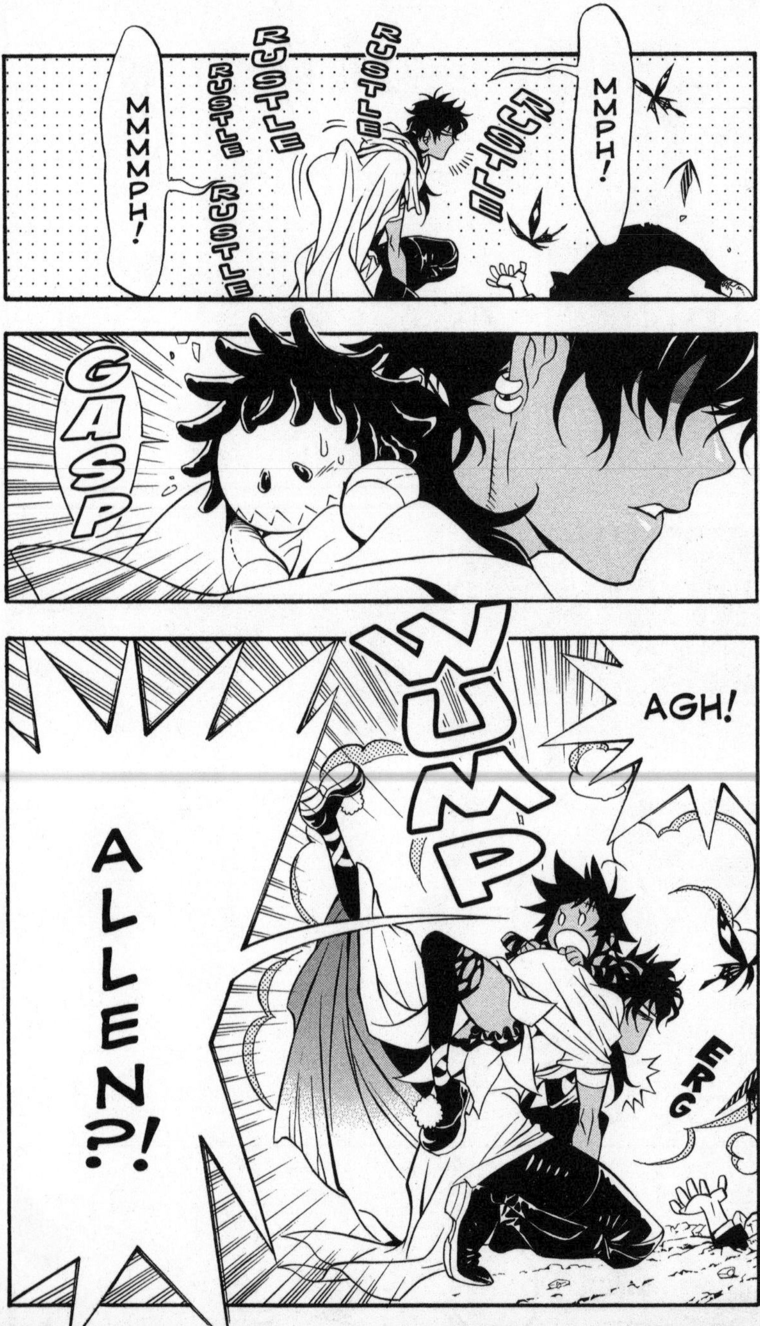

MMPH!
RUSTLE
RUSTLE
RUSTLE
RUSTLE
RUSTLE
MMMMPH!
GASP
AGH!
WUMP
ERG
ALLEN?!

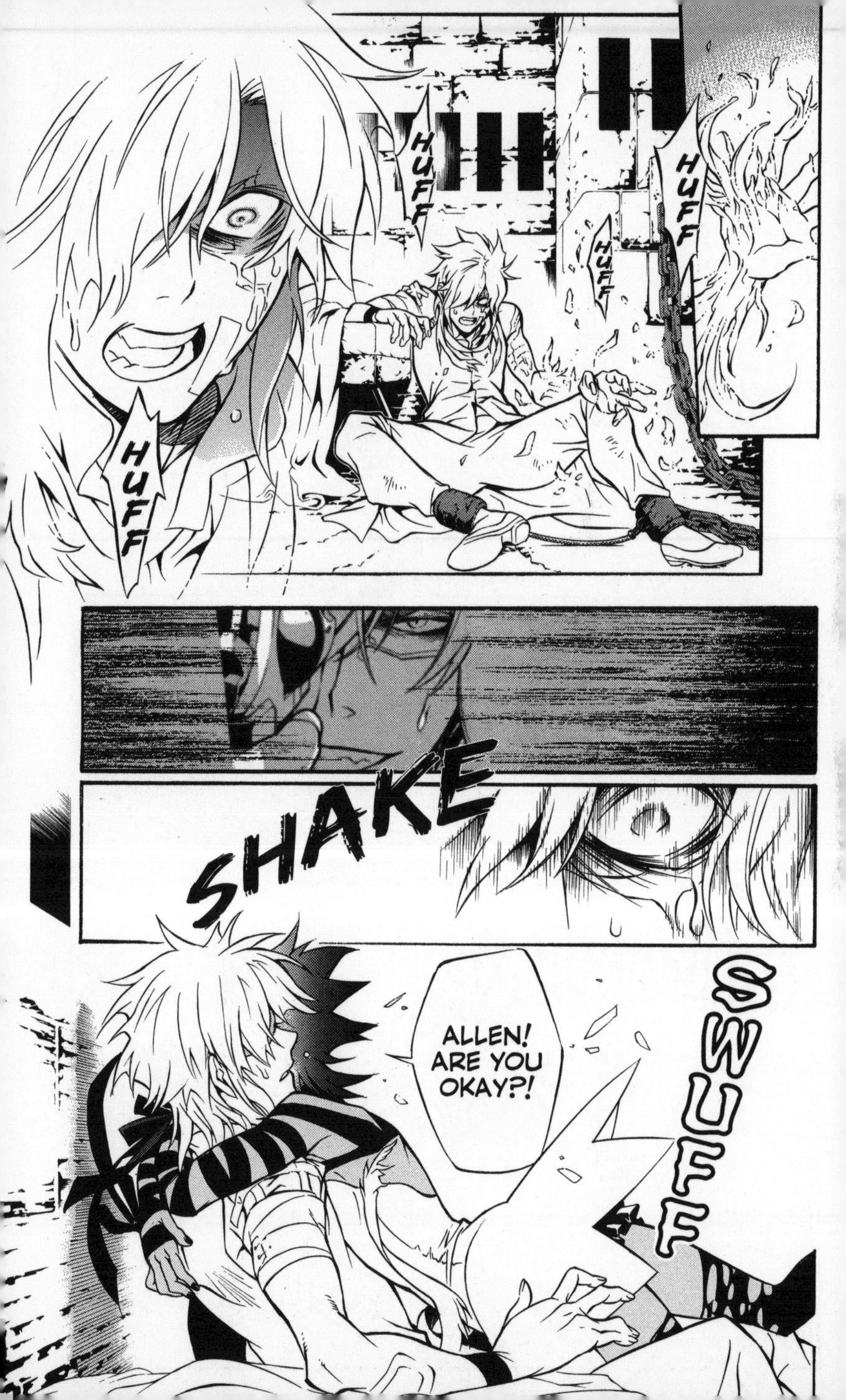

HUFF
HUFF
HUFF
HUFF
SHAKE
SWUFF
ALLEN! ARE YOU OKAY?!

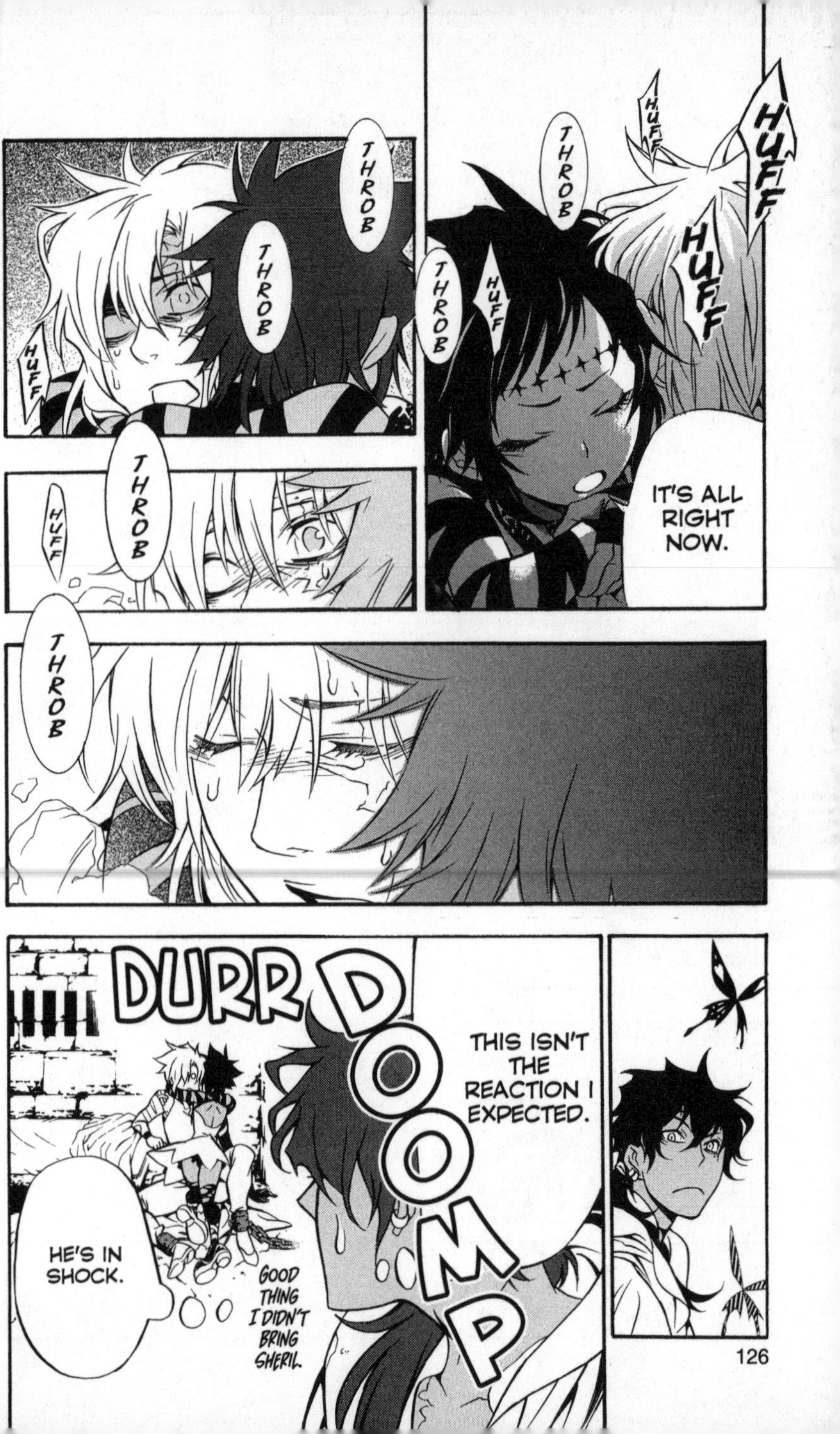
HUFF
HUFF
HUFF
THROB
THROB
HUFF
IT'S ALL RIGHT NOW.
THROB
THROB
HUFF
THROB
HUFF
THROB
DURR
DOOMP
THIS ISN'T THE REACTION I EXPECTED.
HE'S IN SHOCK.
GOOD THING I DIDN'T BRING SHERIL.

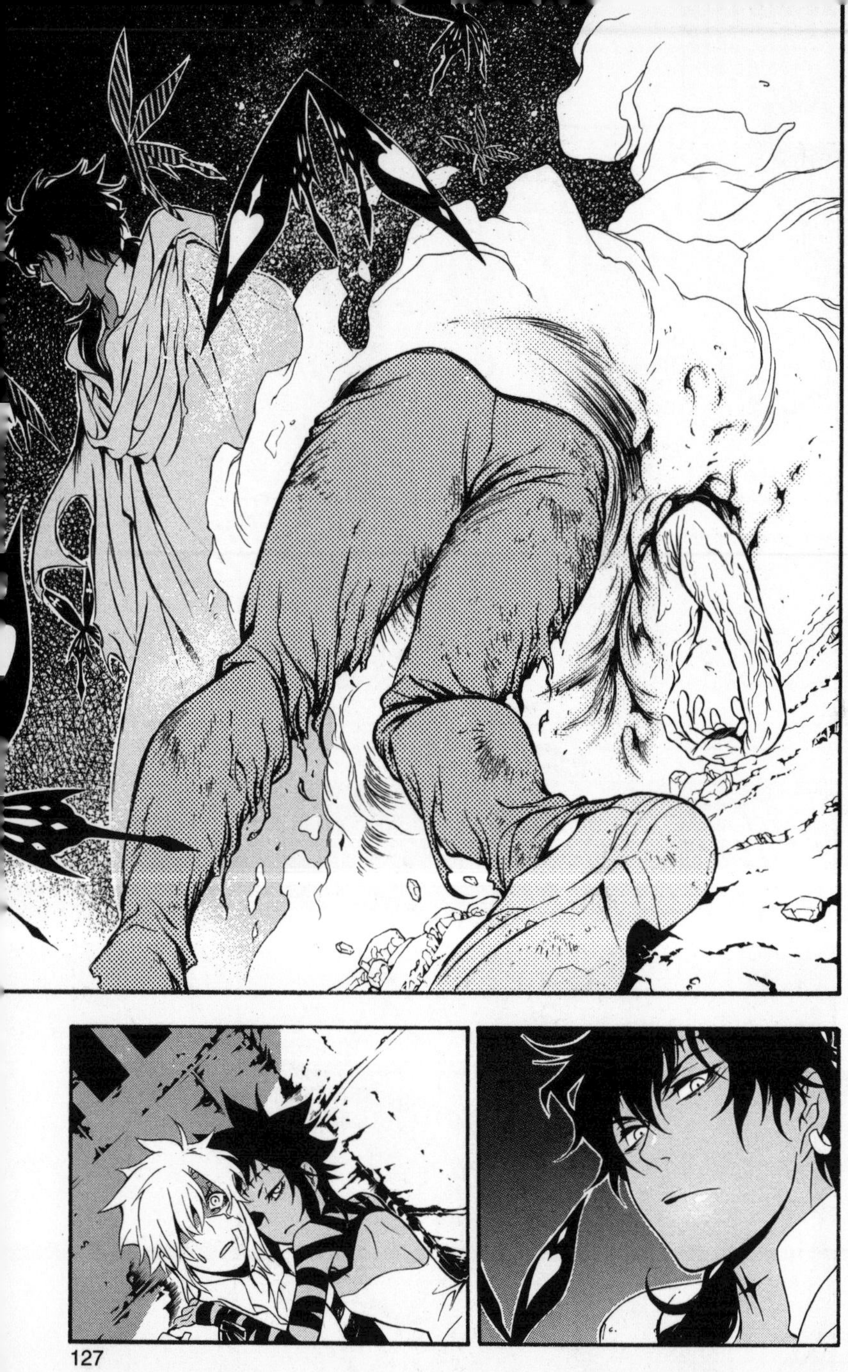

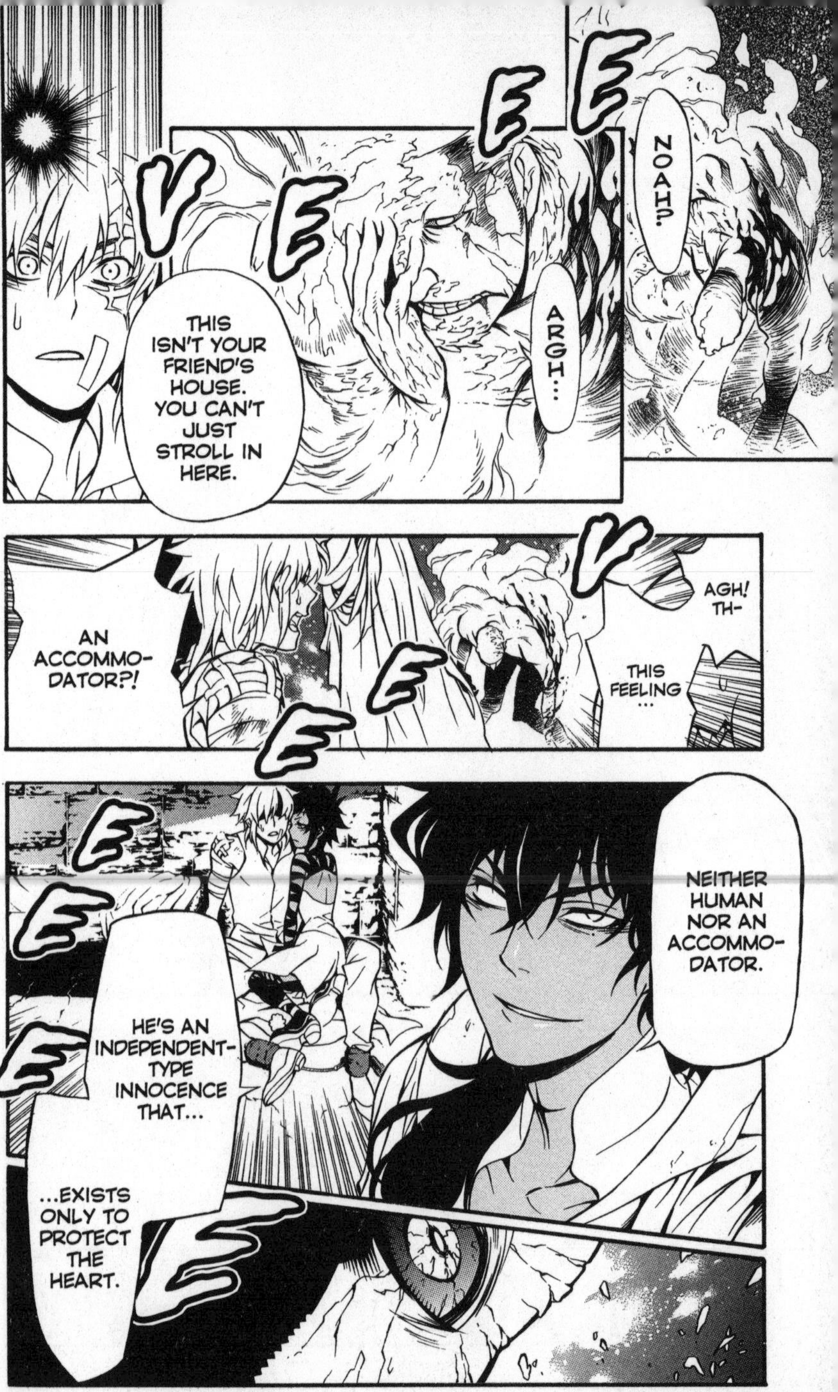
NOAH?
ARGH...
VEEE
THIS ISN'T YOUR FRIEND'S HOUSE. YOU CAN'T JUST STROLL IN HERE.
AGH! TH-
THIS FEELING...
AN ACCOMMO-DATOR?!
VEEEEEE
NEITHER HUMAN NOR AN ACCOMMO-DATOR.
HE'S AN INDEPENDENT-TYPE INNOCENCE THAT...
...EXISTS ONLY TO PROTECT THE HEART.

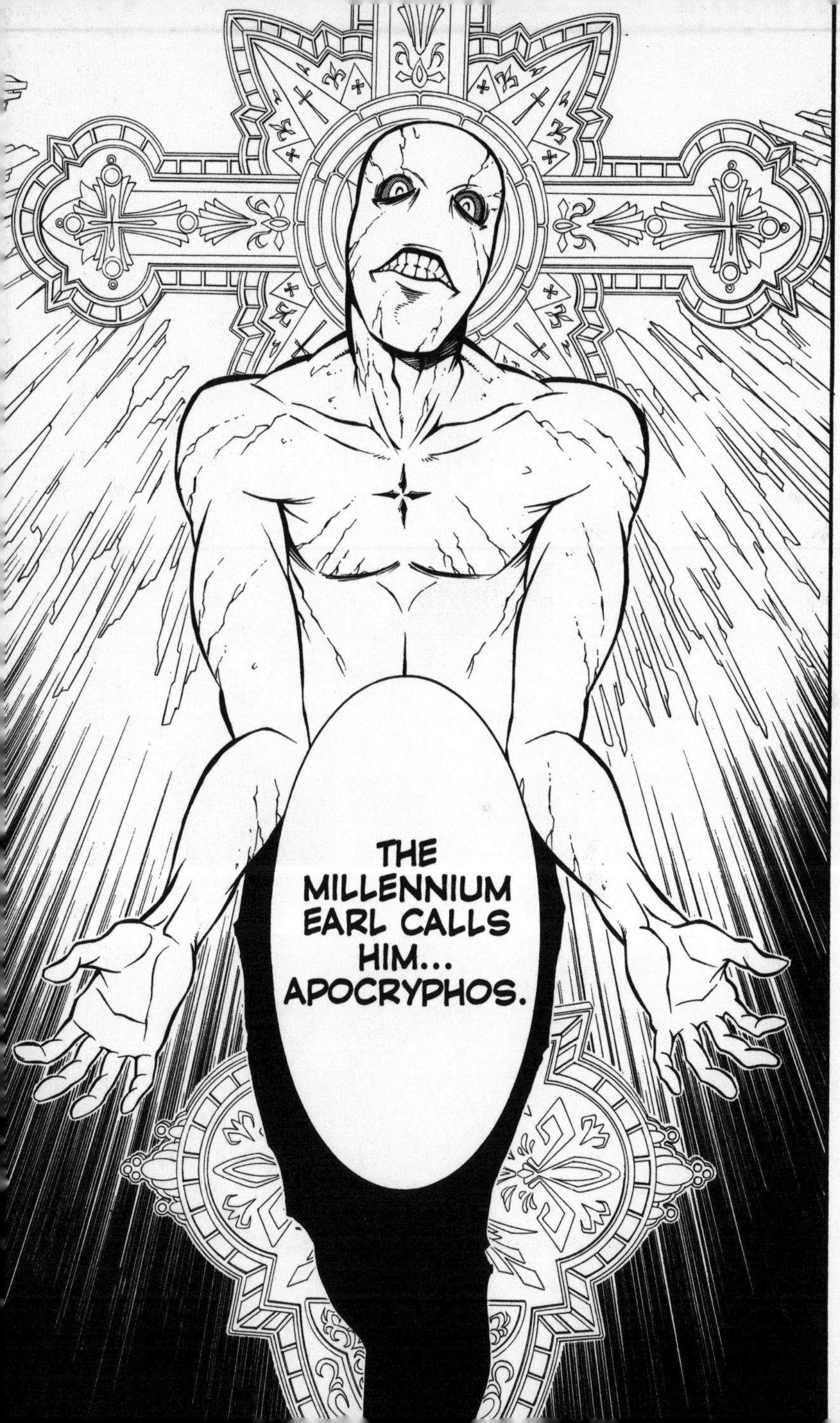
THE MILLENNIUM EARL CALLS HIM... APOCRYPHOS.

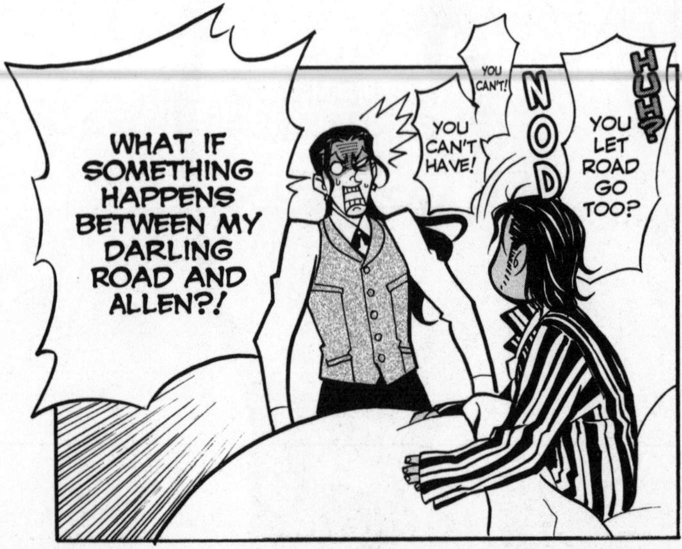
HUH?
YOU LET ROAD GO TOO?
NOD
YOU CAN'T!
YOU CAN'T HAVE!
WHAT IF SOMETHING HAPPENS BETWEEN MY DARLING ROAD AND ALLEN?!

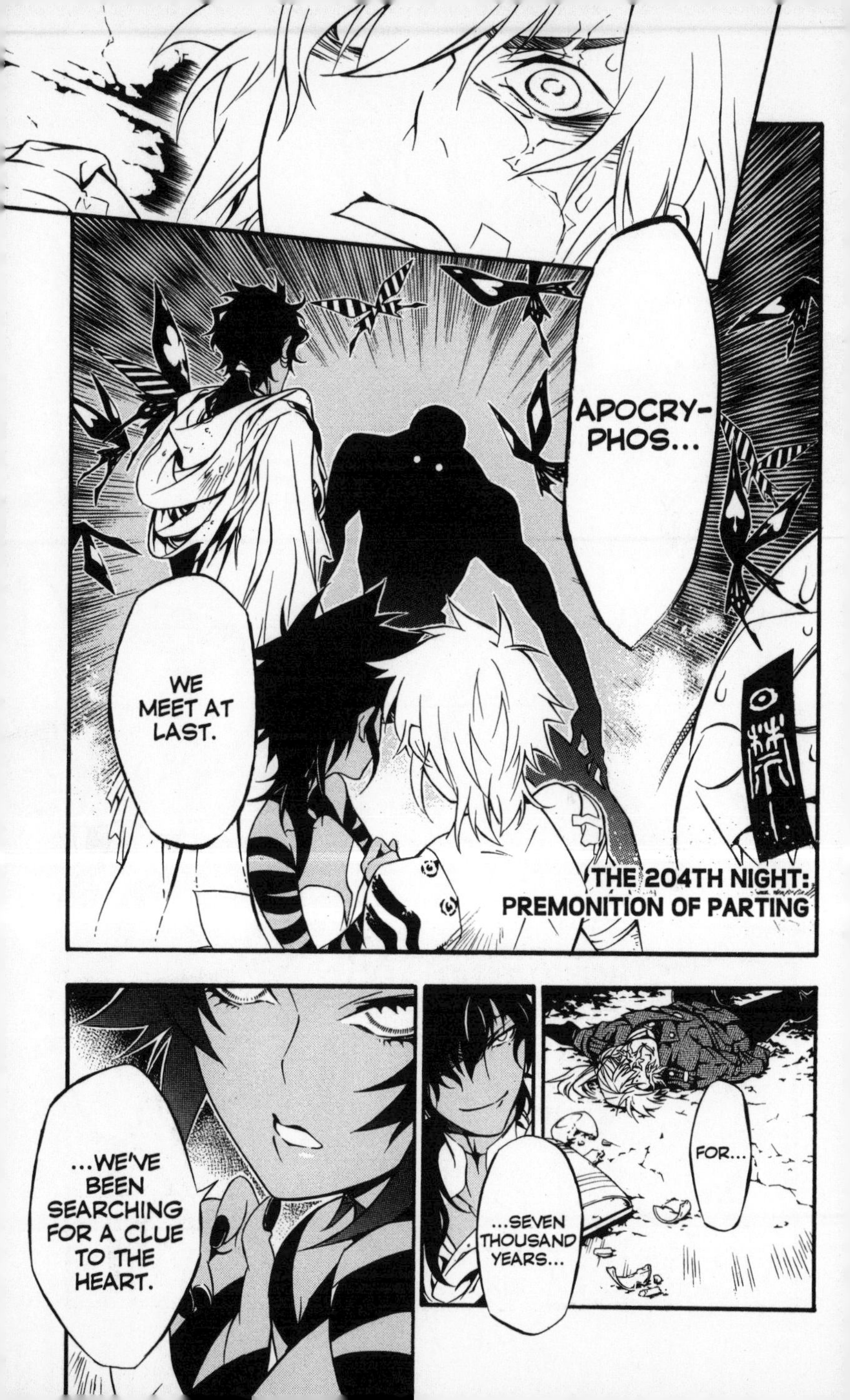
APOCRYPHOS...
WE MEET AT LAST.
THE 204TH NIGHT: PREMONITION OF PARTING
FOR...
...SEVEN THOUSAND YEARS...
...WE'VE BEEN SEARCHING FOR A CLUE TO THE HEART.

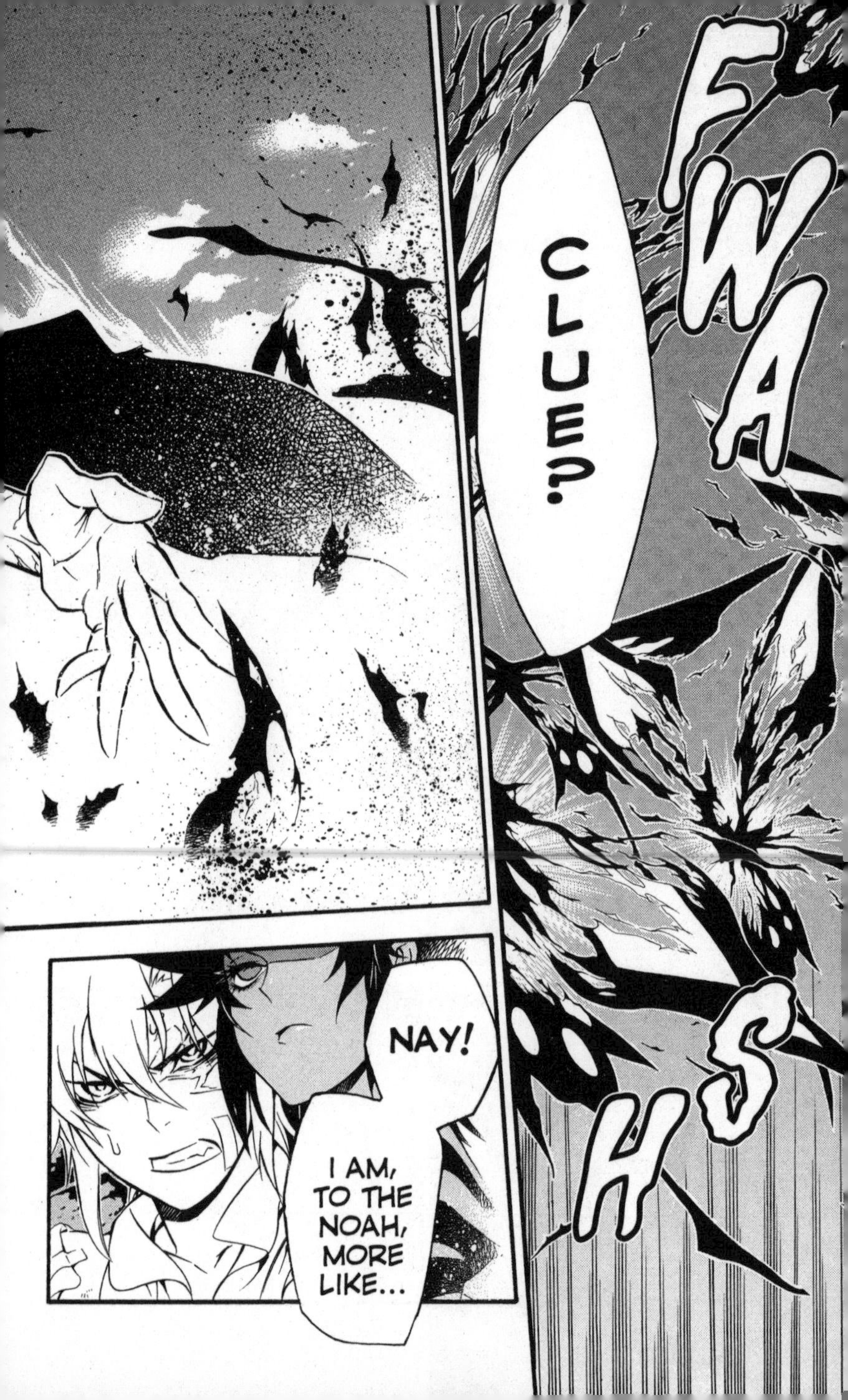
FWASH
CLUE?
NAY!
I AM, TO THE NOAH, MORE LIKE...

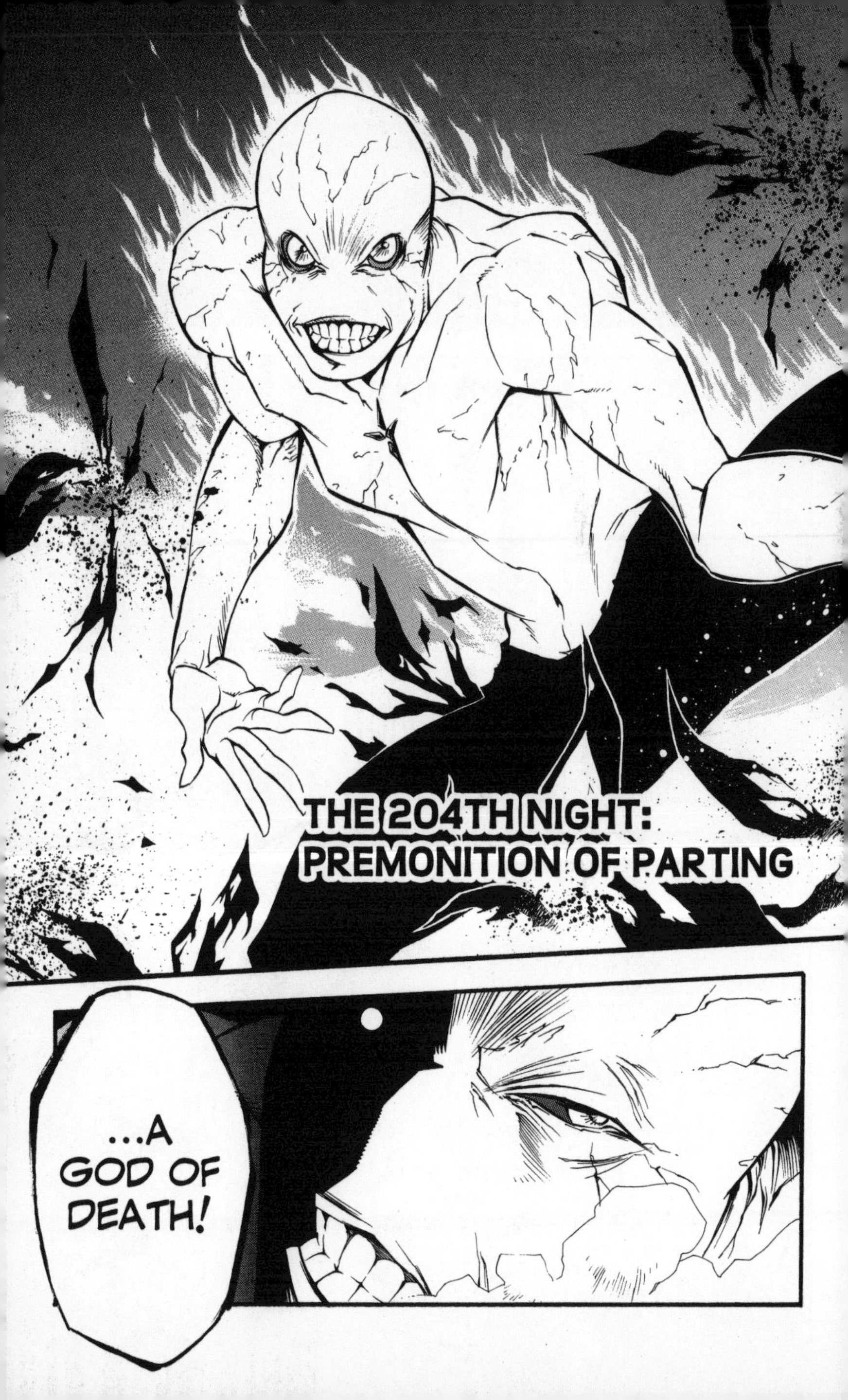
THE 204TH NIGHT:
PREMONITION OF PARTING
...A GOD OF DEATH!

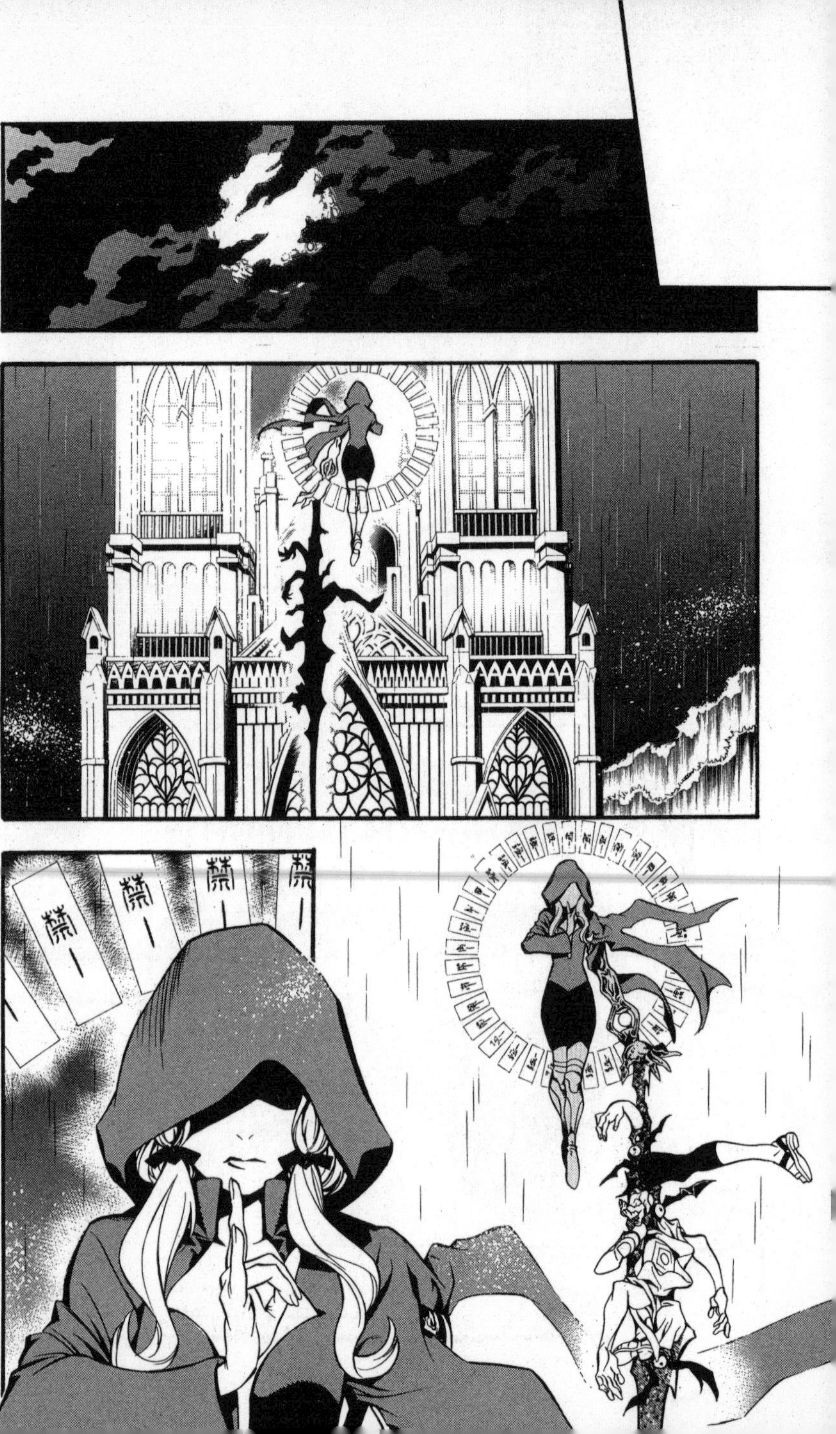
禁
禁
禁
禁

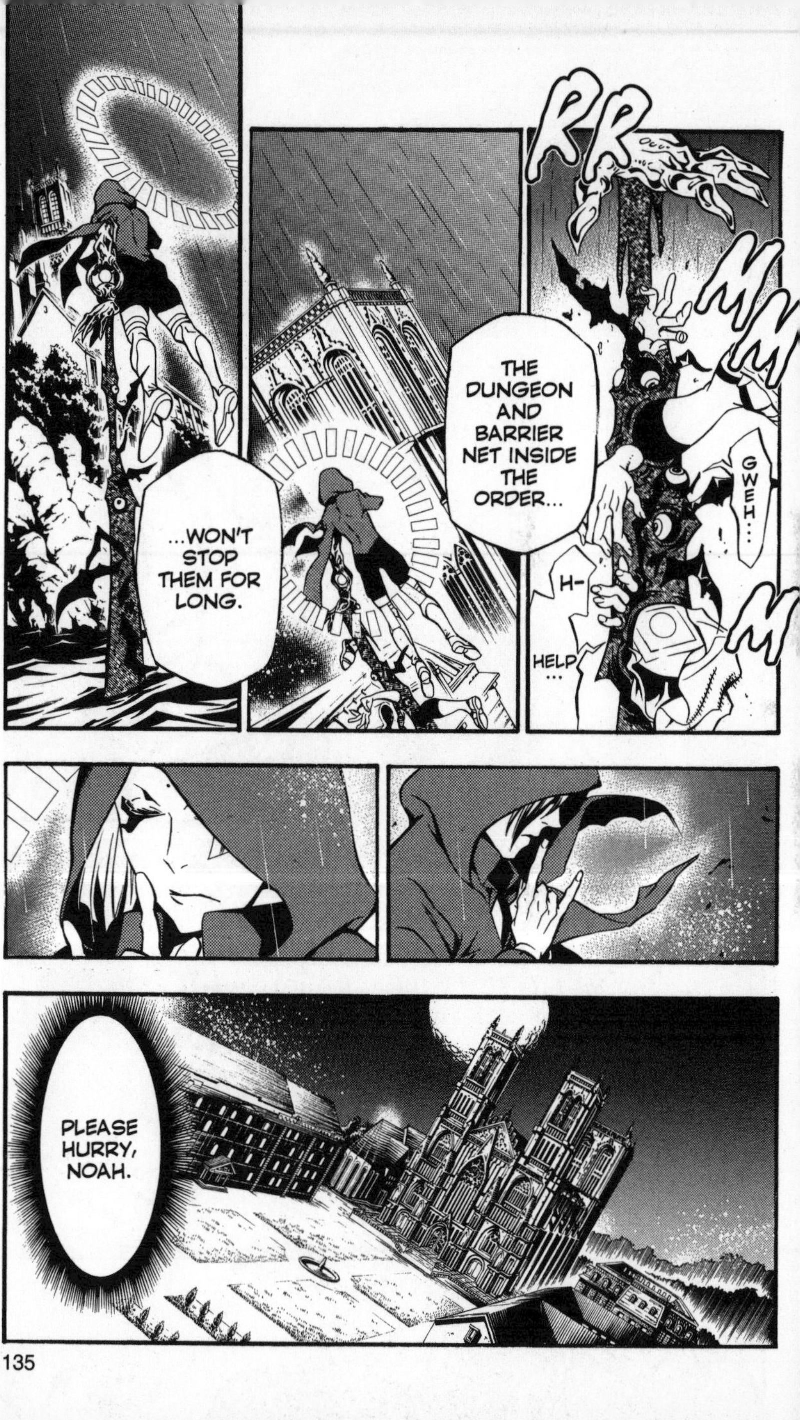
RRMMM
GWEH...
H-
HELP...
THE DUNGEON AND BARRIER NET INSIDE THE ORDER...
...WON'T STOP THEM FOR LONG.
PLEASE HURRY, NOAH.

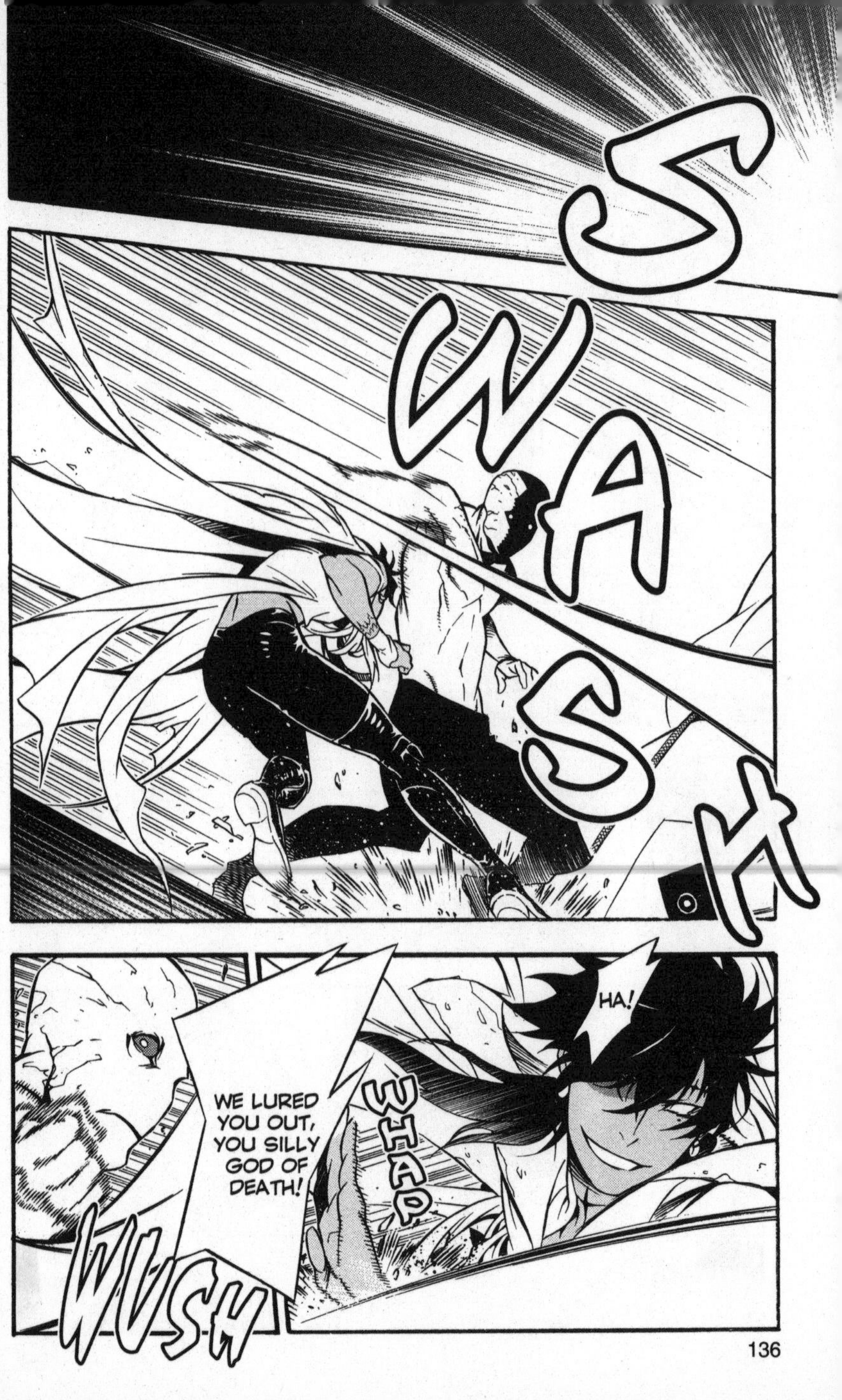
SWASH
HA!
WHAP
WE LURED YOU OUT, YOU SILLY GOD OF DEATH!
WUSH

READ THIS WAY

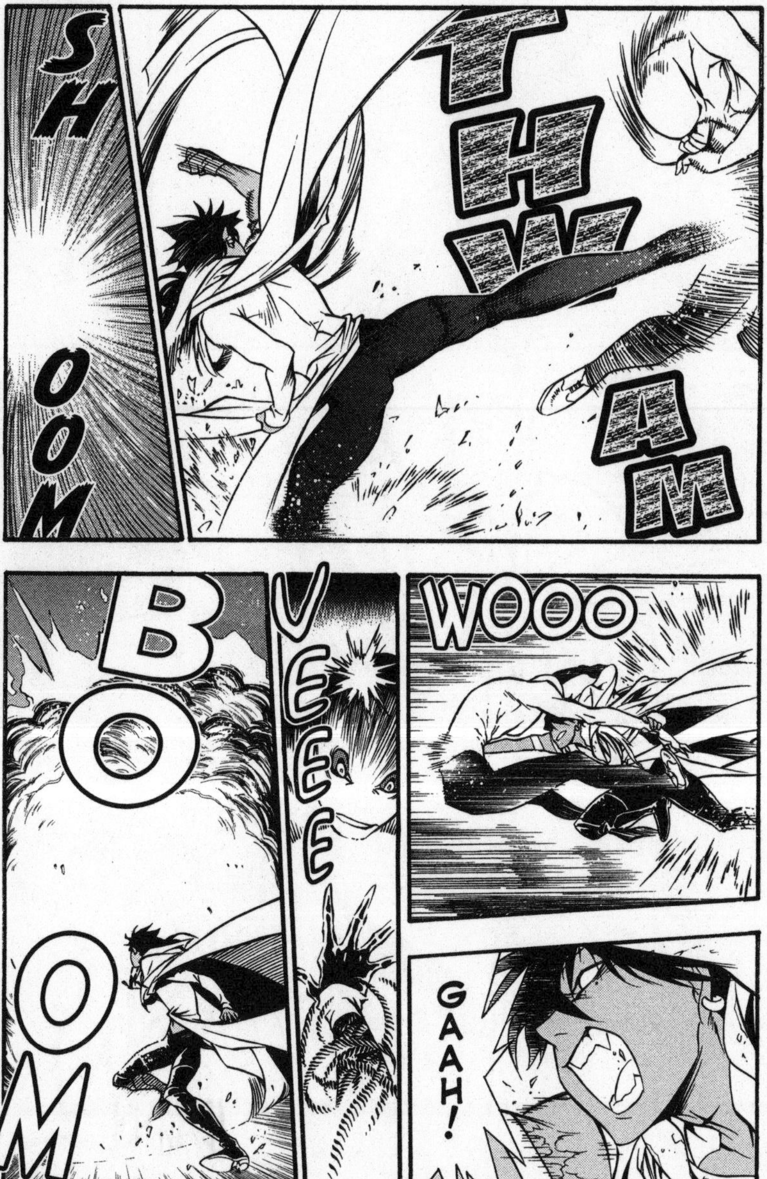
THWAM
SHOOM
WOOO
GAAH!
VEEEE
BOOM

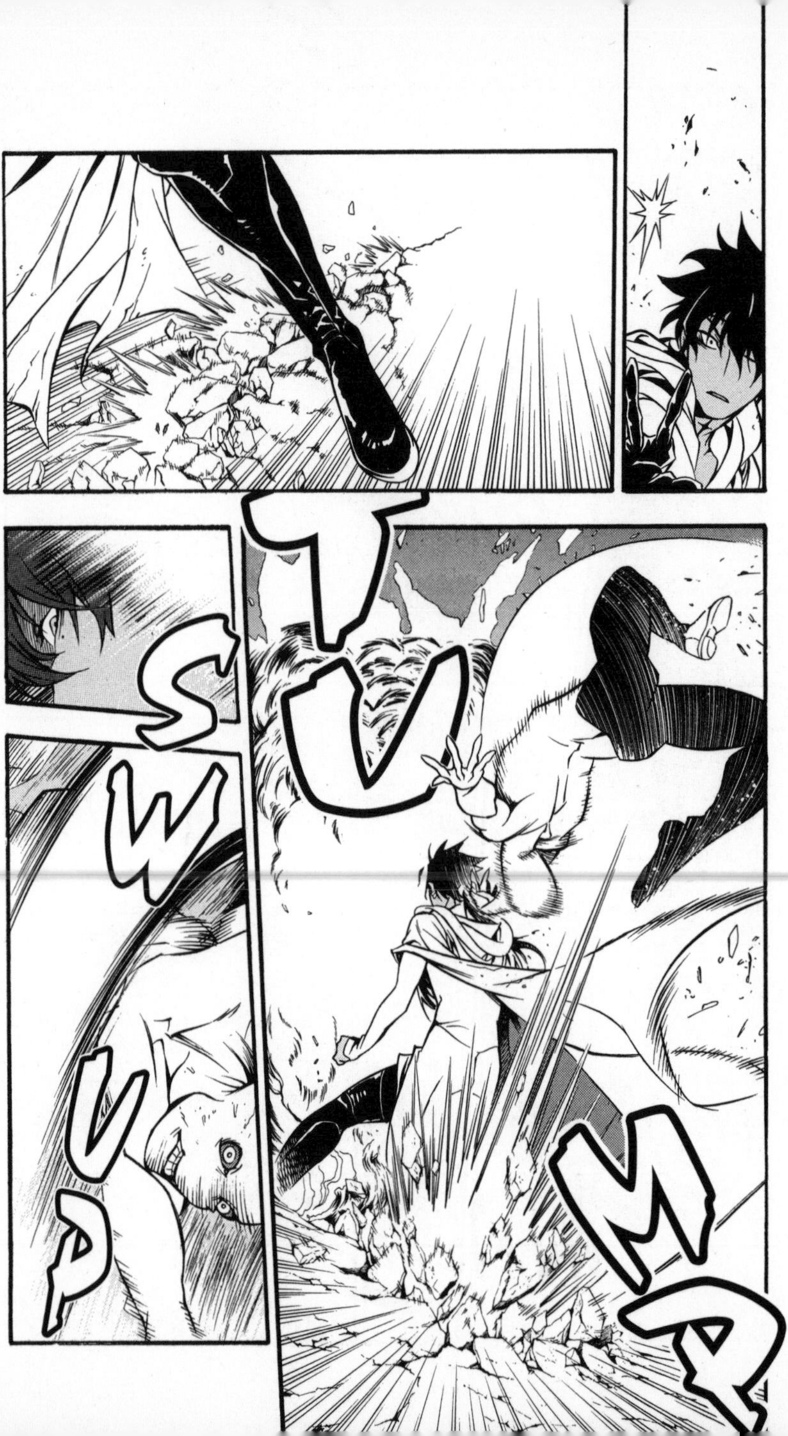

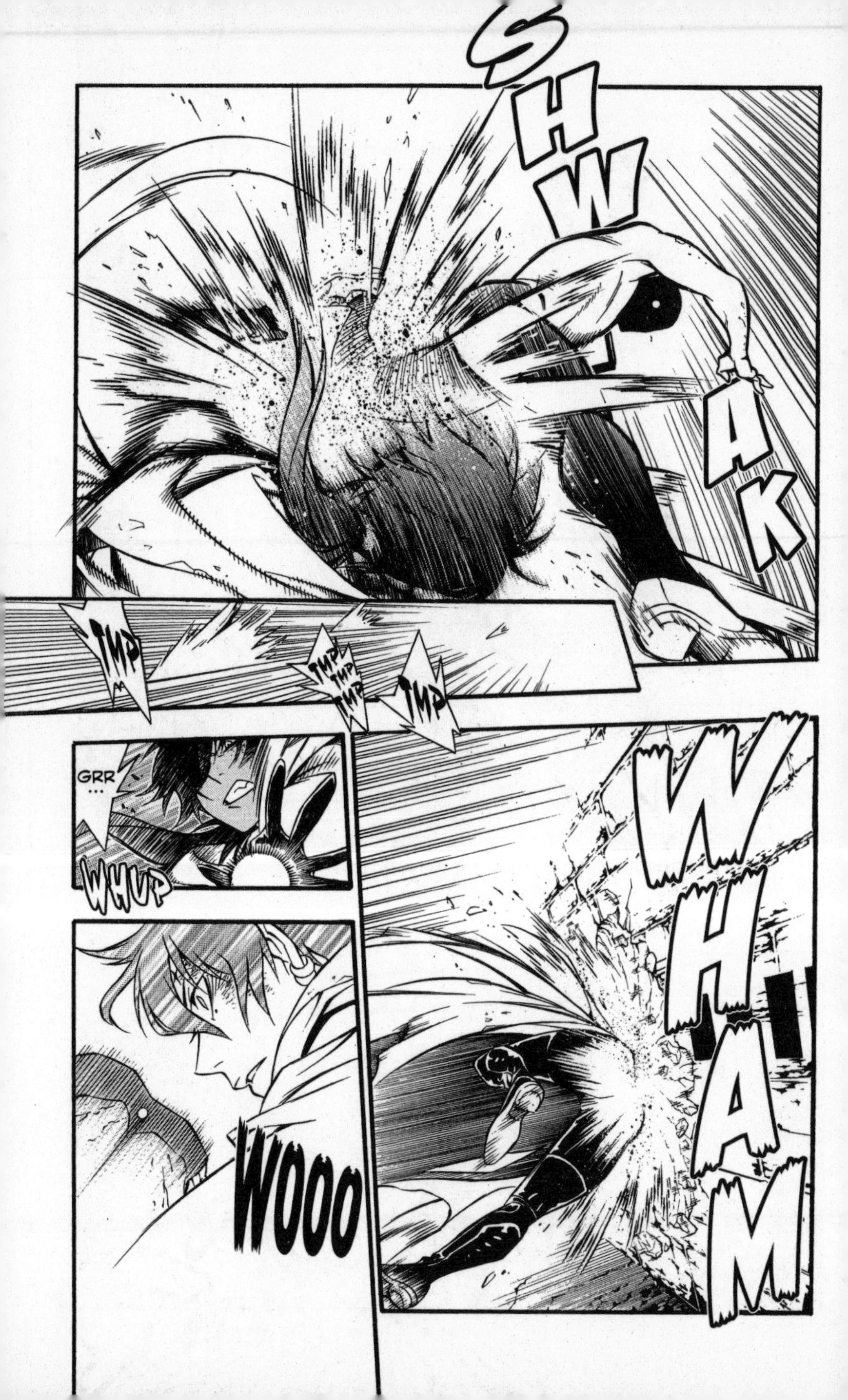
SHWAK
TMP
TMP
TUP
TMP
TMP
WHAM
GRR...
WHUP
WOOO

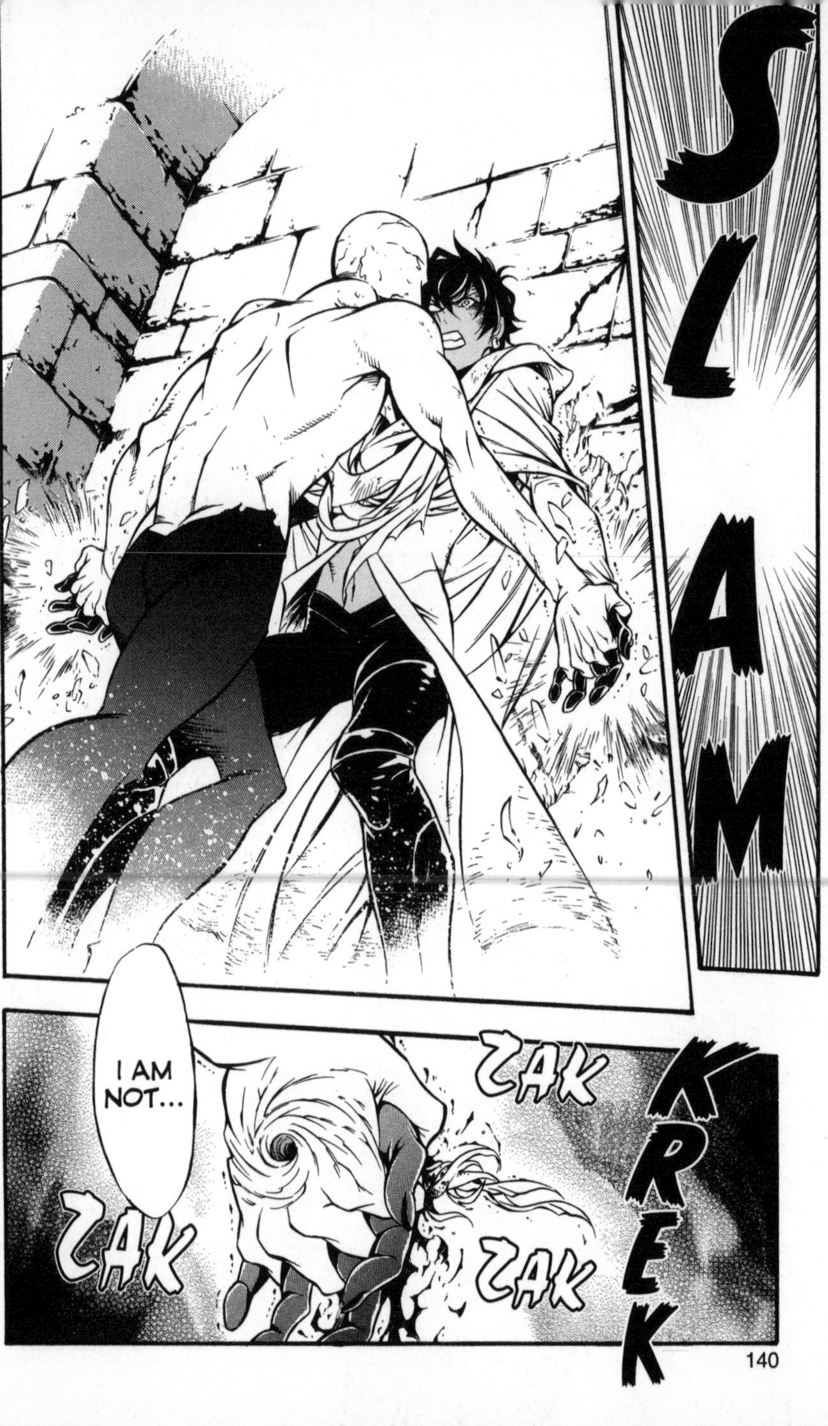
SLAM
KREK
ZAK
I AM NOT...
ZAK
ZAK

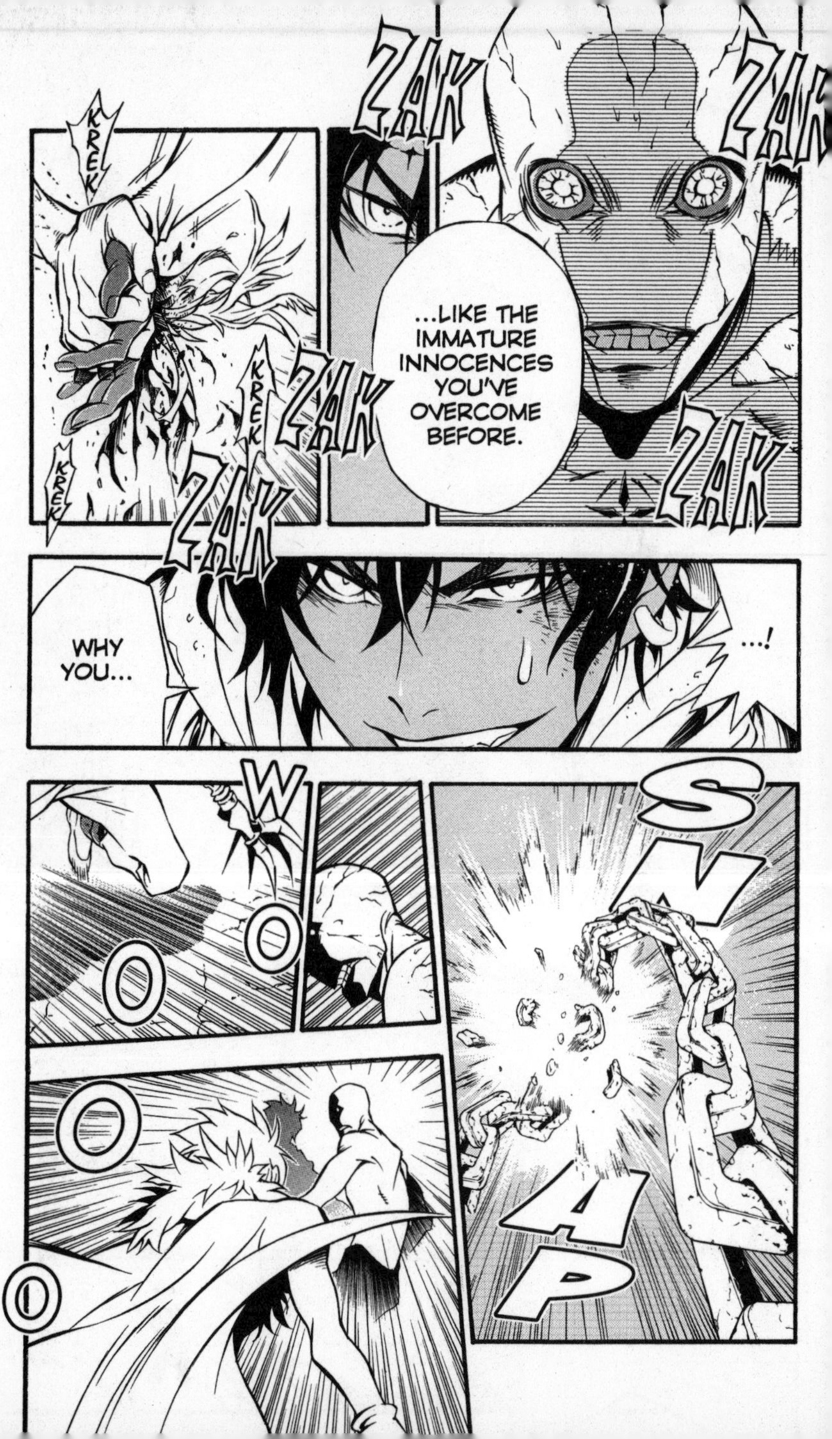
ZAK
ZAK
...LIKE THE IMMATURE INNOCENCES YOU'VE OVERCOME BEFORE.
ZAK
ZAK
ZAK
KREK
KREK
KREK
...!
WHY YOU...
SNAP
WOO
OO

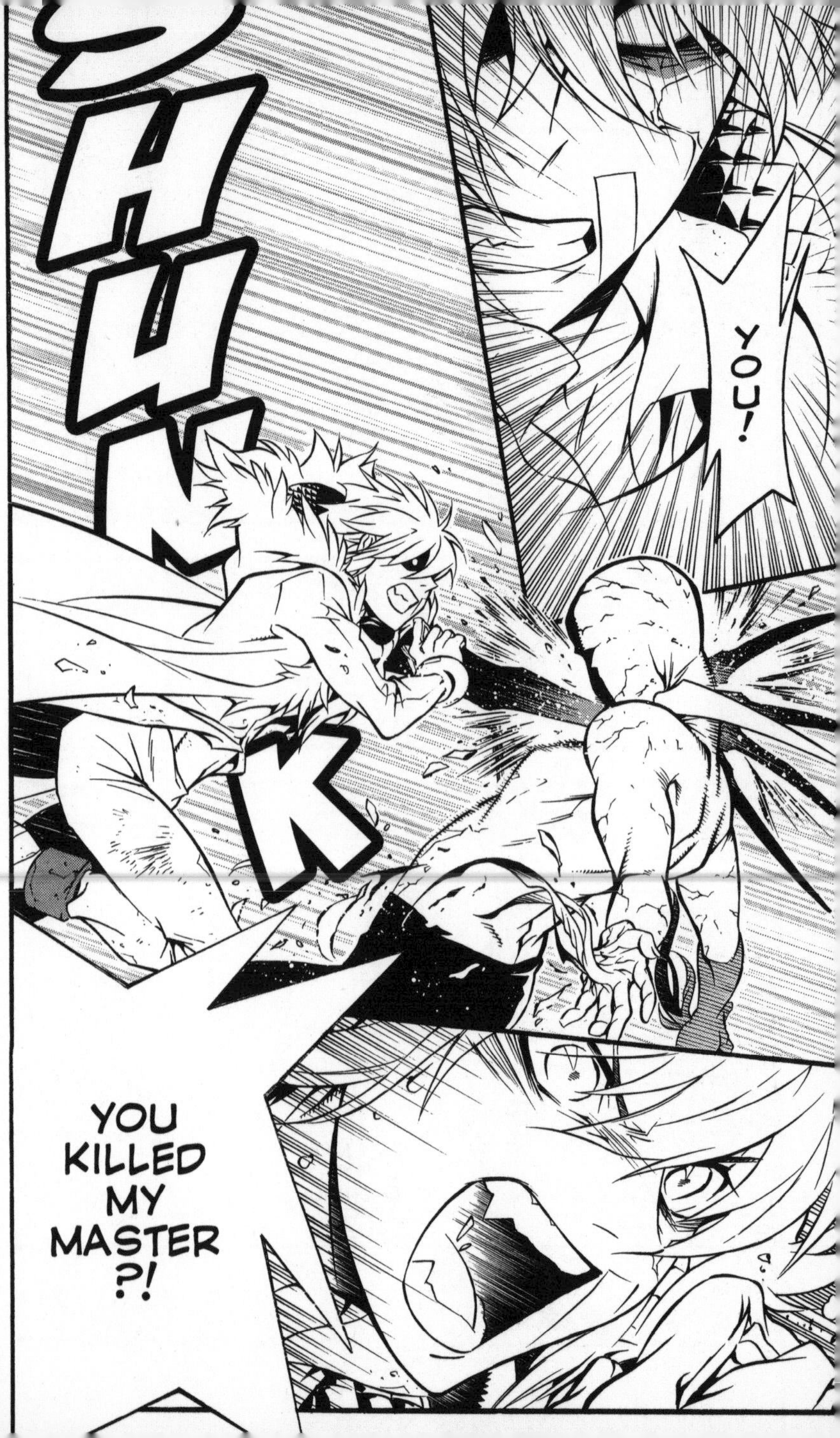
CHUNK
YOU!
YOU KILLED MY MASTER?!

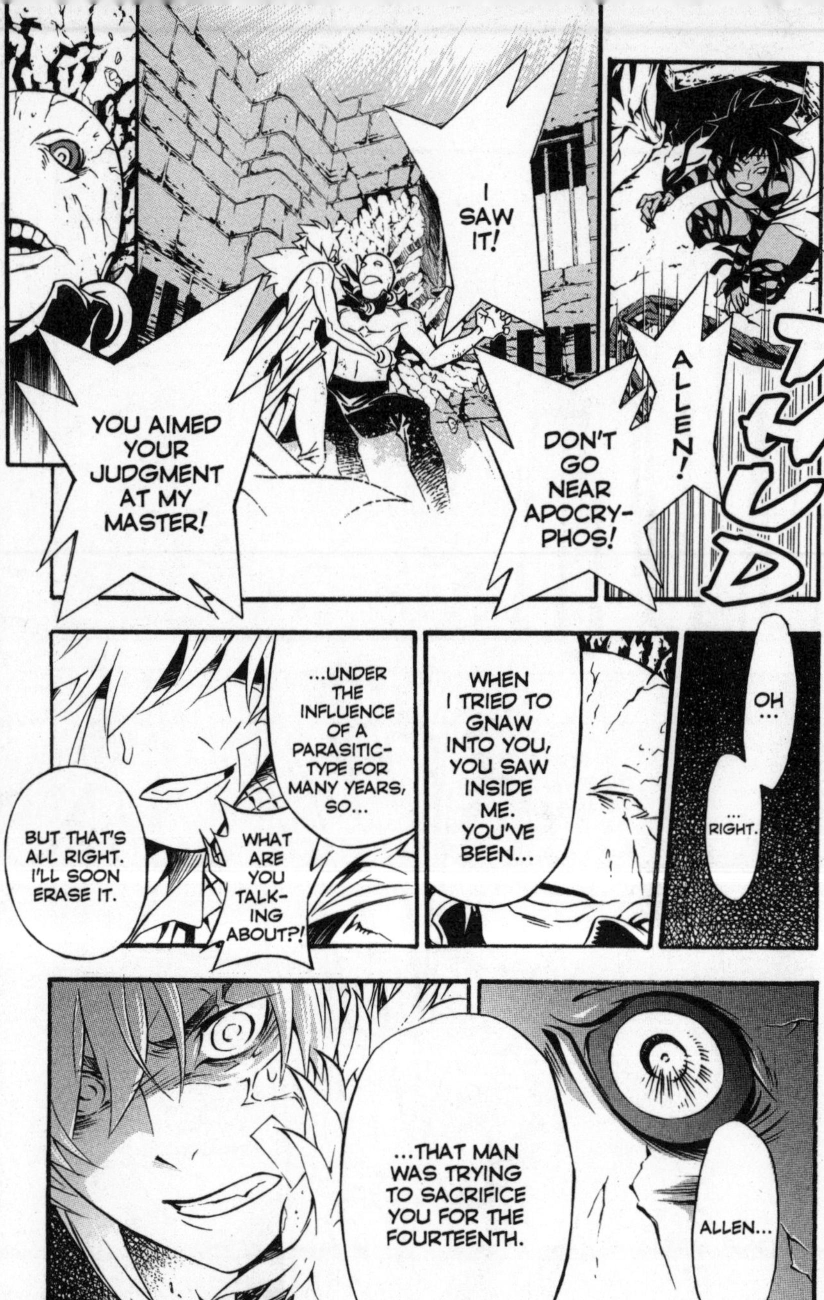
ALLEN!
THUD
DON'T GO NEAR APOCRYPHOS!
I SAW IT!
YOU AIMED YOUR JUDGMENT AT MY MASTER!
OH...
...RIGHT.
WHEN I TRIED TO GNAW INTO YOU, YOU SAW INSIDE ME. YOU'VE BEEN...
...UNDER THE INFLUENCE OF A PARASITIC-TYPE FOR MANY YEARS, SO...
WHAT ARE YOU TALKING ABOUT?!
BUT THAT'S ALL RIGHT. I'LL SOON ERASE IT.
ALLEN...
...THAT MAN WAS TRYING TO SACRIFICE YOU FOR THE FOURTEENTH.

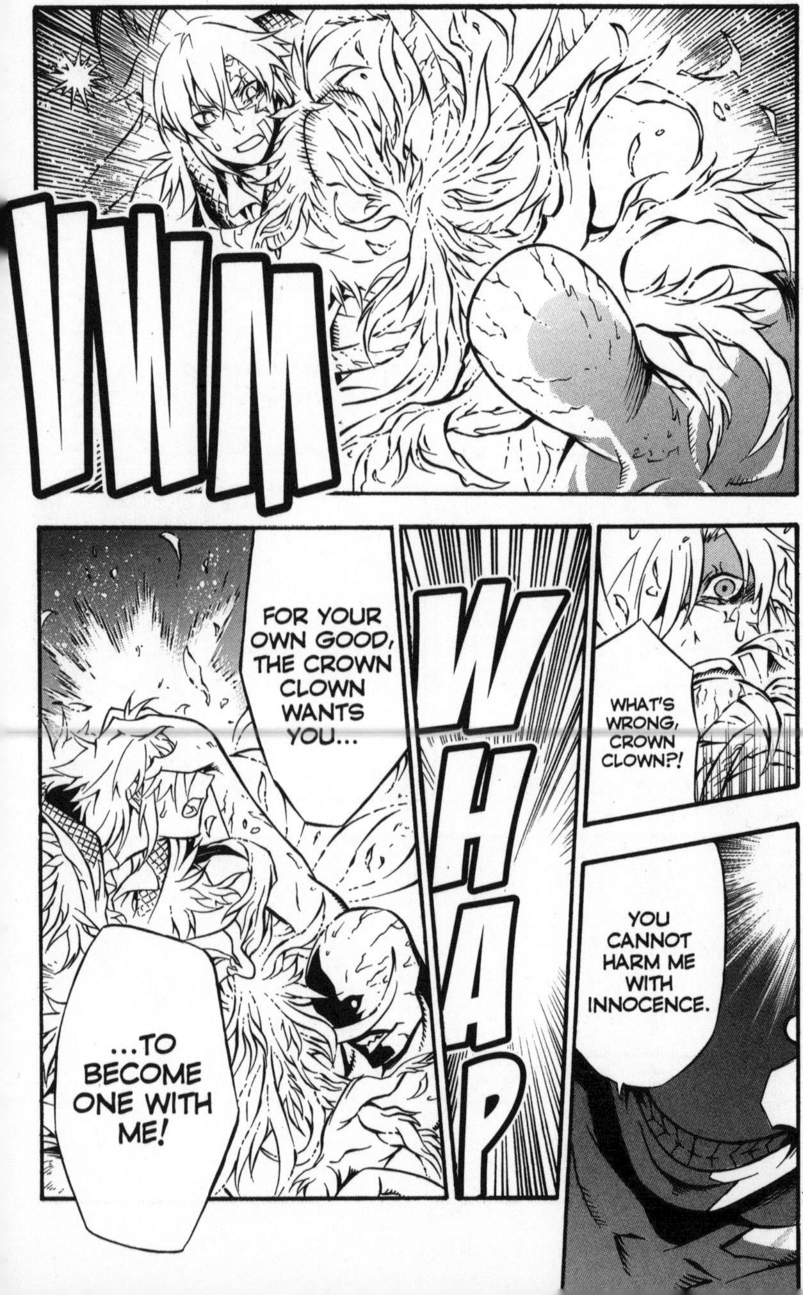
VWM
WHAT'S WRONG, CROWN CLOWN?!
YOU CANNOT HARM ME WITH INNOCENCE.
WHAP
FOR YOUR OWN GOOD, THE CROWN CLOWN WANTS YOU...
...TO BECOME ONE WITH ME!

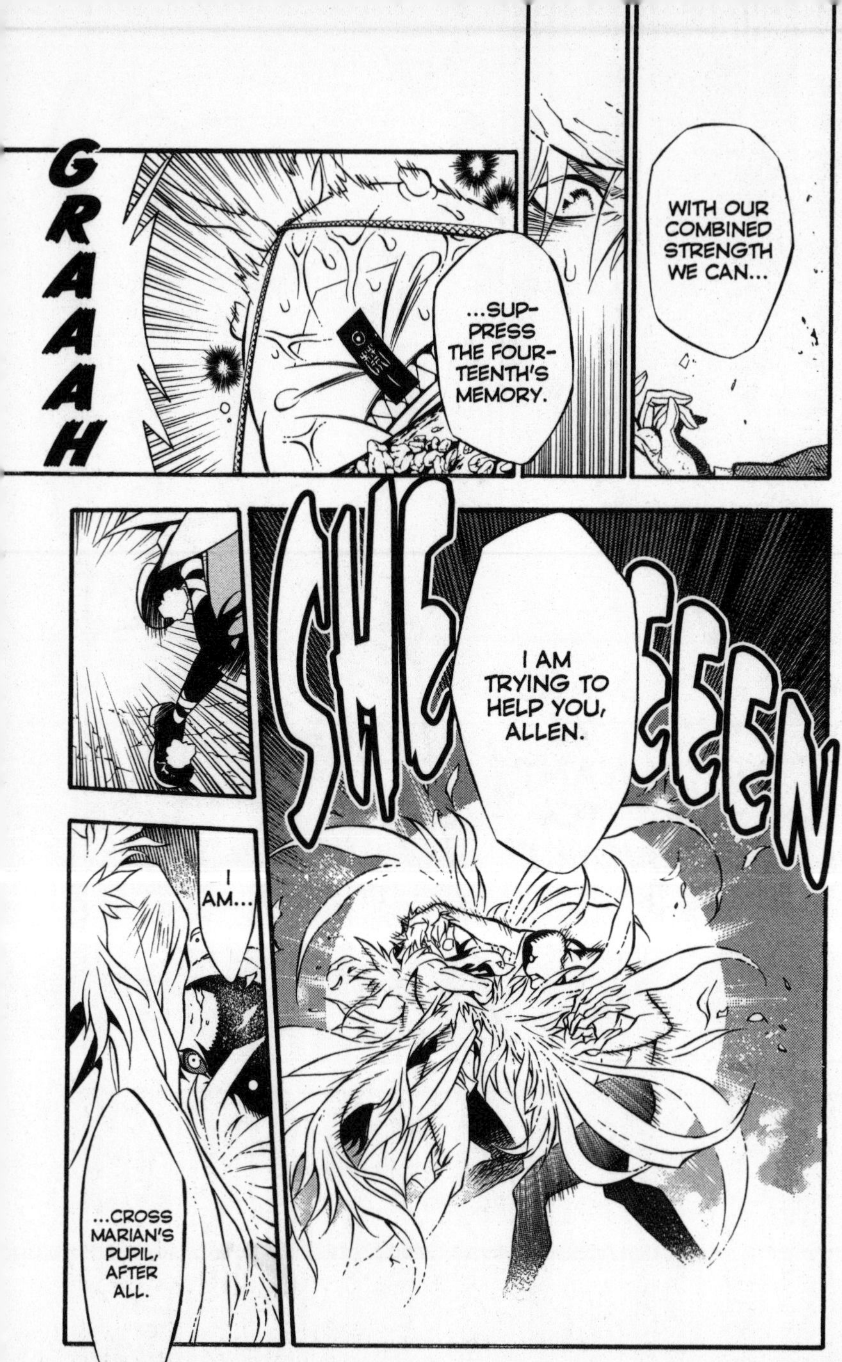
WITH OUR COMBINED STRENGTH WE CAN...
...SUP-PRESS THE FOUR-TEENTH'S MEMORY.
GRAAAAH
I AM TRYING TO HELP YOU, ALLEN.
I AM...
...CROSS MARIAN'S PUPIL, AFTER ALL.

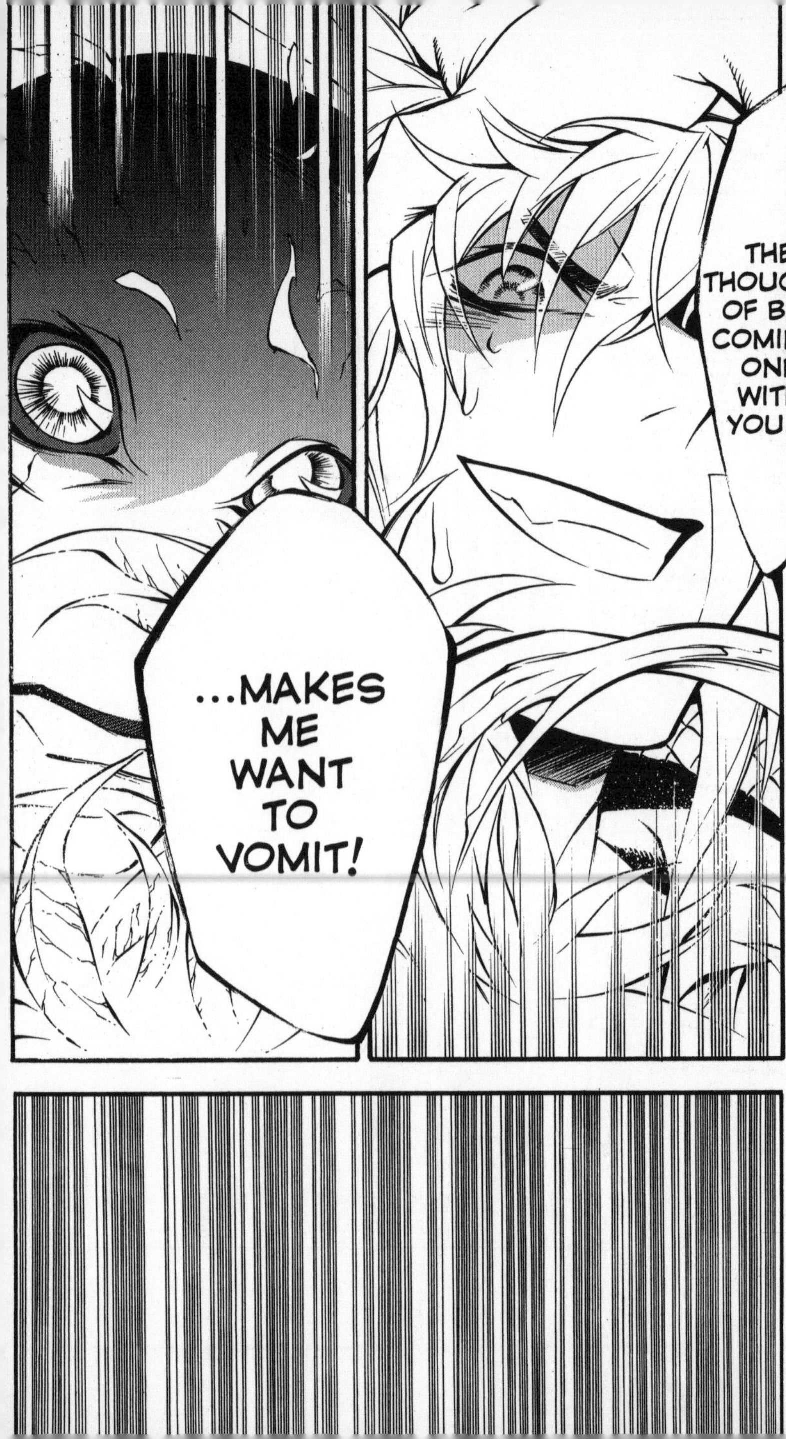
THE THOUGHT OF BE- COMING ONE WITH YOU...
...MAKES ME WANT TO VOMIT!

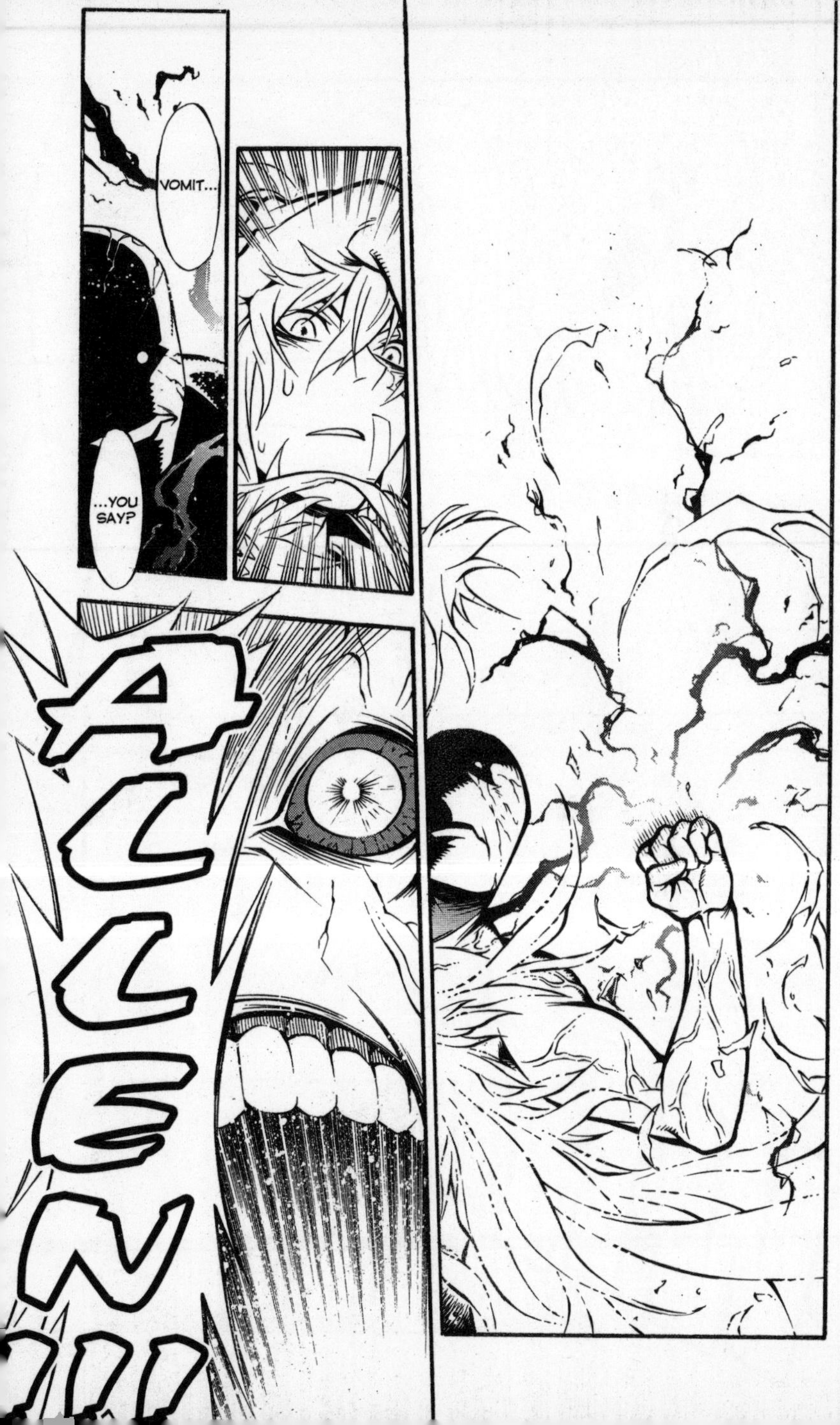
VOMIT...
...YOU SAY?
ALLEN!!!

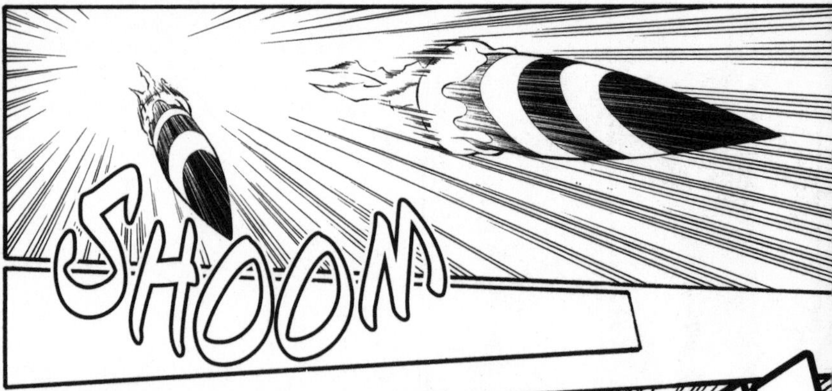
SHOOM

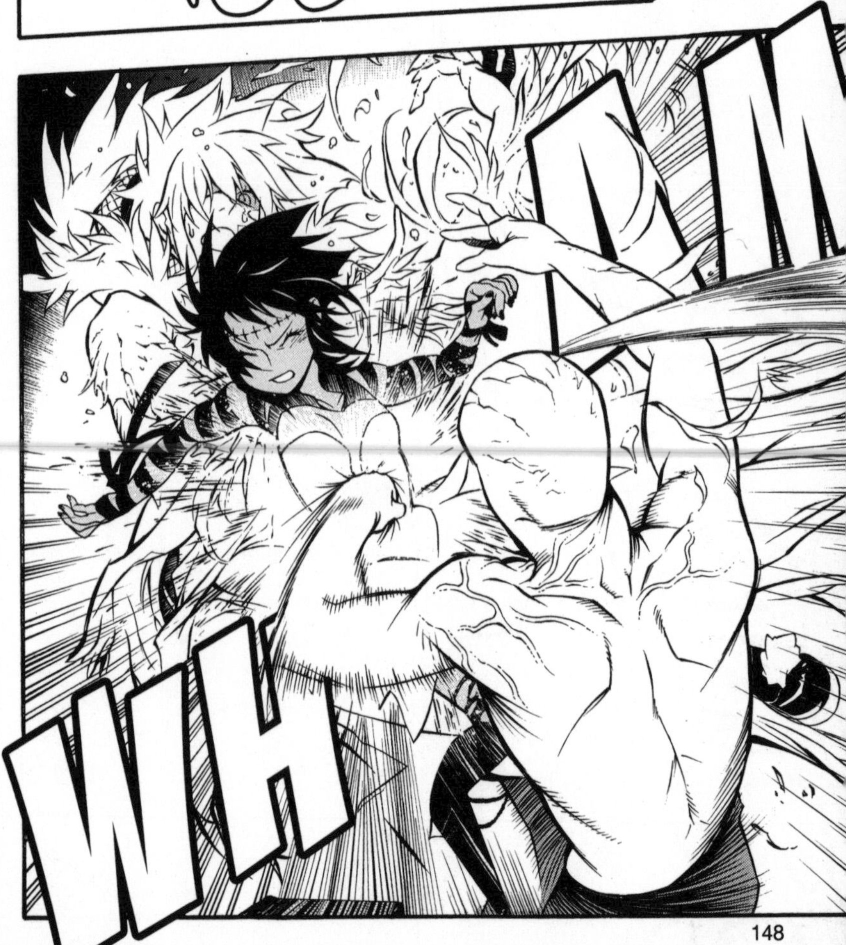
WHAM

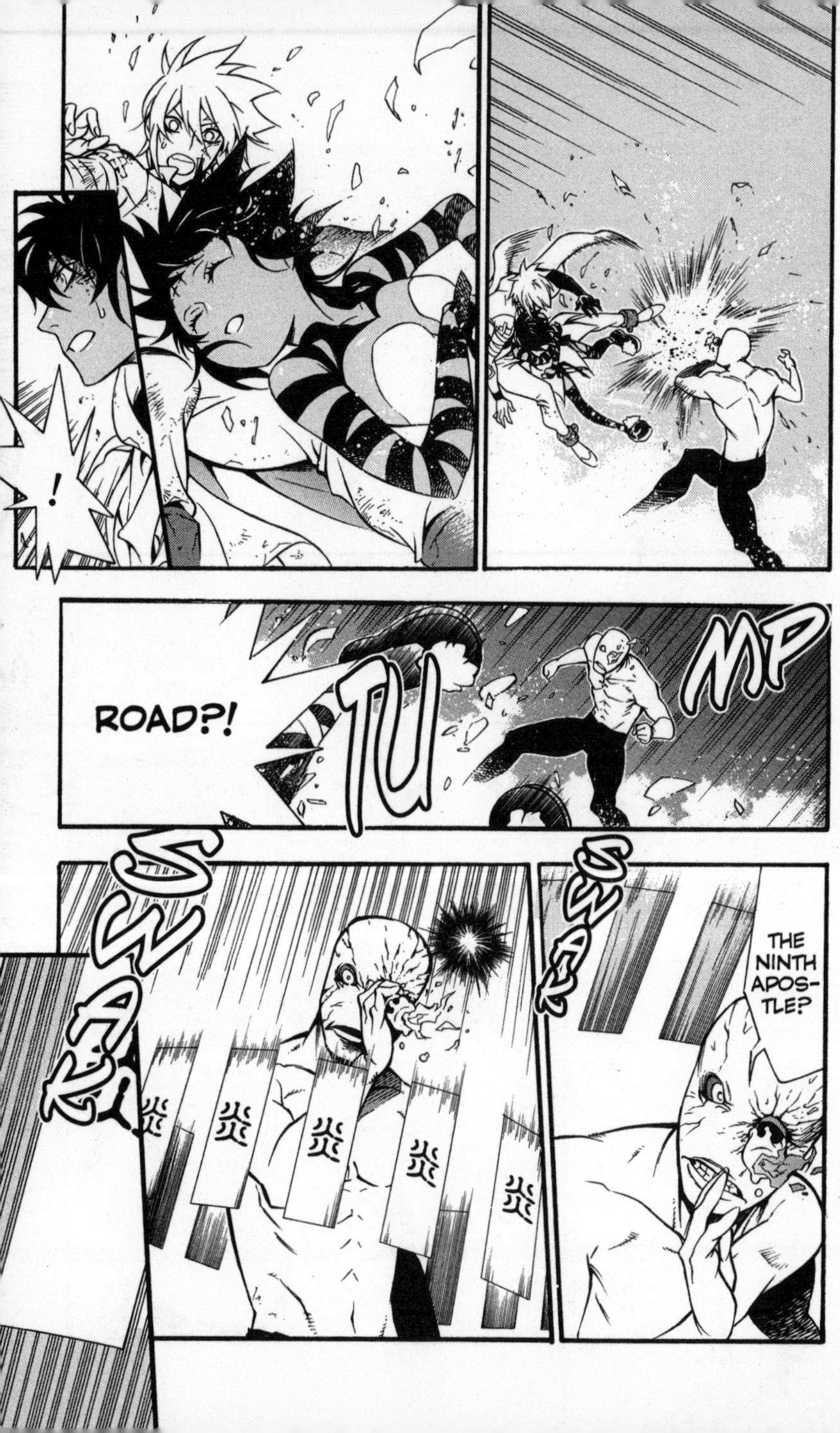
!
TU MP
ROAD?!
SWAK
THE NINTH APOSTLE?
SWAK
炎
炎
炎
炎
炎
炎

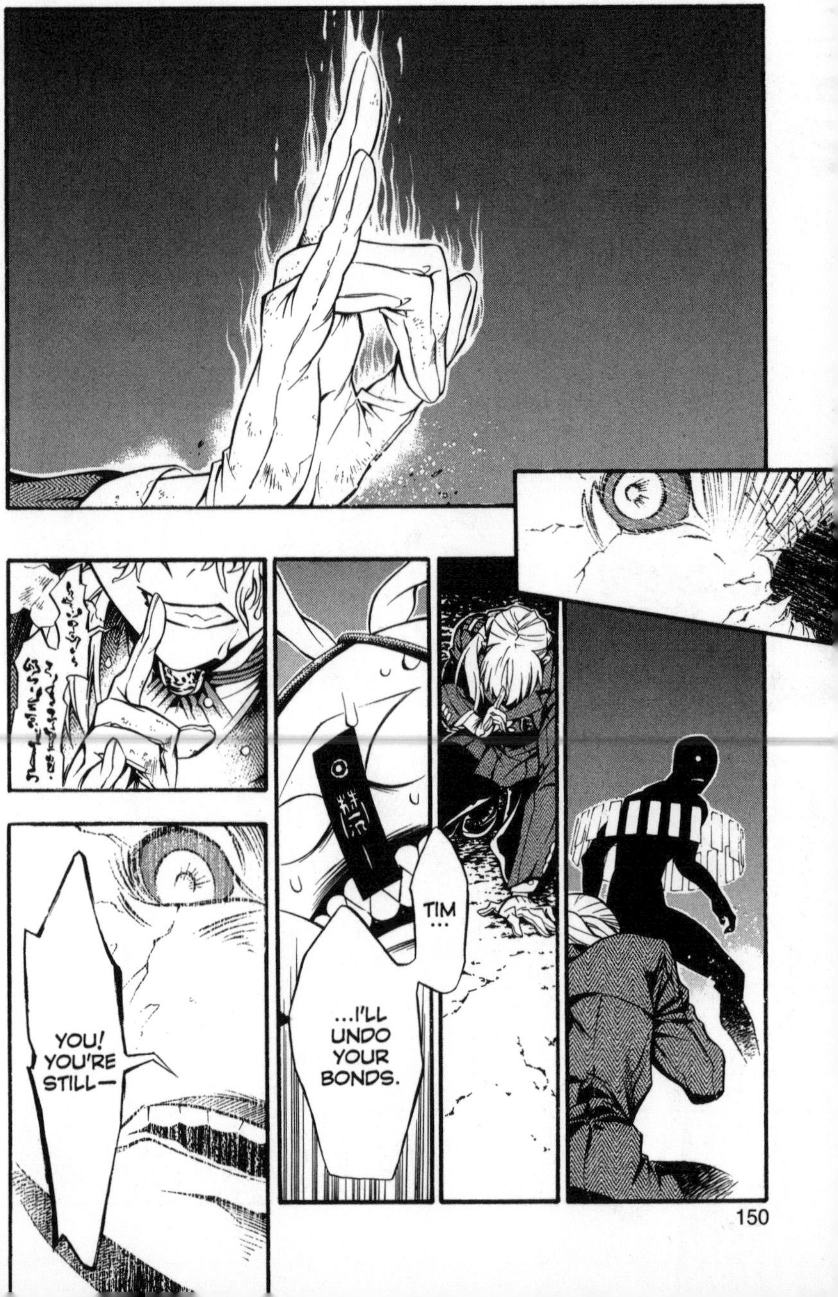
TIM ...
...I'LL UNDO YOUR BONDS.
YOU! YOU'RE STILL—

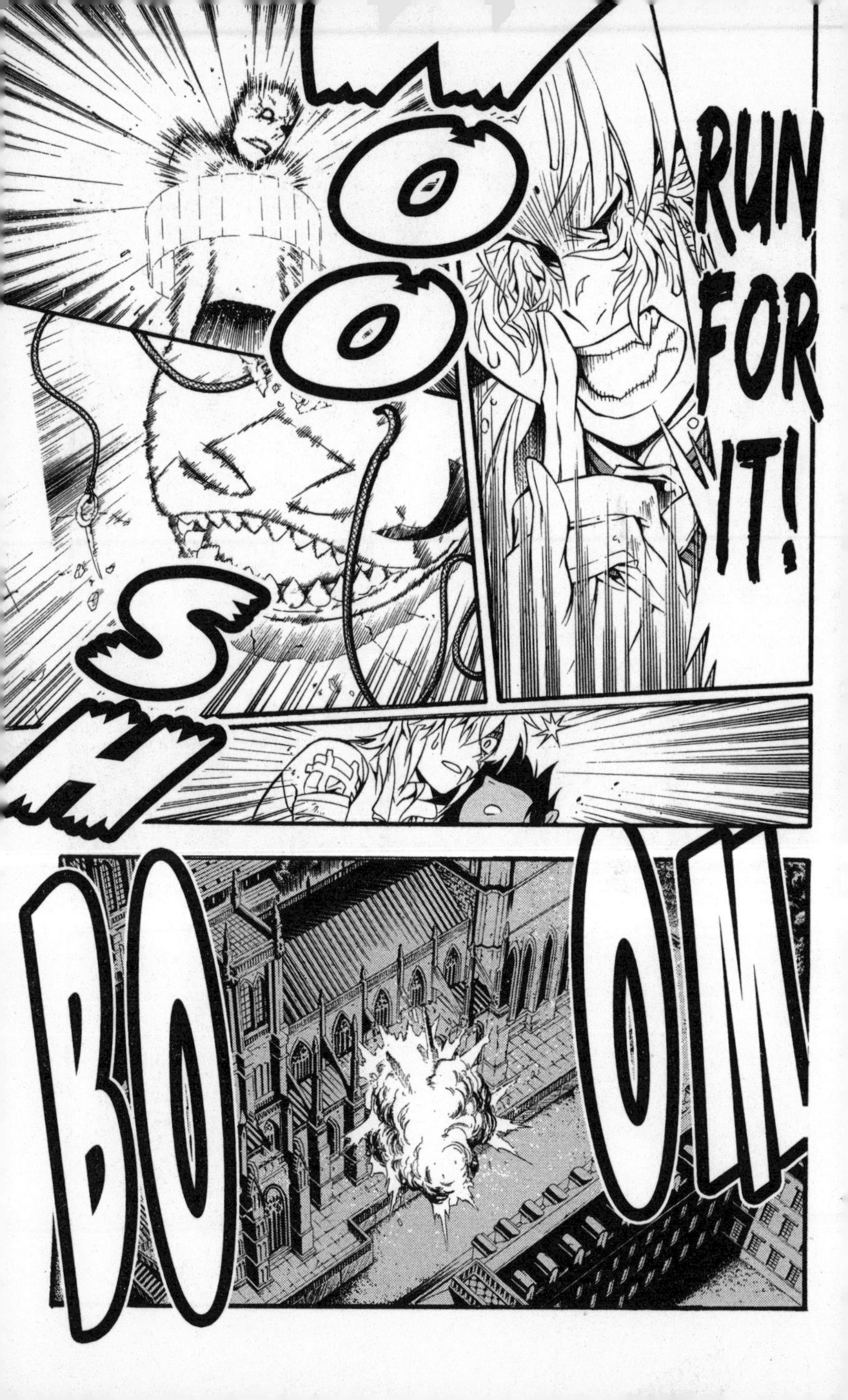
RUN FOR IT!
WOOSH
BOOM

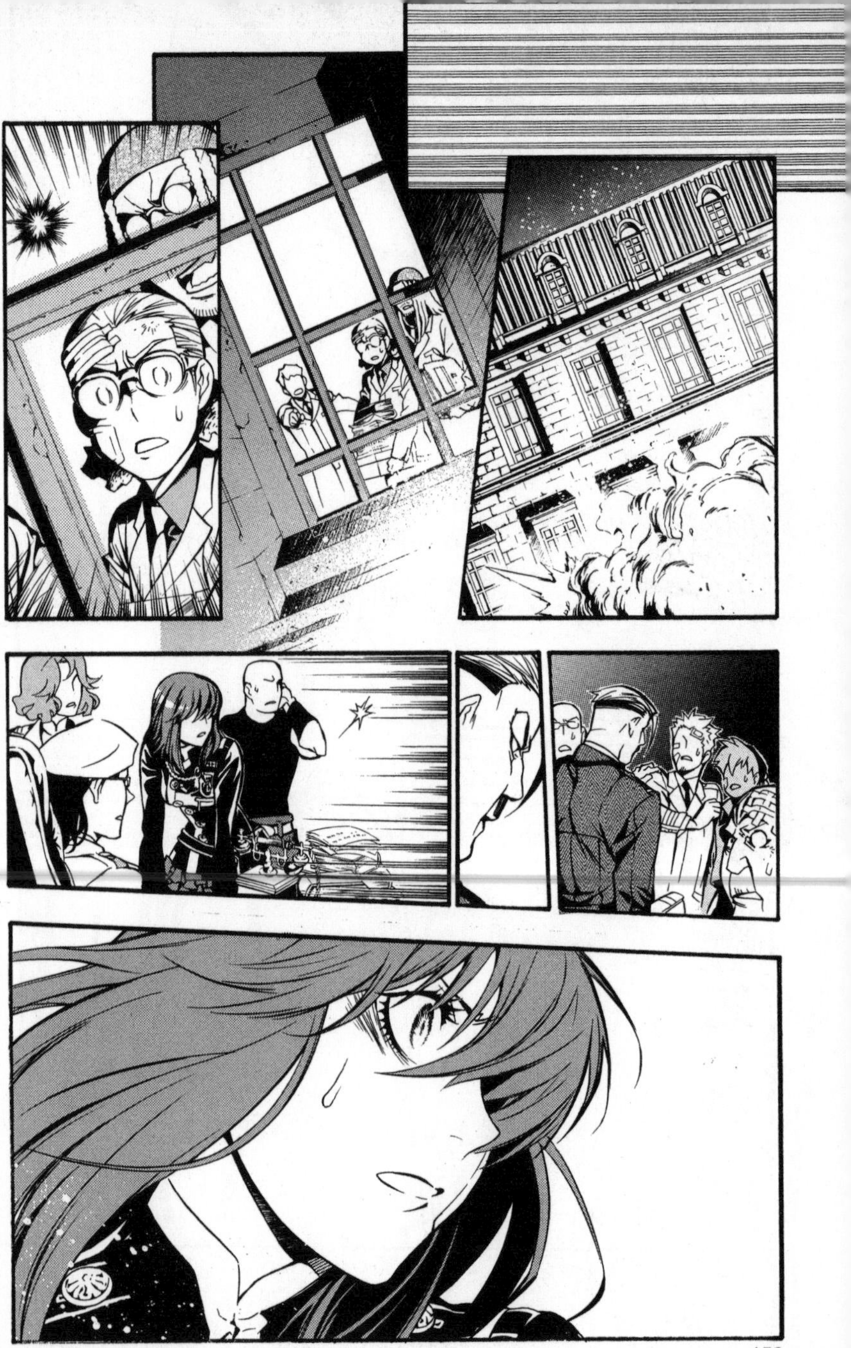

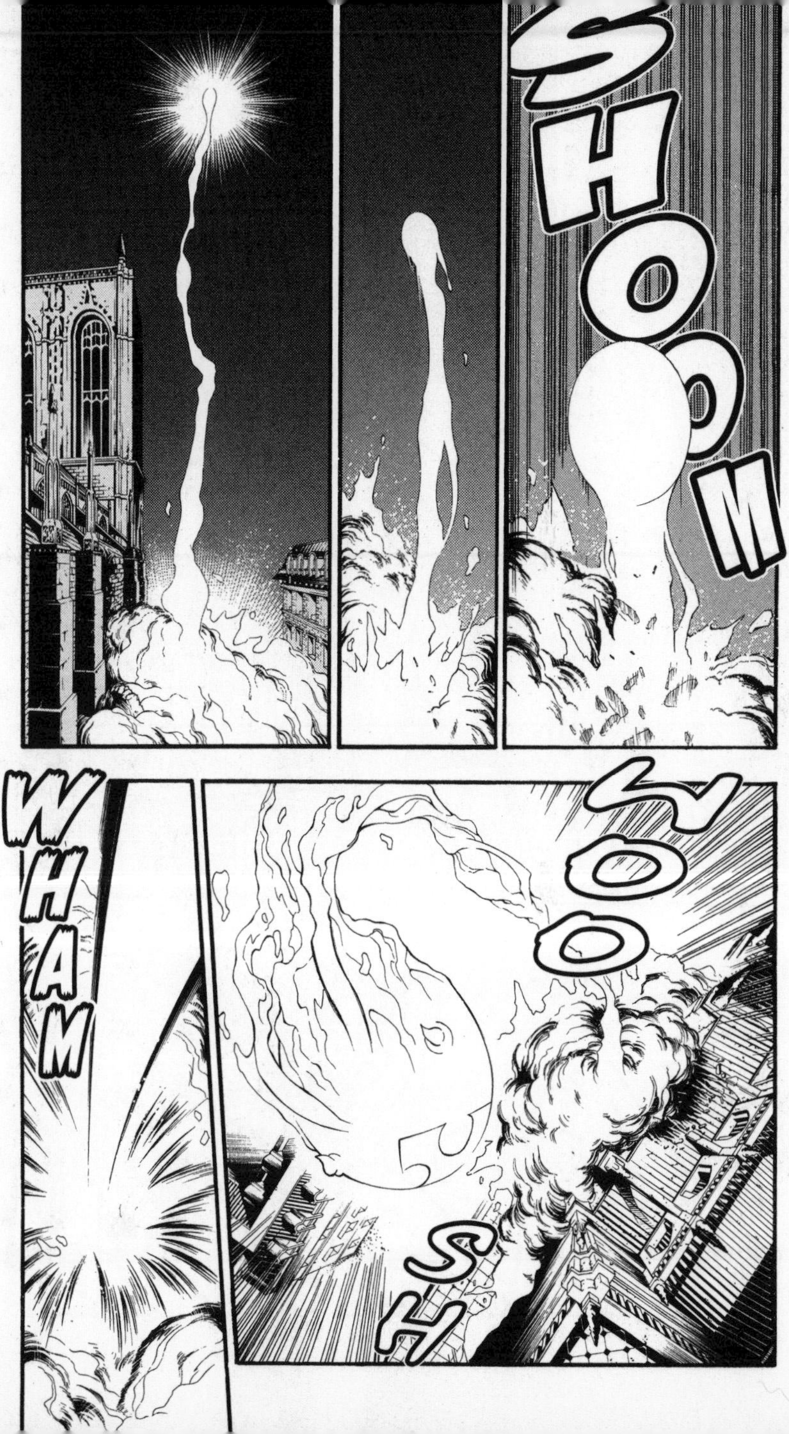
SHOOOM
WOOSH
WHAM

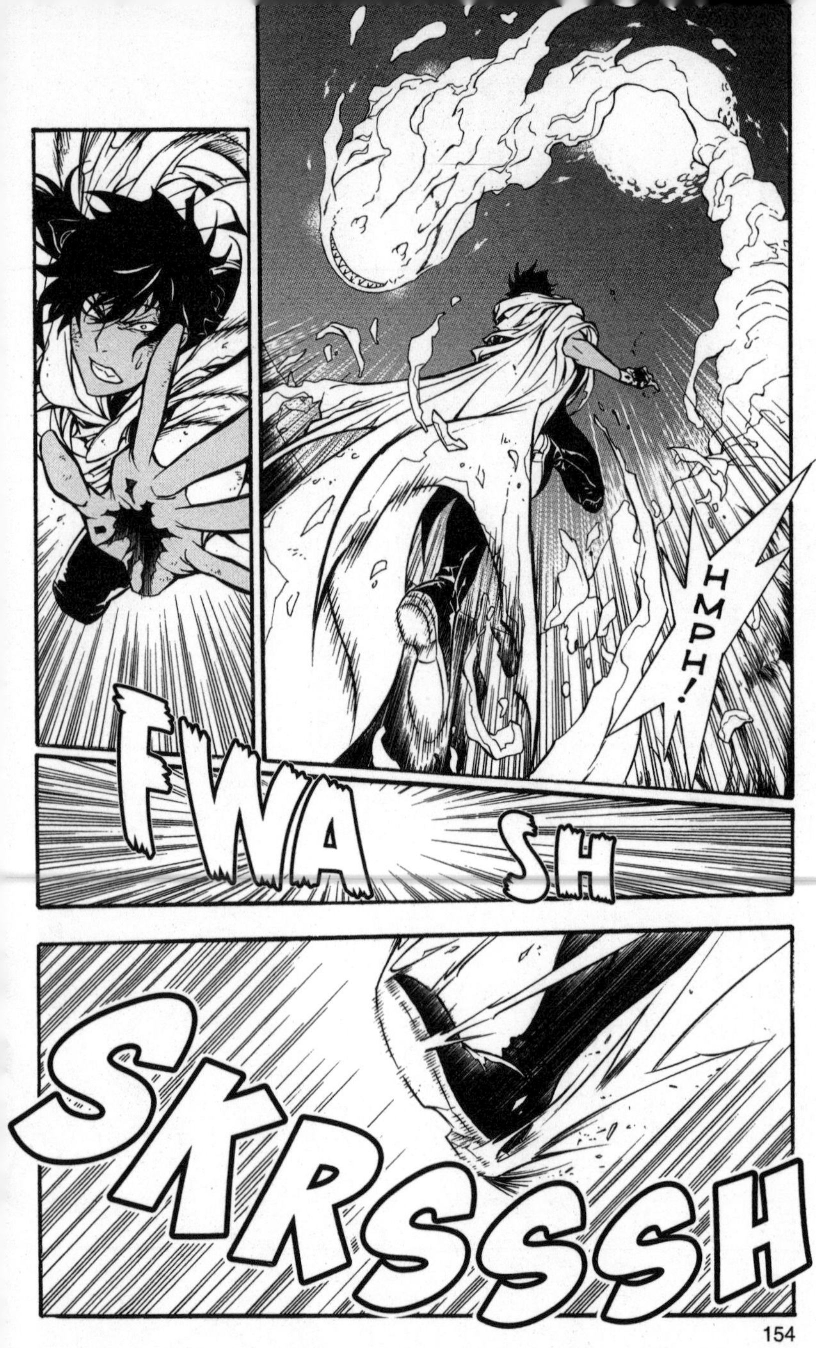
HMPH!
FWASH
SKRSSSH

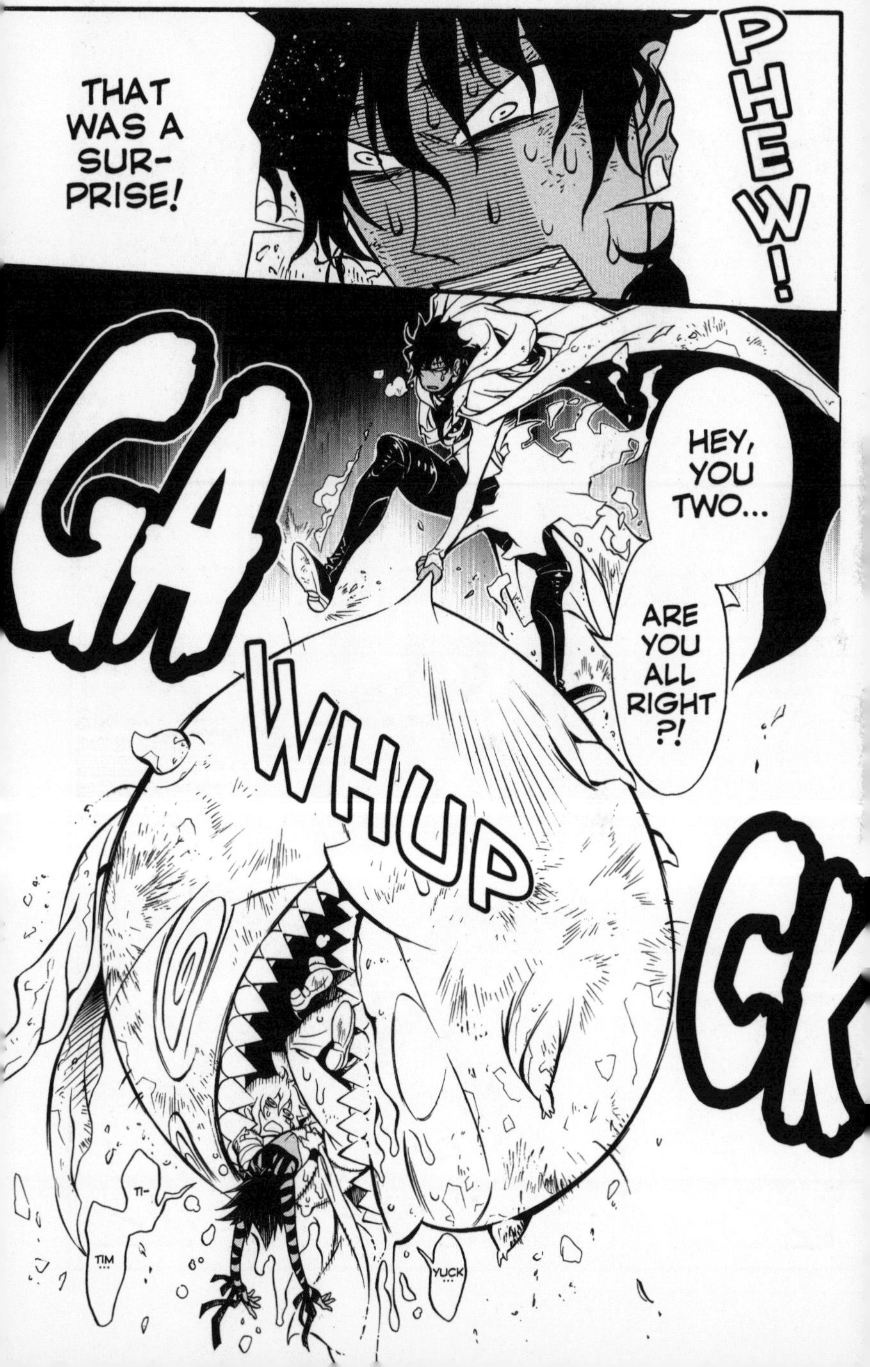
PHEW!
THAT WAS A SURPRISE!
HEY, YOU TWO...
ARE YOU ALL RIGHT?!
GA
WHUP
GK
YUCK...
TI-
TIM...

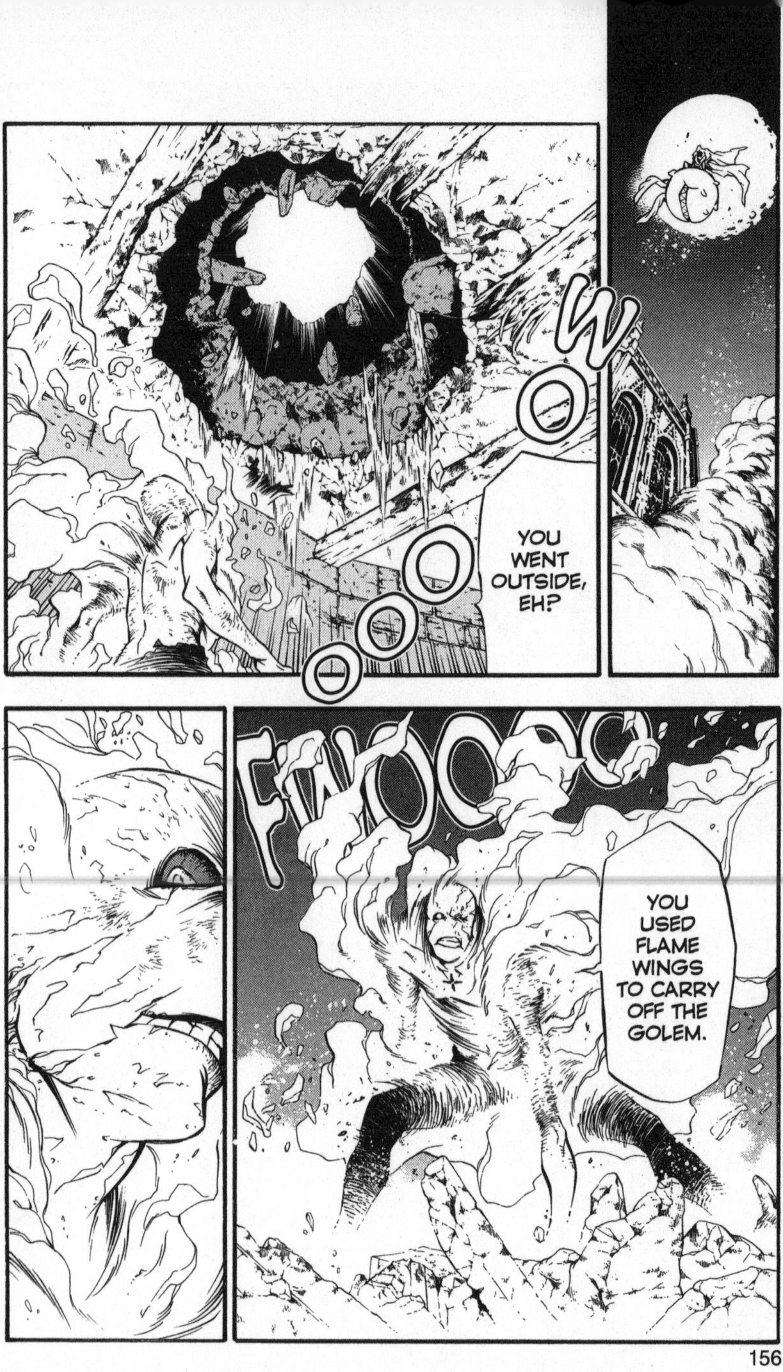
WOOOOO
YOU WENT OUTSIDE, EH?
FWOOOO
YOU USED FLAME WINGS TO CARRY OFF THE GOLEM.

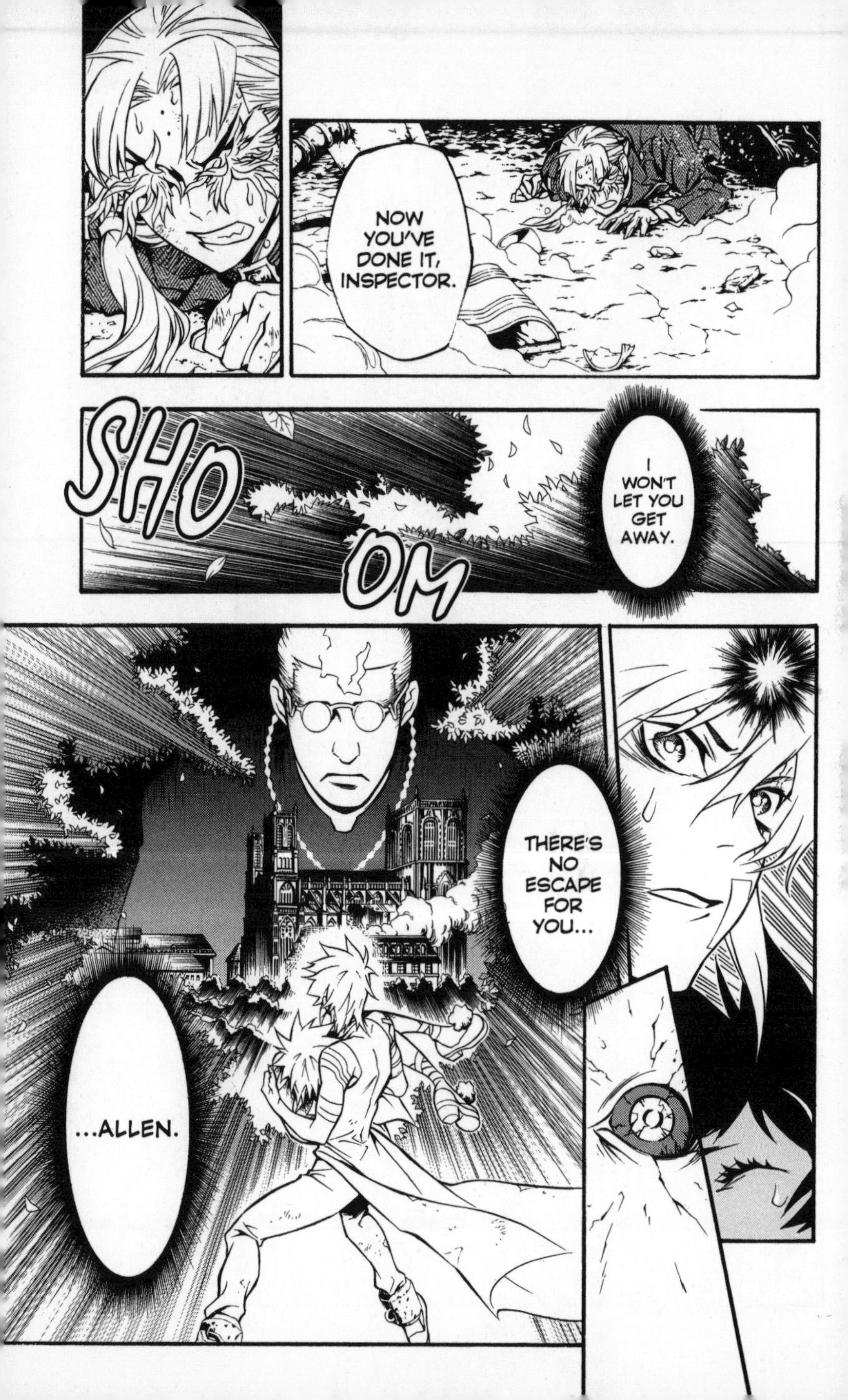
NOW YOU'VE DONE IT, INSPECTOR.
I WON'T LET YOU GET AWAY.
SHOOM
THERE'S NO ESCAPE FOR YOU...
...ALLEN.

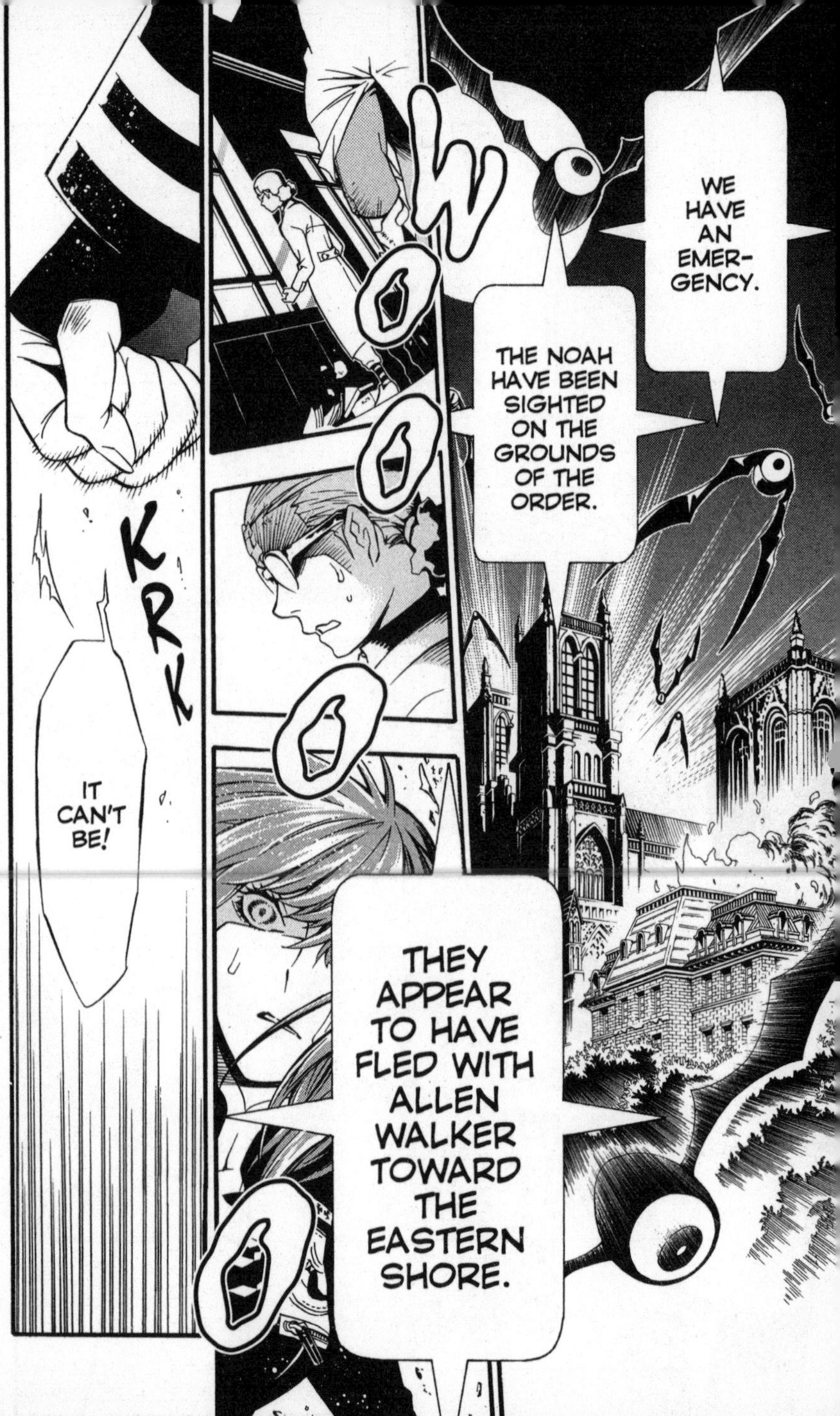
WE HAVE AN EMERGENCY.
THE NOAH HAVE BEEN SIGHTED ON THE GROUNDS OF THE ORDER.
THEY APPEAR TO HAVE FLED WITH ALLEN WALKER TOWARD THE EASTERN SHORE.
WOOOOO
KRK
IT CAN'T BE!

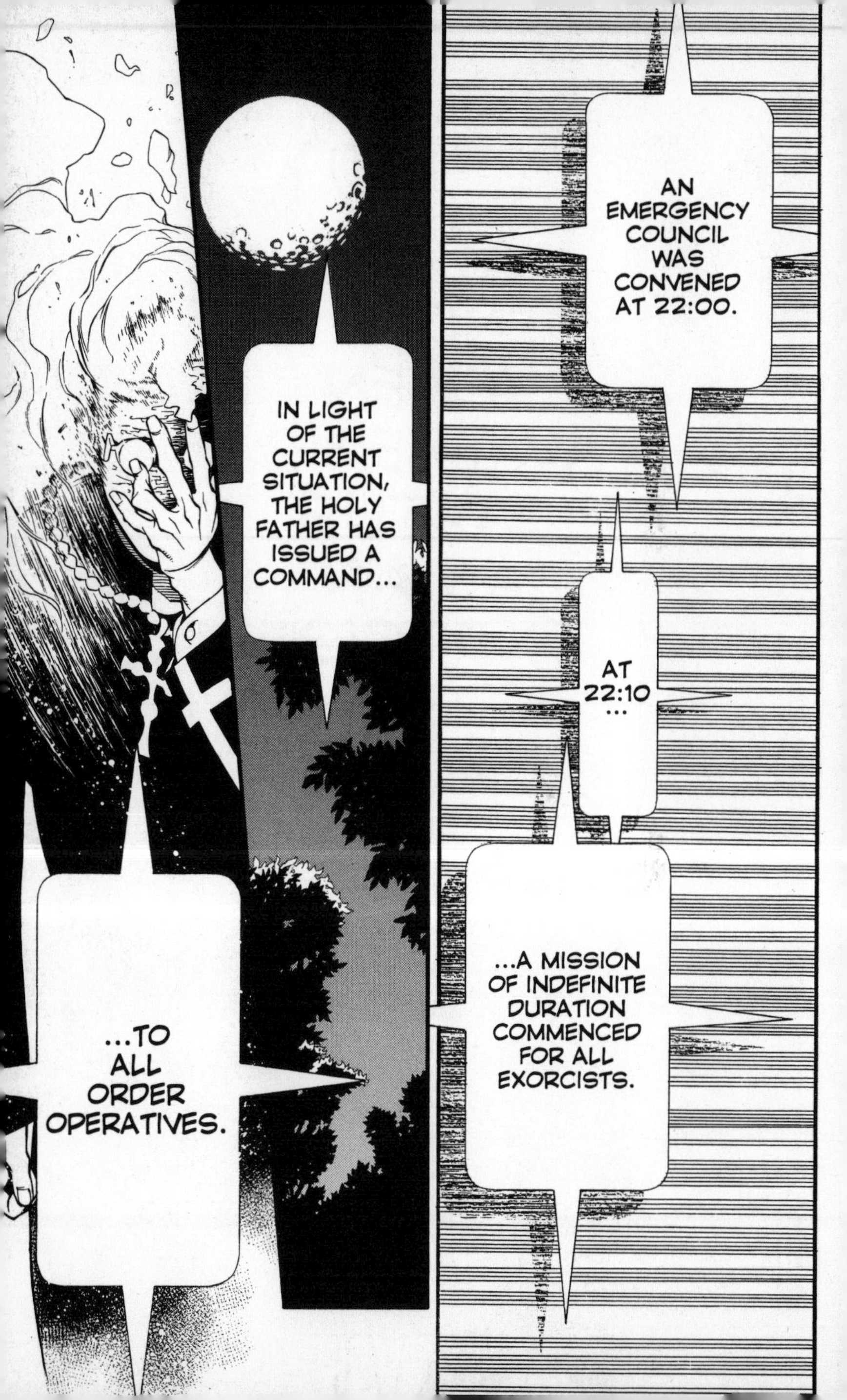
AN EMERGENCY COUNCIL WAS CONVENED AT 22:00.
AT 22:10...
...A MISSION OF INDEFINITE DURATION COMMENCED FOR ALL EXORCISTS.
IN LIGHT OF THE CURRENT SITUATION, THE HOLY FATHER HAS ISSUED A COMMAND...
...TO ALL ORDER OPERATIVES.

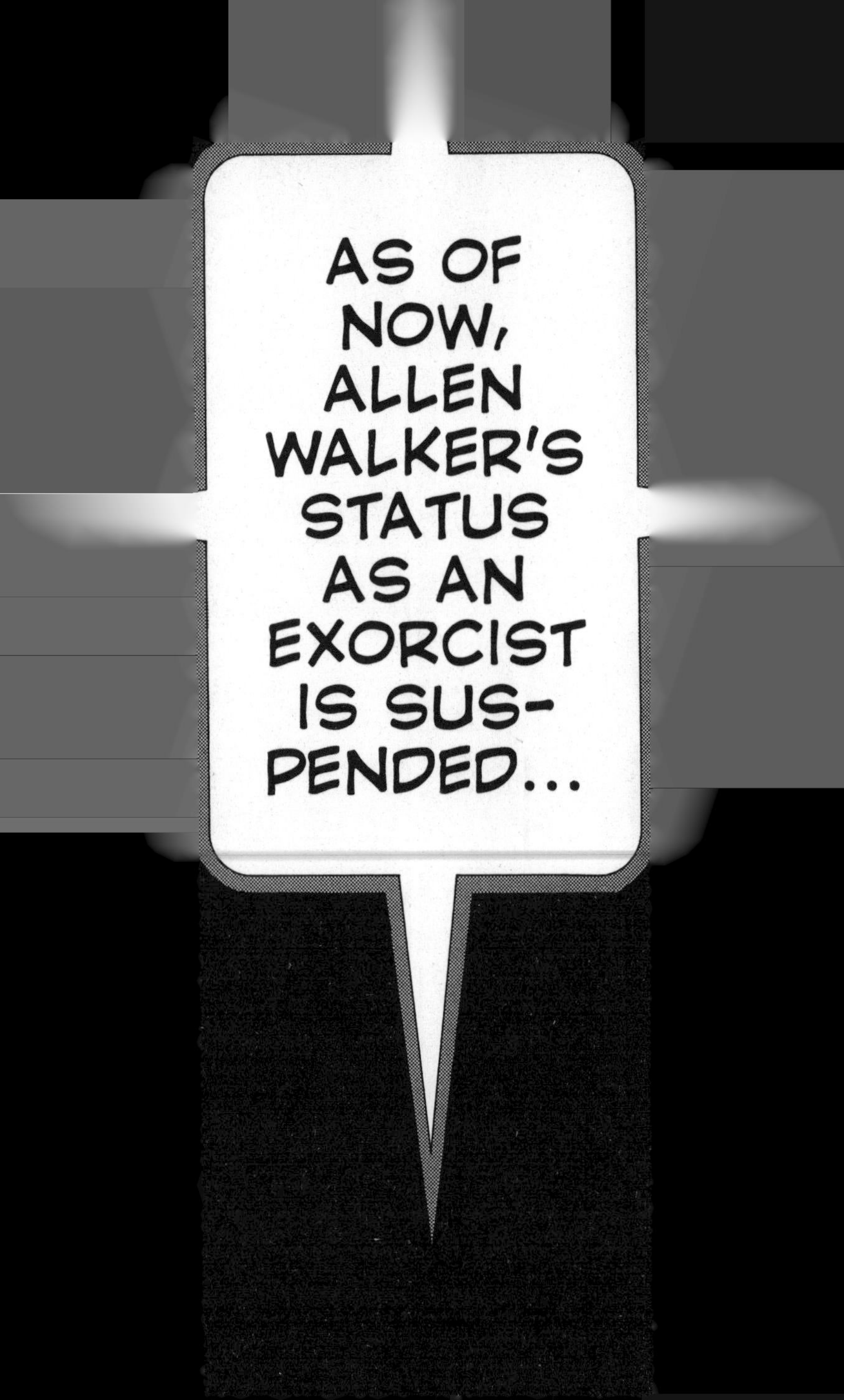
AS OF NOW, ALLEN WALKER'S STATUS AS AN EXORCIST IS SUS-PENDED...

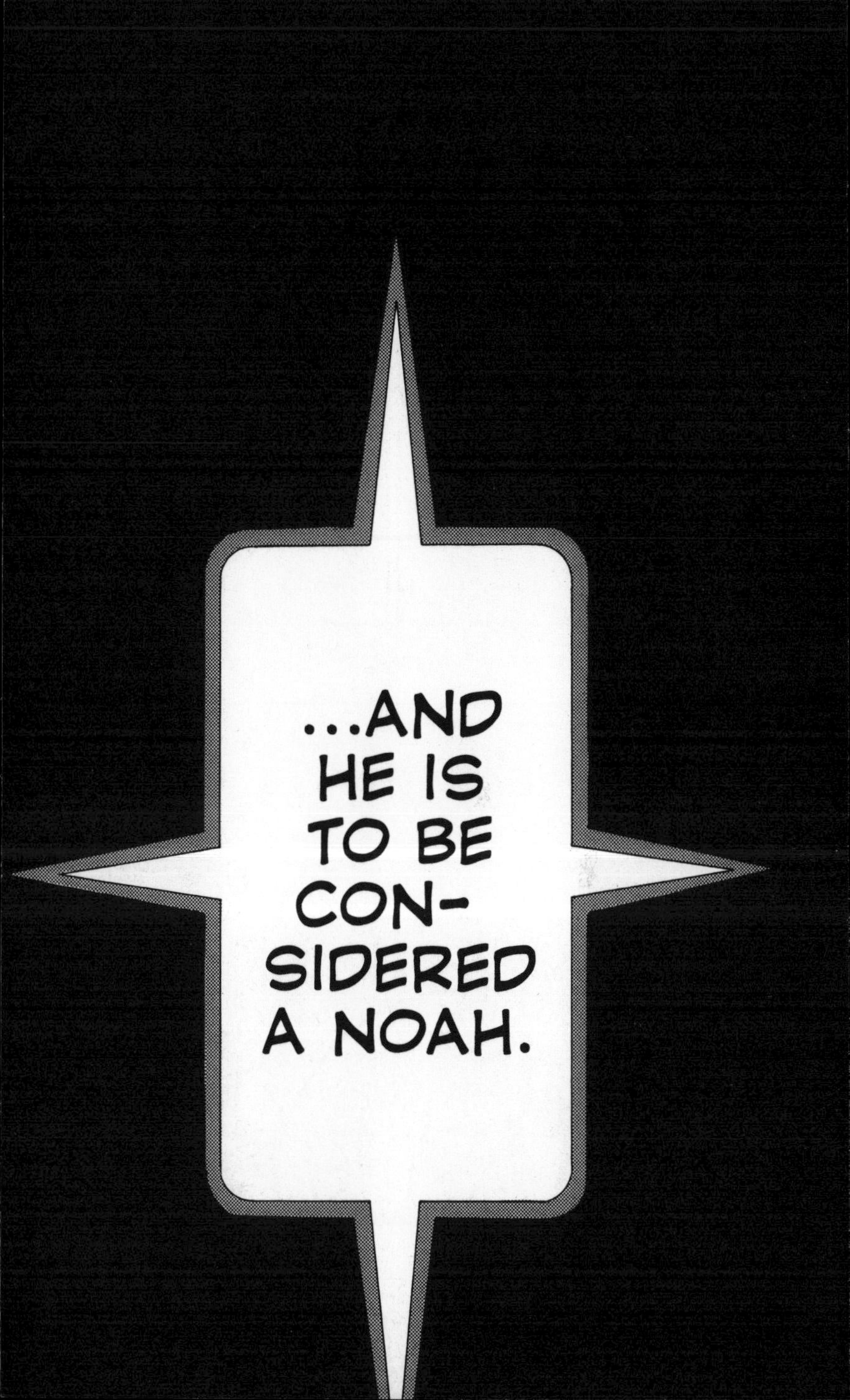
...AND HE IS TO BE CON-SIDERED A NOAH.

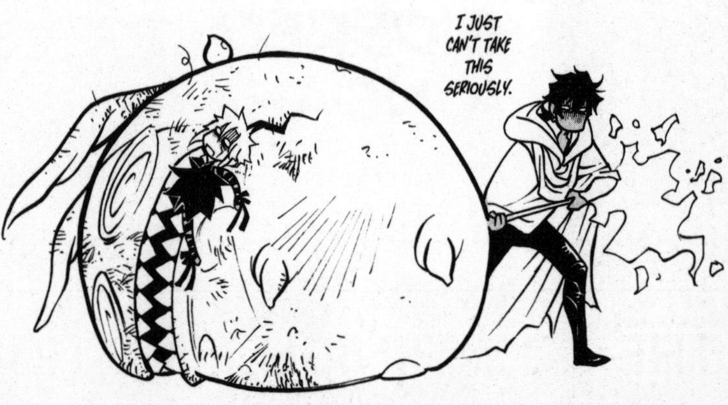
I JUST CAN'T TAKE THIS SERIOUSLY.

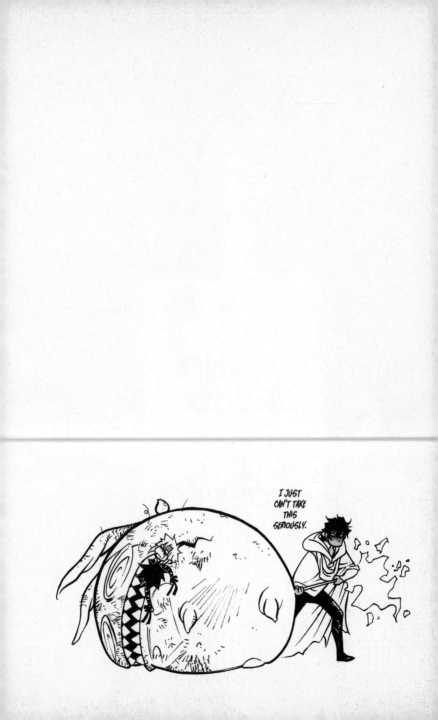

THE 205TH NIGHT: MY HOME

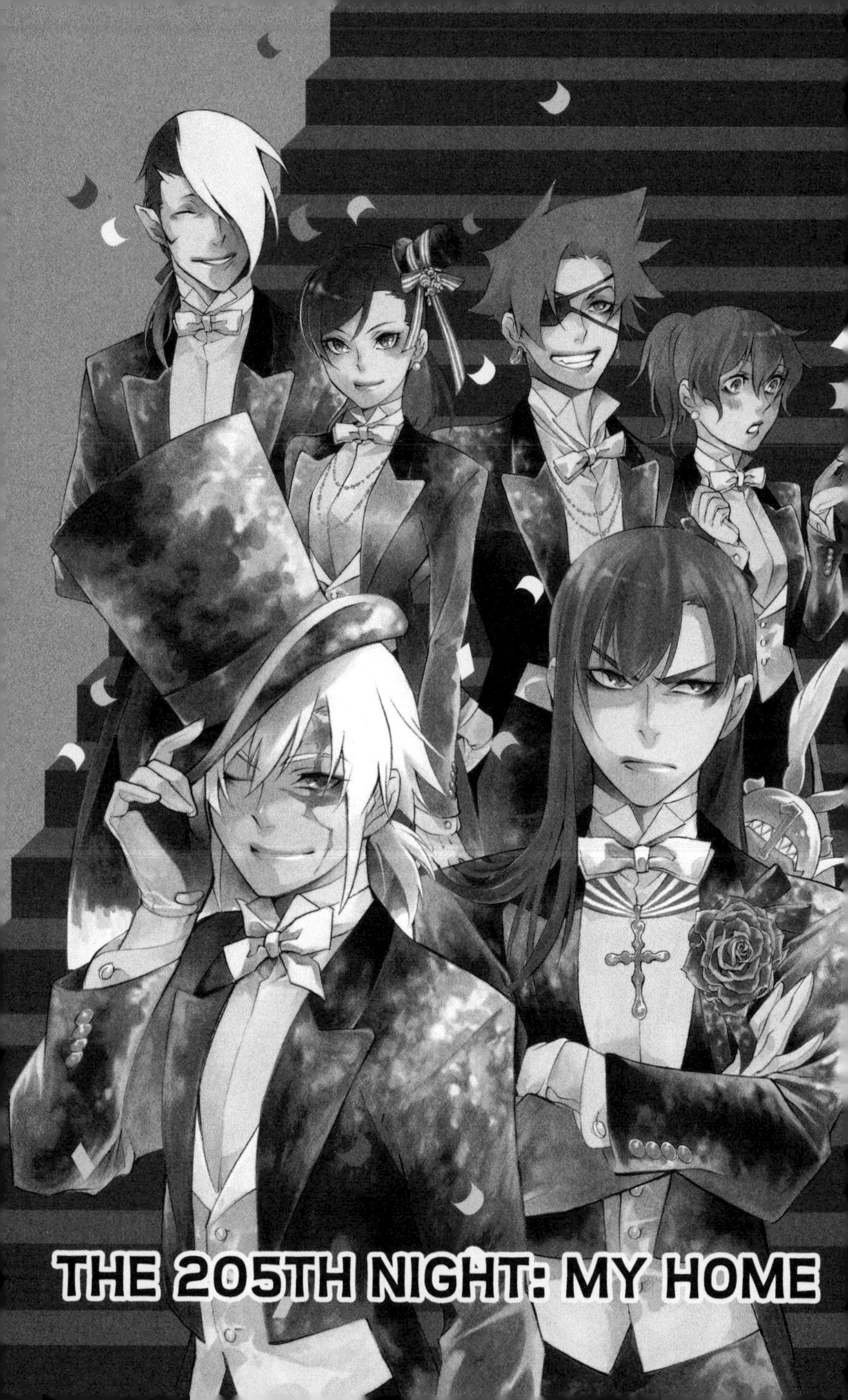

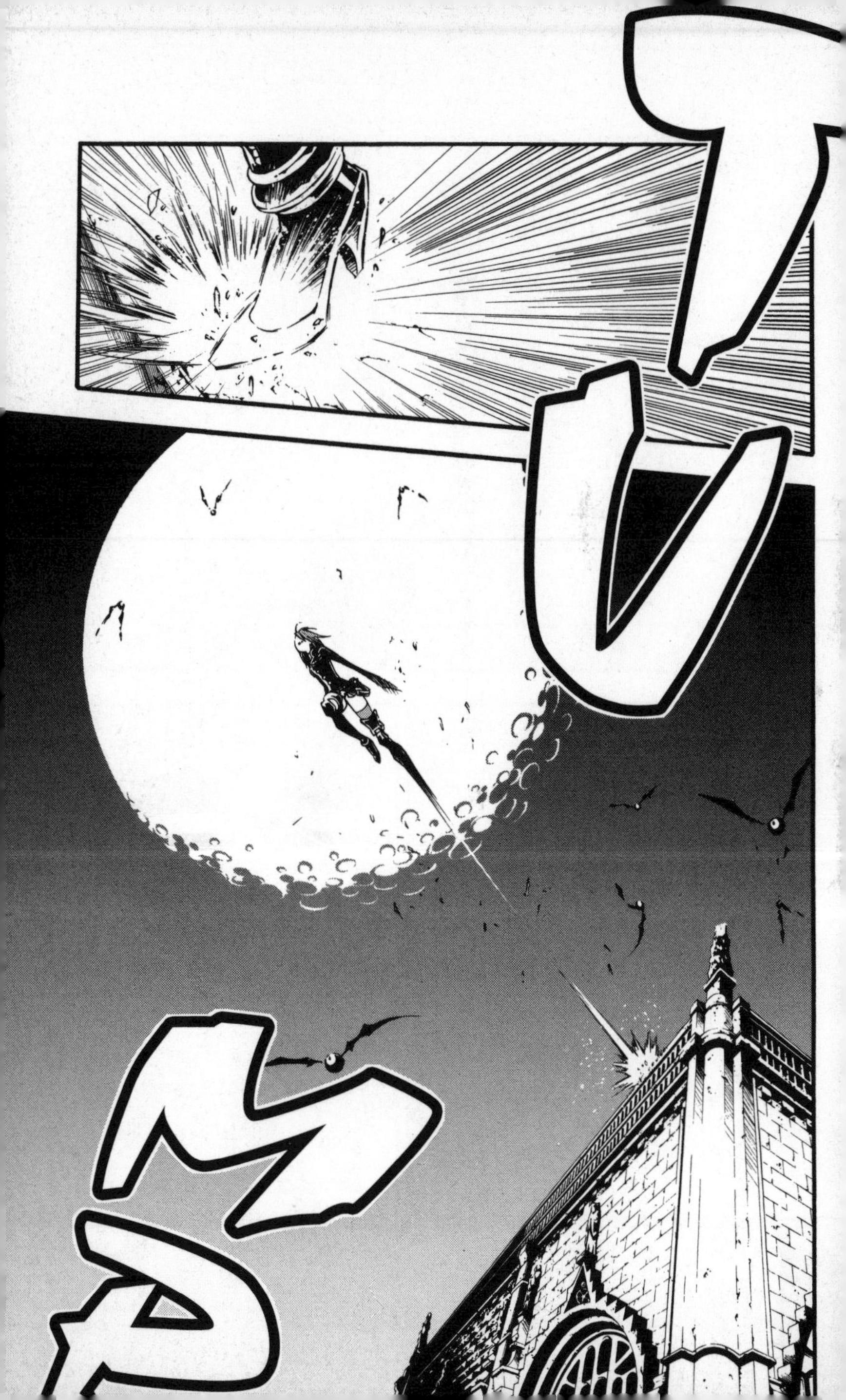

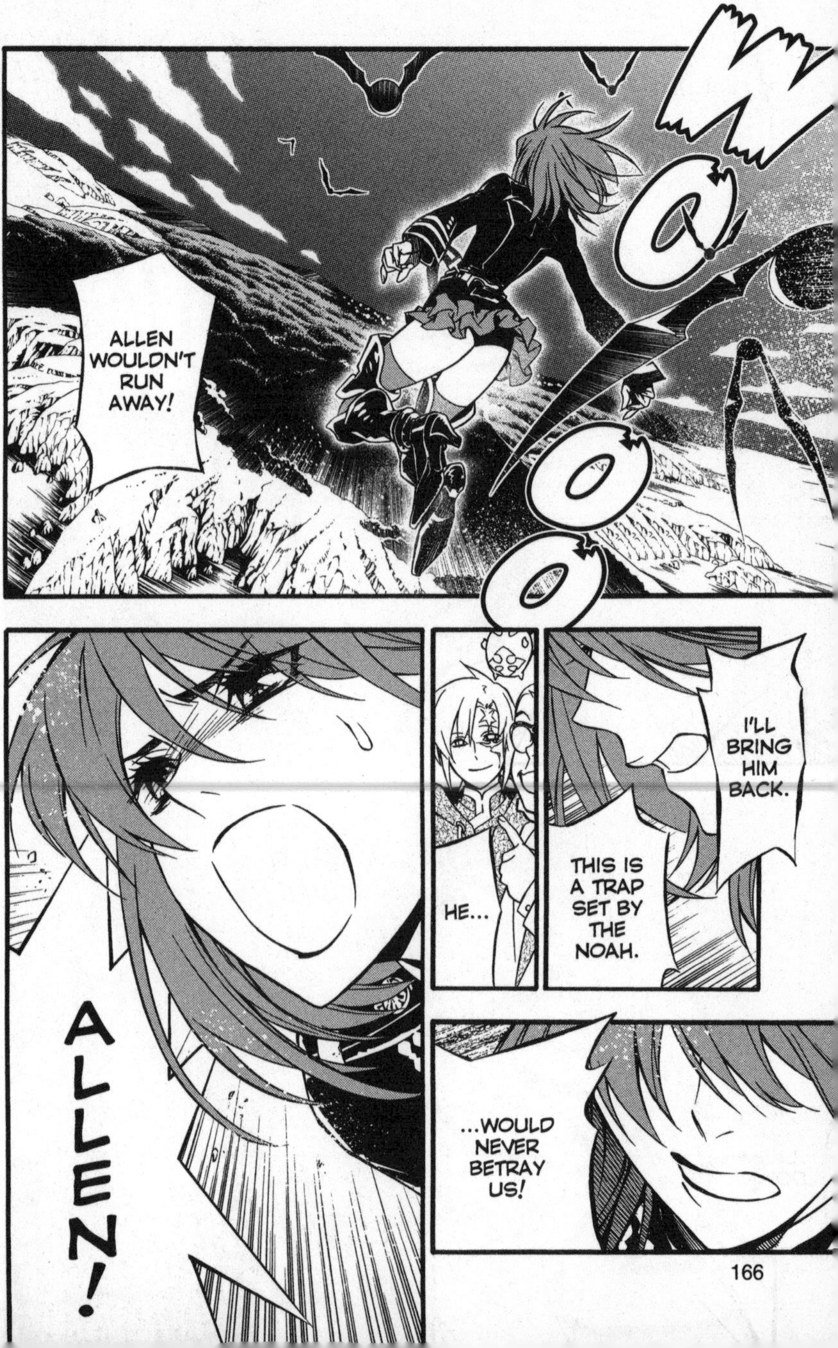
WOOO
ALLEN WOULDN'T RUN AWAY!
I'LL BRING HIM BACK.
THIS IS A TRAP SET BY THE NOAH.
HE...
...WOULD NEVER BETRAY US!
ALLEN!

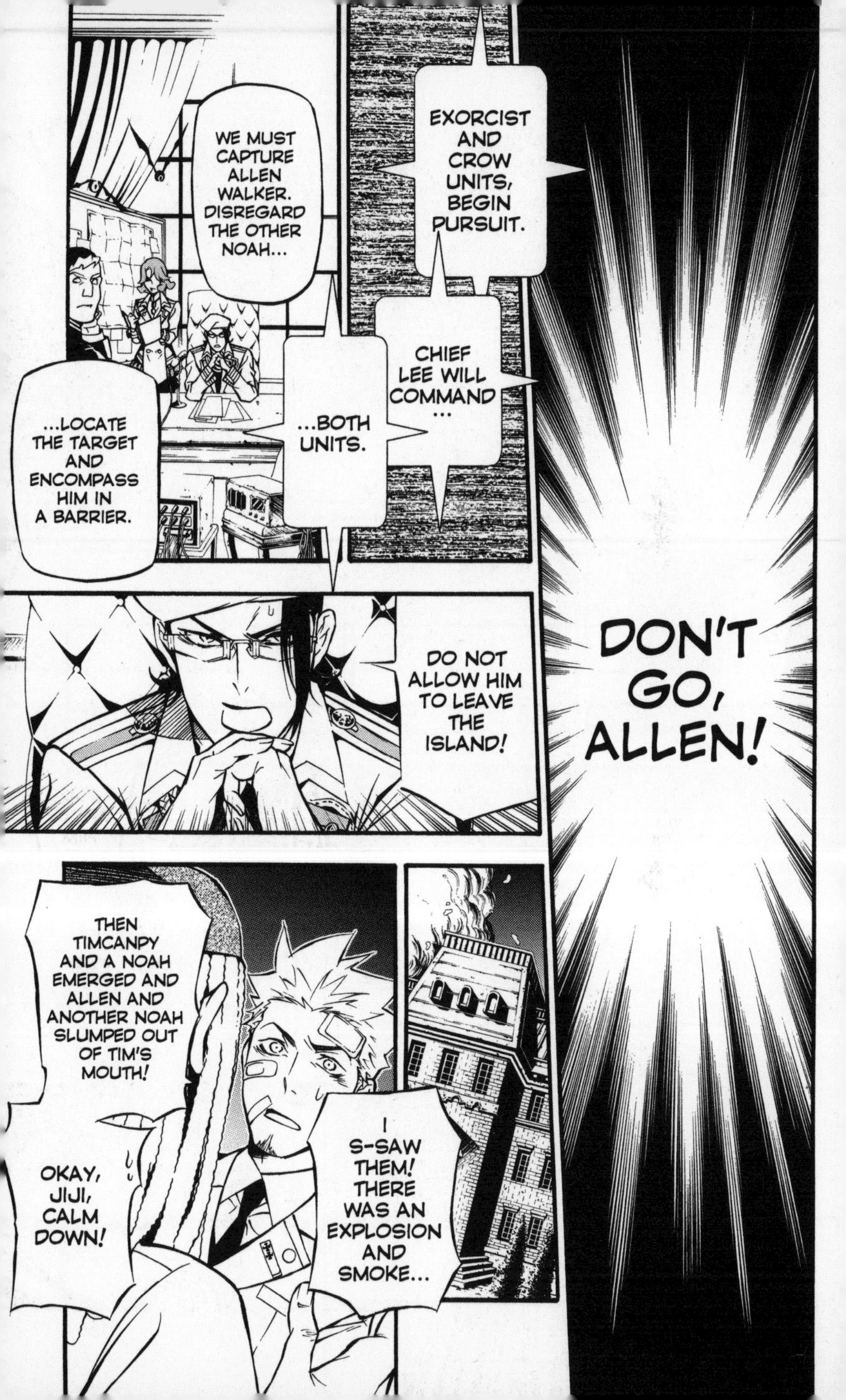
DON'T GO, ALLEN!
EXORCIST AND CROW UNITS, BEGIN PURSUIT.
WE MUST CAPTURE ALLEN WALKER. DISREGARD THE OTHER NOAH...
CHIEF LEE WILL COMMAND...
...BOTH UNITS.
...LOCATE THE TARGET AND ENCOMPASS HIM IN A BARRIER.
DO NOT ALLOW HIM TO LEAVE THE ISLAND!
I S-SAW THEM! THERE WAS AN EXPLOSION AND SMOKE...
THEN TIMCANPY AND A NOAH EMERGED AND ALLEN AND ANOTHER NOAH SLUMPED OUT OF TIM'S MOUTH!
OKAY, JIJI, CALM DOWN!

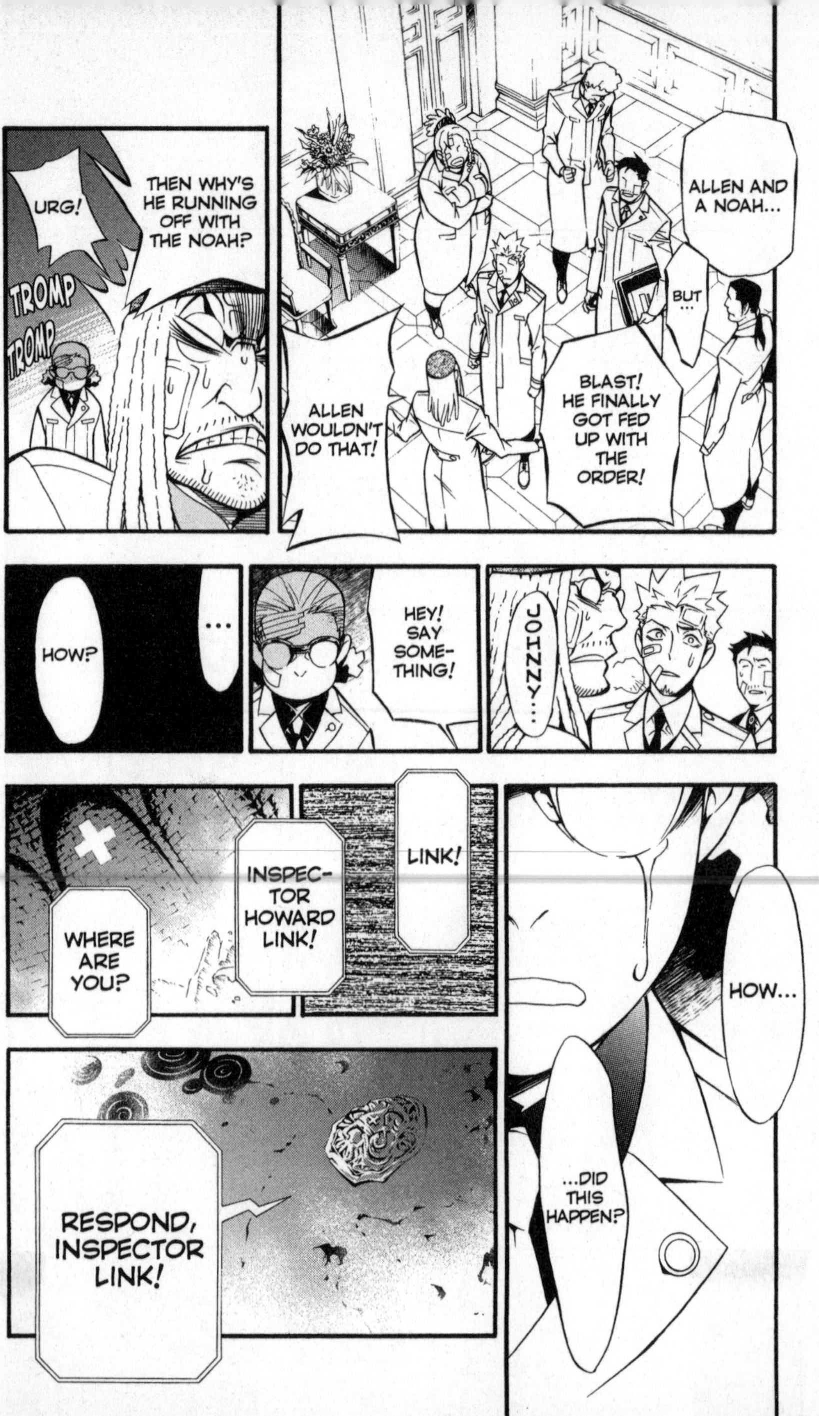

ALLEN AND A NOAH...
BUT ...
BLAST! HE FINALLY GOT FED UP WITH THE ORDER!
ALLEN WOULDN'T DO THAT!
THEN WHY'S HE RUNNING OFF WITH THE NOAH?
URG!
TROMP
TROMP
JOHNNY...
HEY! SAY SOMETHING!
...
HOW?
HOW...
...DID THIS HAPPEN?
LINK!
INSPECTOR HOWARD LINK!
WHERE ARE YOU?
RESPOND, INSPECTOR LINK!

READ THIS WAY

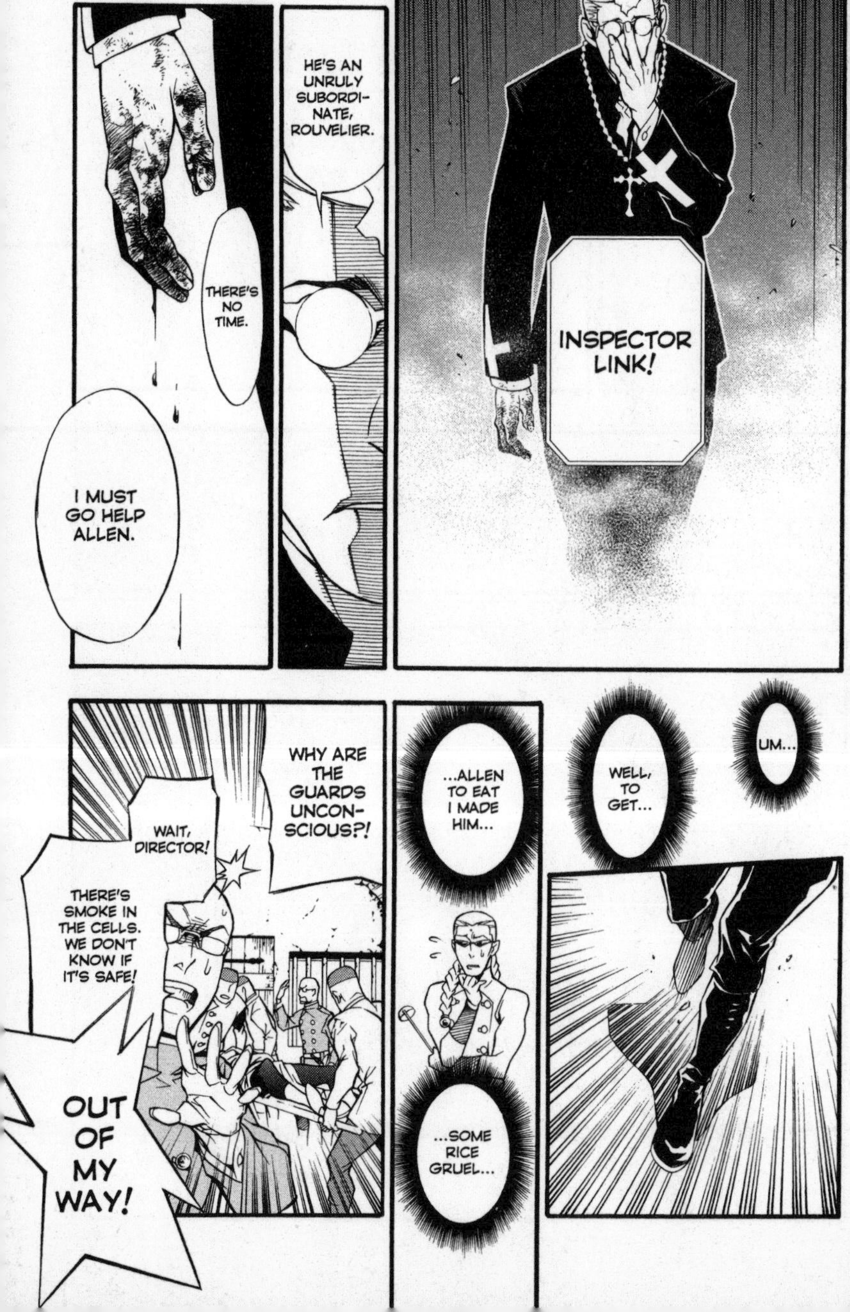
INSPECTOR LINK!
HE'S AN UNRULY SUBORDINATE, ROUVELIER.
THERE'S NO TIME.
I MUST GO HELP ALLEN.
UM...
WELL, TO GET...
...ALLEN TO EAT I MADE HIM...
...SOME RICE GRUEL...
WHY ARE THE GUARDS UNCONSCIOUS?!
WAIT, DIRECTOR!
THERE'S SMOKE IN THE CELLS. WE DON'T KNOW IF IT'S SAFE!
OUT OF MY WAY!

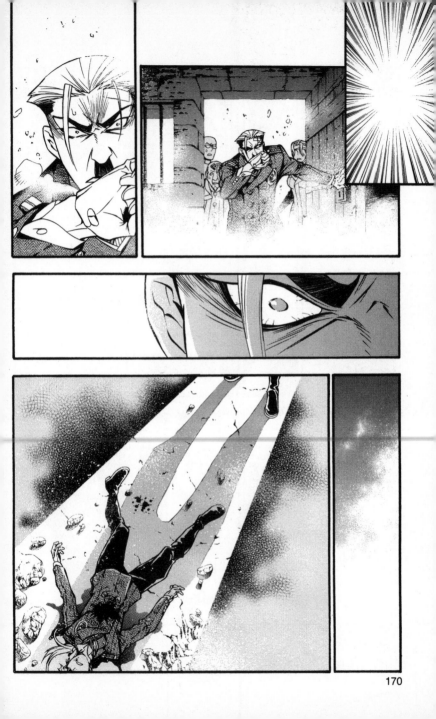

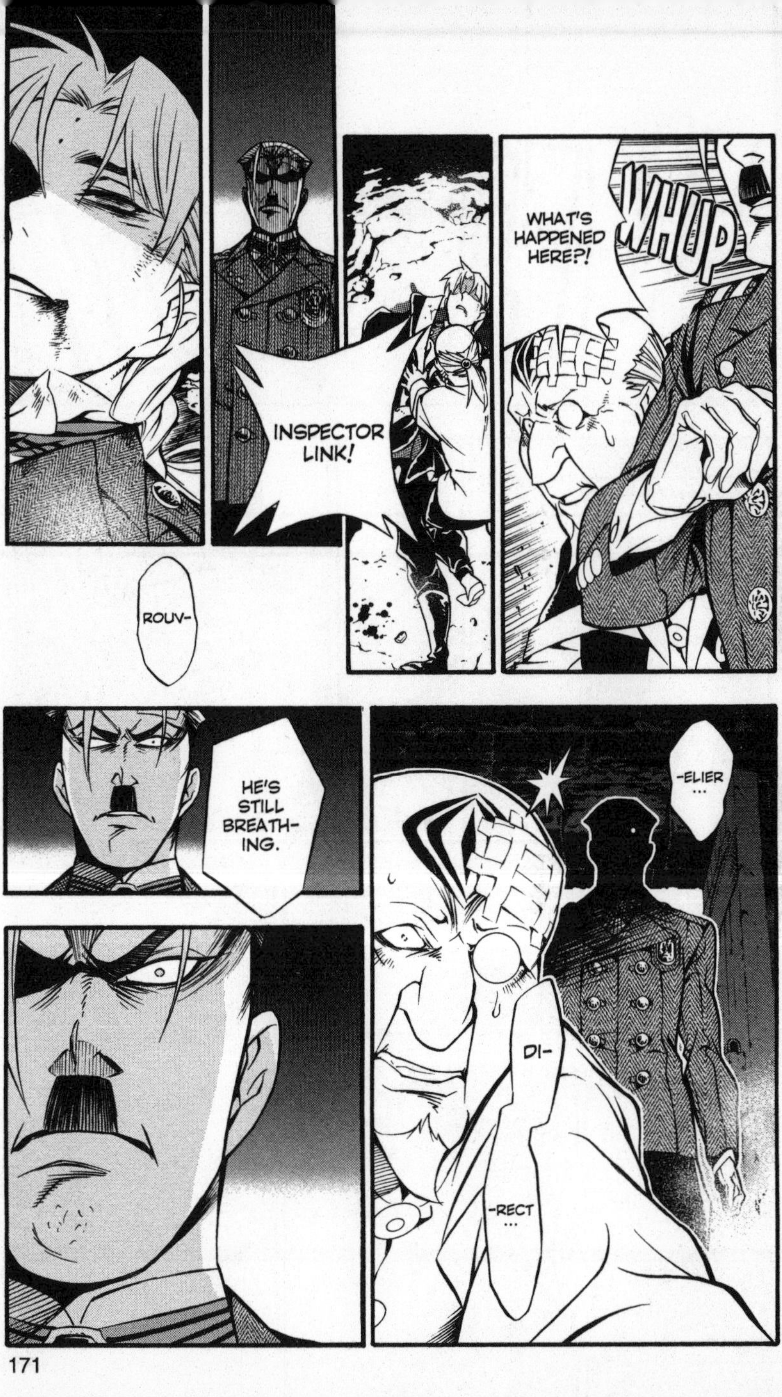
WHUP
WHAT'S HAPPENED HERE?!
INSPECTOR LINK!
ROUV-
-ELIER ...
DI-
-RECT ...
HE'S STILL BREATHING-ING.

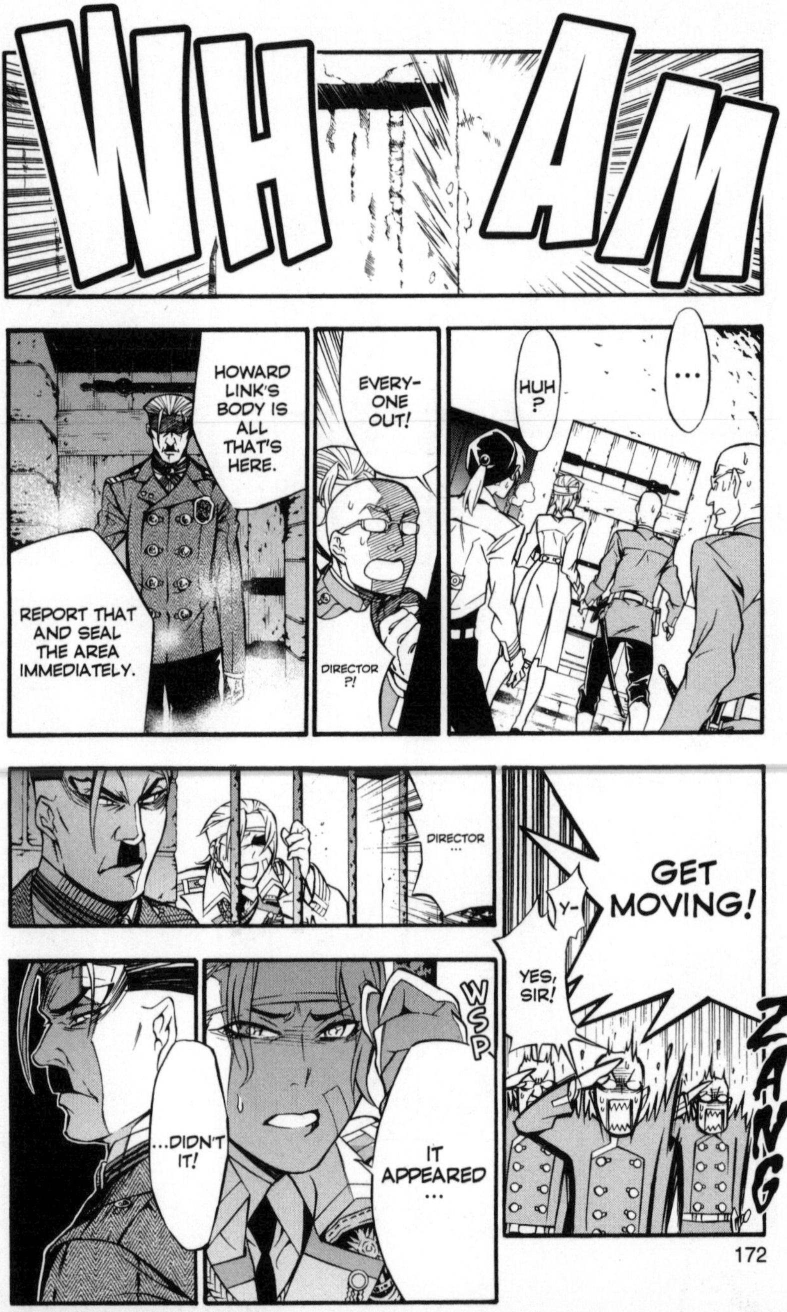
WH AM
...
HUH ?
EVERY-ONE OUT!
DIRECTOR ?!
HOWARD LINK'S BODY IS ALL THAT'S HERE.
REPORT THAT AND SEAL THE AREA IMMEDIATELY.
GET MOVING!
Y-
YES, SIR!
ZANG
DIRECTOR ...
WSP
IT APPEARED ...
...DIDN'T IT!

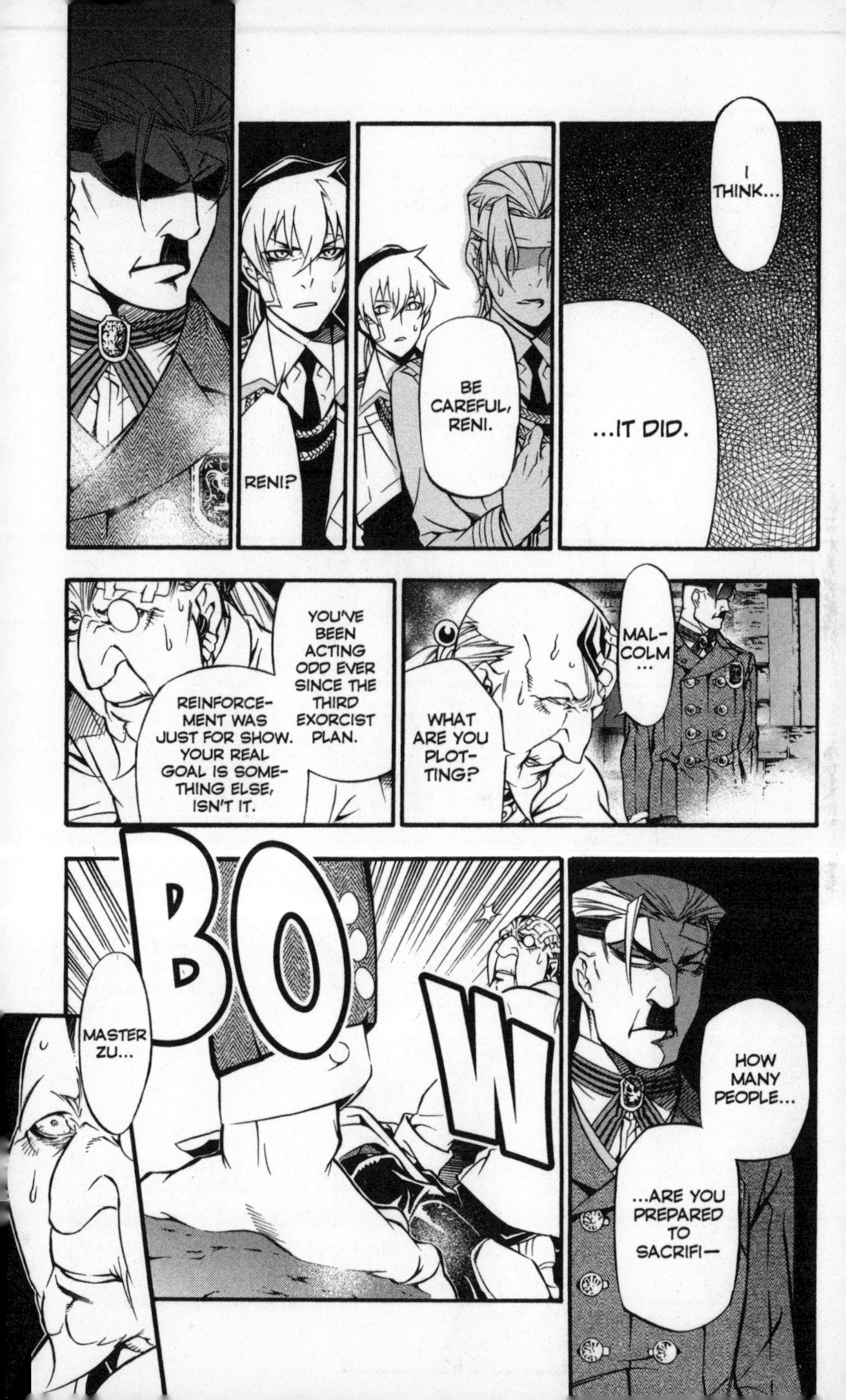

I THINK...
...IT DID.
BE CAREFUL, RENI.
RENI?
MAL-COLM...
WHAT ARE YOU PLOT-TING?
YOU'VE BEEN ACTING ODD EVER SINCE THE THIRD EXORCIST PLAN.
REINFORCE-MENT WAS JUST FOR SHOW. YOUR REAL GOAL IS SOME-THING ELSE, ISN'T IT.
HOW MANY PEOPLE...
...ARE YOU PREPARED TO SACRIFI—
BOW
MASTER ZU...

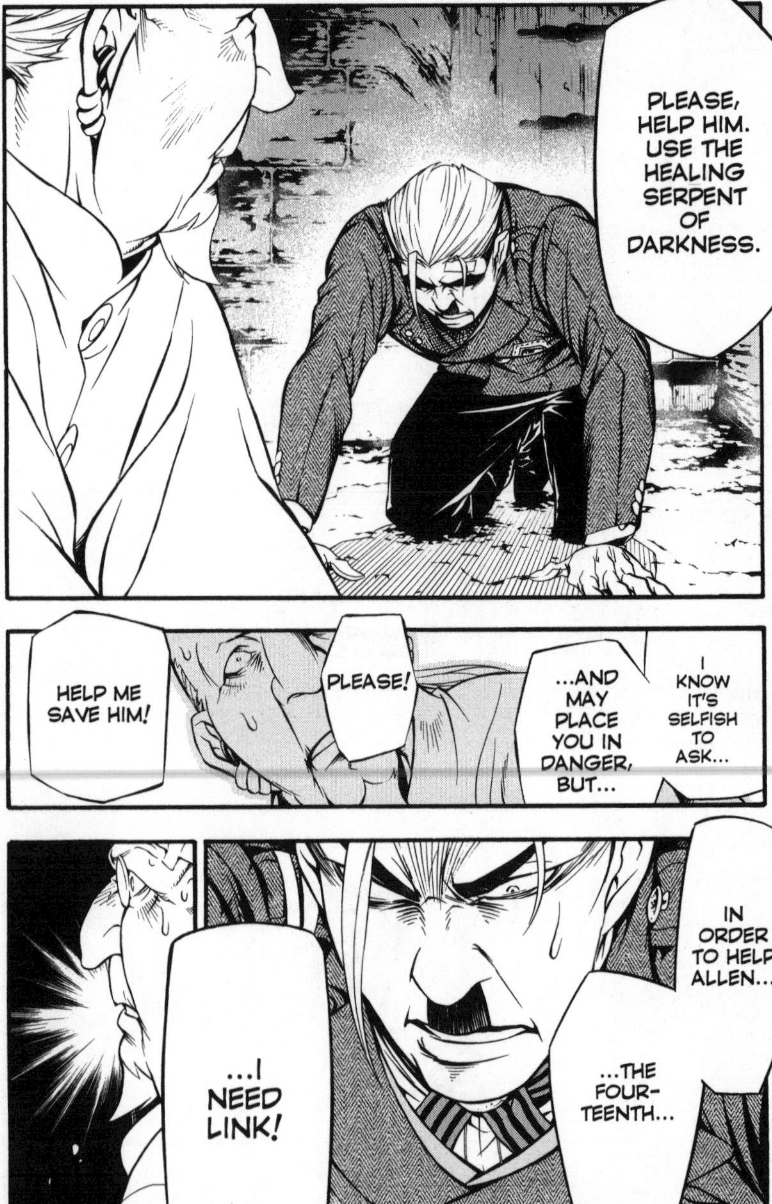
PLEASE, HELP HIM. USE THE HEALING SERPENT OF DARKNESS.
I KNOW IT'S SELFISH TO ASK...
...AND MAY PLACE YOU IN DANGER, BUT...
PLEASE!
HELP ME SAVE HIM!
IN ORDER TO HELP ALLEN...
...THE FOUR-TEENTH...
...I NEED LINK!

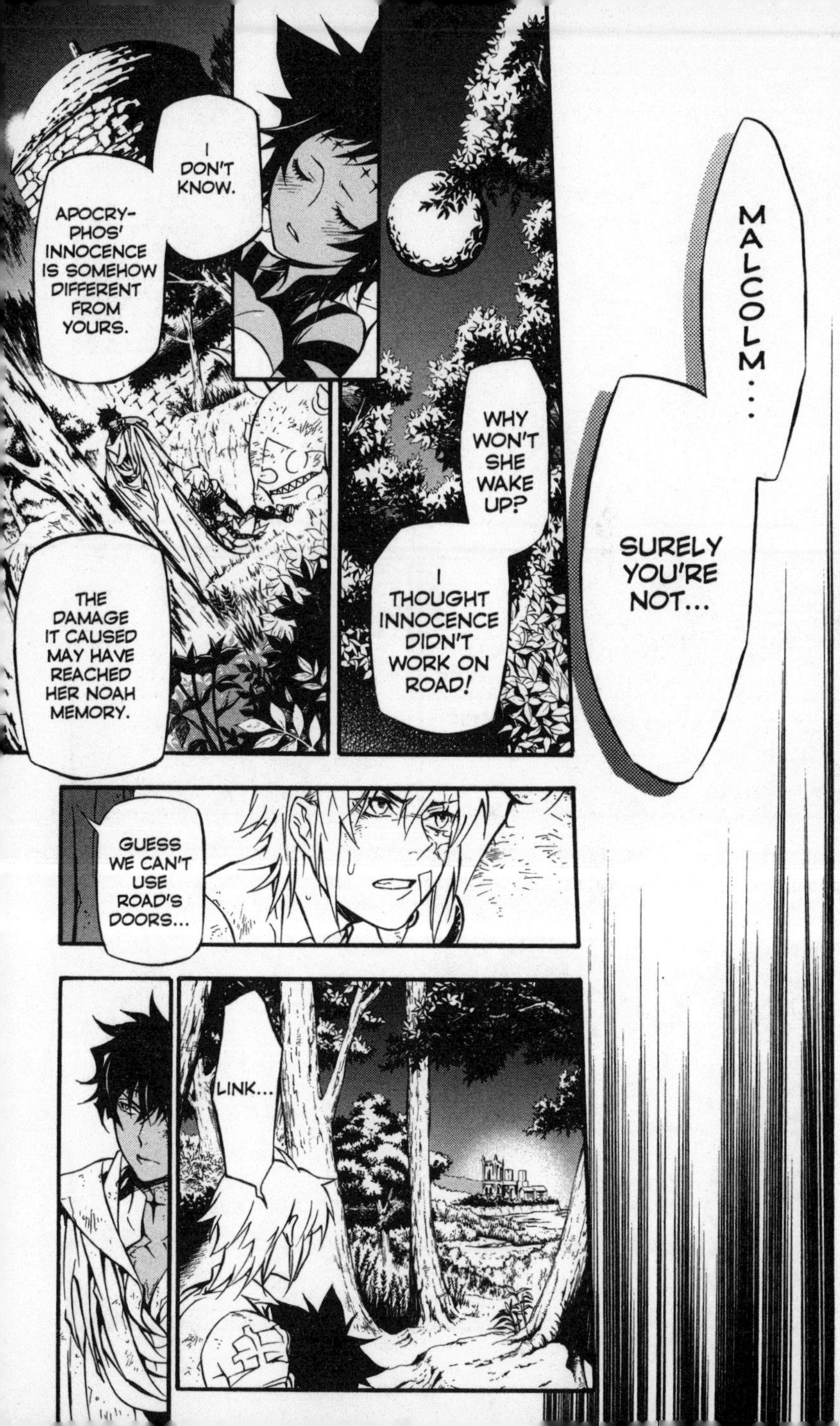
MALCOLM...
SURELY YOU'RE NOT...
WHY WON'T SHE WAKE UP?
I THOUGHT INNOCENCE DIDN'T WORK ON ROAD!
I DON'T KNOW.
APOCRYPHOS' INNOCENCE IS SOMEHOW DIFFERENT FROM YOURS.
THE DAMAGE IT CAUSED MAY HAVE REACHED HER NOAH MEMORY.
GUESS WE CAN'T USE ROAD'S DOORS...
LINK...

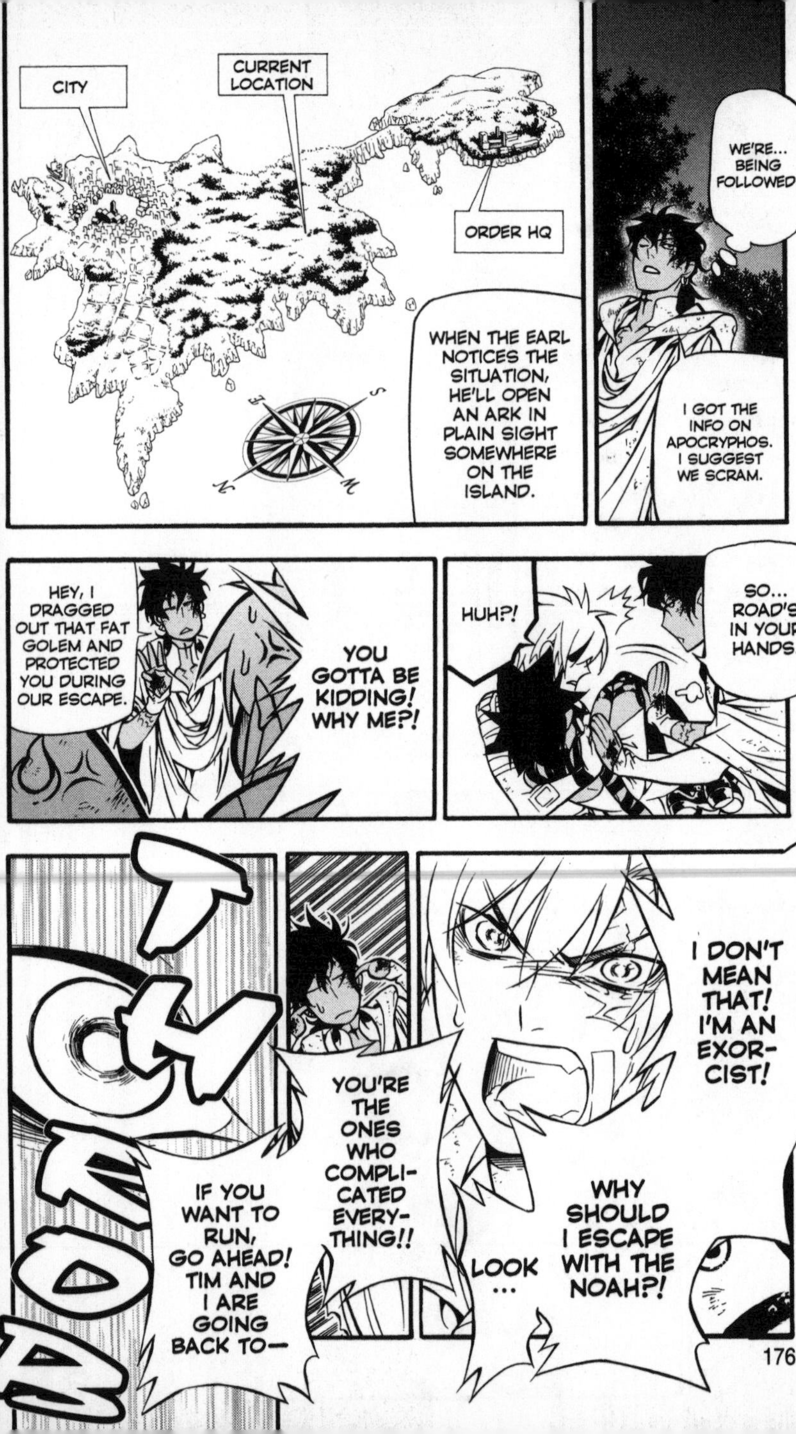
WE'RE... BEING FOLLOWED.
I GOT THE INFO ON APOCRYPHOS. I SUGGEST WE SCRAM.
CURRENT LOCATION
CITY
ORDER HQ
WHEN THE EARL NOTICES THE SITUATION, HE'LL OPEN AN ARK IN PLAIN SIGHT SOMEWHERE ON THE ISLAND.
SO... ROAD'S IN YOUR HANDS.
HUH?!
YOU GOTTA BE KIDDING! WHY ME?!
HEY, I DRAGGED OUT THAT FAT GOLEM AND PROTECTED YOU DURING OUR ESCAPE.
I DON'T MEAN THAT! I'M AN EXOR-CIST!
WHY SHOULD I ESCAPE WITH THE NOAH?!
LOOK...
YOU'RE THE ONES WHO COMPLI-CATED EVERY-THING!!
IF YOU WANT TO RUN, GO AHEAD! TIM AND I ARE GOING BACK TO—

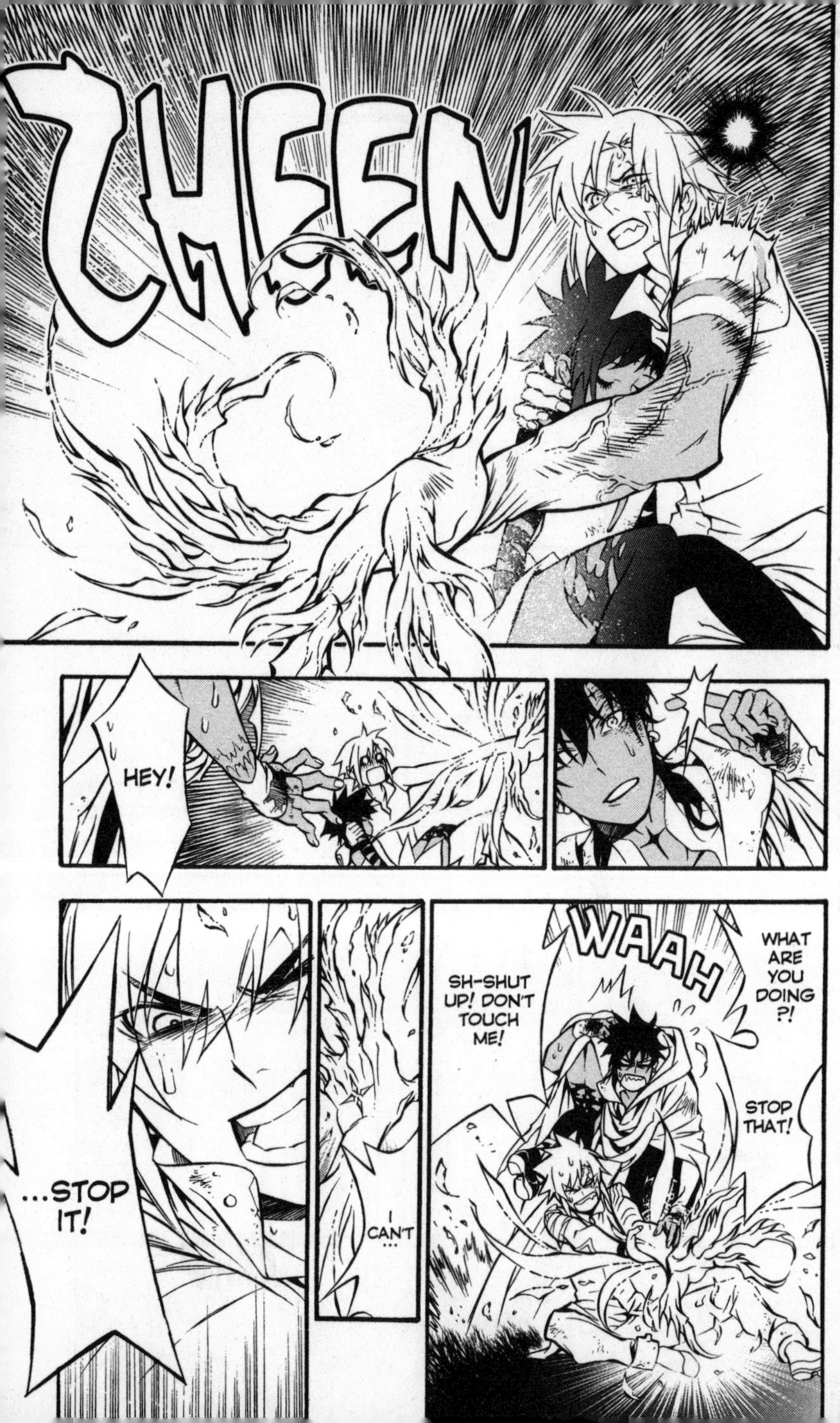
CHEEN
HEY!
WAAH
WHAT ARE YOU DOING ?!
SH-SHUT UP! DON'T TOUCH ME!
STOP THAT!
I CAN'T ...
...STOP IT!

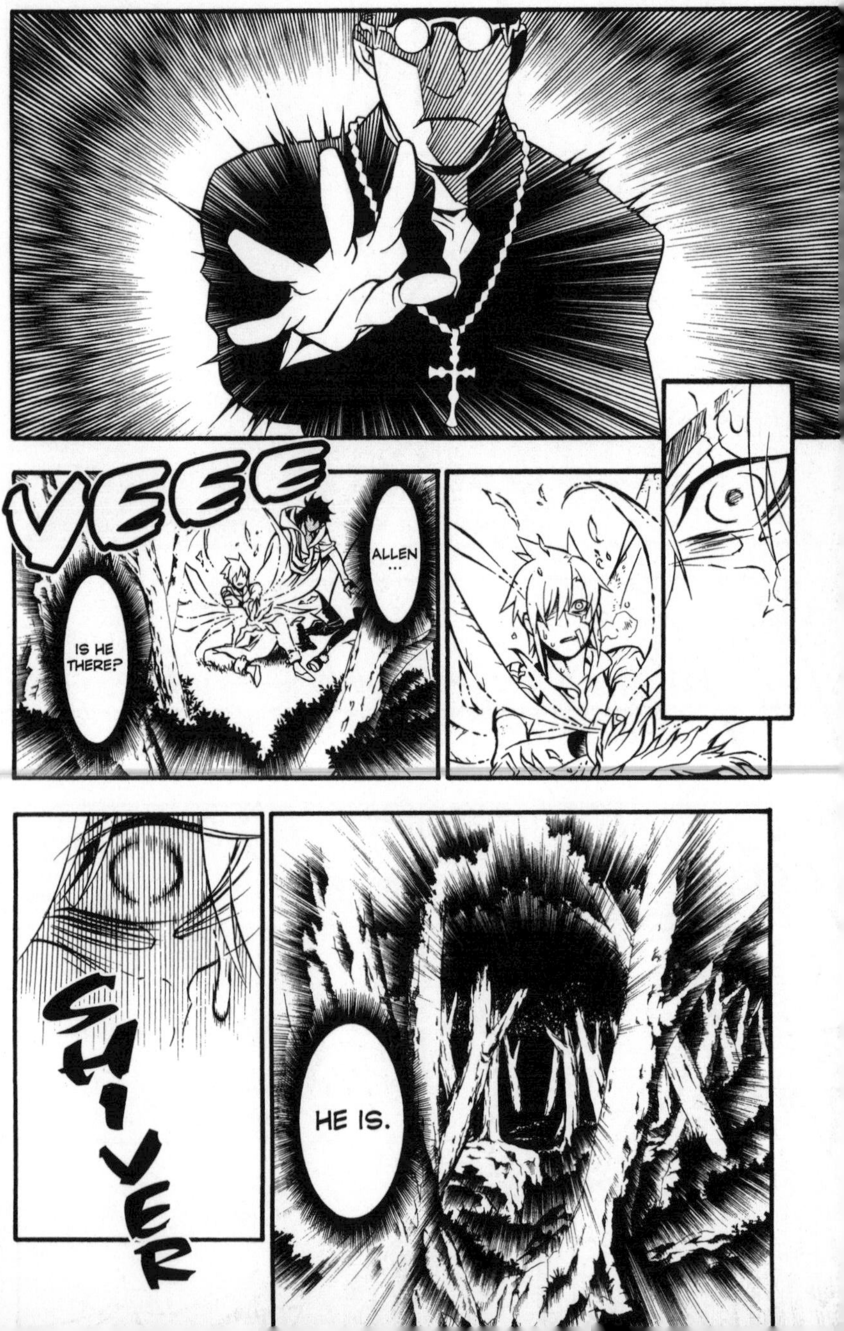

ALLEN ...
VEEE
IS HE THERE?
HE IS.
SHIVER

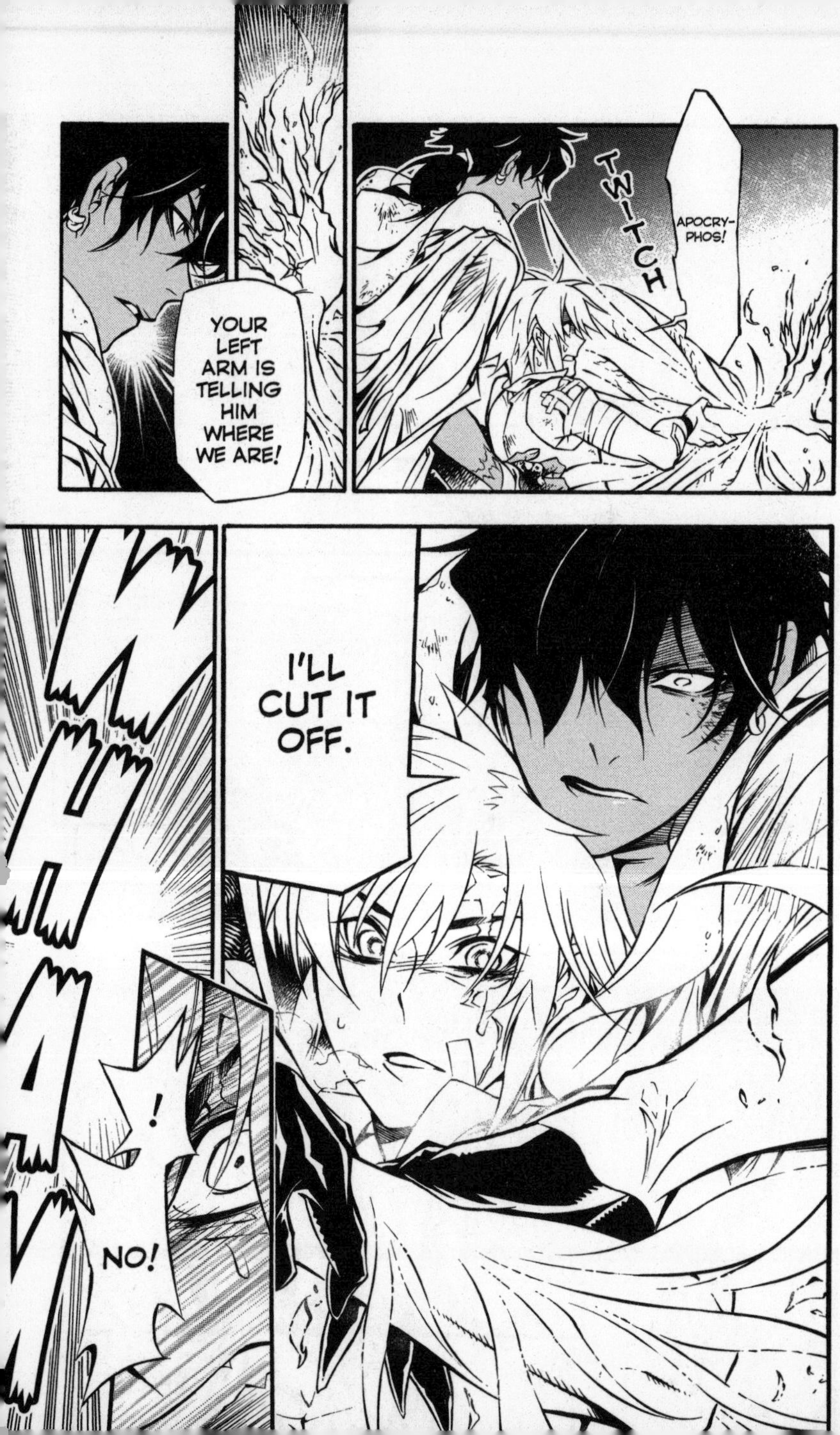
TWITCH
APOCRYPHOS!
YOUR LEFT ARM IS TELLING HIM WHERE WE ARE!
I'LL CUT IT OFF.
!
NO!

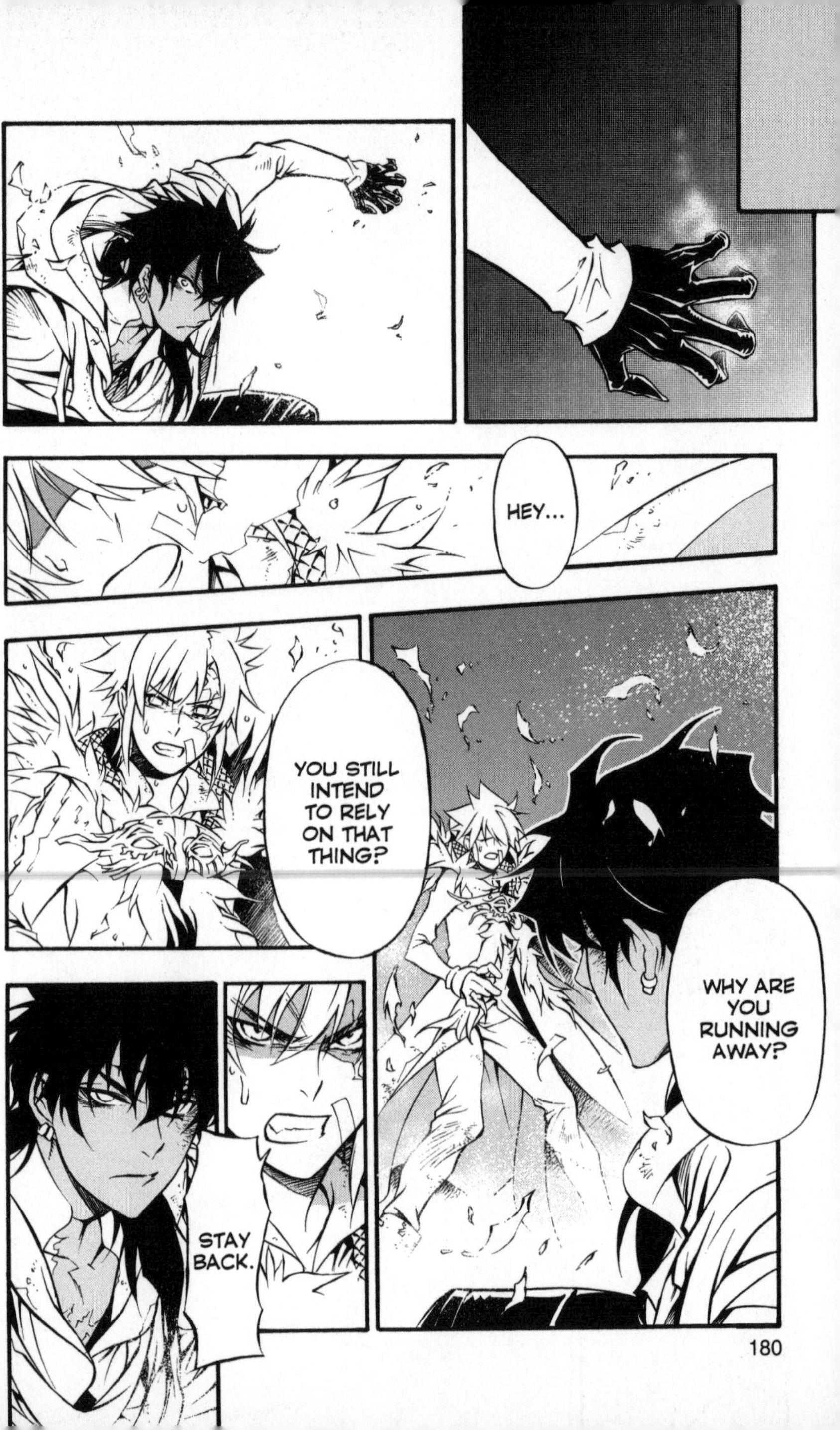
HEY...
WHY ARE YOU RUNNING AWAY?
YOU STILL INTEND TO RELY ON THAT THING?
STAY BACK.

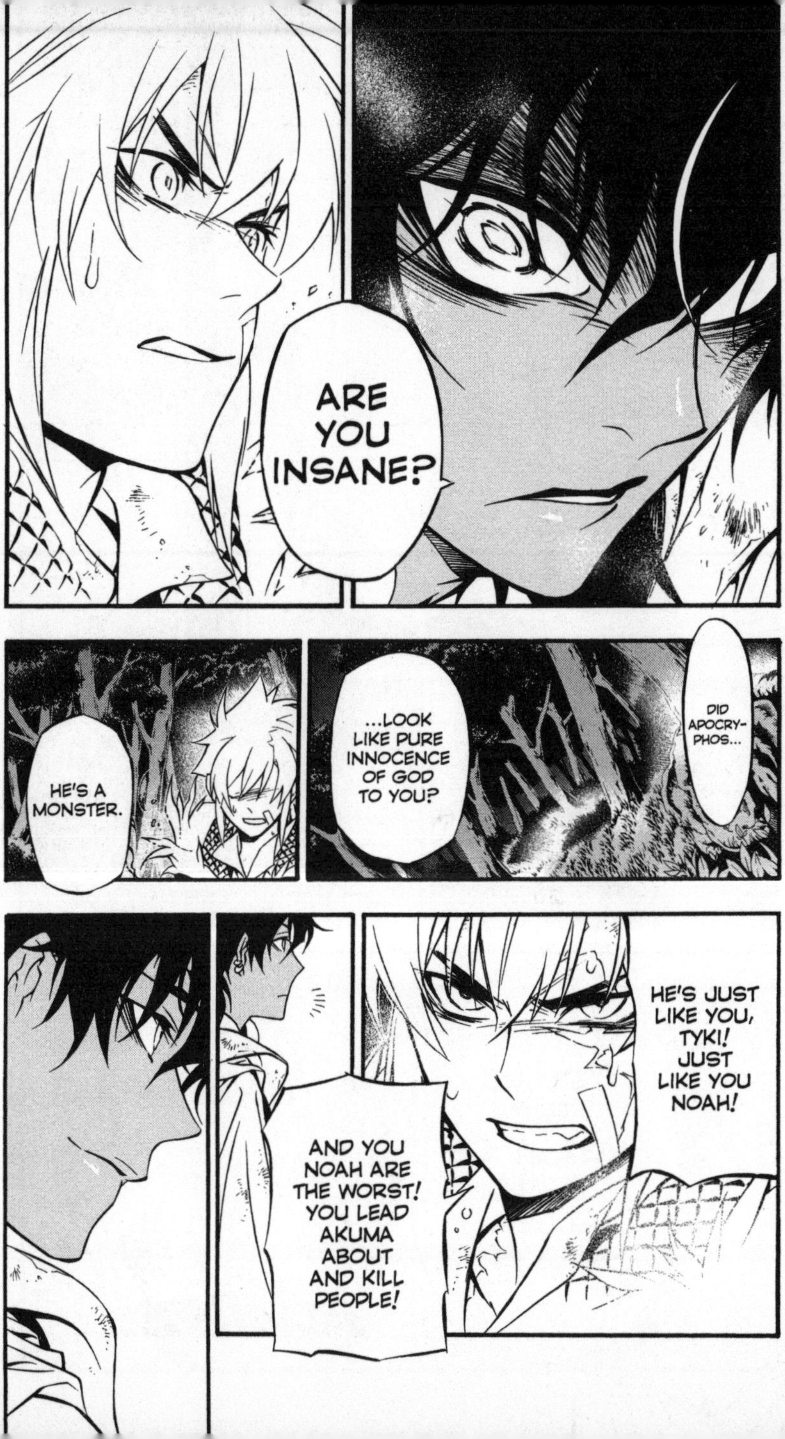
ARE YOU INSANE?
DID APOCRYPHOS...
...LOOK LIKE PURE INNOCENCE OF GOD TO YOU?
HE'S A MONSTER.
HE'S JUST LIKE YOU, TYKI! JUST LIKE YOU NOAH!
AND YOU NOAH ARE THE WORST! YOU LEAD AKUMA ABOUT AND KILL PEOPLE!

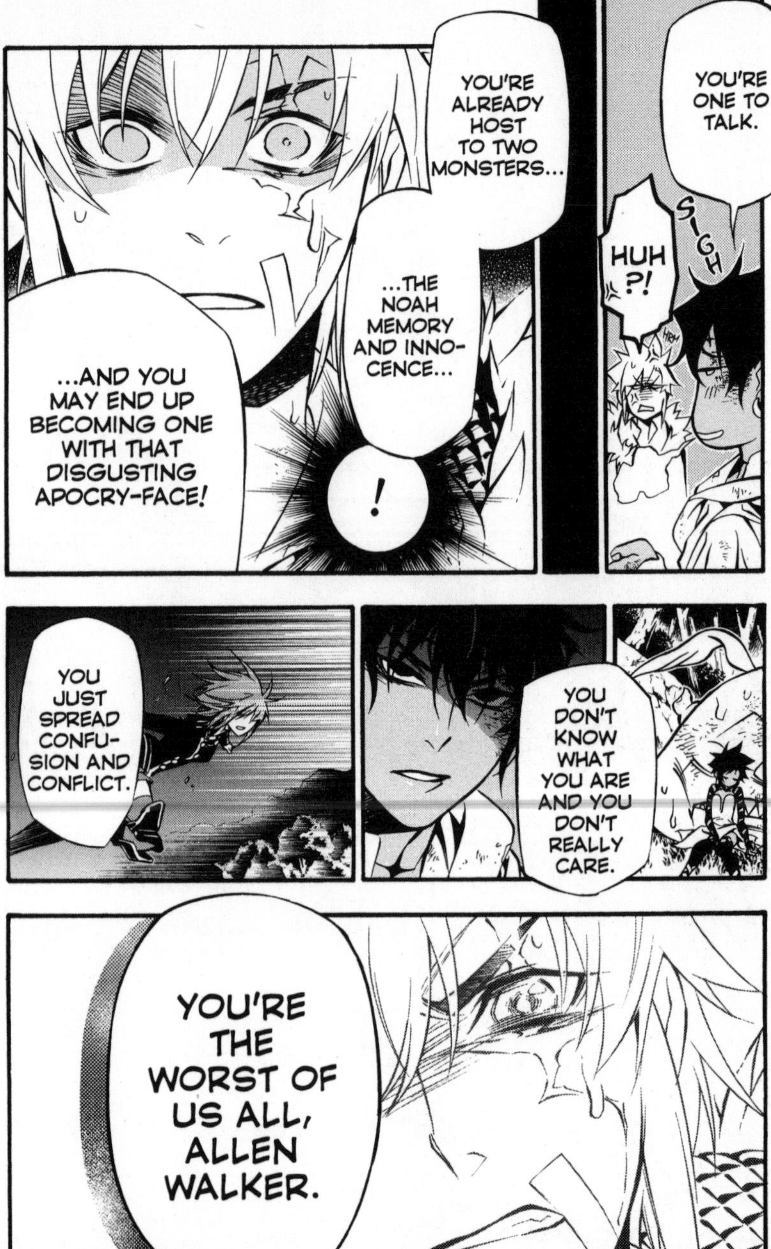

YOU'RE ONE TO TALK.
SIGH
HUH?!
HRM
YOU'RE ALREADY HOST TO TWO MONSTERS...
...THE NOAH MEMORY AND INNO-CENCE...
!
...AND YOU MAY END UP BECOMING ONE WITH THAT DISGUSTING APOCRY-FACE!
YOU DON'T KNOW WHAT YOU ARE AND YOU DON'T REALLY CARE.
YOU JUST SPREAD CONFU-SION AND CONFLICT.
YOU'RE THE WORST OF US ALL, ALLEN WALKER.

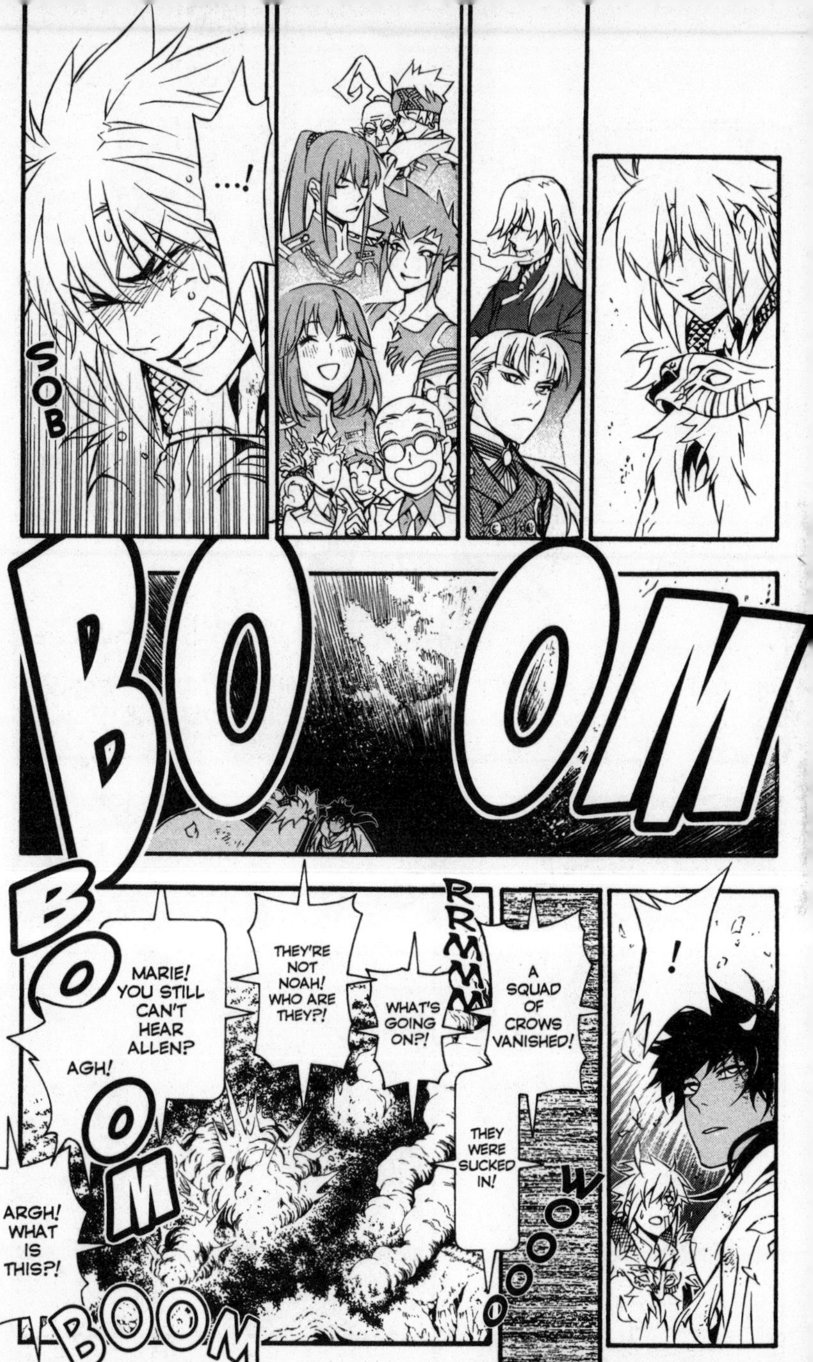
...!
SOB
BOOM
!
RRMMM
A SQUAD OF CROWS VANISHED!
THEY WERE SUCKED IN!
WOOOOO
WHAT'S GOING ON?!
THEY'RE NOT NOAH! WHO ARE THEY?!
MARIE! YOU STILL CAN'T HEAR ALLEN?
AGH!
BOOM
ARGH! WHAT IS THIS?!
BOOM

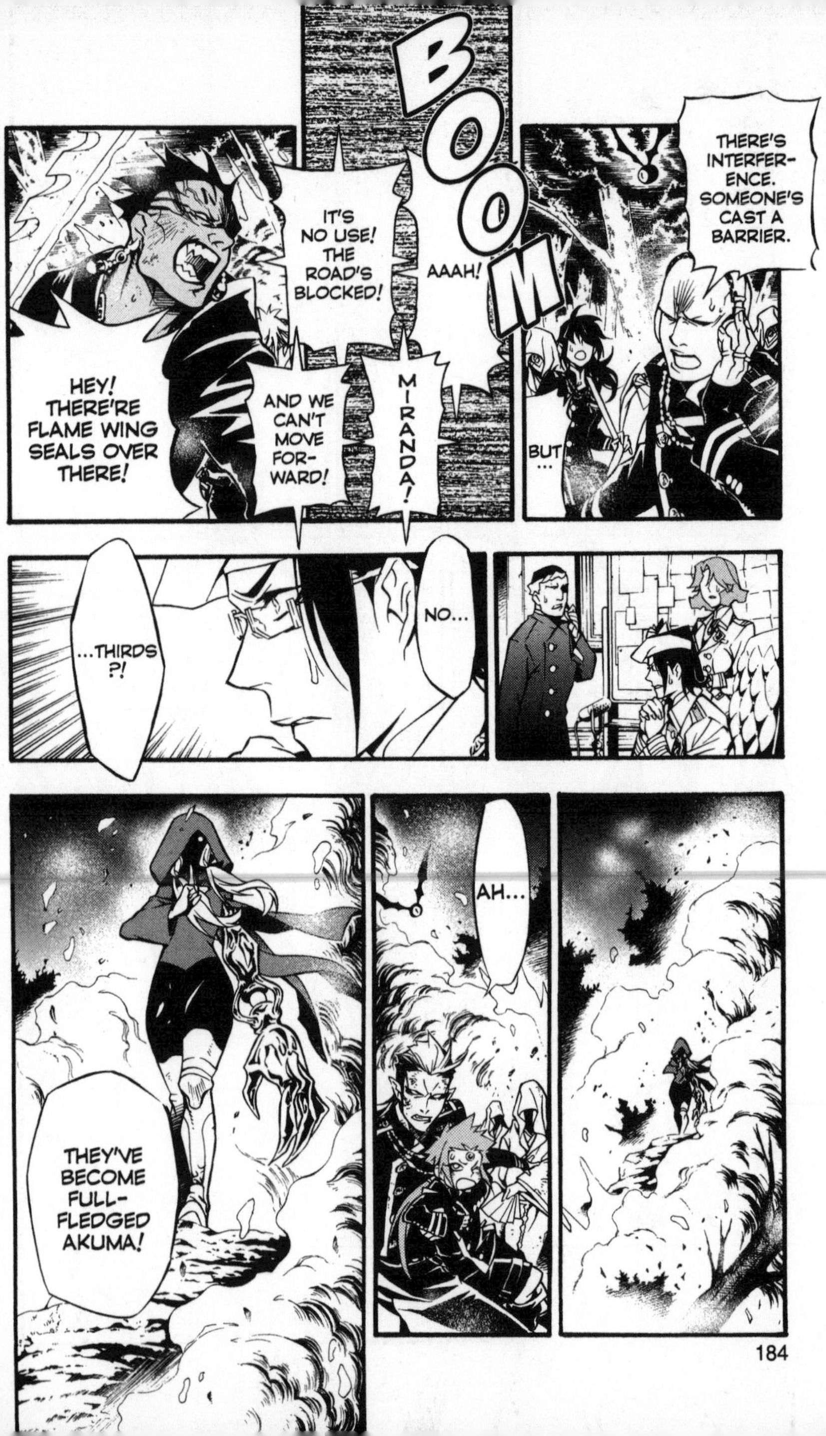
THERE'S INTERFERENCE. SOMEONE'S CAST A BARRIER.
BUT...
BOOM
AAAH!
MIRANDA!
IT'S NO USE! THE ROAD'S BLOCKED!
AND WE CAN'T MOVE FORWARD!
HEY! THERE'RE FLAME WING SEALS OVER THERE!
NO...
...THIRDS?!
AH...
THEY'VE BECOME FULL-FLEDGED AKUMA!

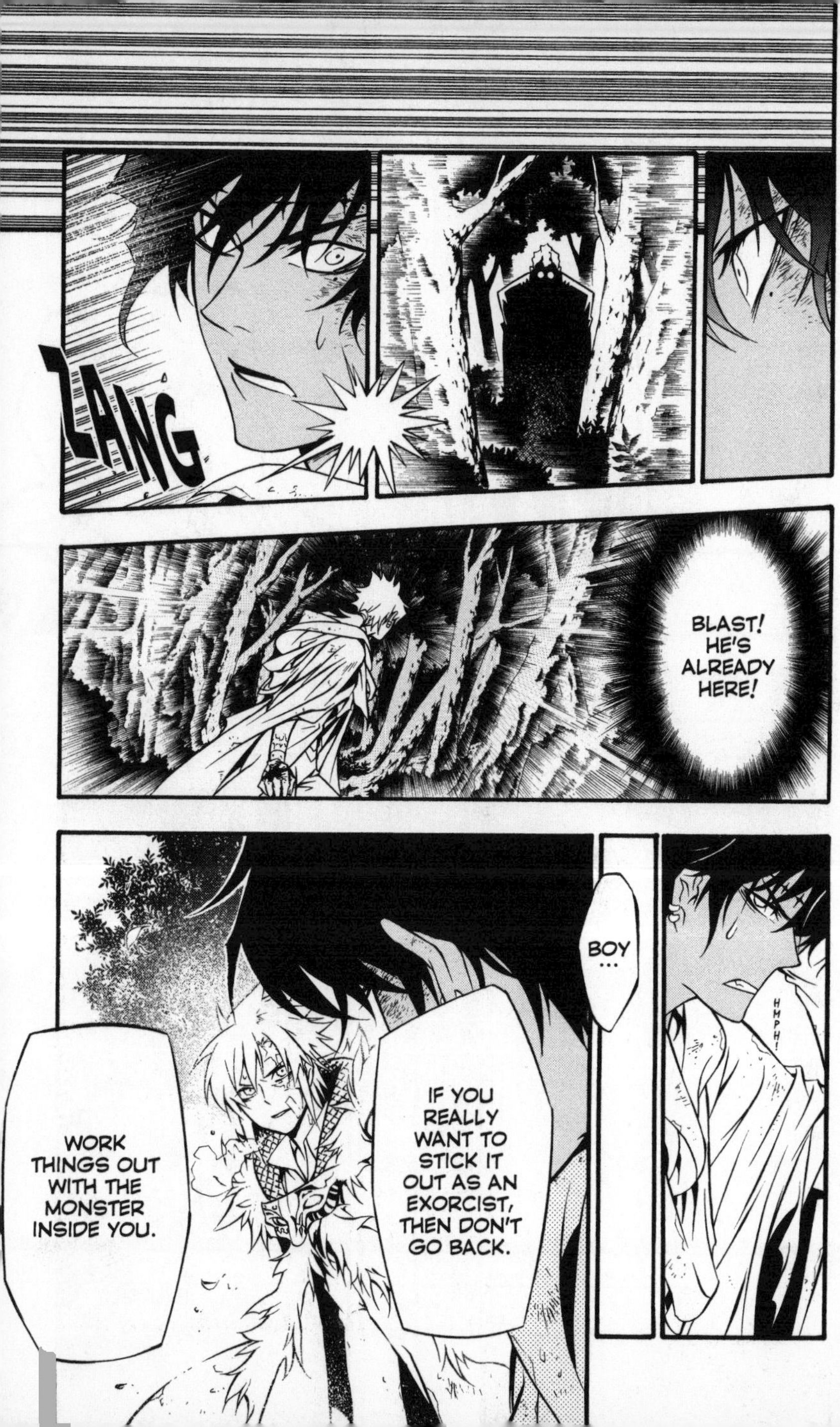
ZANG
BLAST! HE'S ALREADY HERE!
BOY...
HMPH!
IF YOU REALLY WANT TO STICK IT OUT AS AN EXORCIST, THEN DON'T GO BACK.
WORK THINGS OUT WITH THE MONSTER INSIDE YOU.

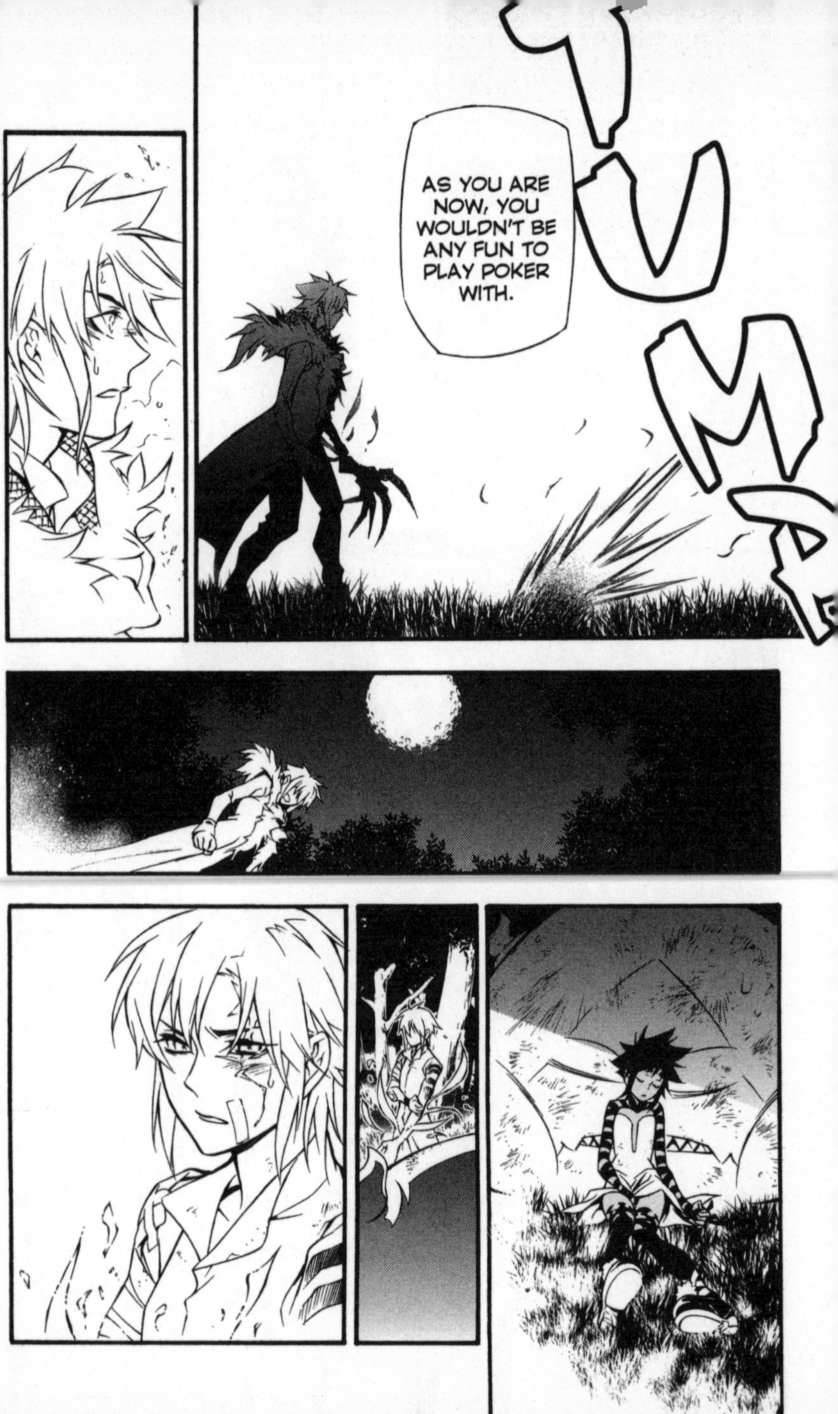
AS YOU ARE NOW, YOU WOULDN'T BE ANY FUN TO PLAY POKER WITH.

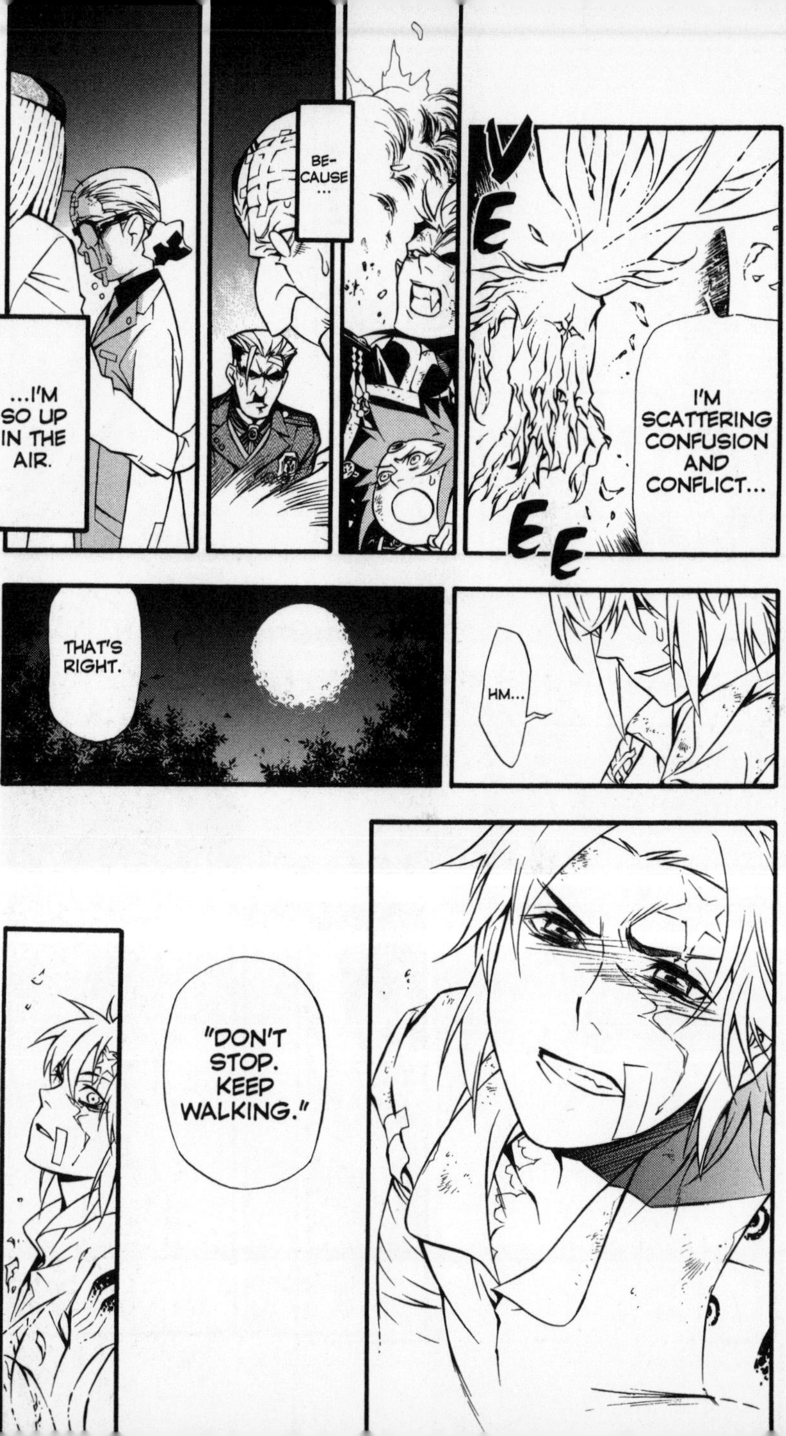
VEEE
I'M SCATTERING CONFUSION AND CONFLICT...
BE-CAUSE...
...I'M SO UP IN THE AIR.
HM...
THAT'S RIGHT.
"DON'T STOP. KEEP WALKING."

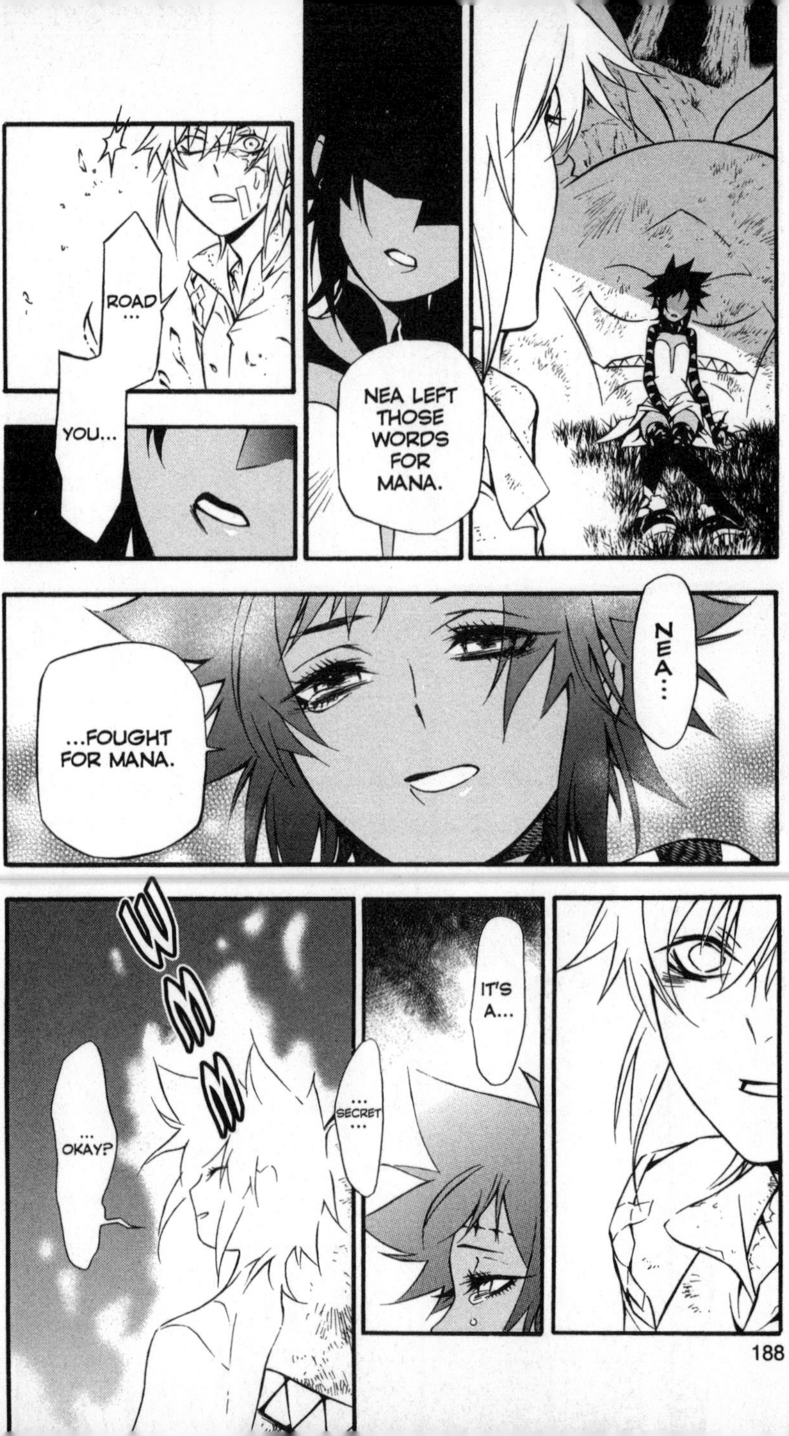
NEA LEFT THOSE WORDS FOR MANA.
ROAD...
YOU...
NEA...
...FOUGHT FOR MANA.
IT'S A...
...SECRET...
...OKAY?

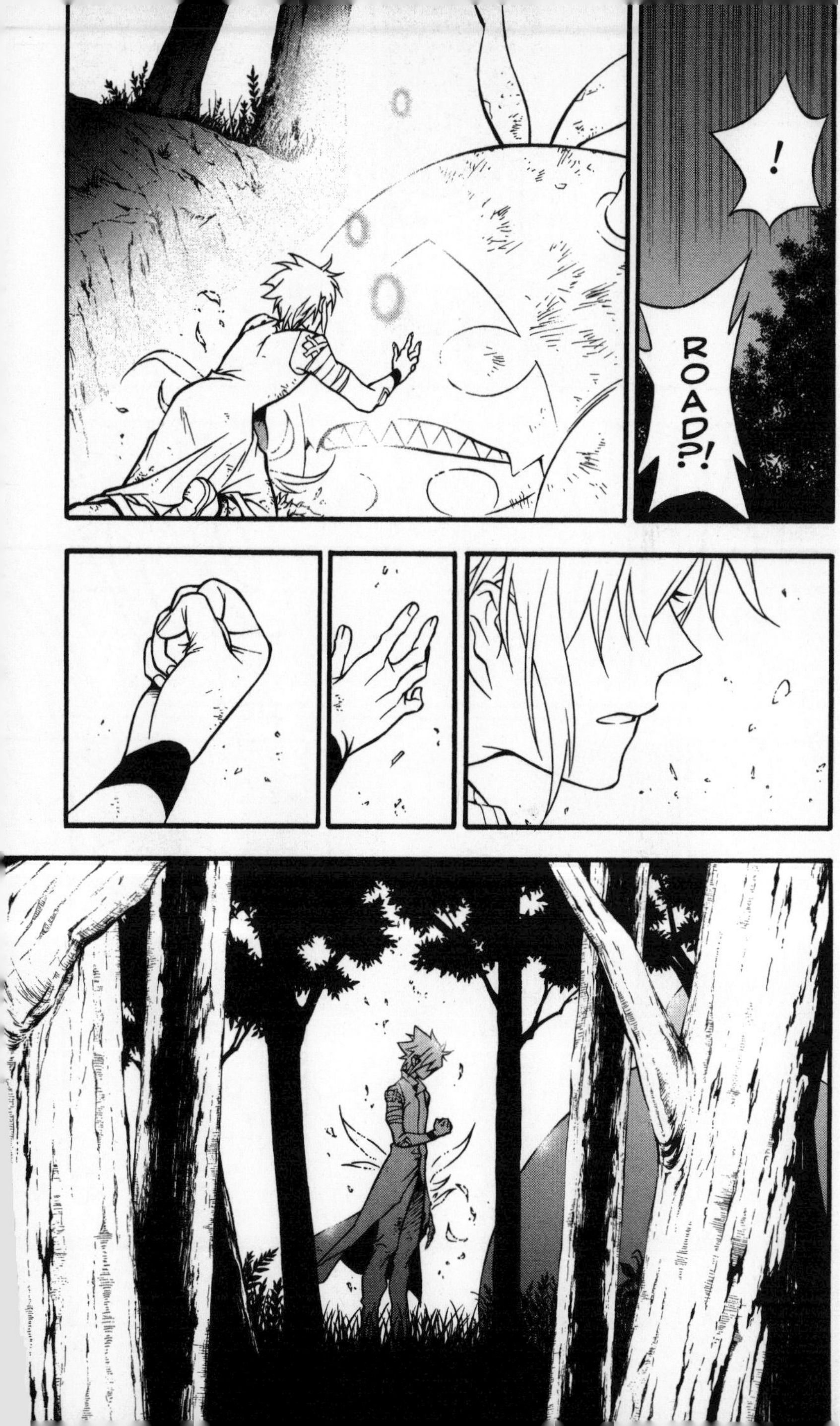
!
ROAD?!

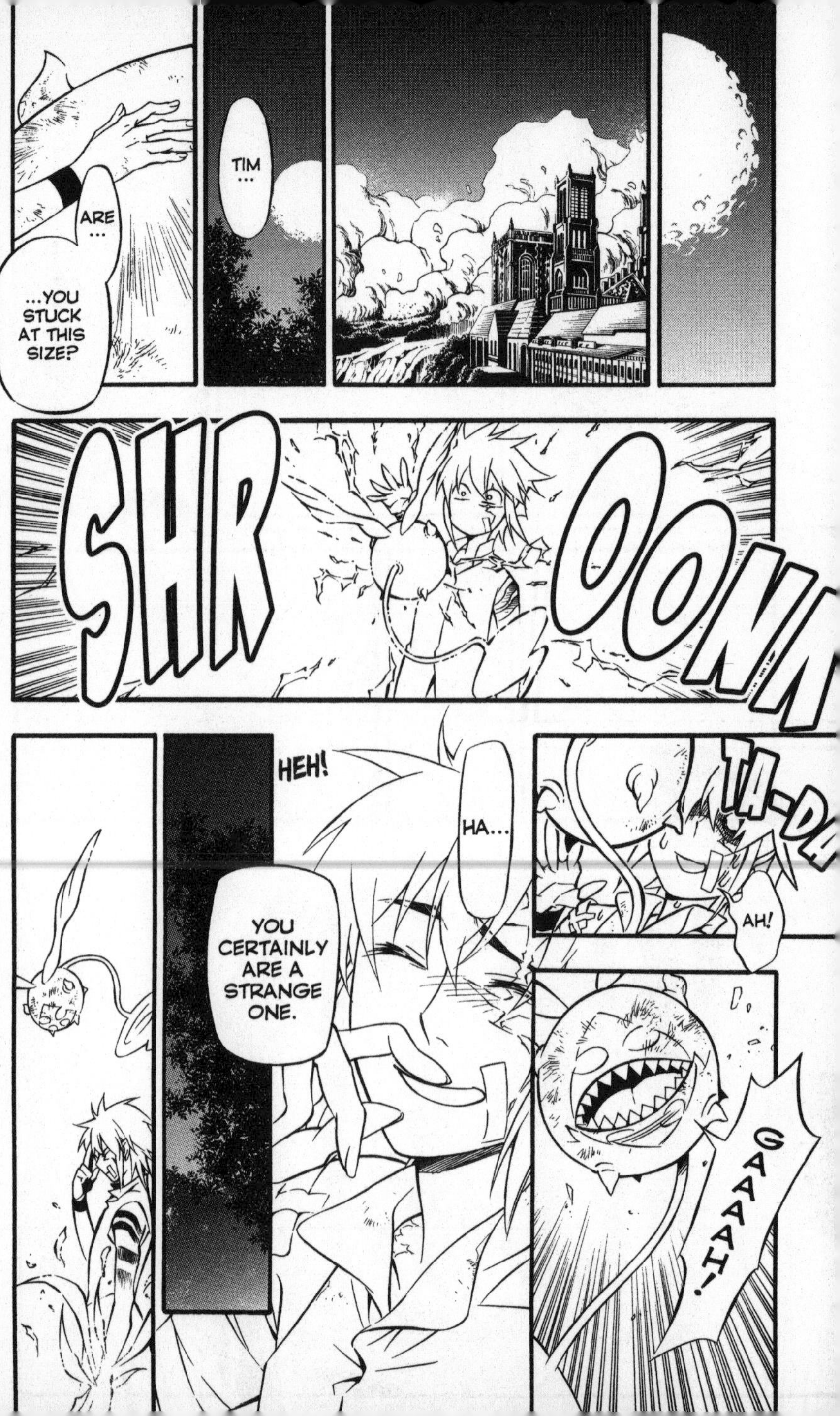
TIM...
ARE...
...YOU STUCK AT THIS SIZE?
SHR
OONN
TA-DA
AH!
GAAAAH!
HEH!
HA...
YOU CERTAINLY ARE A STRANGE ONE.

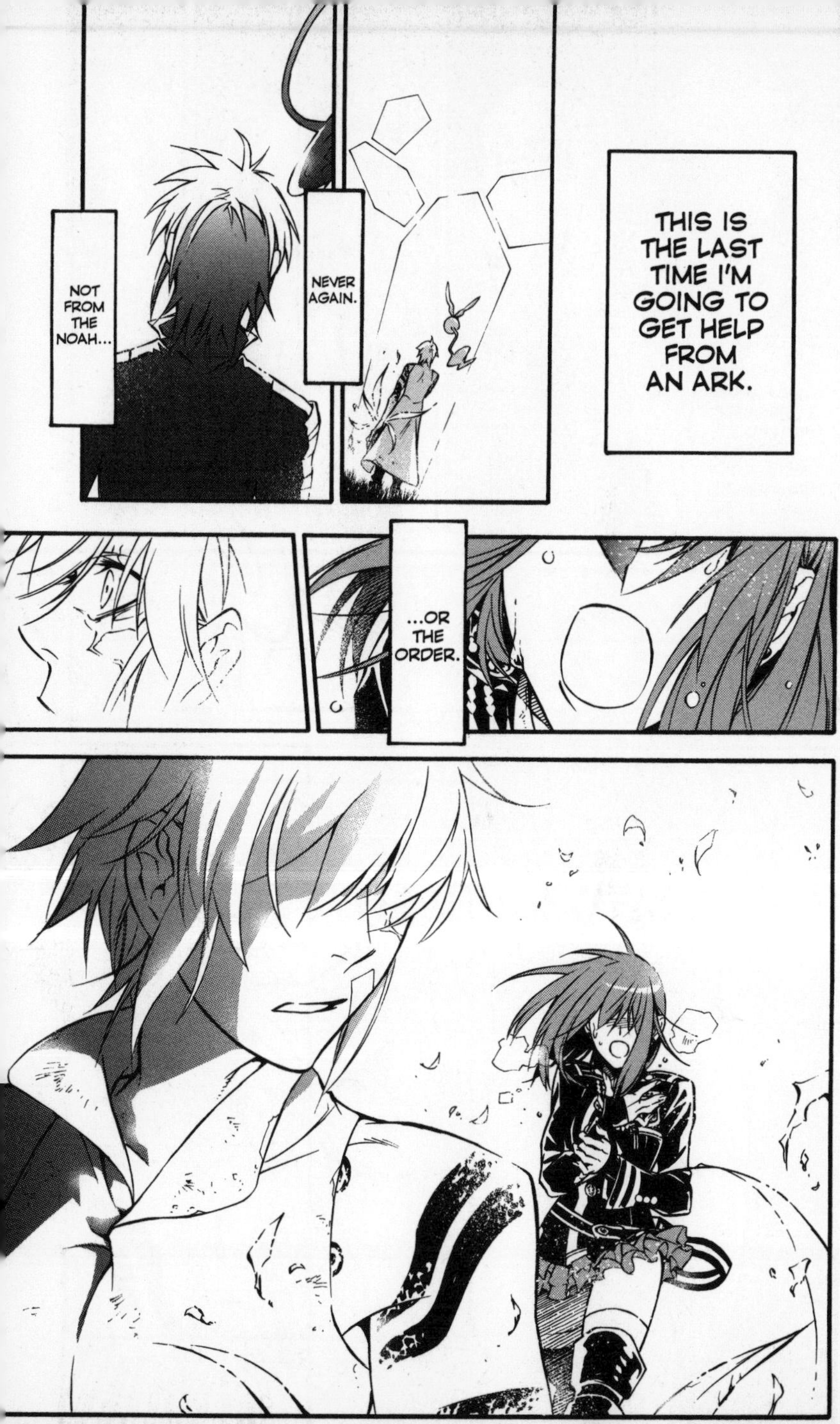
THIS IS THE LAST TIME I'M GOING TO GET HELP FROM AN ARK.
NEVER AGAIN.
NOT FROM THE NOAH...
...OR THE ORDER.

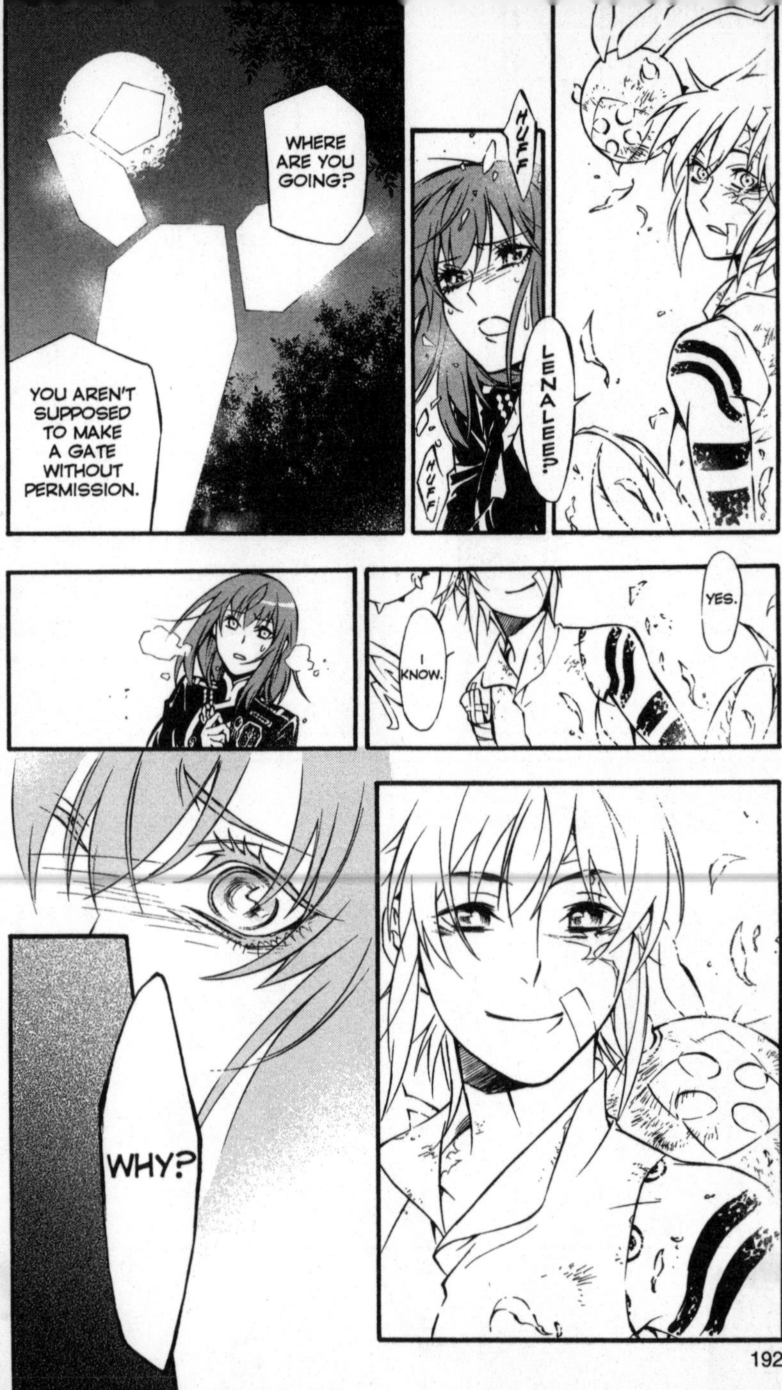
HUFF
LENALEE?
HUFF
WHERE ARE YOU GOING?
YOU AREN'T SUPPOSED TO MAKE A GATE WITHOUT PERMISSION.
YES.
I KNOW.
WHY?

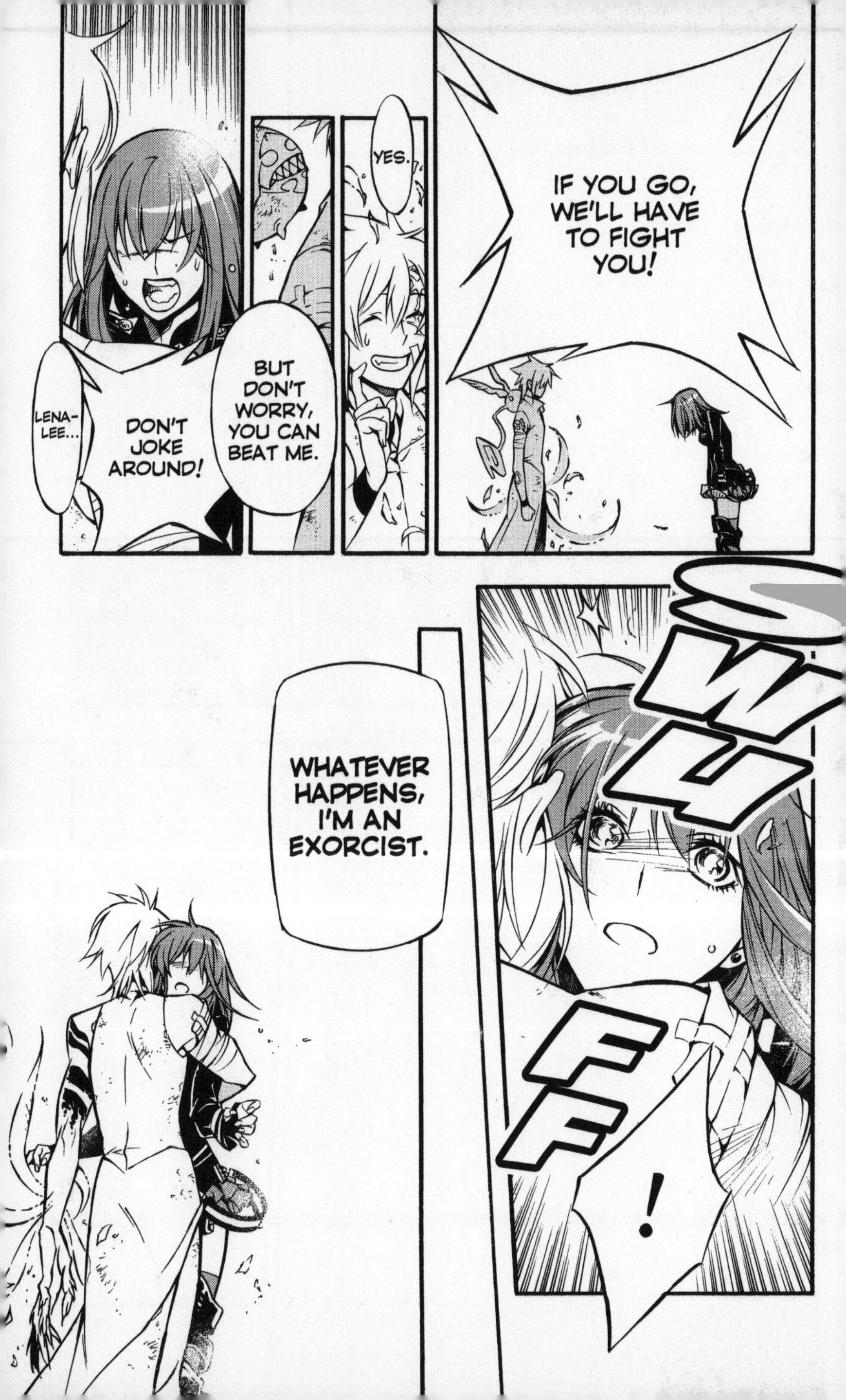
IF YOU GO, WE'LL HAVE TO FIGHT YOU!
YES.
BUT DON'T WORRY, YOU CAN BEAT ME.
DON'T JOKE AROUND!
LENA-LEE...
SWUFF
!
WHATEVER HAPPENS, I'M AN EXORCIST.

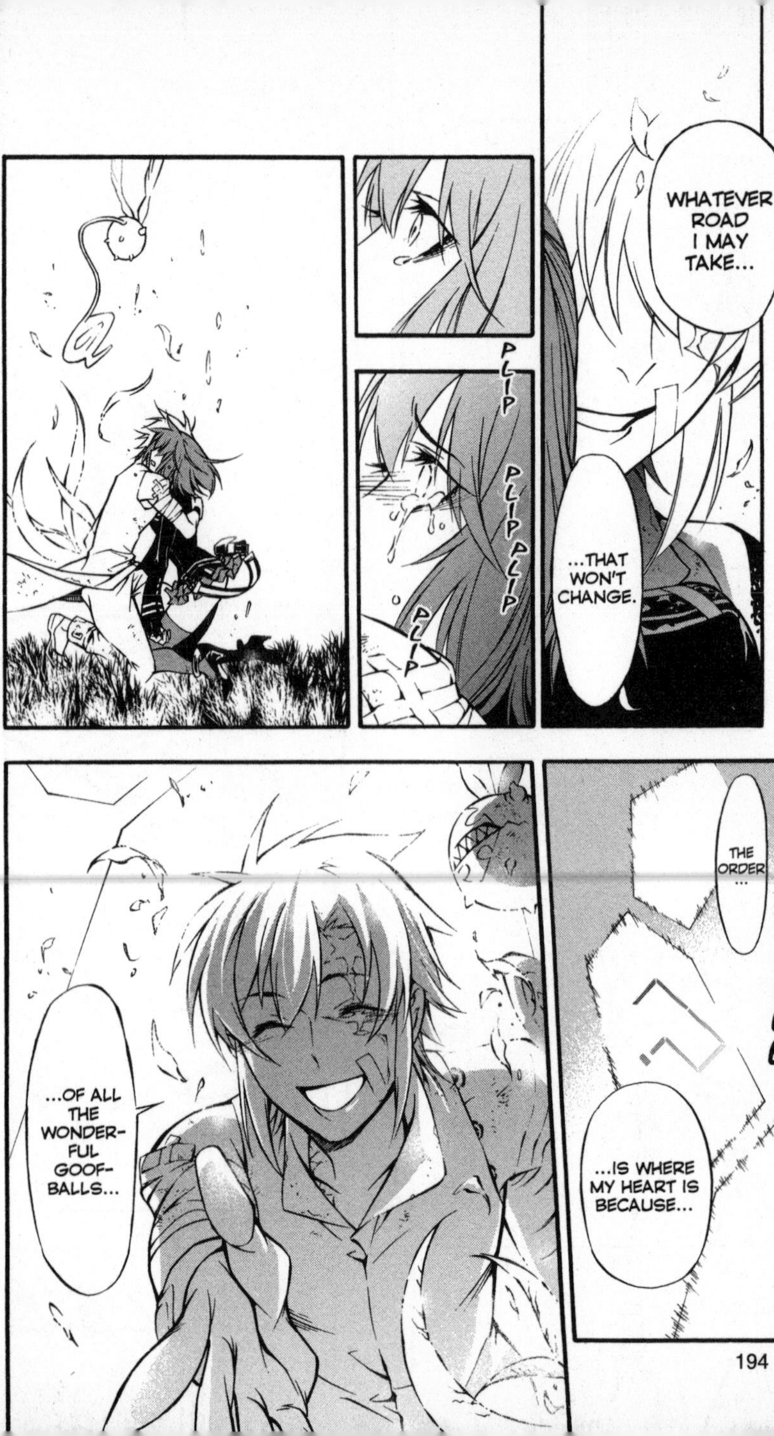
WHATEVER ROAD I MAY TAKE...
...THAT WON'T CHANGE.
PLIP PLIP PLIP PLIP PLIP
THE ORDER...
VEEEE
...IS WHERE MY HEART IS BECAUSE...
...OF ALL THE WONDERFUL GOOFBALLS...

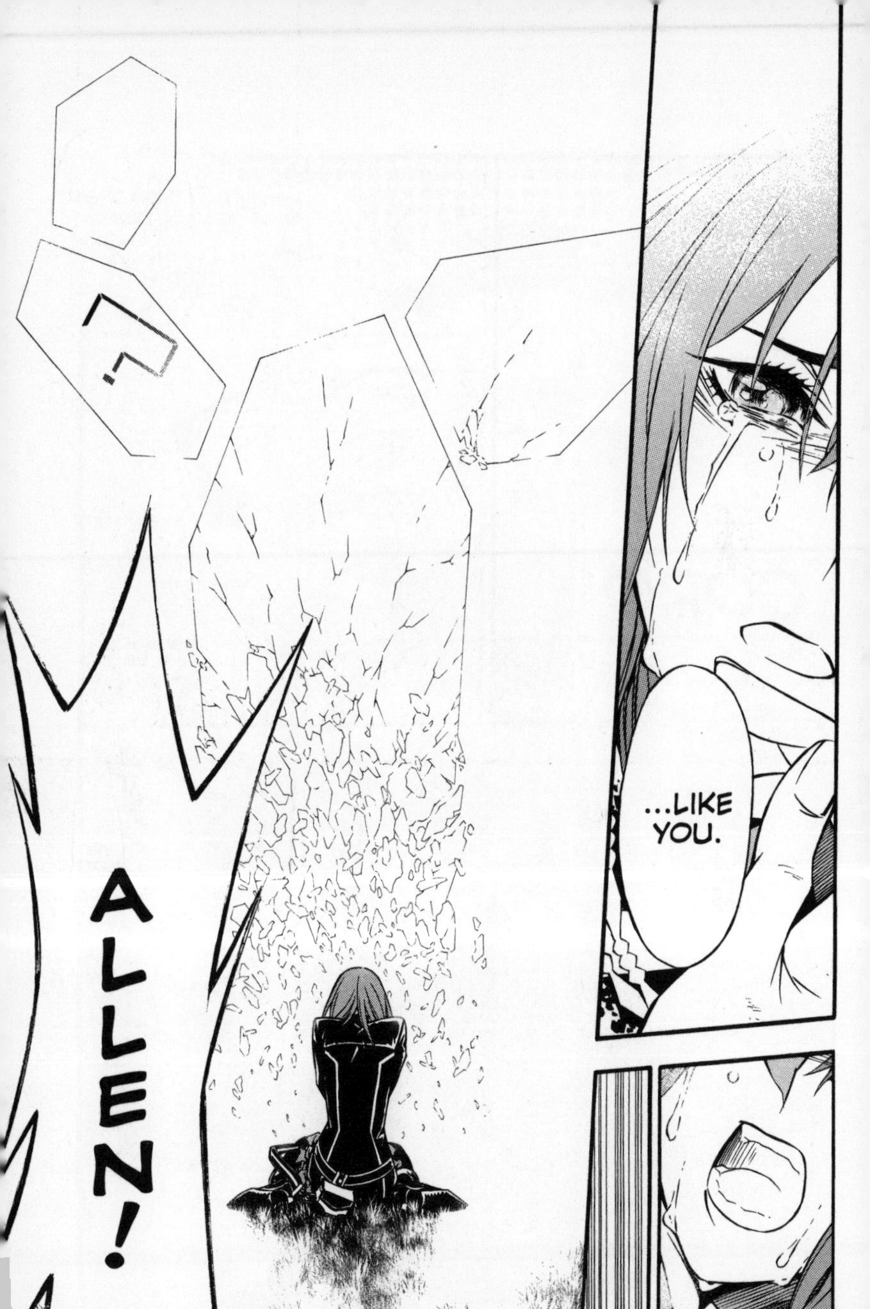
...LIKE YOU.
!?
ALLEN!
VOL. 22 FATE (END)

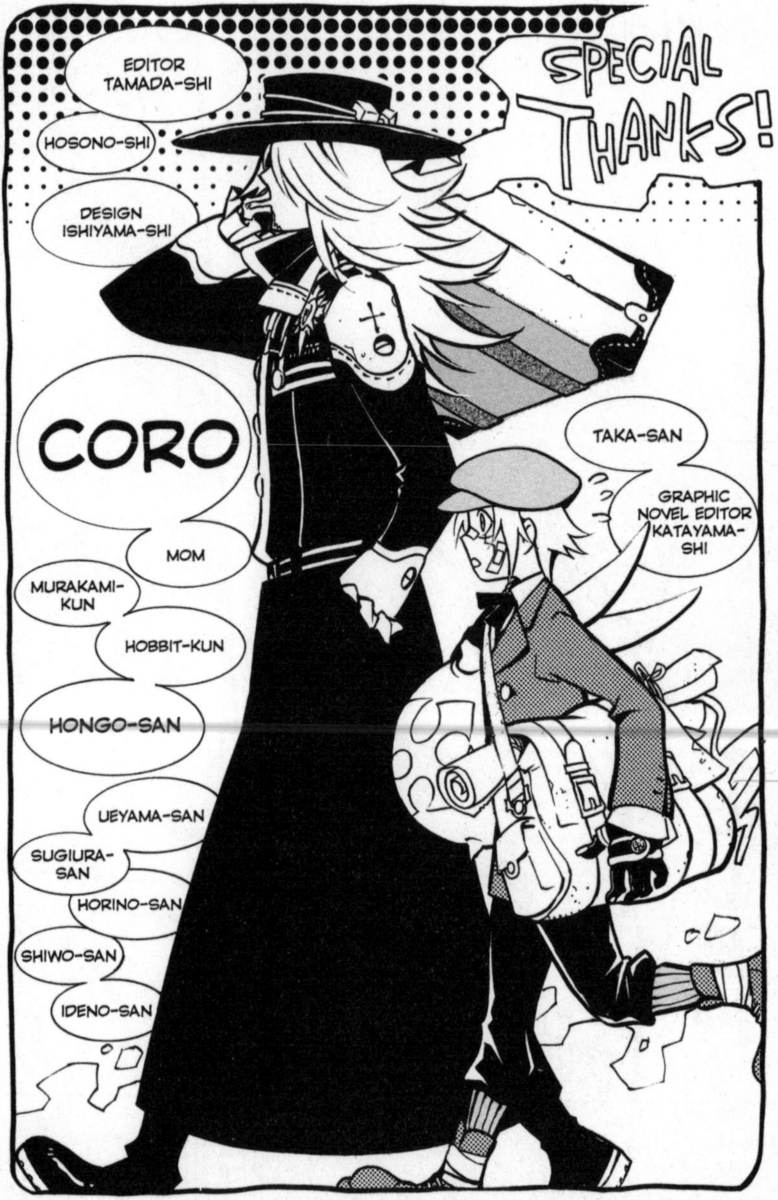
SPECIAL THANKS!
EDITOR TAMADA-SHI
HOSONO-SHI
DESIGN ISHIYAMA-SHI
TAKA-SAN
GRAPHIC NOVEL EDITOR KATAYAMA-SHI
CORO
MOM
MURAKAMI-KUN
HOBBIT-KUN
HONGO-SAN
UEYAMA-SAN
SUGIURA-SAN
HORINO-SAN
SHIWO-SAN
IDENO-SAN

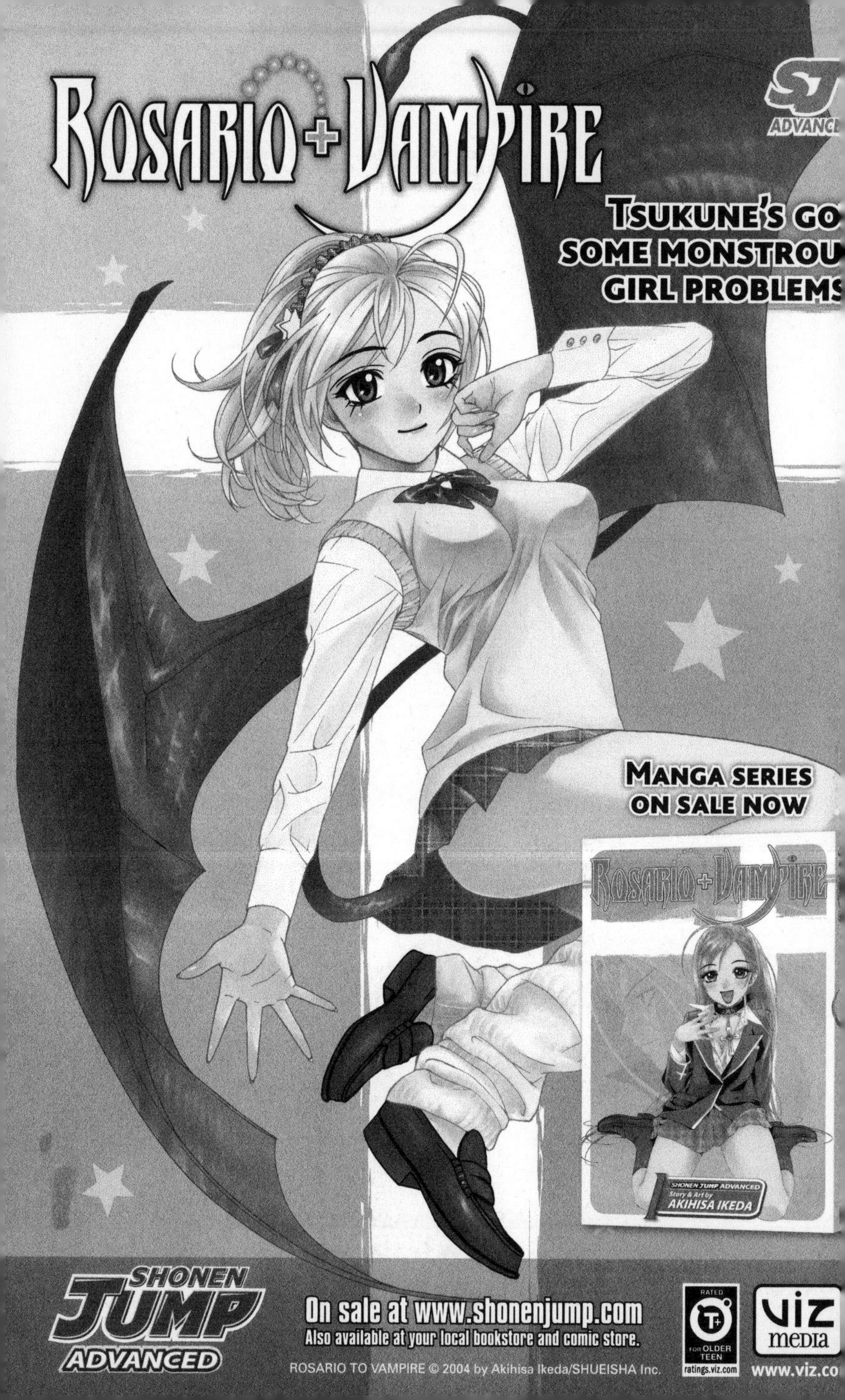
ROSARIO+VAMPIRE
SJ ADVANCE
TSUKUNE'S GO
SOME MONSTROU
GIRL PROBLEMS
MANGA SERIES
ON SALE NOW
ROSARIO+VAMPIRE
SHONEN JUMP ADVANCED
Story & Art by
AKIHISA IKEDA
SHONEN JUMP ADVANCED
On sale at www.shonenjump.com
Also available at your local bookstore and comic store.
ROSARIO TO VAMPIRE © 2004 by Akihisa Ikeda/SHUEISHA Inc.
RATED T+ FOR OLDER TEEN
ratings.viz.com
viz media
www.viz.co

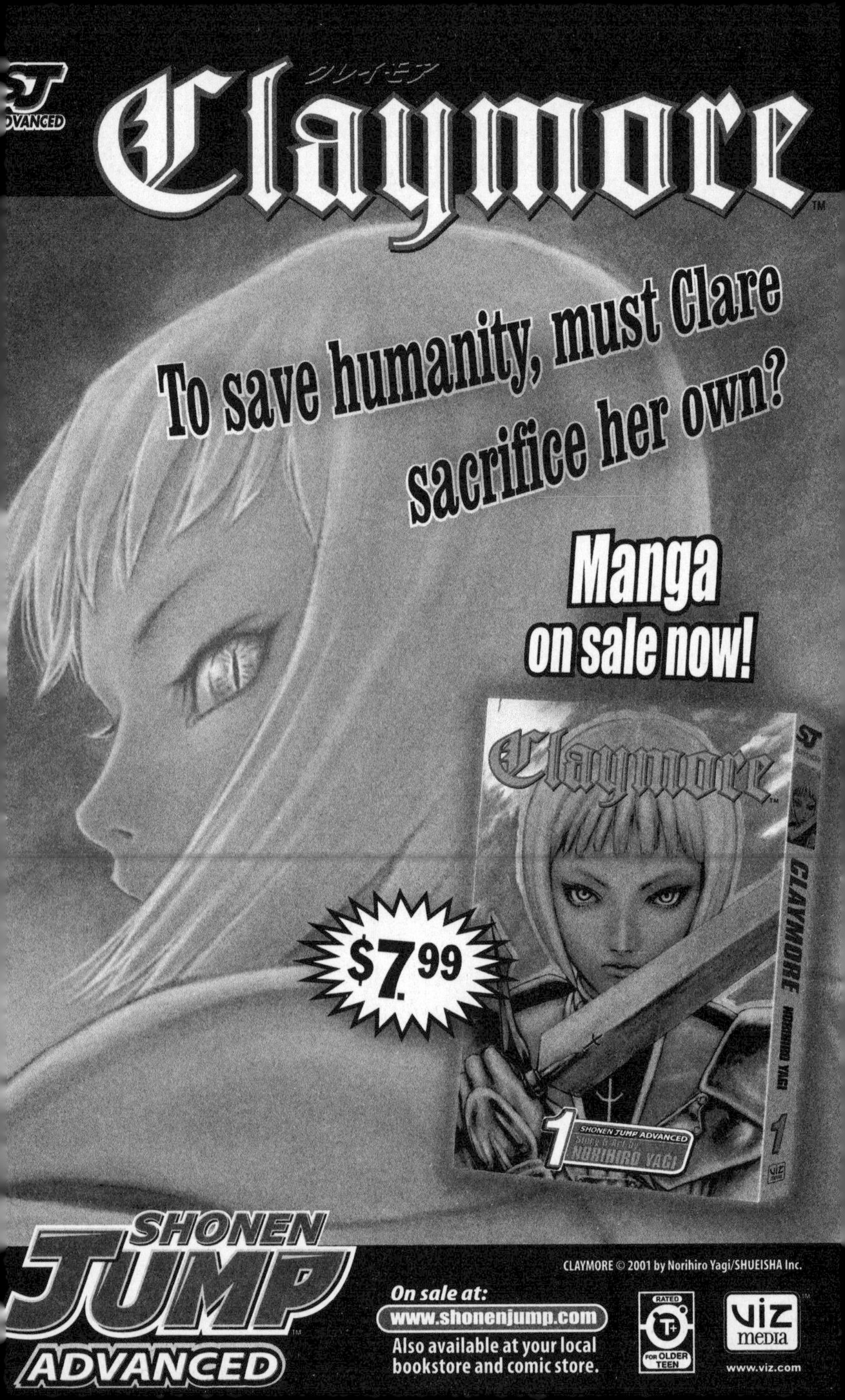
SJ ADVANCED
Claymore™
To save humanity, must Clare sacrifice her own?
Manga on sale now!
$7.99
Claymore™
CLAYMORE
NORIHIRO YAGI
1
SHONEN JUMP ADVANCED
Story & Art by
NORIHIRO YAGI
SHONEN JUMP™ ADVANCED
CLAYMORE © 2001 by Norihiro Yagi/SHUEISHA Inc.
On sale at:
www.shonenjump.com
Also available at your local bookstore and comic store.
RATED T+ FOR OLDER TEEN
VIZ media
www.viz.com

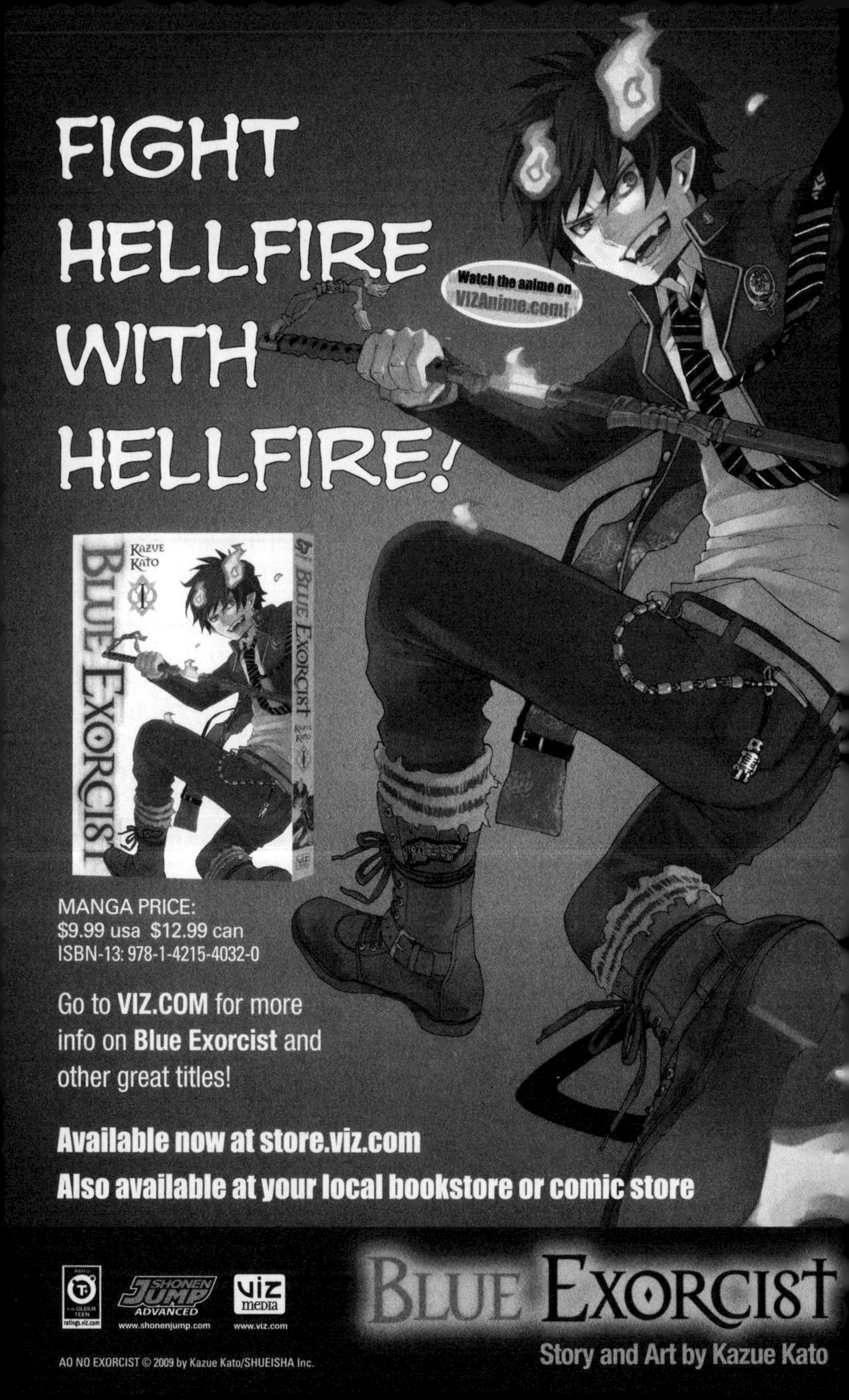
FIGHT HELLFIRE WITH HELLFIRE!
Watch the anime on VIZAnime.com!
Kazue Kato
Blue Exorcist
1
MANGA PRICE:
$9.99 usa $12.99 can
ISBN-13: 978-1-4215-4032-0
Go to VIZ.COM for more info on Blue Exorcist and other great titles!
Available now at store.viz.com
Also available at your local bookstore or comic store
Shonen Jump Advanced
www.shonenjump.com
viz media
www.viz.com
Blue Exorcist
Story and Art by Kazue Kato
AO NO EXORCIST © 2009 by Kazue Kato/SHUEISHA Inc.

You're Reading in the Wrong Direction!!

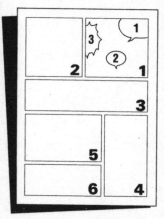

Whoops! Guess what? You're starting at the wrong end of the comic!

It's true! In keeping with the original Japanese format, **D.Gray-man** is meant to be read from right to left, starting in the upper-right corner.

Unlike English, which is read from left to right, Japanese is read from right to left, meaning action, sound effects and word-balloon order are completely reversed... something which can make readers unfamiliar with Japanese feel pretty backwards themselves. For this reason, manga or Japanese comics published in the U.S. in English have sometimes been published "flopped"—that is, printed in exact reverse order, as though seen from the other side of a mirror.

By flopping pages, U.S. publishers can avoid confusing readers, but the compromise is not without its downside. For one thing, a character in a flopped manga series who once wore in the original Japanese version a T-shirt emblazoned with "M A Y" (as in "the merry month of") now wears one which reads "Y A M"! Additionally, many manga creators in Japan are themselves unhappy with the process, as some feel the mirror-imaging of their art skews their original intentions.

We are proud to bring you Katsura Hoshino's **D.Gray-man** in the original unflopped format. For now, though, turn to the other side of the book and let the adventure begin...!

—Editor